24 HOUR COMICS

Edited by
Scott McCloud

D1437570

About Comics   Thousand Oaks, California

Published by About Comics

ISBN: 0-9716338-4-3

First printing - April 2004

1 2 3 4 5 6 7 8 9 09 08 07 06 05 04

For more information about About Comics, head over to www.AboutComics.com

Printed in Canada

TABLE OF CONTENTS

Introduction
by
Scott McCloud

The Idea

THE FIRST 24-HOUR COMIC was a scary experience. As far as I knew, no one had ever done anything like it, and as far as I knew, it couldn't be done - least of all by me.

It all began in the summer of 1990. I was convinced at the time that I was the second-slowest artist in comics. The slowest, by his own half-joking estimate, was my pal Steve "Glacier" Bissette who, at the time, was producing at a rate of a little over a page a month. They were beautiful pages, some of the best of their day, but at that rate, it was no way to make a living.

Steve had a home in Vermont with his family; my wife Ivy and I lived in Somerville, Massachusetts; but we found frequent excuses to hook up with Steve for occasions both business and social. In July of that year, he was doing a signing at Newbury Comics in Cambridge (a hybrid comics/music store) so Ivy and I drove into town to meet him.

When we arrived at the store, Steve was doing sketches. Readers would saunter up and ask for a drawing of, say, Betty Page and Wonder Woman on Swamp Thing's shoulders surrounded by 26 Samurai on the slopes of Mount Fuji and sure enough, that's what Steve would give them. I watched in awe as Steve drew. His hands ripped across the page at blinding speed, turning out masterful pen and ink renderings that would make

Heinrich Kley weep with envy. I thought: Why would this guy ever have troubles with deadlines??; he's an incredible draftsman! I'll bet he could do a full length comic in a day if he wanted to. Why, I'll bet he —

[Lightbulb clicks on over my head.]

Suddenly, I knew what Steve needed to do. And I knew that I could only get him to do it, if I did it too. Thus the deal was struck. Steve and I made a mutual vow that we would each do a complete 24-page comic in a single day at some point before August 31st. My original idea had been midnight to midnight, but Steve's semi-nocturnal schedule was best suited to the more flexible 24-hour rule so that's what we finally settled on.

The First

Procrastinators that we were, Steve and I both put off our 24-hour comics until our self-imposed deadline of August 31st. That morning at 6 am I stumbled out of bed and began to draw.

To the left of my drawing desk, I had a small stack of random art books that I had grabbed the day before on a methodical walk through the Somerville Library. Big photos of Donatello sculptures. Pre-Columbian Masks. Hopper. Some Russian painter I'd never heard of... Anything that I thought might stimulate my visual imagination.

I kept my drawing supplies simple: 2-ply kid-finish bristol board, a mechanical pencil, an eraser, a straight edge and japanese felt brushes.

Oh yeah, and a two liter bottle of Dr. Pepper.

I vaguely remember Ivy coming and going that day. I think she was actually rehearsing for something or another with some friends. Or was it a lingerie party? Bad movie night? It's all a blur.

Feeling increasingly alone and silly, I called Steve to see how his own comic was coming along, but I discovered he couldn't do it that day after all because of family obligations. This made me feel even more alone and silly of course, but I kept going anyway. Bleary eyes, sore hands and an aching back began calling attention to themselves, but I was determined to see it through. I liked the way the bizarre, improvisational comic was coming out (though God knows, it was no masterpiece) and I wanted to see how it ended.

I finished at about 11:30pm, throwing in a cover so that when we showed off each other's comics, I could brag that I did one more page than Steve did.

In the end, Steve kept his bargain, completing his far better "A Life in Black and White" on August 36th. Steve — even though he knew nothing about mine beyond its existence — also threw in an extra cover page in hopes of doing me one better. Each of us had drawn a complete 25-page, 24-hour comic.

Both of us were exhausted and exhilerated by the experience. We'd agreed beforehand not to think about printing the things until after the fact, but having reaped the benefits of our art-as-therapy and basking in the afterglow of it all, Steve suggested printing them in his *Taboo* anthology and I agreed. Steve also showed or sent photocopies of his comics to some friends.

And that was that. Steve got back to his various projects, I returned to drawing my overdue *Zot!* issues. The 24-hour comics we did were fun, but now there was serious work to do. Steve and I returned to our respective lives and put the idea behind us.

We had no idea what we were starting.

The Virus

One of the photocopies Steve made was sent to Kitchener, Ontario where it was received with interest by *Cerebus* creator Dave Sim. Dave liked what he saw enough that he decided to created his own 24-hour comic and sent copies to Steve and I. He also printed or previewed all three comics in the back pages of *Cerebus* and publicized the dare far and wide.

Our friend Rick provided the fourth in the series, but with a twist. His dream-diary "Rare Bit Fiends" was completed in a series of short morning sessions. The results were indeed the product of less than 24 hours, but not a full-blown unbroken session. As it happened, this was the first installment of what eventually became an actual full-sized comic book series by Rick.

Writer Neil Gaiman was next to pick up the bug. Neil was just getting rolling on his groundbreaking *Sandman* series at the time and hadn't drawn a thing in 14 years, but he bravely gave it a go anyway. Though he couldn't make the 24-page mark, he still managed to turn in one of the most literate and funny of all the 24-hour comics, filled with several memorable I-don't-know-how-to-draw-this-so-I'll draw-something-else-instead panels. Neil's effort gave birth to the so-called "Gaiman variation": If you get to 24 hours and you're not done, end it there.

Teenage Mutant Ninja Turtles co-creator Kevin Eastman also gave it a try. Kevin would later print his story under the title "No Guts, No Glory". (The original title was "Fuck the Dead" but Kevin decided that perhaps that wouldn't be as easy to market for some reason). Kevin fell short at the 24-hour mark, but forged on an additional 26 hours for a total of 50, giving us the "Eastman Variation": If you get to 24 hours and you're not done, **keep going until you are!**

Once news of the six comics got out, thanks in large part to the exposure in *Cerebus*, there was no stopping the idea. In the 14 years since that fateful day, nearly four hundred 24-hour comics have come to my attention directly. The total number may be closer to twice that, but at this point the idea has drifted far from home-as all good inventions do-and the parental connection is getting increasingly remote. Many don't even know where it all started, lost in the mists of comic book lore and legend, along with why The Thing was all lumpy in those early issues of *Fantastic Four*.

Recent years have even seen the emergence of 24-hour group events, the largest of which at the time of this writing may be the Australia-based "OzComics 24-Hour Challenge" which pulled in over 40 participants from around the continent and beyond. Where this trend will lead is anyone's guess, but if it continues, the number of 24-hour comics in existence might be dramatically higher in just a few years.

Students have drawn them. Friends have drawn them. Even my own daughter (at the tender age of nine) took it upon herself to create a 24-hour comic and succeeded — and then did another one less than a year later! I've listed those that I can at the "24-Hour Comics Index" on my site but I have trouble keeping up with the ever-growing list.

See for yourself at www.scottmccloud.com/inventions/24hr/index/index.html

The Mutatations

As if the story of the 24-Hour Comic wasn't remarkable enough, the virus began mutating in the mid to late 90s.

After hearing about the 24-hour Comics from a friend, Tina Fallon of Crux Productions in New York, proposed the idea of 24-hour Plays as an event for an upcoming Fringe Festival. Her hyper-compression of the theatrical process proved so exhilarating for the participants that it was done again and again and has become something of a tradition in the following years (I later found out that my old friend, the legendary Brian Dewan, had been a writer for one of the first, though he had no idea it was related to my comics at the time). As happened with the comics, Tina's idea soon spread beyond Crux and eventually beyond New York to other cities and even countries. There had been over 300 24-Hour plays as of May 2002.

In 1998, my wife Ivy and five of her former teen improv students (now grown) teamed-up to bring the process full-circle by putting on a 24-hour play of their own. While Tina's New York invention had packed all of the elements of the theatrical business (including 8 x 10's, auditions, full written scripts, etc.) into a 24 hour period to create very short plays, Ivy and her "kids" took a route closer to the comics tradition and created and performed a full 70 minute play all by themselves in the 24-hour period.

The 24-Hour Plays in turn inspired the massive 48-Hour Film Project (at *www.48hourfilm.com*), while the comics helped spawn a

24-Hour animation website and 24-Hour Website Challenge. There's even an Album-in-a-Day movement. Coincidence? Yeah, okay, maybe that one is. But still...

The Dare

So, do you draw? You know, it really it worth it. C'mon...

Want to know the rules? Here we go.

THE GOAL: To create a complete 24 page comic book in 24 continuous hours.

That means *everything*: Story, finished art, lettering, colors (if you want 'em), paste-up, everything! Once pen hits paper, the clock starts ticking. 24 hours later, the pen lifts off the paper, never to descend again. Even proofreading has to occur in the 24 hour period. [Computer-generated comics are fine of course, same principles apply.]

No sketches, designs, plot summaries or any other kind of direct preparation can precede the 24 hour period. Indirect preparation such as assembling tools, reference materials, food, music etc. is fine.

Your pages can be any size, any material. Carve 'em in stone; print 'em with rubber stamps; draw 'em on your kitchen walls with a magic marker. Anything.

The 24 hours are continuous. You can take a nap if you like, but the clock will continue to tick. If you get to 24 hours and you're not done, either end it there ("the Gaiman Variation") or keep going until you're done ("the Eastman Variation"). I consider both of these "Noble Failure Variants" and true 24 hour comics in spirit; but you must sincerely intend to do the 24 pages in 24 hours at the outset.

THE ONLINE VARIATION: The above applies to printed comics or online comics with "pages" but if you'd like to try a 24-hour Online Comic that doesn't break down into pages (like the expanded canvas approach I use in most of my own webcomics) then try this: At least 100 panels and it has to be done, formatted and online within the 24-hour period.

When you're done, send me a photocopy (or link, in the case of webcomics). Yes, this is actually one of the "rules," (sometimes referred to as the "Rumpelstiltskin" rule.) Inventor's prerogative! Send your copies (successes and failures alike) to:

Scott McCloud
Box 115
Newbury Park CA 91319

Then use my forms on the 24-Hour Index Page to get your name listed with the proud and the few!

Suggestions

At one hour per page, some treat the 24-hour comic as a minimalist excercise — how little can you put on a page and still have it be comics — but I like to think of it in the opposite way; how much can you draw in an hour?! If you think about it, the answer is a lot! Figuring six panels per page that's ten minutes per panel. Try it yourself. [Yeah, right now!] Draw a box about 3 inches wide, 2 inches tall, set a timer for ten minutes and see how much you can draw. You might surprise yourself.

As far as planning goes, you can think about it beforehand, but I recommend improvisation as the most satisfying route. Perhaps have some randomizer at startup (like Pictionary cards, a Tarot Card Deck or a child's picture book of household objects) to actually prevent you from knowing what the story will be about beforehand. The less you plan, the less likely you are to get frustrated.

Some have found the exercise is especially fun to do in big groups. Some even chronicle the food they ate, the music they listened to, etc. Doing it alone can be kind of bleak, but also have a cool rite-of-passage feeling to it. Your choice.

My strongest suggestion: Do it! It's fun, it's exciting, it's mind-altering, it'll teach you all kinds of cool stuff about yourself and - best of all - it's only one day, so what have you got to lose?

Scott McCloud
Newbury Park, California
February 2004

a life in black and white

by SR BISSETTE
© 9/5/90

STEVE BISSETTE

Steve Bissette's "A Life in Black and White" showcases Steve's dark sense of humor to great effect. It's also a showcase for the sorts of desperate tortured gyrations the artistic mind can undergoe when the clock is ticking and the body is screaming in vain to just lie down and rest.

When drawing an ordinary comic, it takes days or even weeks to execute a visual idea that may have come to mind fully-formed in 60 seconds; meaning that the execution of the page is usually a rational, conscious affair like fixing a bicycle or washing the dishes. But when your hands are closing in on the next panel and *you haven't even figured out what that next panel is going to be yet,* your mind has to call on the emergency back-up generator of the subconscious—at which point things can get very interesting indeed. Check out Steve's choice of visuals for Marty's "angel" for an idea of what I'm talking about. (No, not yet; no peeking!)

When Steve draws fast, his lines have a savage, screaming, punk-ass *rightness* to them; the way that the vocals of Jack White (of The White Stripes) always seem to be on the verge of swerving out of control, yet still drive straight into the note every time. Although it includes the occasional "white-cow-in-a-snowstorm"-style dodge, Steve's deliciously nasty tale also boasts some marvellously detailed grotesqueries; including, lest you miss it, a rather striking portrait of an ill-fated penis, as well as my personal favorite, our protagonist's sad, panoramic graduation picture. I've read it a dozen times and always manage to find something new.

"A Life in Black and White" was the first 24-hour comic I saw after my own attempt and it's still one of my favorites.

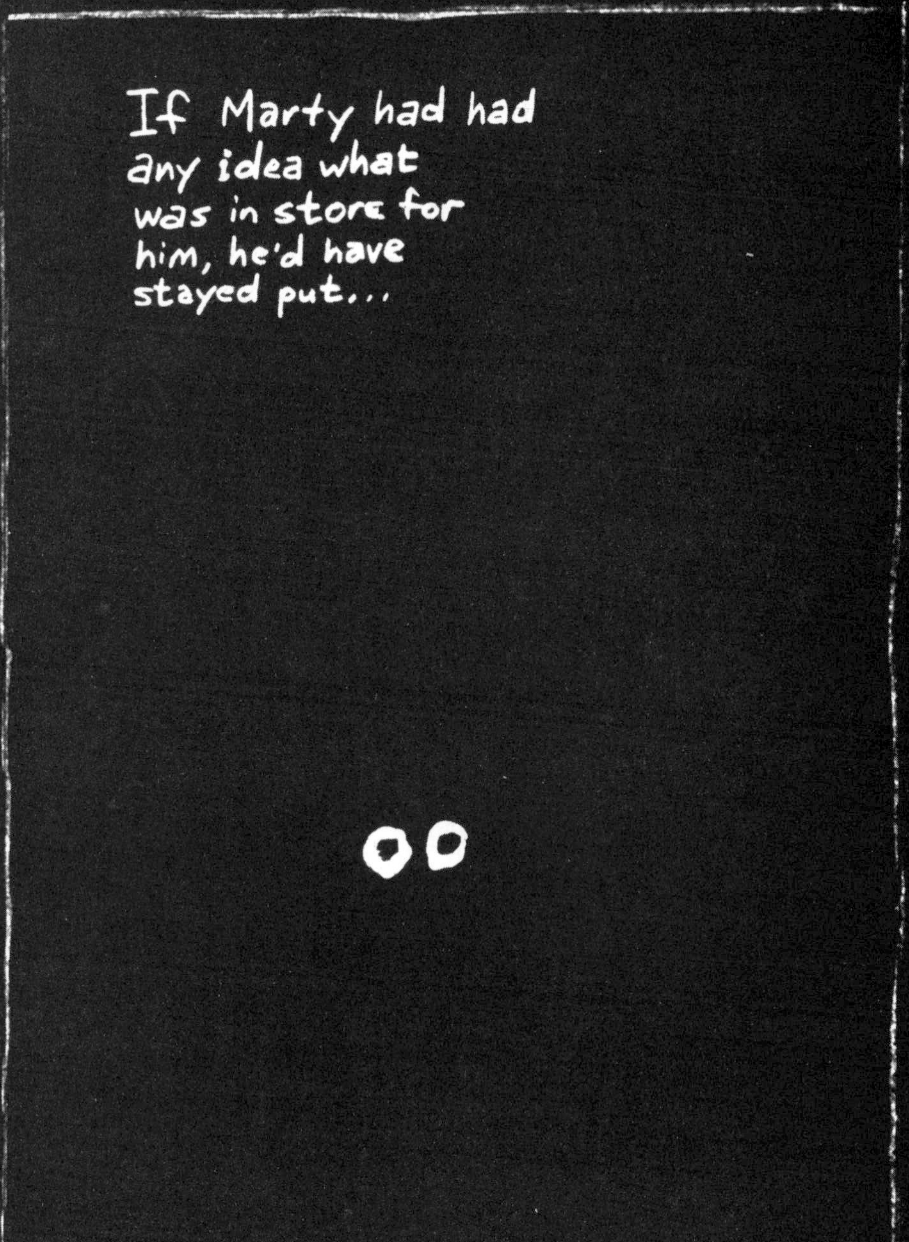
If Marty had had any idea what was in store for him, he'd have stayed put...

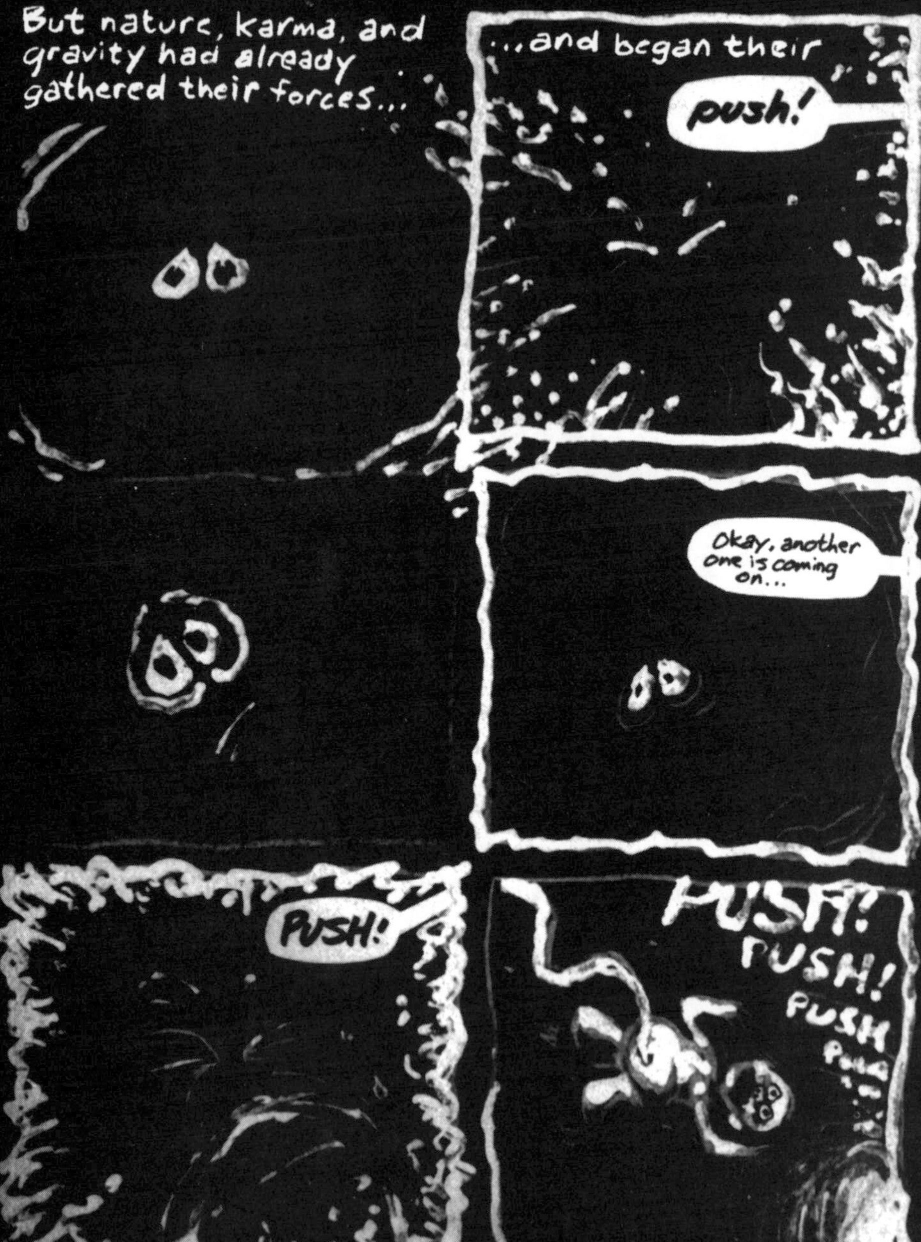
But nature, karma, and gravity had already gathered their forces...
...and began their
push!
Okay, another one is coming on...
PUSH!
PUSH!
PUSH!
PUSH
Things got worse.

The doctor dropped Marty on his fragile little skull.
He was fitted for a glass eye and a metal plate was surgically implanted.
What a l'il monkey!
Of course, as Marty grew, the plate and eye had to be regularly replaced.
Surgery became a way of life, but Marty had the niftiest marbles in the neighborhood (that wasn't of any importance yet).
PING!
Things got worse. Marty's first word was 'lawyer'.
A freak accident cost Marty his right arm.
Dishwasher

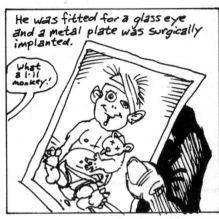

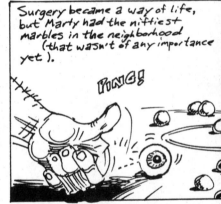

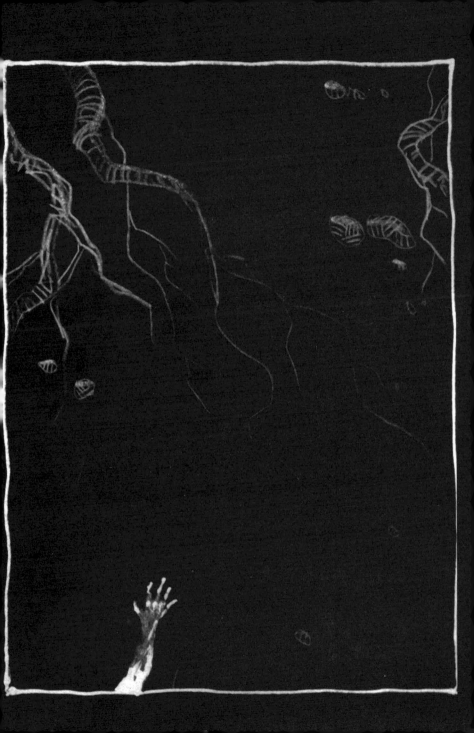

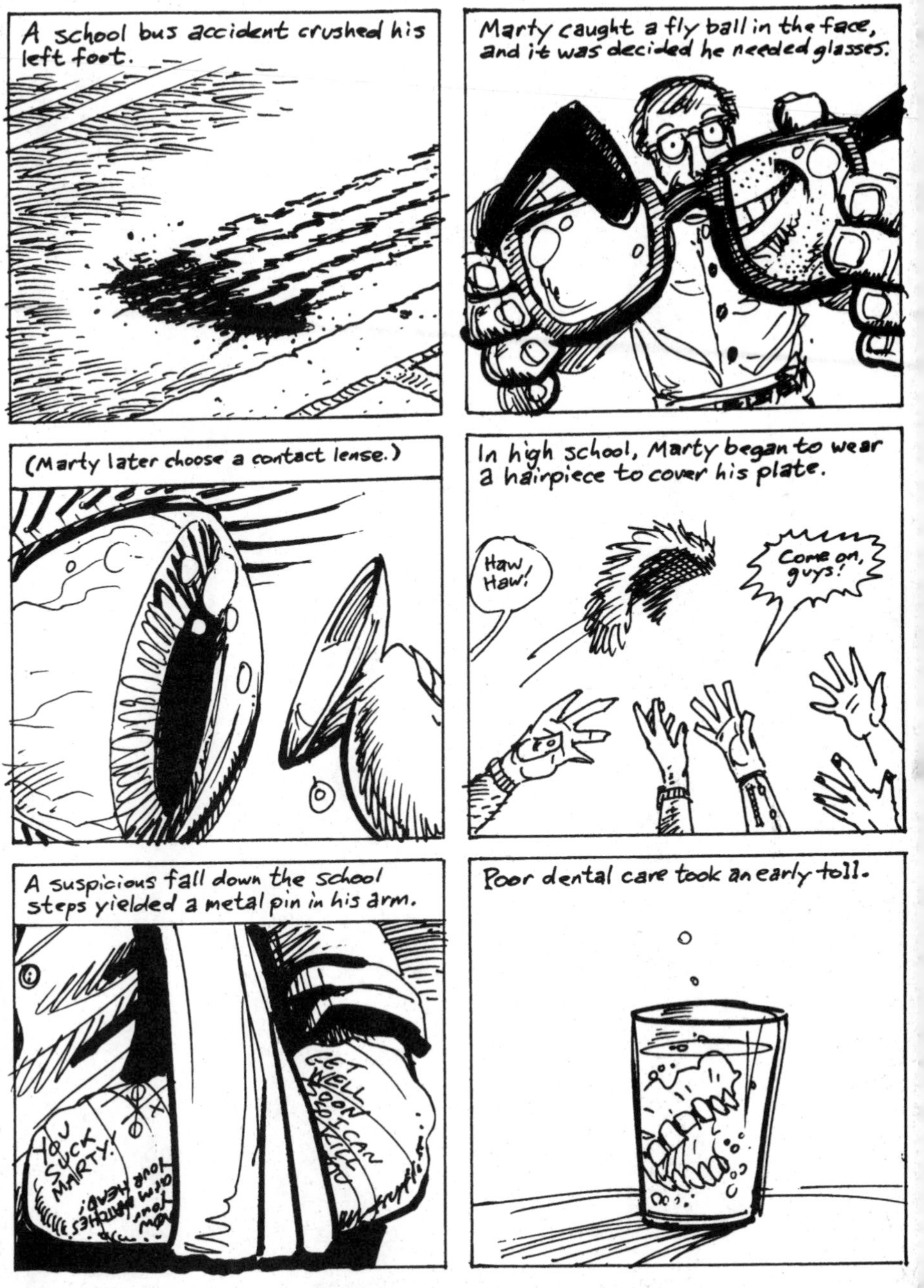
A school bus accident crushed his left foot.
Marty caught a fly ball in the face, and it was decided he needed glasses.
(Marty later choose a contact lense.)
In high school, Marty began to wear a hairpiece to cover his plate.
Haw Haw!
Come on, guys!
A suspicious fall down the school steps yielded a metal pin in his arm.
YOU SUCK MARTY!
GET WELL SOON SO I CAN
Poor dental care took an early toll.

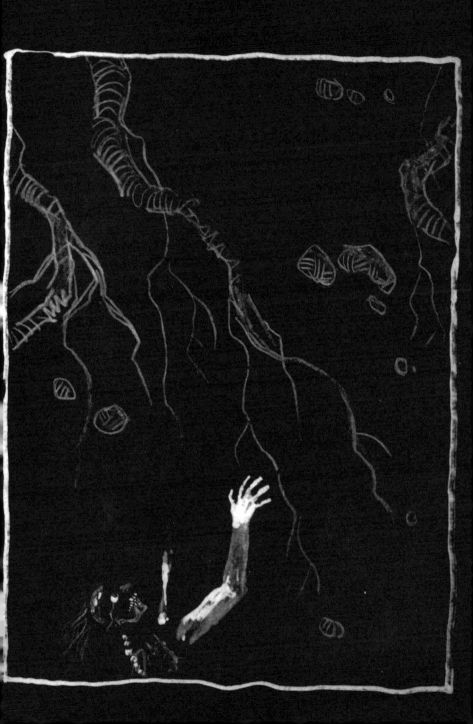

Marty survived high school, graduating with honors.

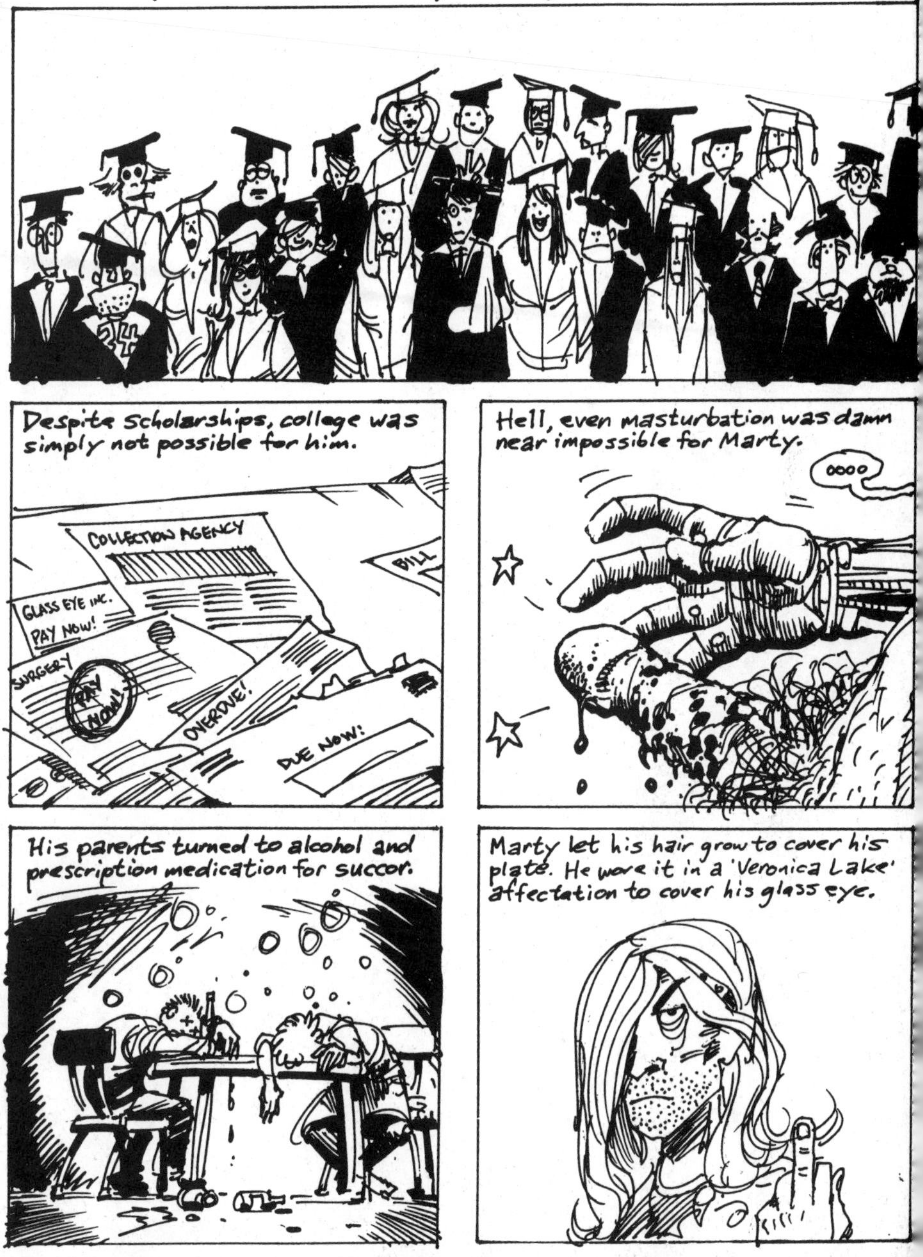
Despite scholarships, college was simply not possible for him.
COLLECTION AGENCY
BILL
GLASS EYE INC.
PAY NOW!
SURGERY
PAY NOW!
OVERDUE!
DUE NOW!
Hell, even masturbation was damn near impossible for Marty.
oooo
His parents turned to alcohol and prescription medication for succor.
Marty let his hair grow to cover his plate. He wore it in a 'Veronica Lake' affectation to cover his glass eye.

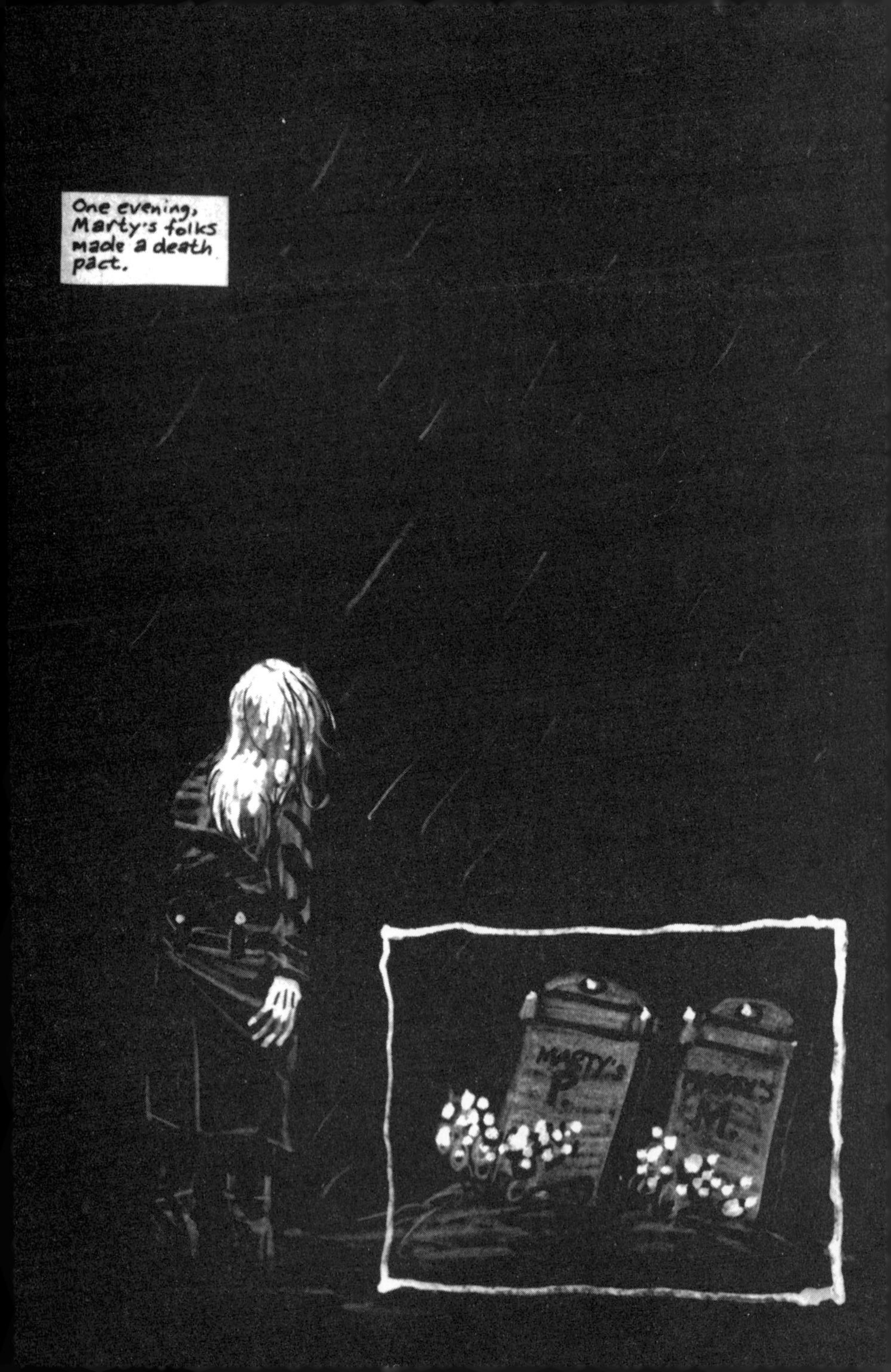
One evening, Marty's folks made a death pact.
MARTY'S P.

Things rapidly went downhill after the funeral.

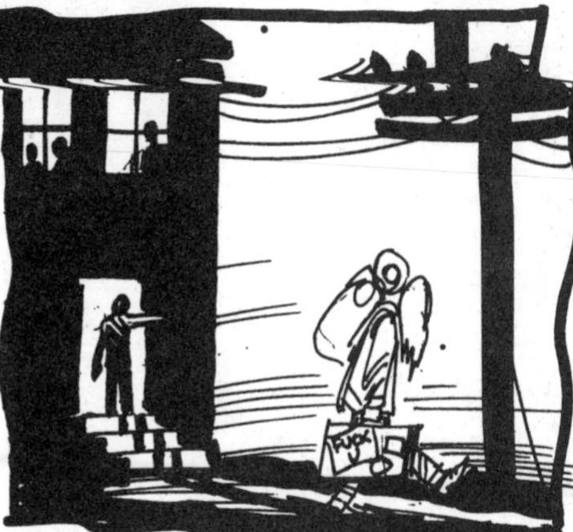
FUCK

With creditors hounding him, Marty was rejected by a succession of dimly remembered relatives.

Dejected and utterly alone, Marty shaved his head and sought escape in an escalating haze of drugs, depravity, and self-abuse.

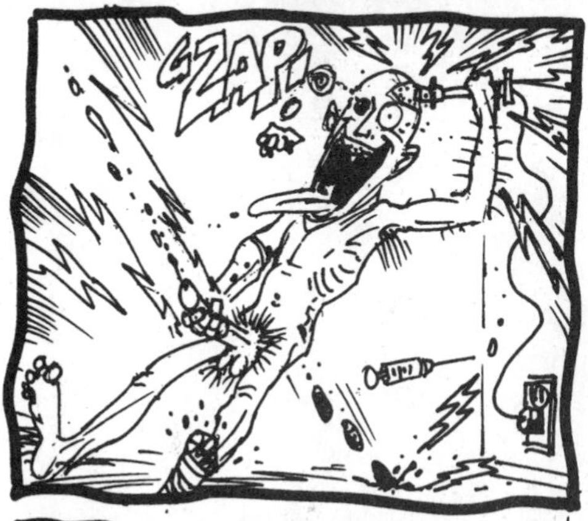

The authorities found him on the street, nude and near-comatose. His artificial arm was gone and his kidneys were failing.

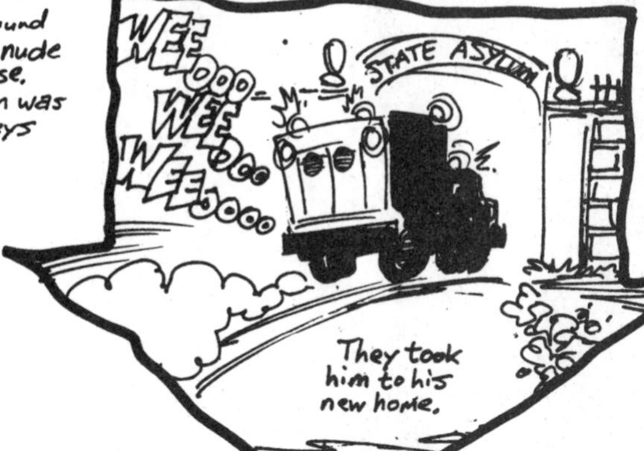
STATE ASYLUM
They took him to his new home.

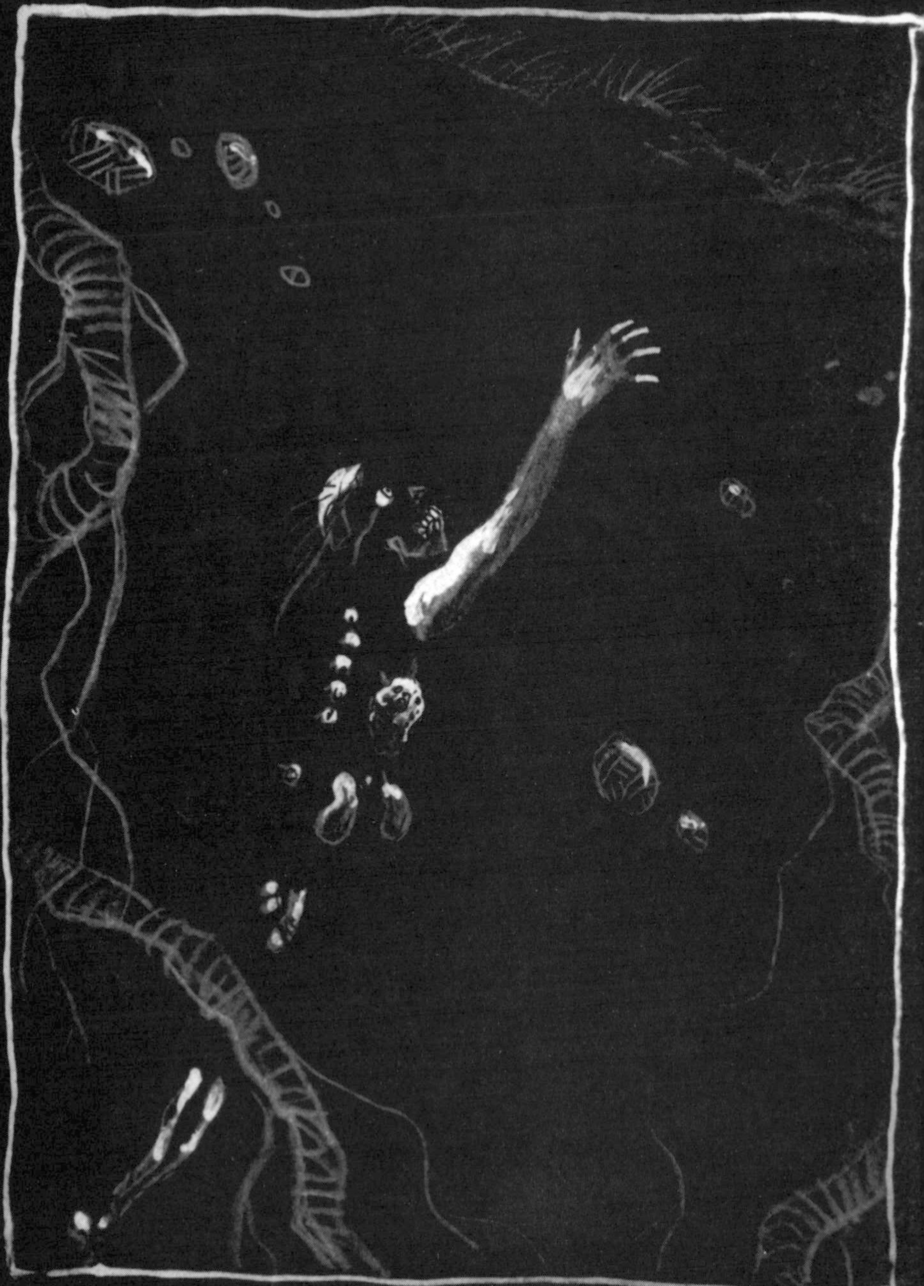

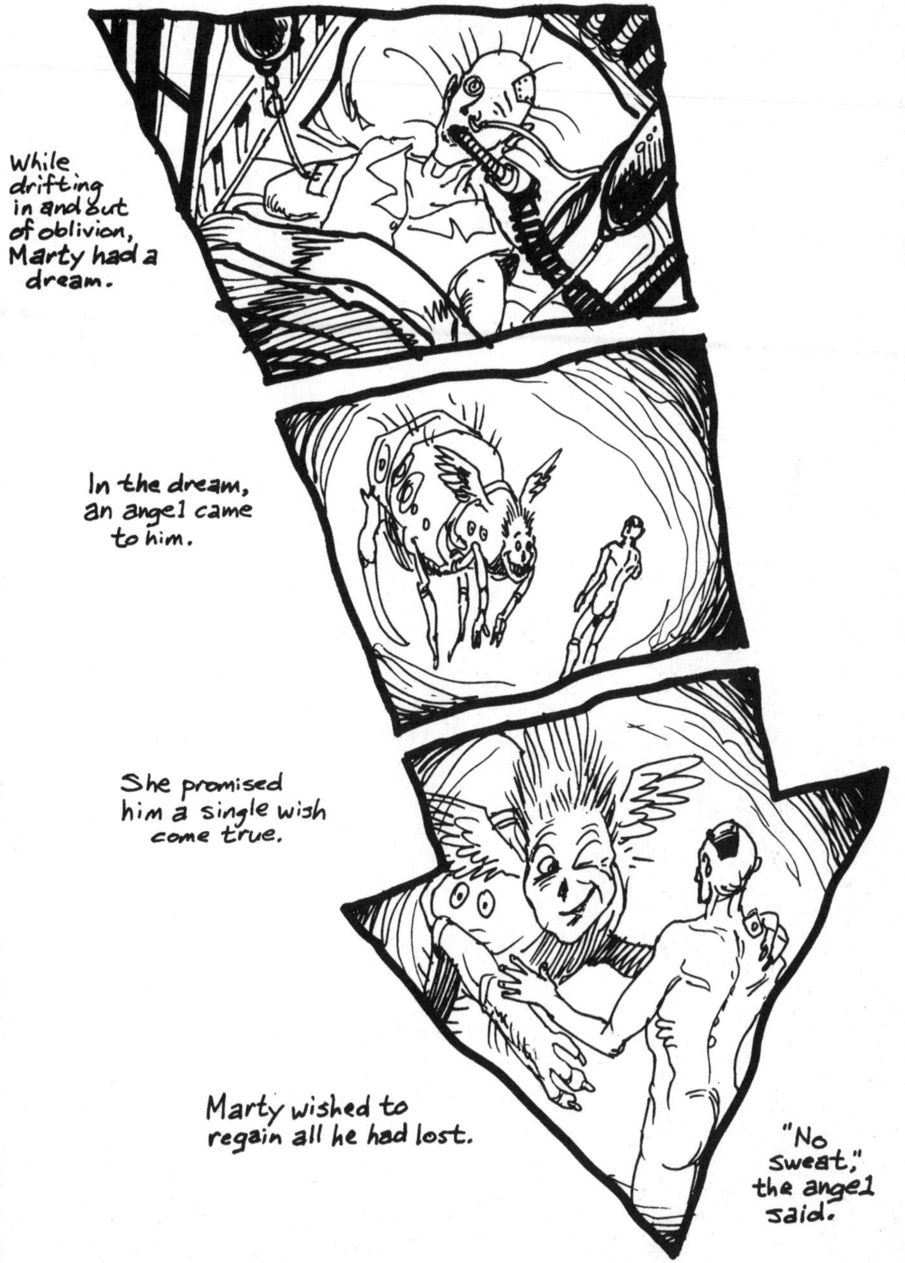

While drifting in and out of oblivion, Marty had a dream.
In the dream, an angel came to him.
She promised him a single wish come true.
Marty wished to regain all he had lost.
"No sweat," the angel said.

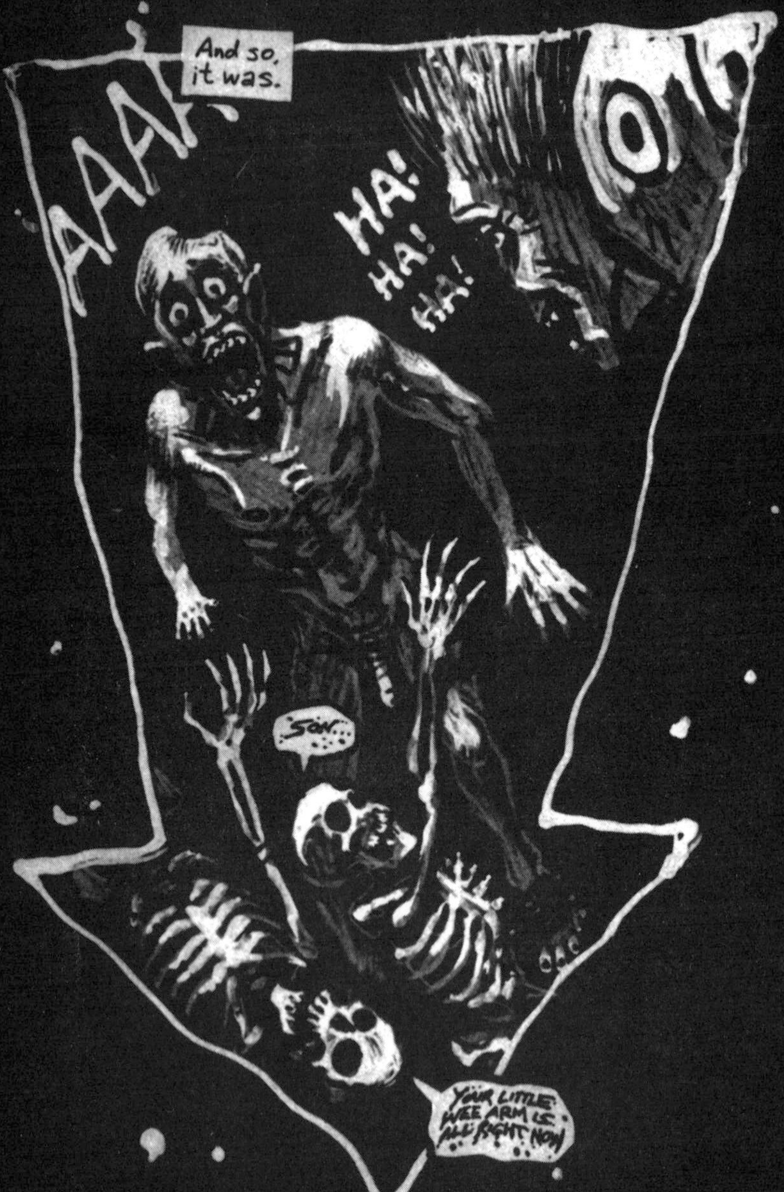
And so, it was.
AAA
HA! HA! HA!
SON
YOUR LITTLE WEE ARM IS ALL RIGHT NOW

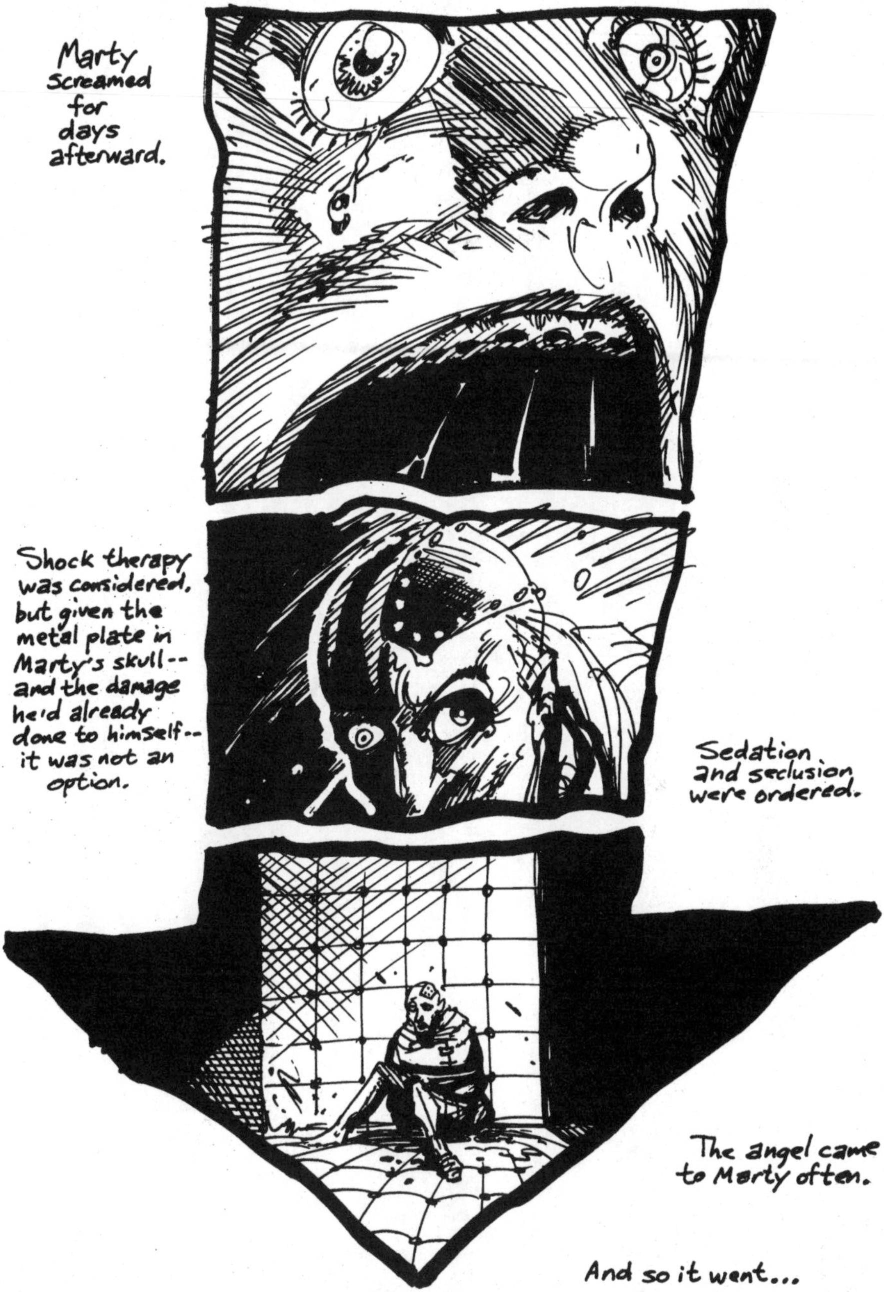
Marty screamed for days afterward.
Shock therapy was considered, but given the metal plate in Marty's skull-- and the damage he'd already done to himself-- it was not an option.
Sedation and seclusion were ordered.
The angel came to Marty often.
And so it went...

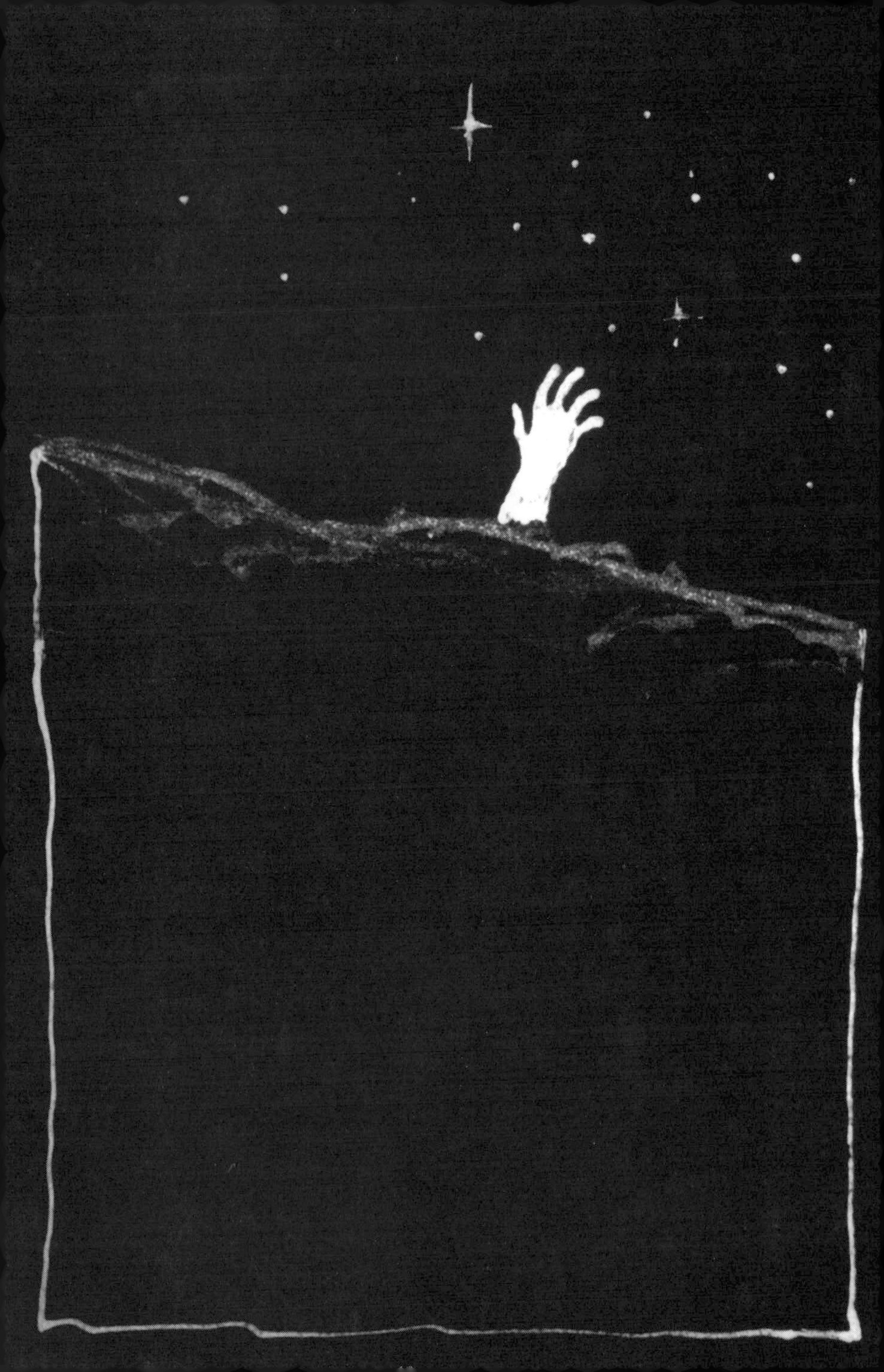

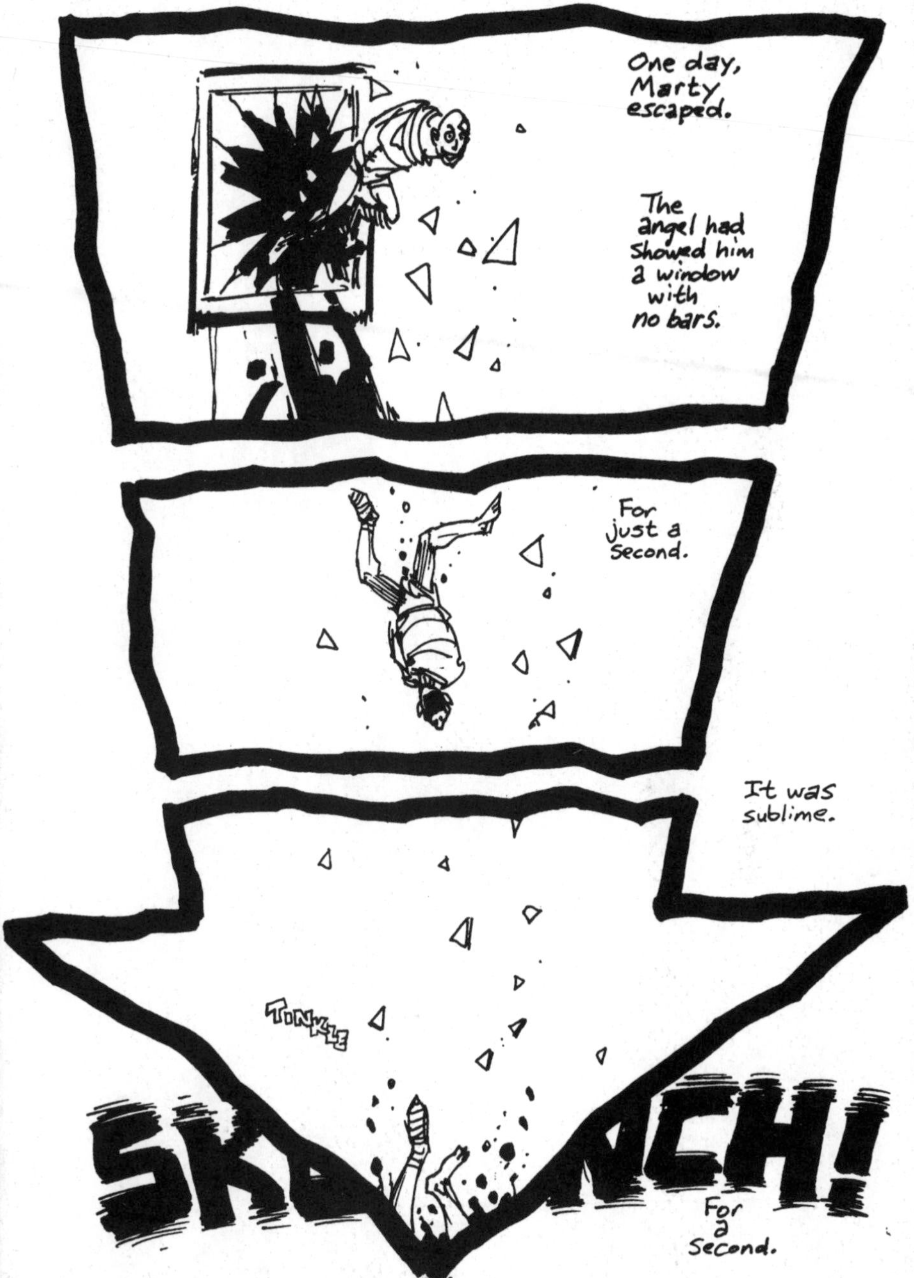

One day, Marty escaped.
The angel had showed him a window with no bars.
For just a second.
It was sublime.
TINKLE
SKR NCH!
For a second.

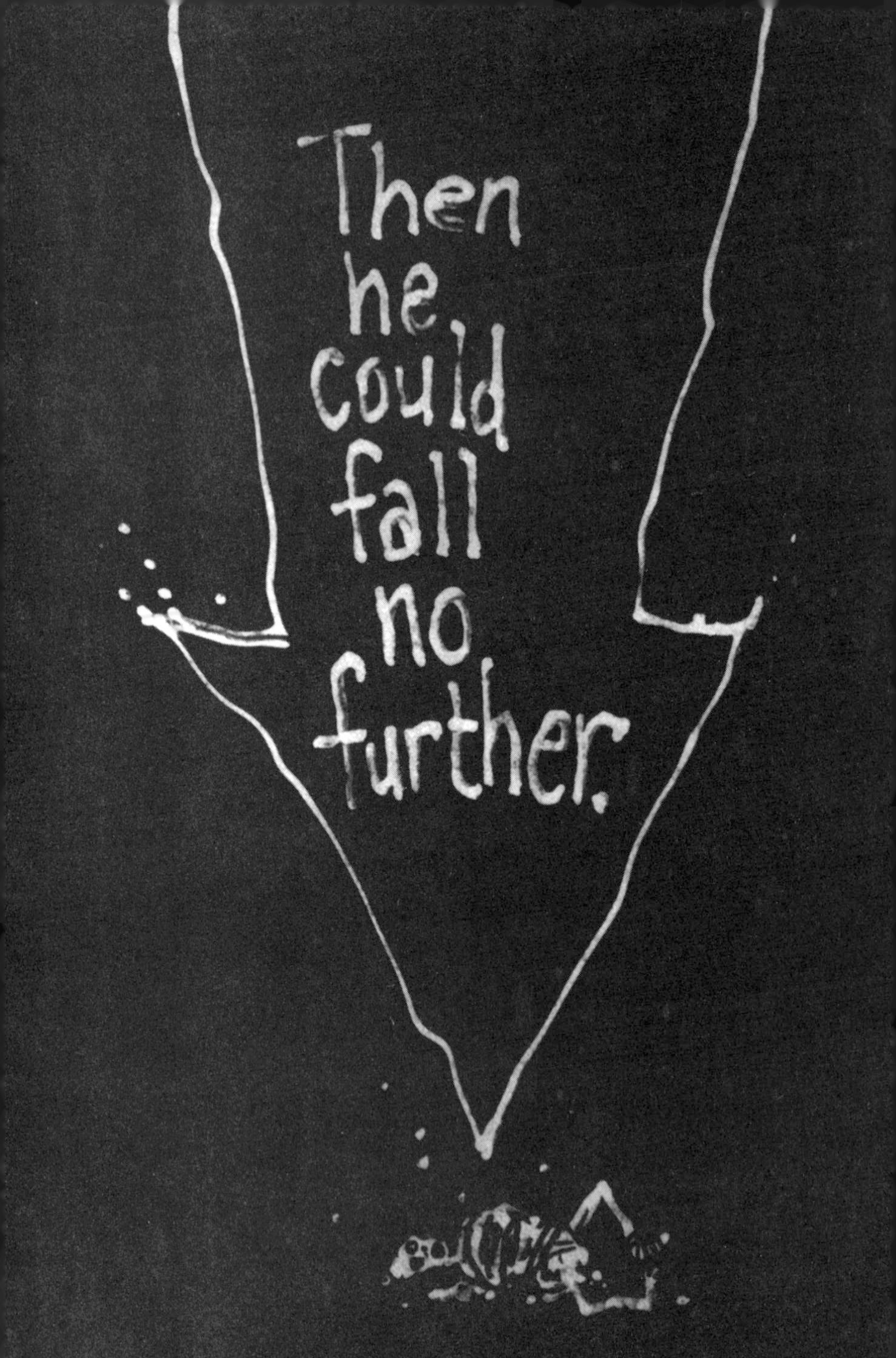
Then
he
could
fall
no
further.

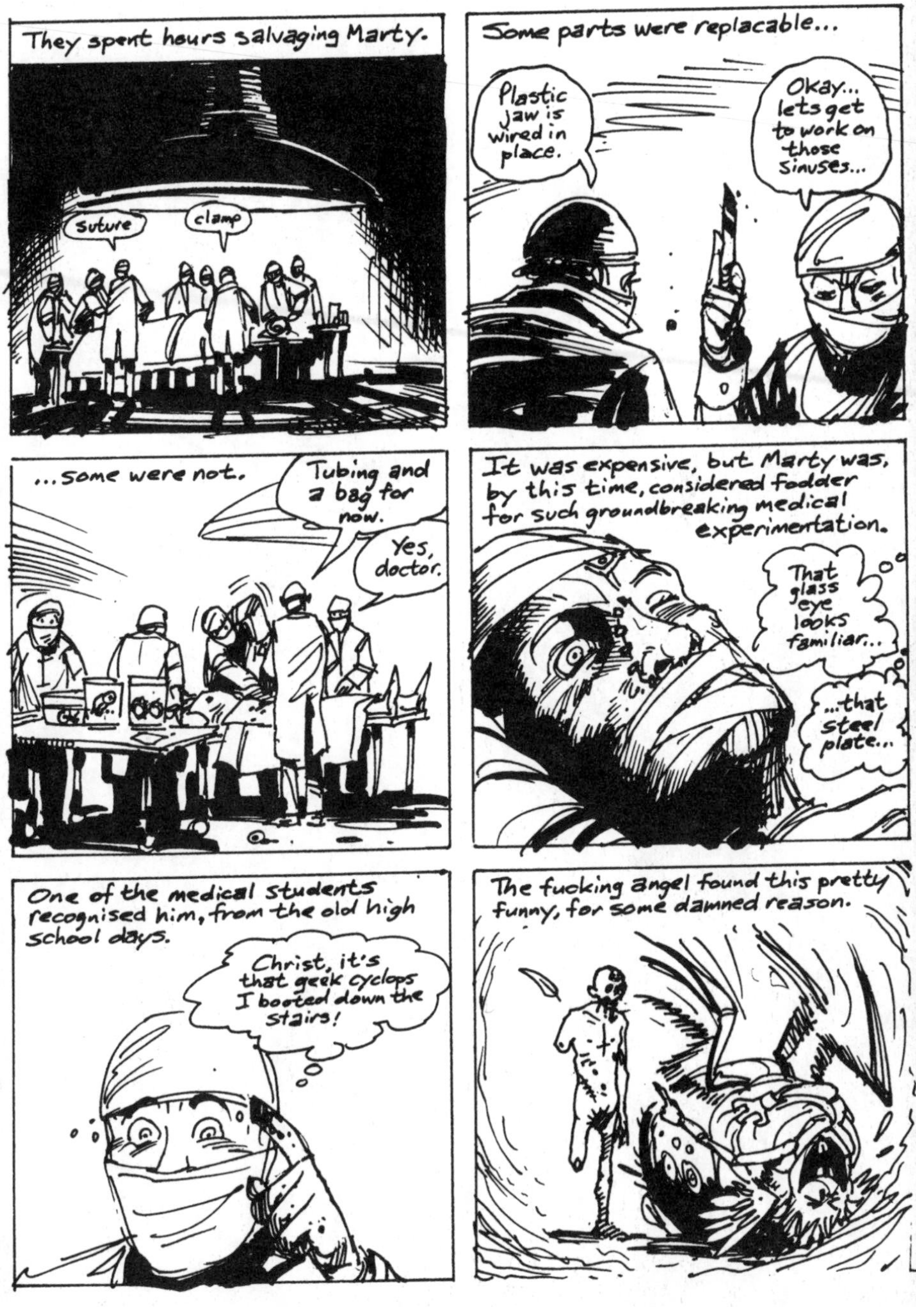
They spent hours salvaging Marty.
suture
clamp
Some parts were replacable...
Plastic jaw is wired in place.
Okay... lets get to work on those sinuses...
...some were not.
Tubing and a bag for now.
Yes, doctor.
It was expensive, but Marty was, by this time, considered fodder for such groundbreaking medical experimentation.
That glass eye looks familiar...
...that steel plate...
One of the medical students recognised him, from the old high school days.
Christ, it's that geek cyclops I booted down the stairs!
The fucking angel found this pretty funny, for some damned reason.

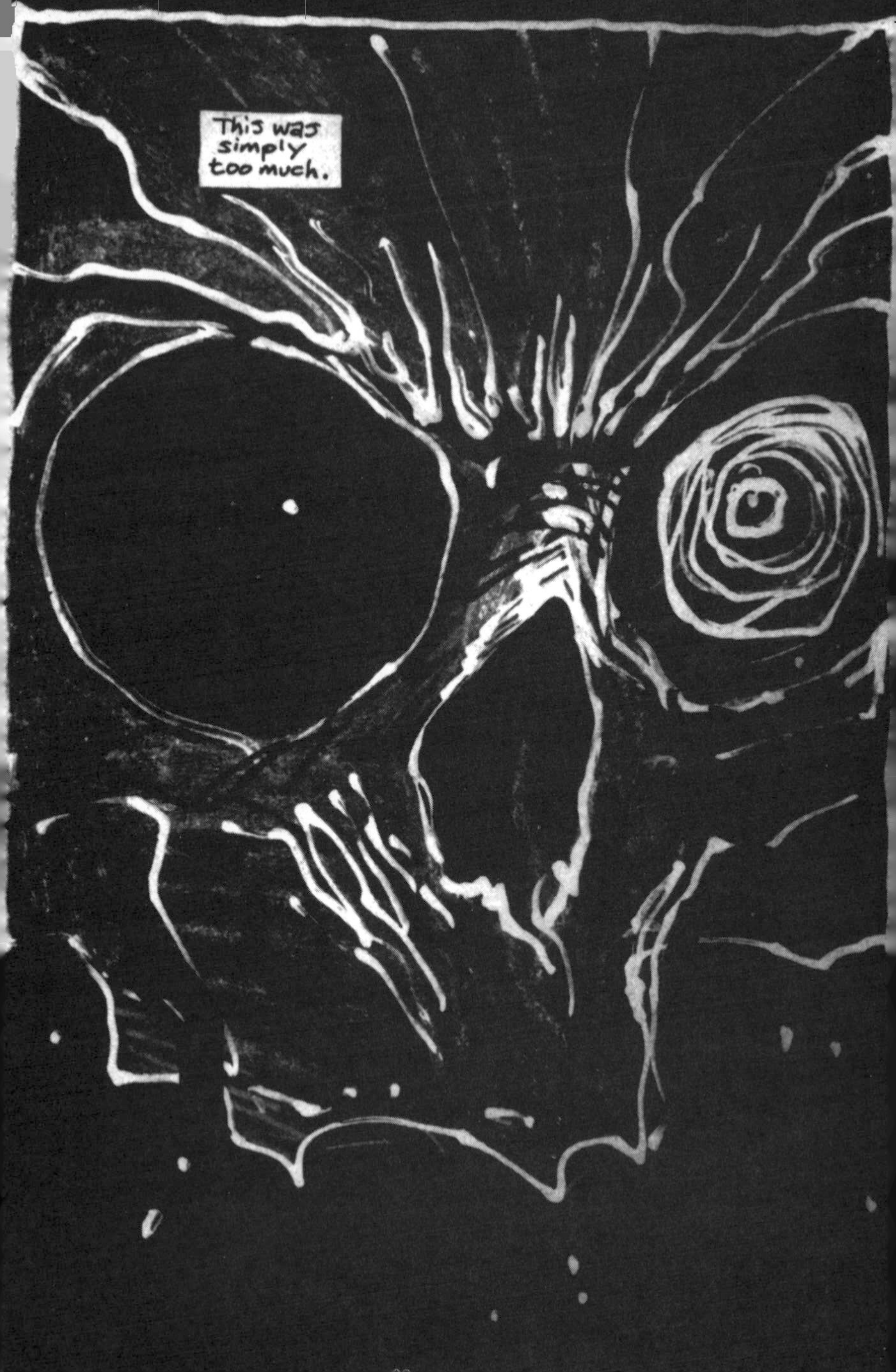
This was simply too much.

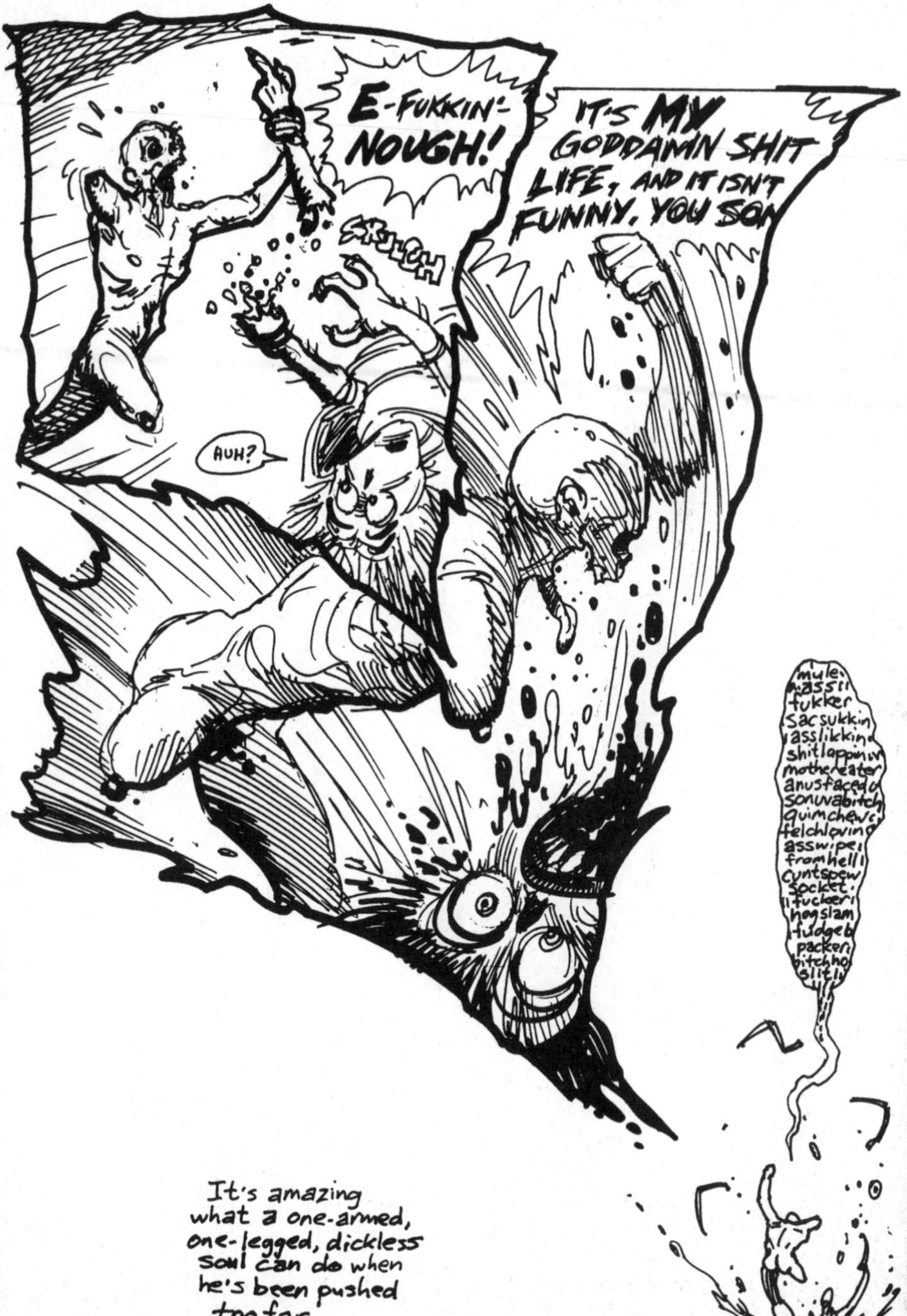
E-FUKKIN'-NOUGH!
IT'S MY GODDAMN SHIT LIFE, AND IT ISN'T FUNNY, YOU SON
SKULCH
AUH?
mule-ass fukker sacsukkin asslikkin shitlappin mothereater anusfaced sonuvabitch quimchew felchlovin asswipe from hell cuntspew socket fucker hogslam fudge packer bitchho slit
It's amazing what a one-armed, one-legged, dickless soul can do when he's been pushed too far.

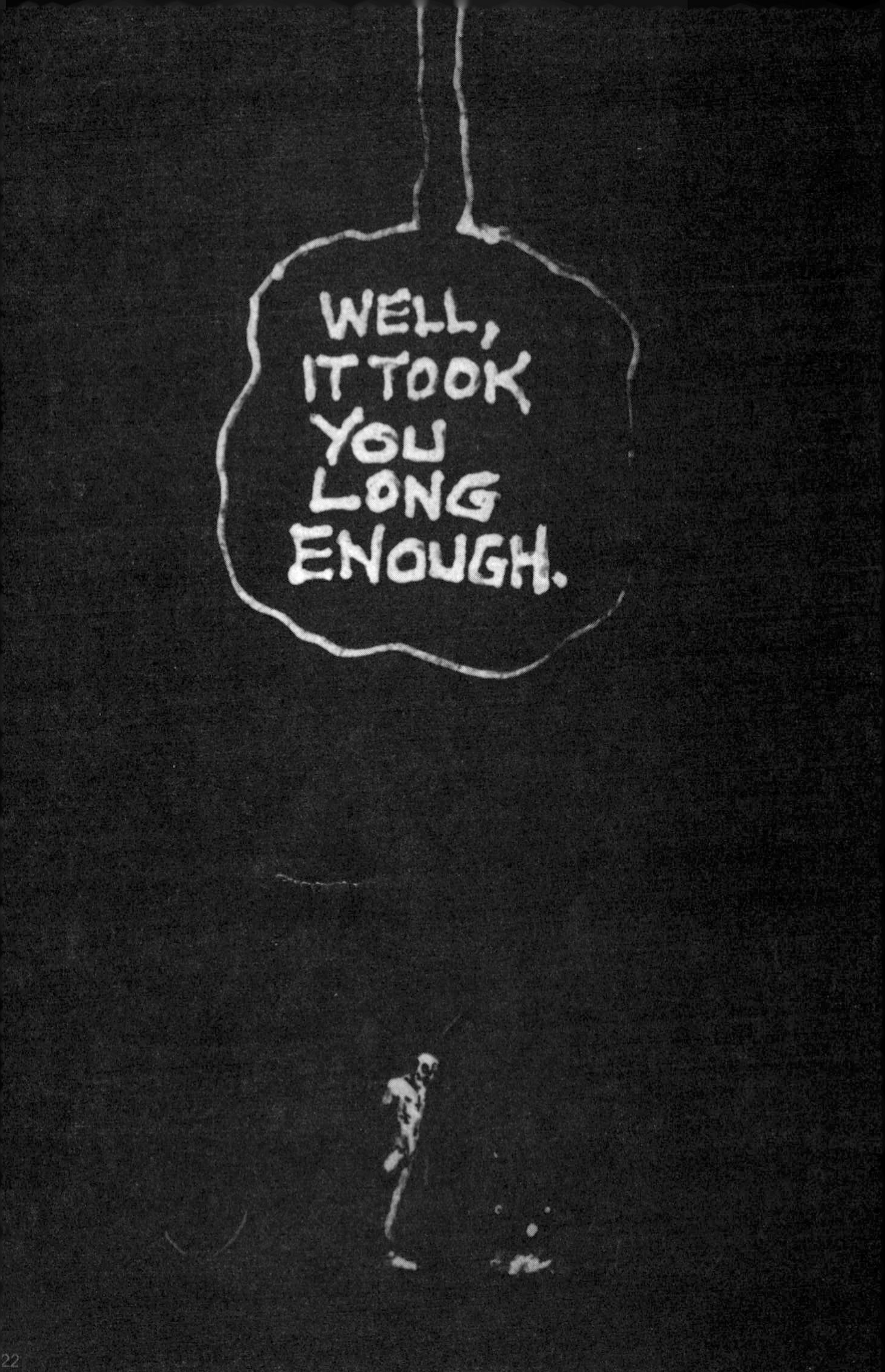
WELL, IT TOOK YOU LONG ENOUGH.

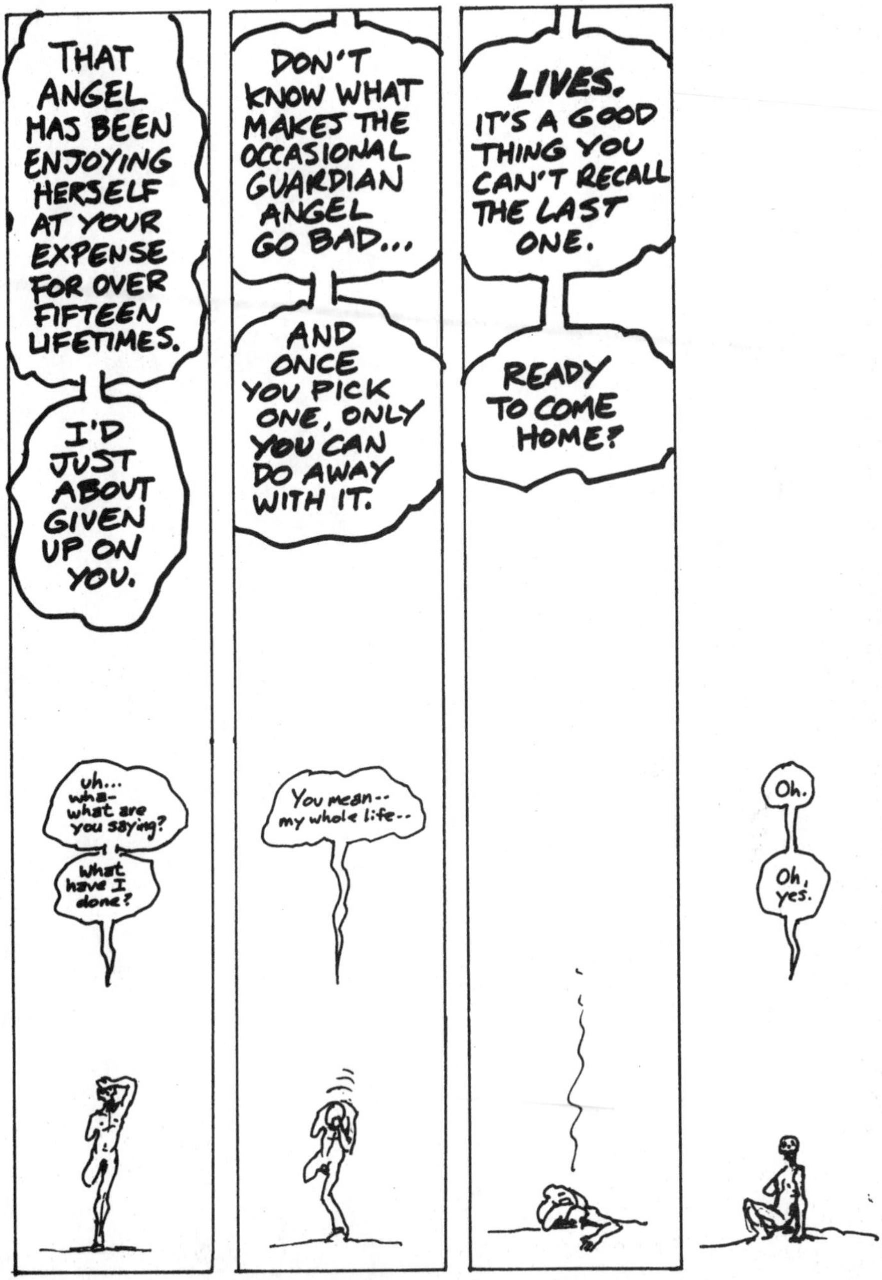
THAT ANGEL HAS BEEN ENJOYING HERSELF AT YOUR EXPENSE FOR OVER FIFTEEN LIFETIMES.
I'D JUST ABOUT GIVEN UP ON YOU.
uh... wha- what are you saying?
What have I done?
DON'T KNOW WHAT MAKES THE OCCASIONAL GUARDIAN ANGEL GO BAD...
AND ONCE YOU PICK ONE, ONLY YOU CAN DO AWAY WITH IT.
You mean-- my whole life--
LIVES. IT'S A GOOD THING YOU CAN'T RECALL THE LAST ONE.
READY TO COME HOME?
Oh.
Oh, yes.

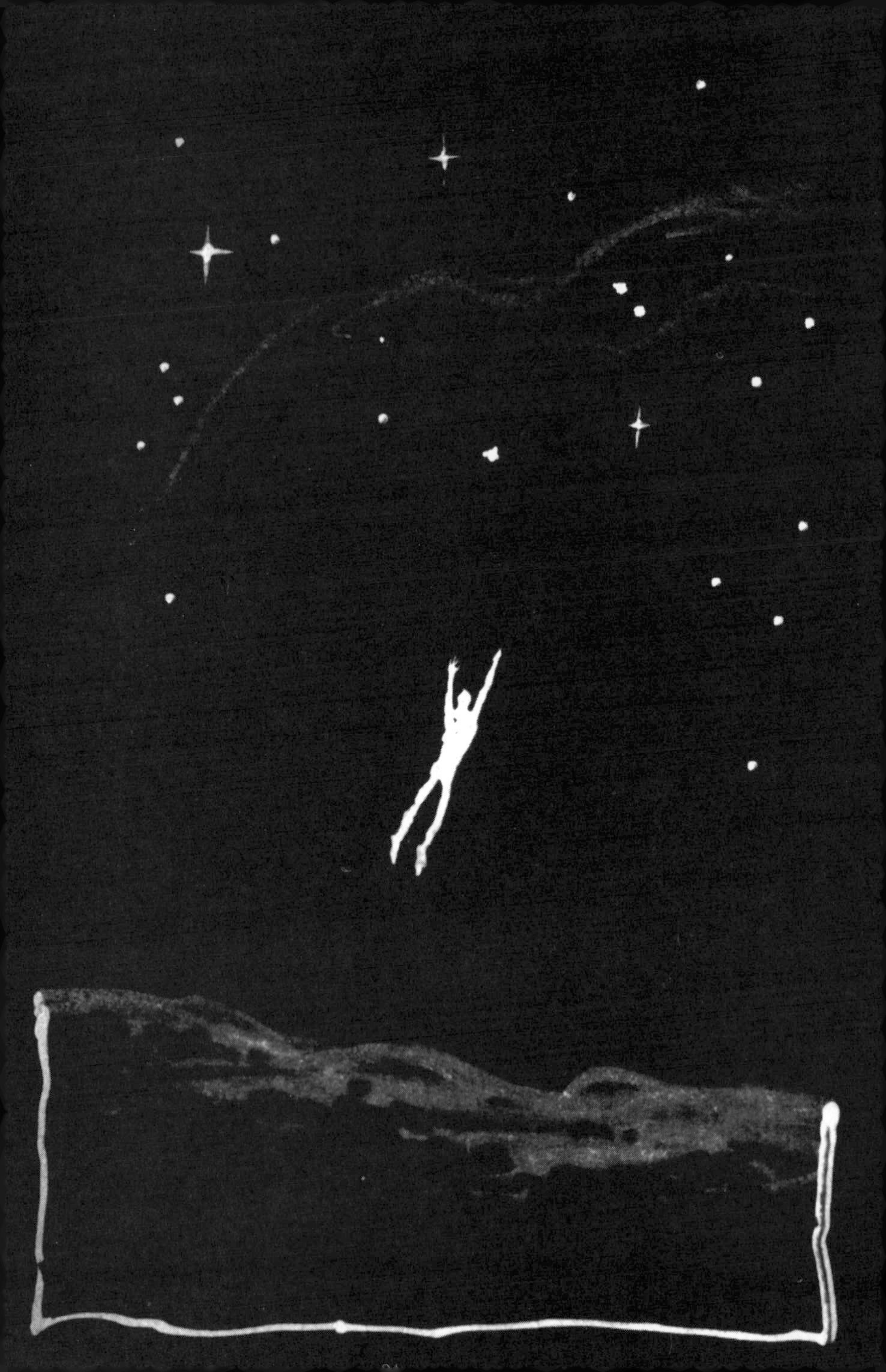

Marty died on the operating table.

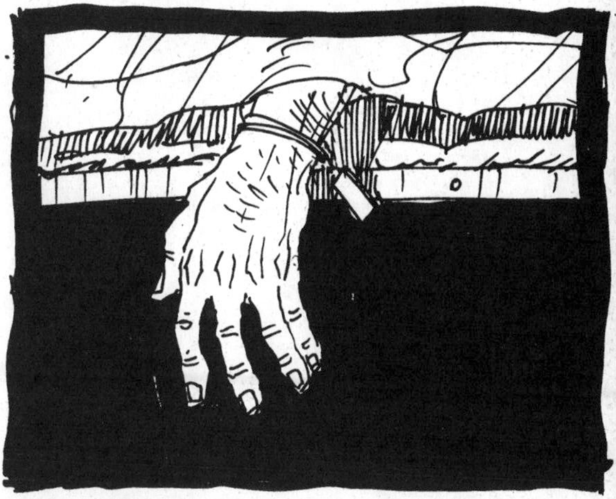

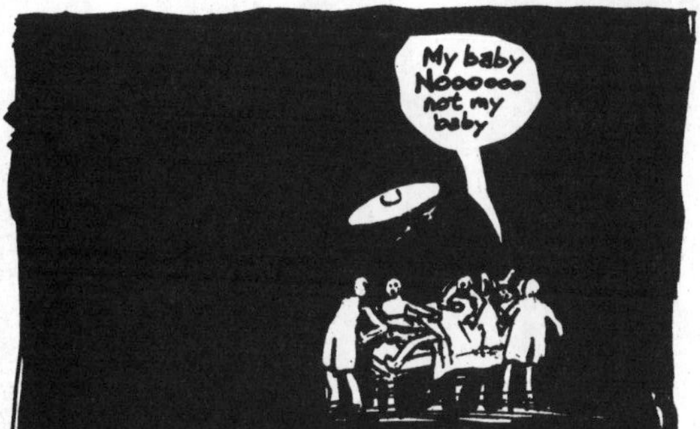
My baby Noooooo not my baby

In the maternity ward, a child was delivered stillborn.

Marty and the child were buried together without circumstance.

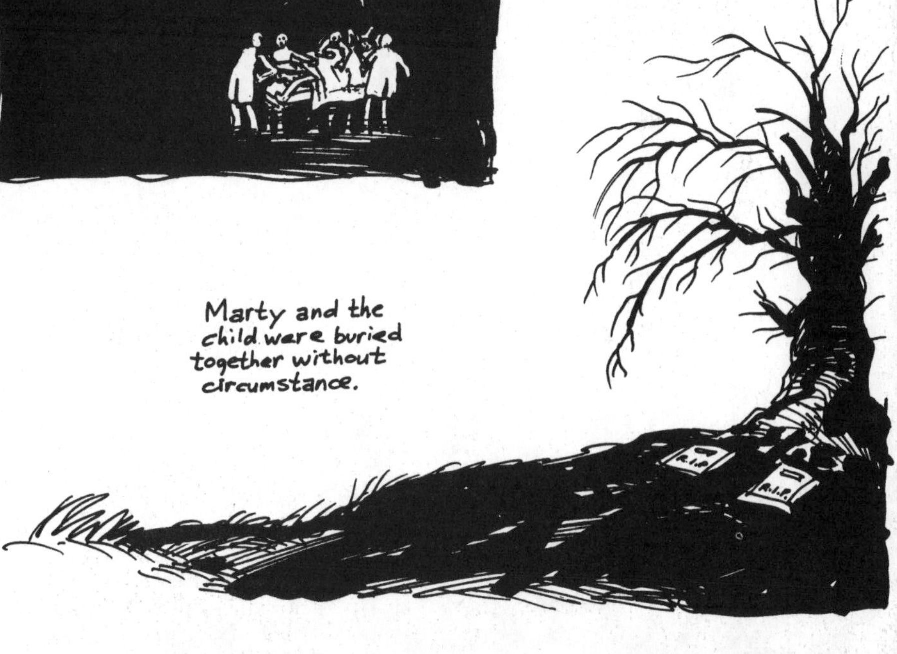
R.I.P.
R.I.P.

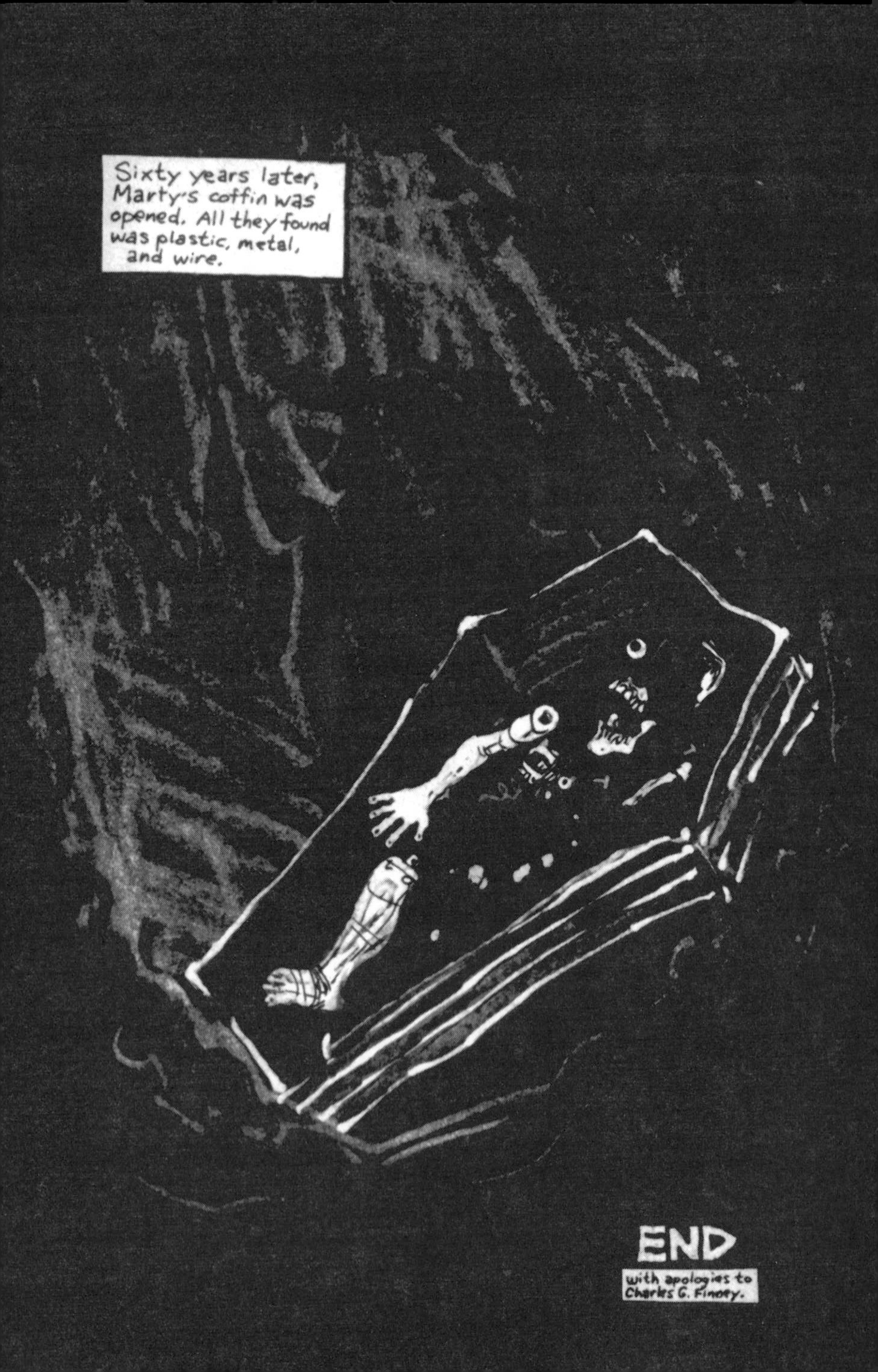
Sixty years later, Marty's coffin was opened. All they found was plastic, metal, and wire.
END
with apologies to Charles G. Finney.

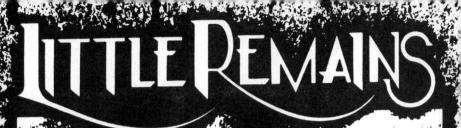

Little Remains

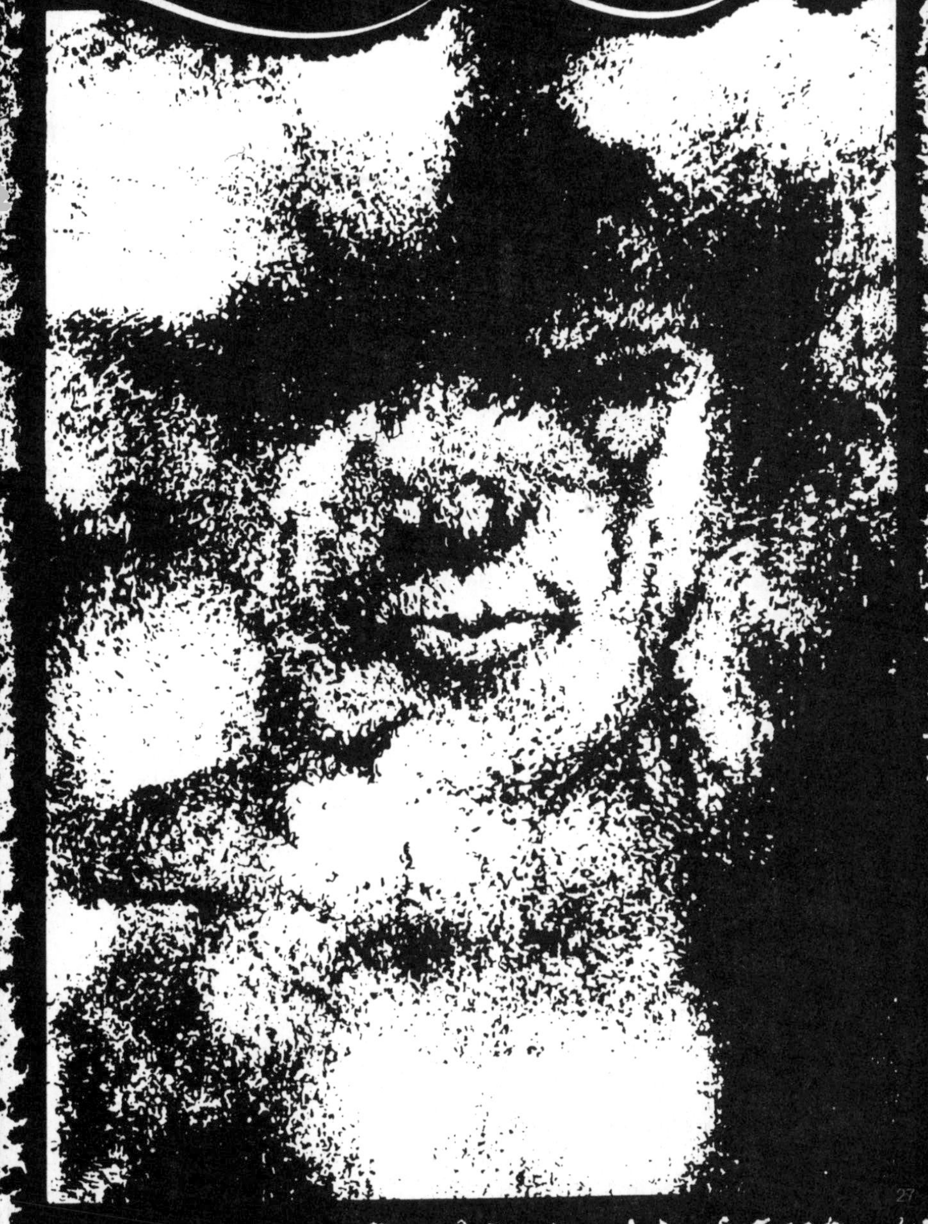

ALEX GRECIAN

Of all the 24-hour comics that have come across my desk, Alex Grecian's "Little Remains" is among the most complete and self-contained. A sweet, melancholy tale with some genuinely clever twists. Alex also distinguishes himself by having one of the better excuses for not quite making the 24 hour deadline:

"The day I started, the ceiling fo the apartment below mine caved in. Men in powder blue workshirts invaded my home and spent two days tearing my bathroom apart, tramping through every room to test the floors and doing everything else they could to annoy and distract me."

Because of those meddling gods of home repair, Alex was doomed to sit at his drawing board for a day and half before finishing, but—and this is important—he also "didn't take any naps" in full compliance with Noble Failure Variant #2 (The Eastman Variation: If you get to 24 hours and you're still not done, *keep going until you are*).

Perhaps, in part because of the extra hours, Alex's art is consistent throughout and never looks like it's running to catch up. The rendering isn't elaborate, but it's solid and effective, and it looks the same on page 24 as it does on page 1; one of the most basic pre-requisites for creating comics that allow the reader to get lost in the world of the story.

Enjoy getting lost in this one.

LITTLE REMAINS

A 24 HOUR COMIC

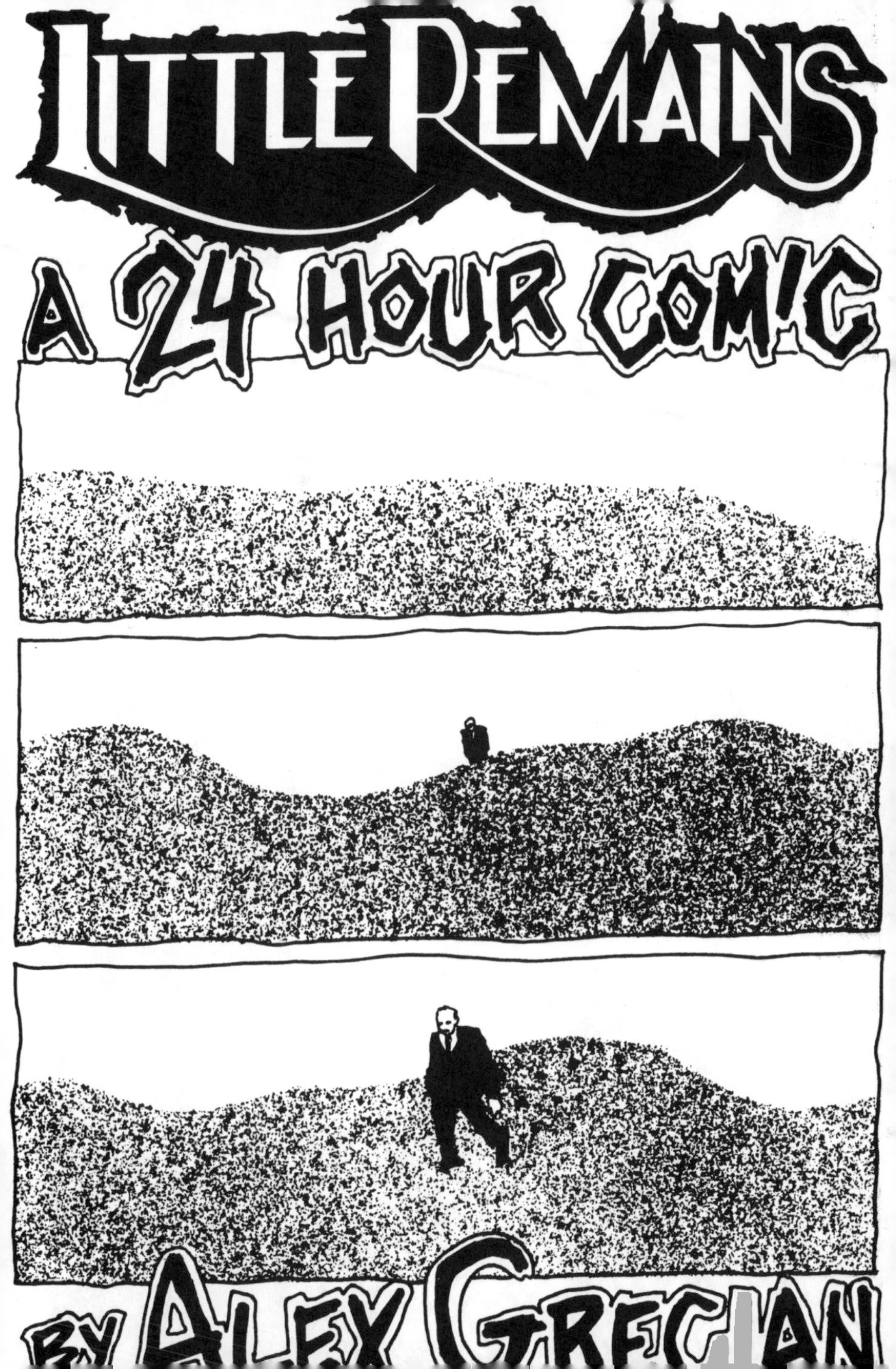

BY ALEX GRECIAN

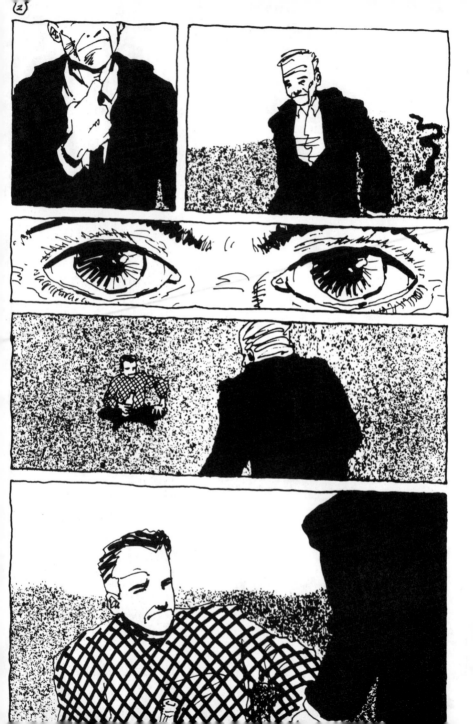

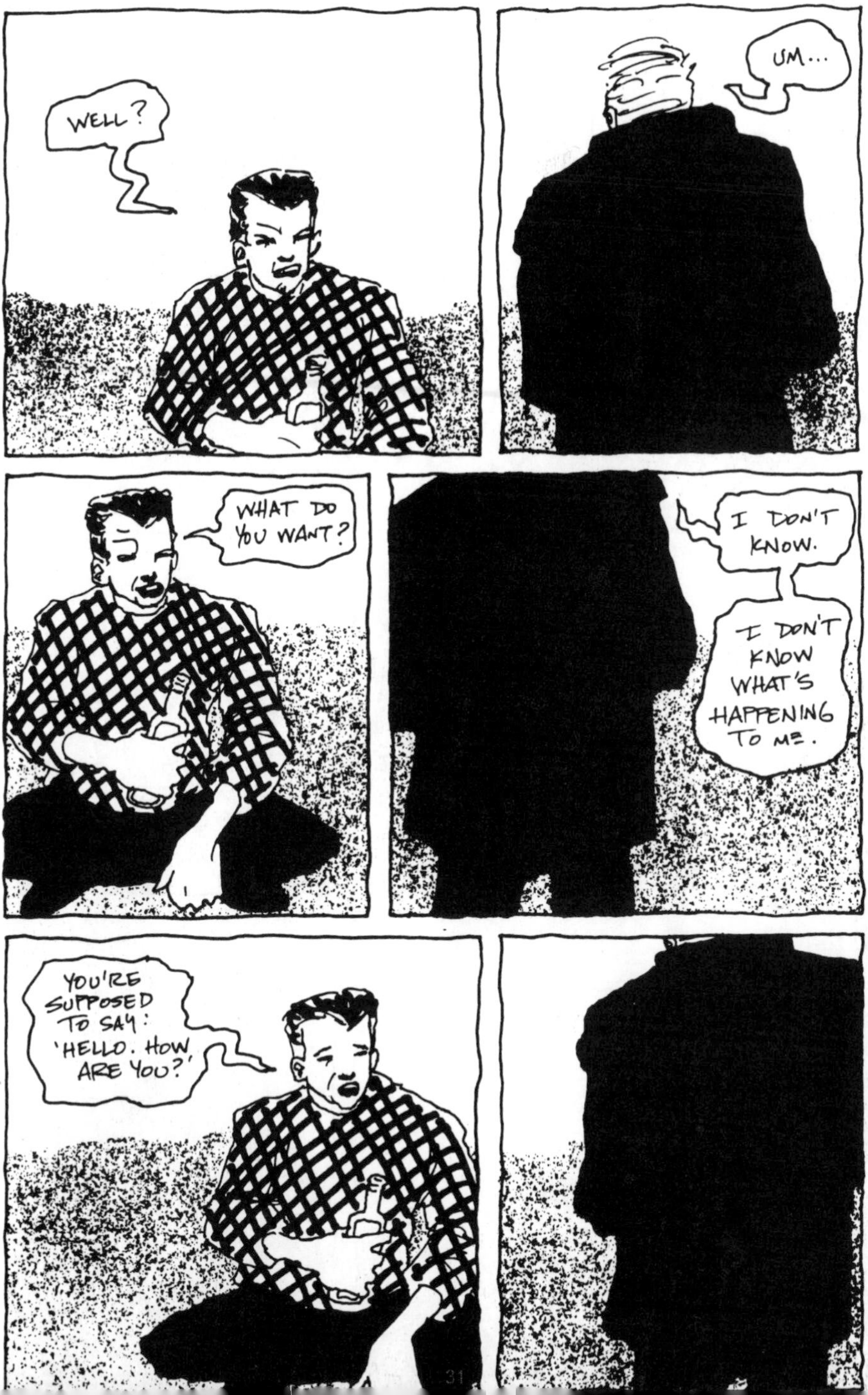
WELL?
UM...
WHAT DO YOU WANT?
I DON'T KNOW.
I DON'T KNOW WHAT'S HAPPENING TO ME.
YOU'RE SUPPOSED TO SAY: 'HELLO. HOW ARE YOU?'

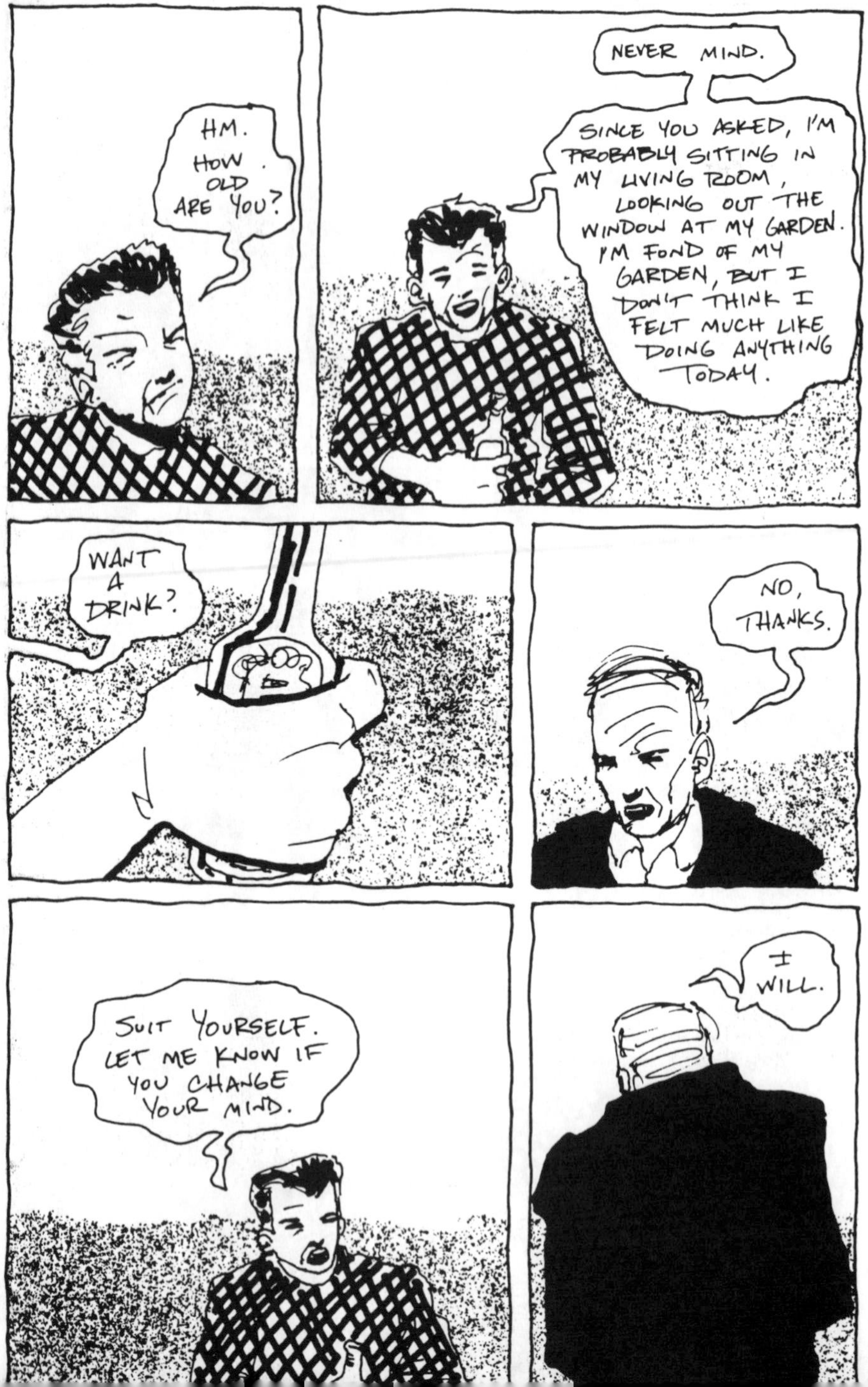
HM. HOW OLD ARE YOU?
NEVER MIND.
SINCE YOU ASKED, I'M PROBABLY SITTING IN MY LIVING ROOM, LOOKING OUT THE WINDOW AT MY GARDEN. I'M FOND OF MY GARDEN, BUT I DON'T THINK I FELT MUCH LIKE DOING ANYTHING TODAY.
WANT A DRINK?
NO, THANKS.
SUIT YOURSELF. LET ME KNOW IF YOU CHANGE YOUR MIND.
I WILL.

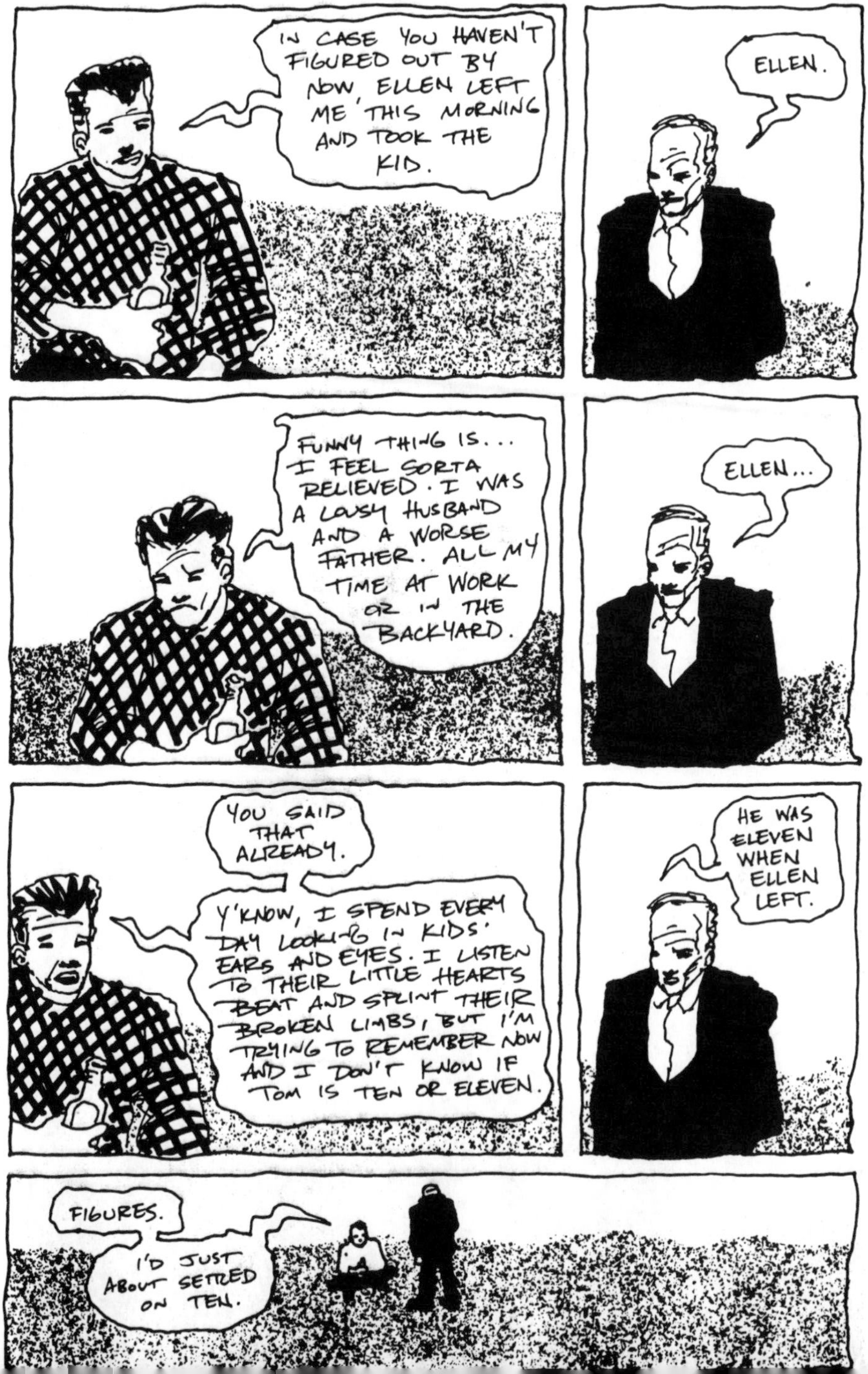
IN CASE YOU HAVEN'T FIGURED OUT BY NOW, ELLEN LEFT ME THIS MORNING AND TOOK THE KID.
ELLEN.
FUNNY THING IS... I FEEL SORTA RELIEVED. I WAS A LOUSY HUSBAND AND A WORSE FATHER. ALL MY TIME AT WORK OR IN THE BACKYARD.
ELLEN...
YOU SAID THAT ALREADY.
Y'KNOW, I SPEND EVERY DAY LOOKING IN KIDS' EARS AND EYES. I LISTEN TO THEIR LITTLE HEARTS BEAT AND SPLINT THEIR BROKEN LIMBS, BUT I'M TRYING TO REMEMBER NOW AND I DON'T KNOW IF TOM IS TEN OR ELEVEN.
HE WAS ELEVEN WHEN ELLEN LEFT.
FIGURES.
I'D JUST ABOUT SETTLED ON TEN.

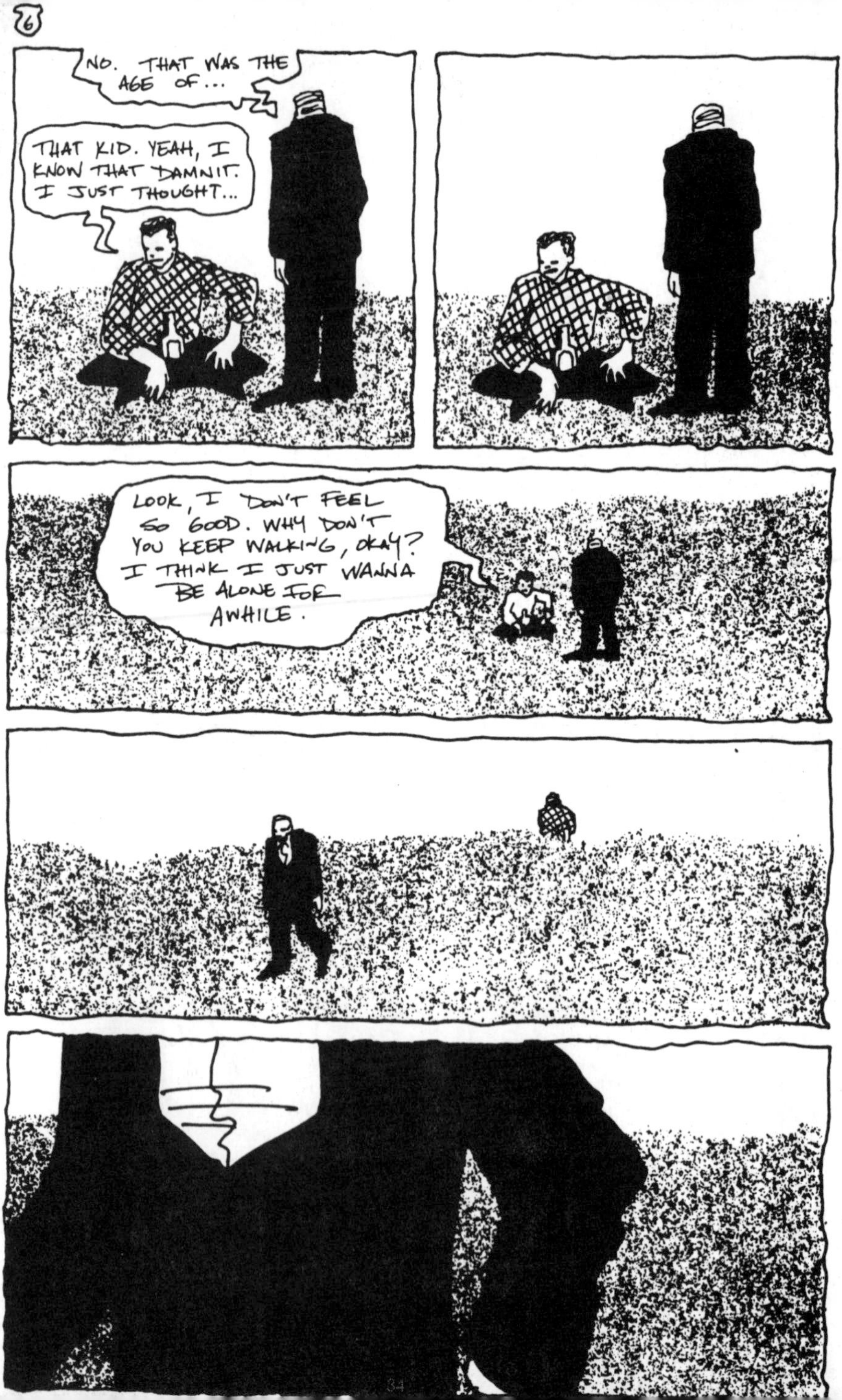
6
NO. THAT WAS THE AGE OF...
THAT KID. YEAH, I KNOW THAT DAMNIT. I JUST THOUGHT...
LOOK, I DON'T FEEL SO GOOD. WHY DON'T YOU KEEP WALKING, OKAY? I THINK I JUST WANNA BE ALONE FOR AWHILE.

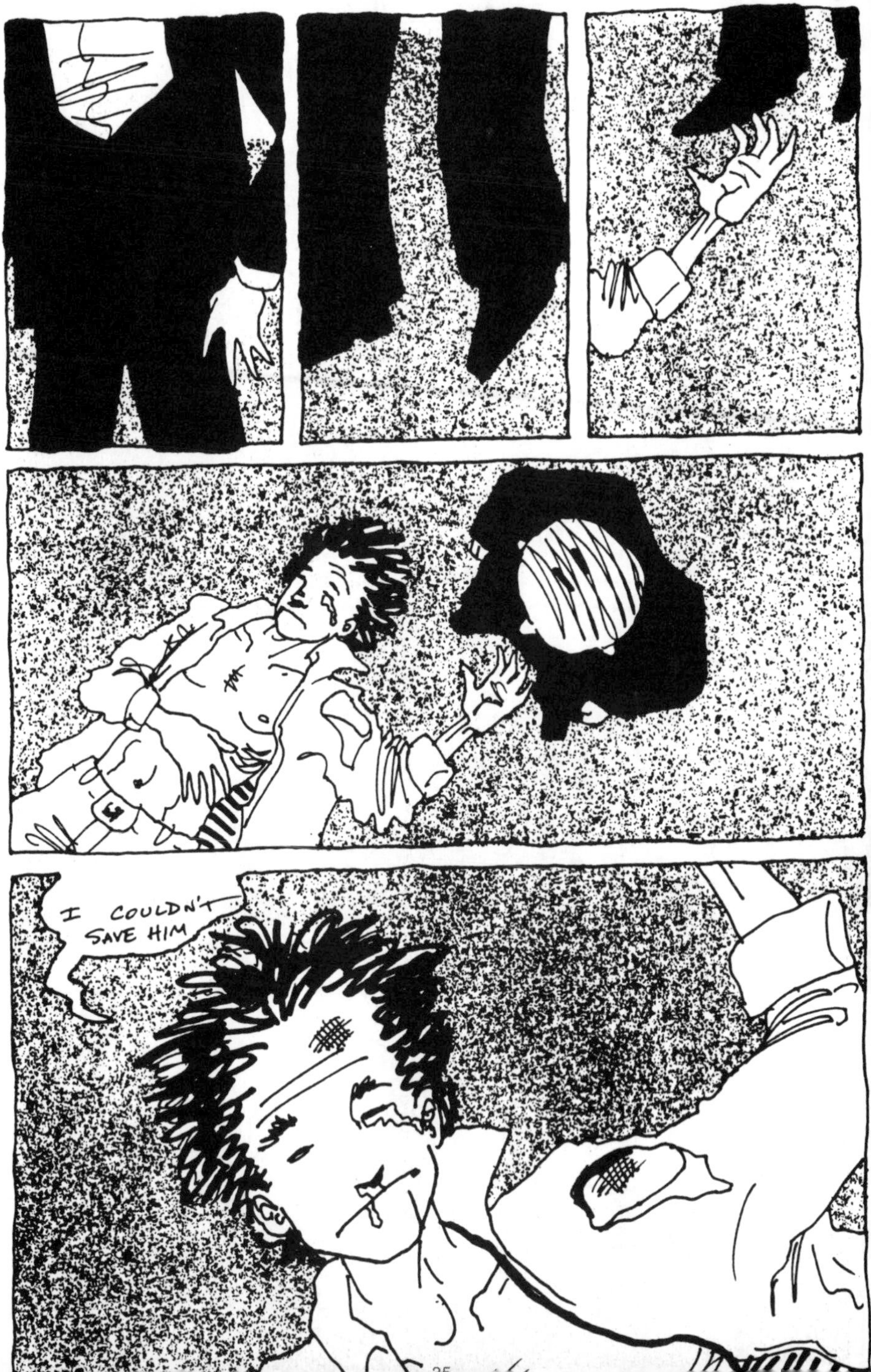
I COULDN'T SAVE HIM

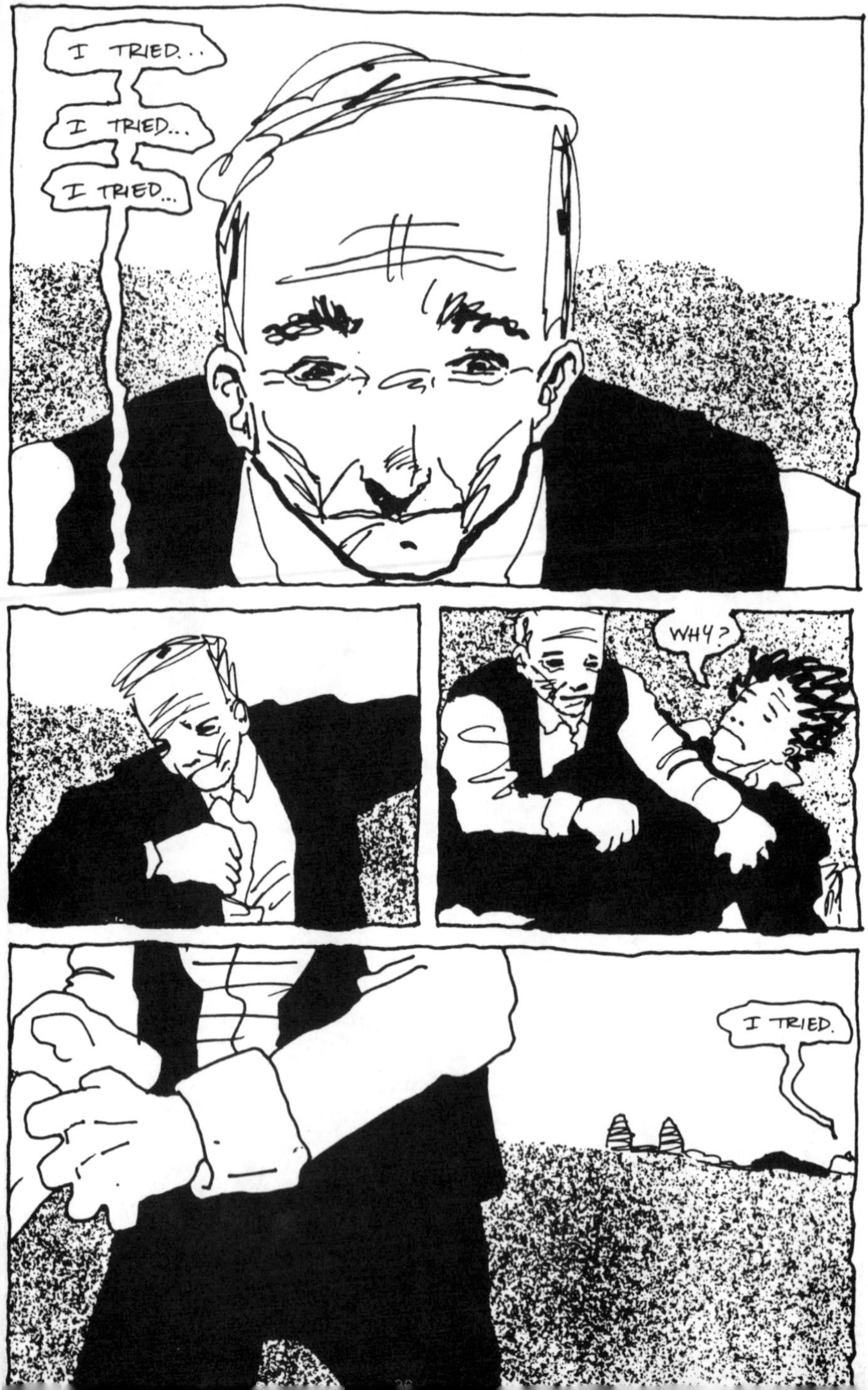
I TRIED...
I TRIED...
I TRIED...
WHY?
I TRIED.

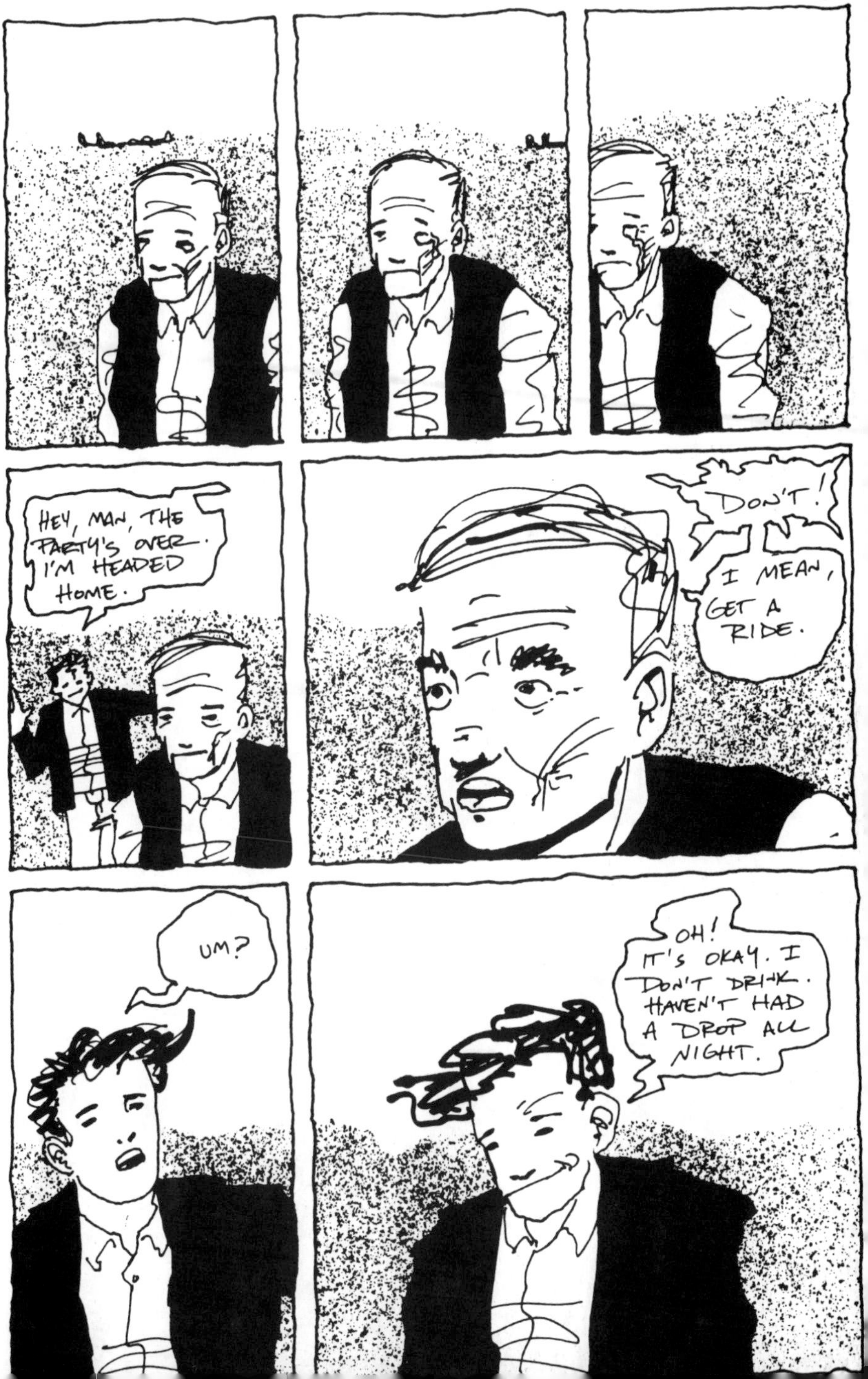
HEY, MAN, THE PARTY'S OVER. I'M HEADED HOME.
DON'T!
I MEAN, GET A RIDE.
UM?
OH! IT'S OKAY. I DON'T DRINK. HAVEN'T HAD A DROP ALL NIGHT.

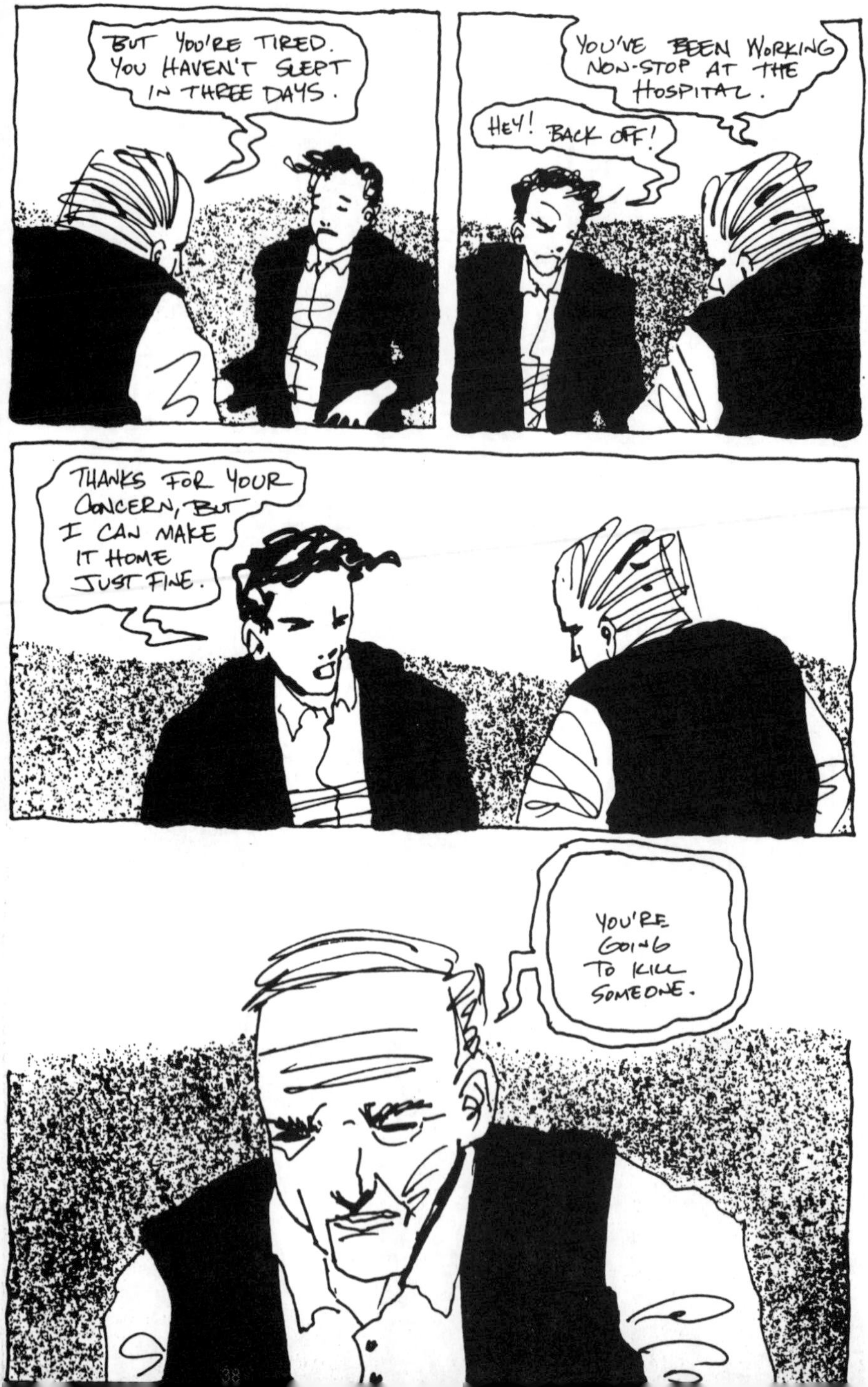
BUT YOU'RE TIRED. YOU HAVEN'T SLEPT IN THREE DAYS.
YOU'VE BEEN WORKING NON-STOP AT THE HOSPITAL.
HEY! BACK OFF!
THANKS FOR YOUR CONCERN, BUT I CAN MAKE IT HOME JUST FINE.
YOU'RE GOING TO KILL SOMEONE.

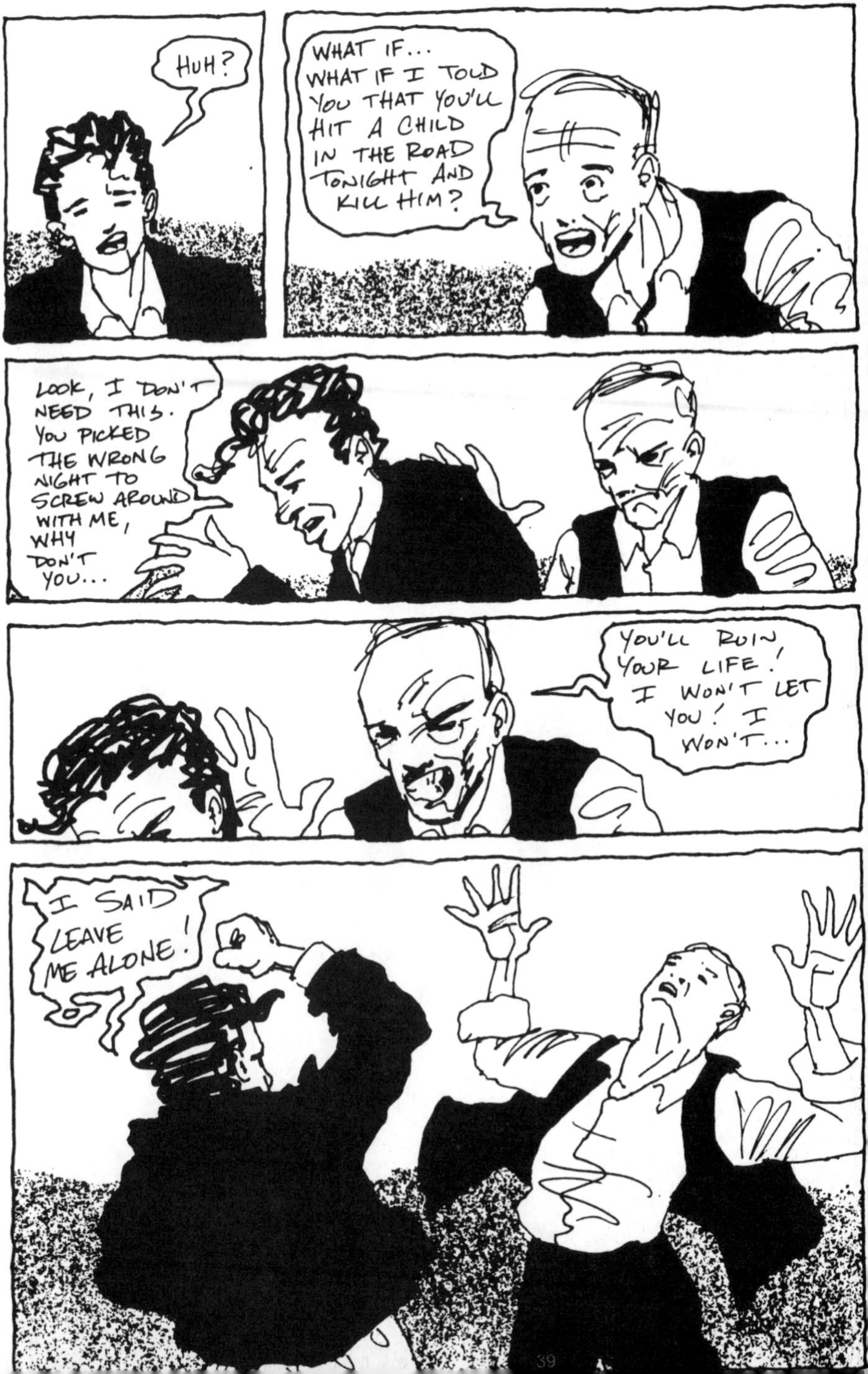
HUH?
WHAT IF... WHAT IF I TOLD YOU THAT YOU'LL HIT A CHILD IN THE ROAD TONIGHT AND KILL HIM?
LOOK, I DON'T NEED THIS. YOU PICKED THE WRONG NIGHT TO SCREW AROUND WITH ME, WHY DON'T YOU...
YOU'LL RUIN YOUR LIFE! I WON'T LET YOU! I WON'T...
I SAID LEAVE ME ALONE!

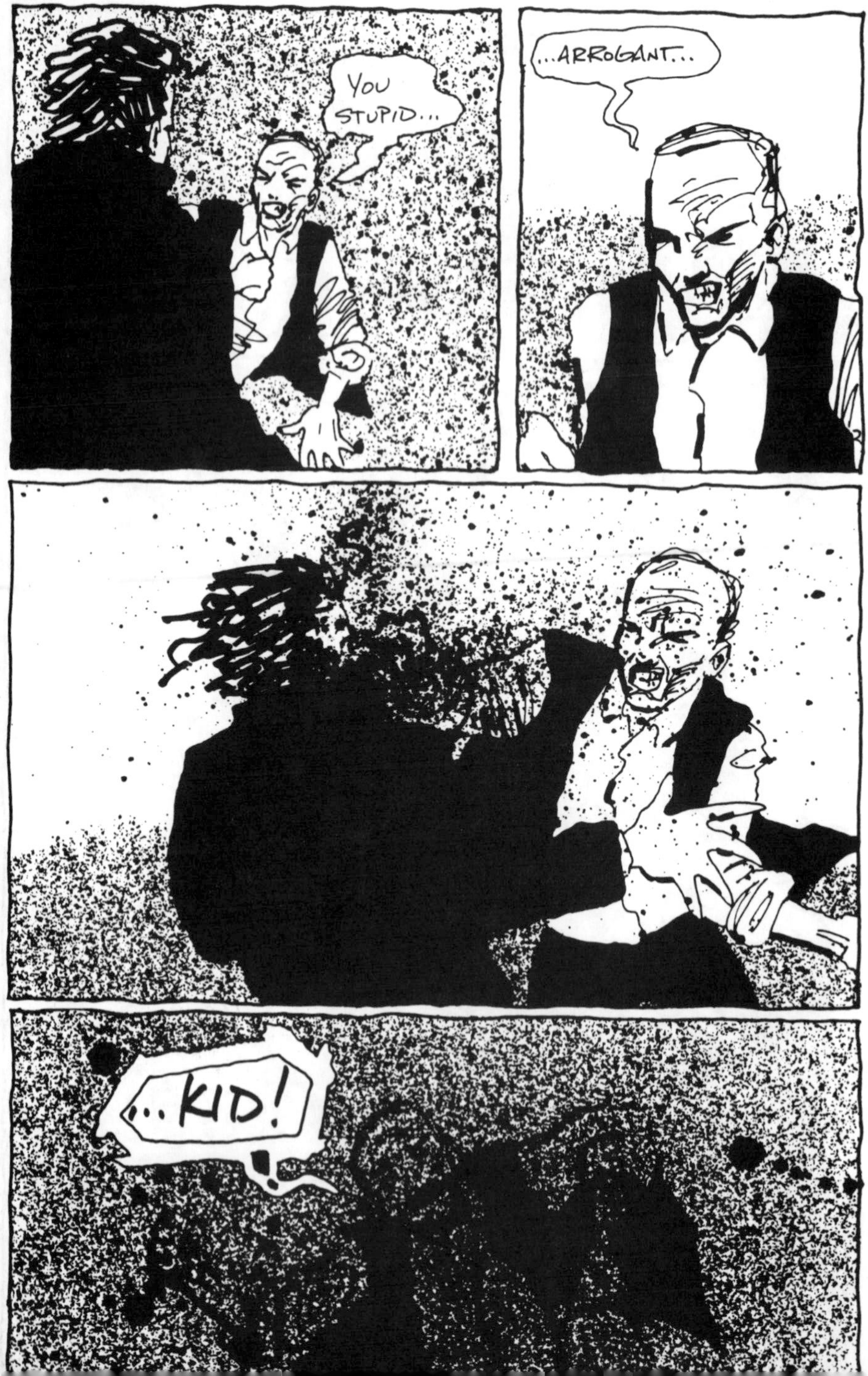
YOU STUPID...
...ARROGANT...
...KID!

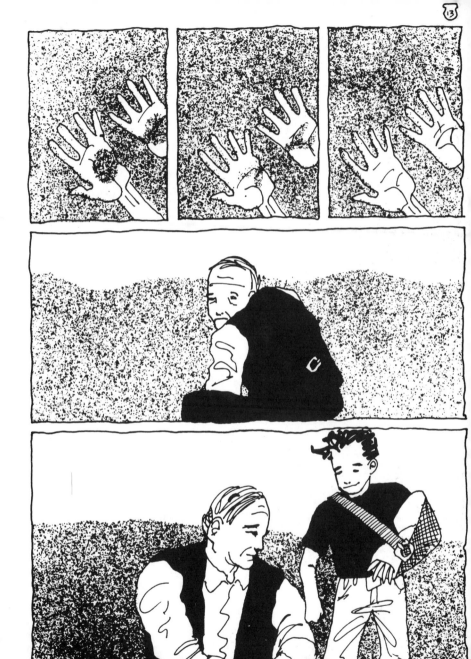

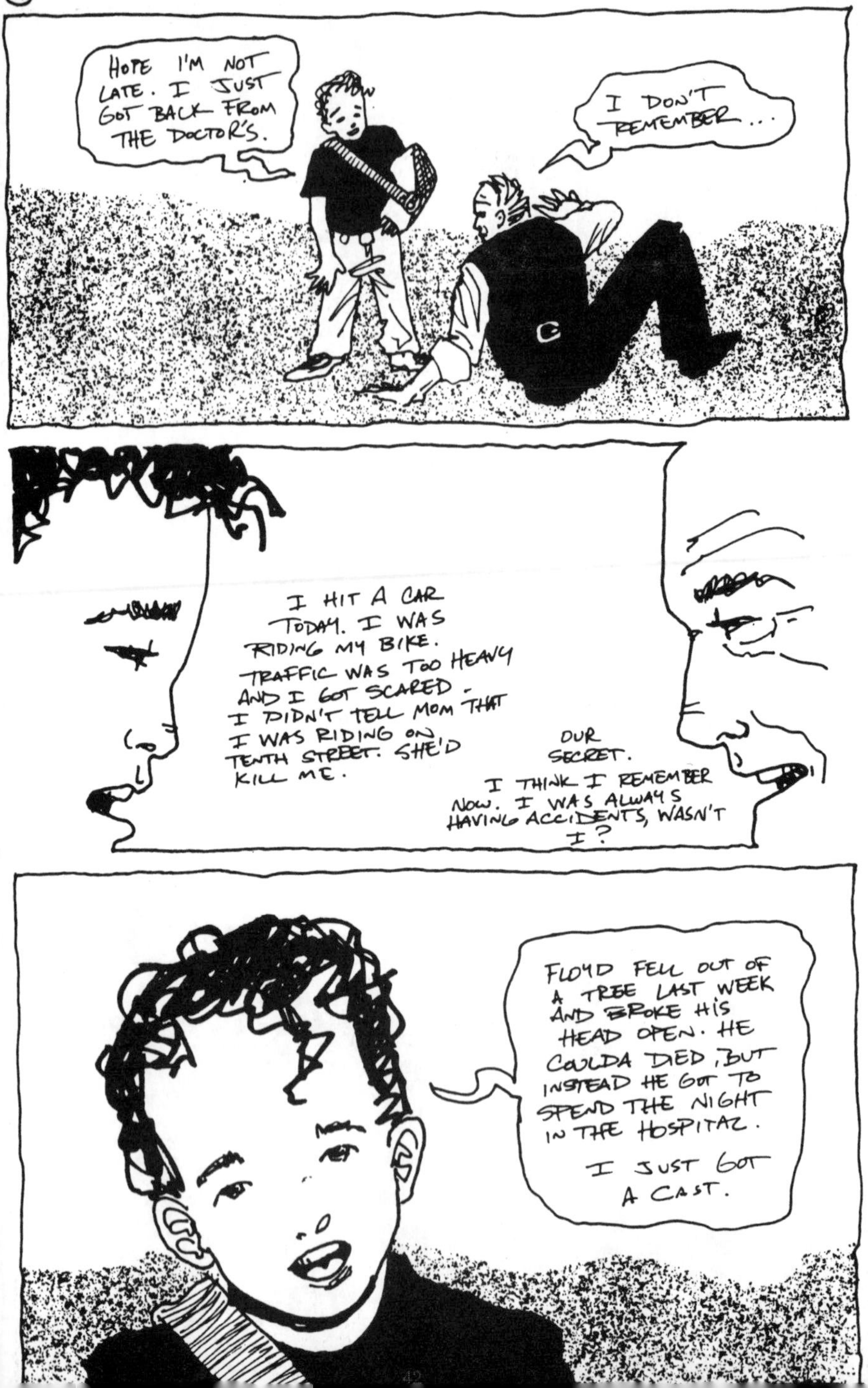
HOPE I'M NOT LATE. I JUST GOT BACK FROM THE DOCTOR'S.
I DON'T REMEMBER...
I HIT A CAR TODAY. I WAS RIDING MY BIKE. TRAFFIC WAS TOO HEAVY AND I GOT SCARED. I DIDN'T TELL MOM THAT I WAS RIDING ON TENTH STREET. SHE'D KILL ME.
OUR SECRET.
I THINK I REMEMBER NOW. I WAS ALWAYS HAVING ACCIDENTS, WASN'T I?
FLOYD FELL OUT OF A TREE LAST WEEK AND BROKE HIS HEAD OPEN. HE COULDA DIED, BUT INSTEAD HE GOT TO SPEND THE NIGHT IN THE HOSPITAL.
I JUST GOT A CAST.

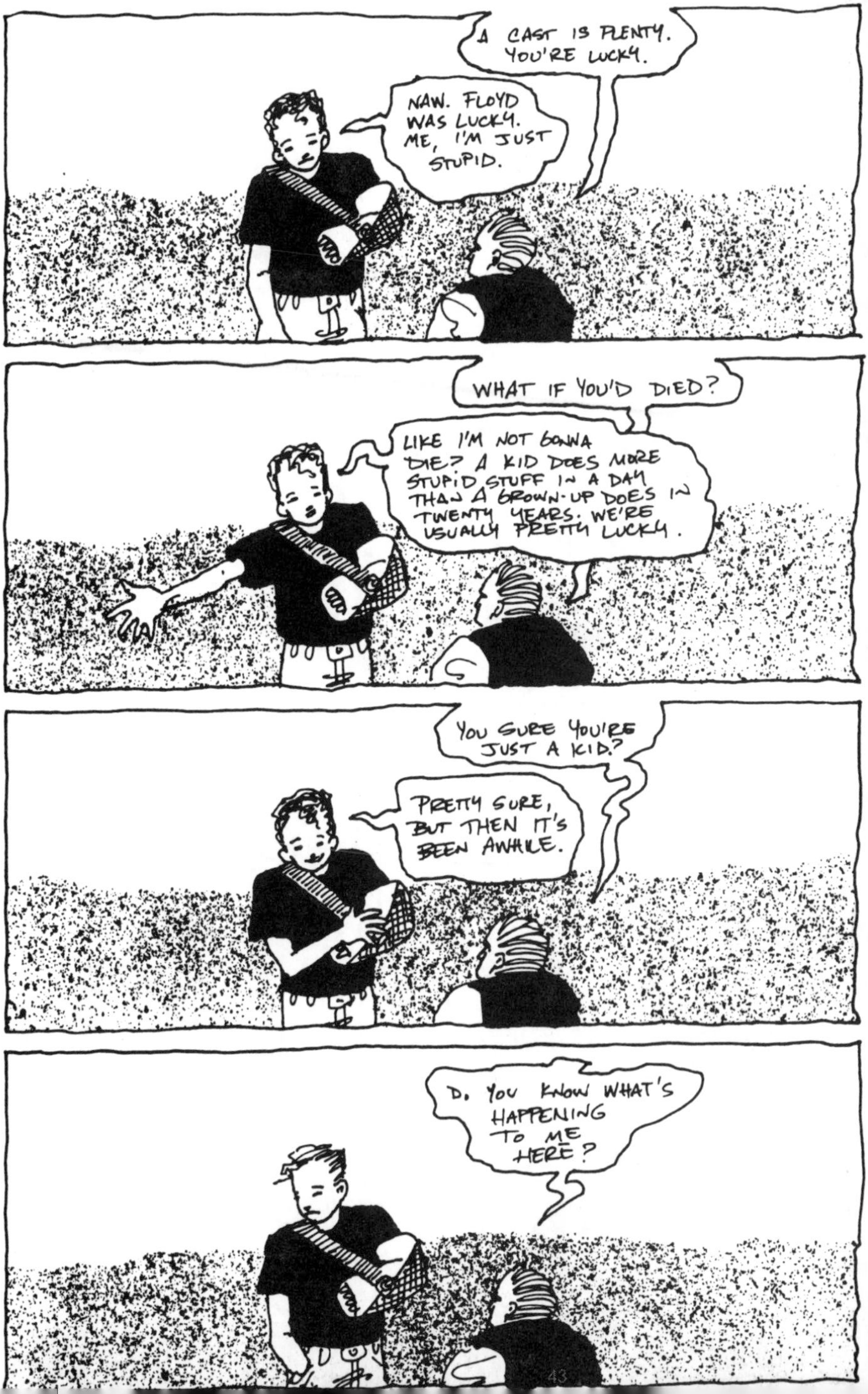
A CAST IS PLENTY. YOU'RE LUCKY.
NAW. FLOYD WAS LUCKY. ME, I'M JUST STUPID.
WHAT IF YOU'D DIED?
LIKE I'M NOT GONNA DIE? A KID DOES MORE STUPID STUFF IN A DAY THAN A GROWN-UP DOES IN TWENTY YEARS. WE'RE USUALLY PRETTY LUCKY.
YOU SURE YOU'RE JUST A KID?
PRETTY SURE, BUT THEN IT'S BEEN AWHILE.
D. YOU KNOW WHAT'S HAPPENING TO ME HERE?

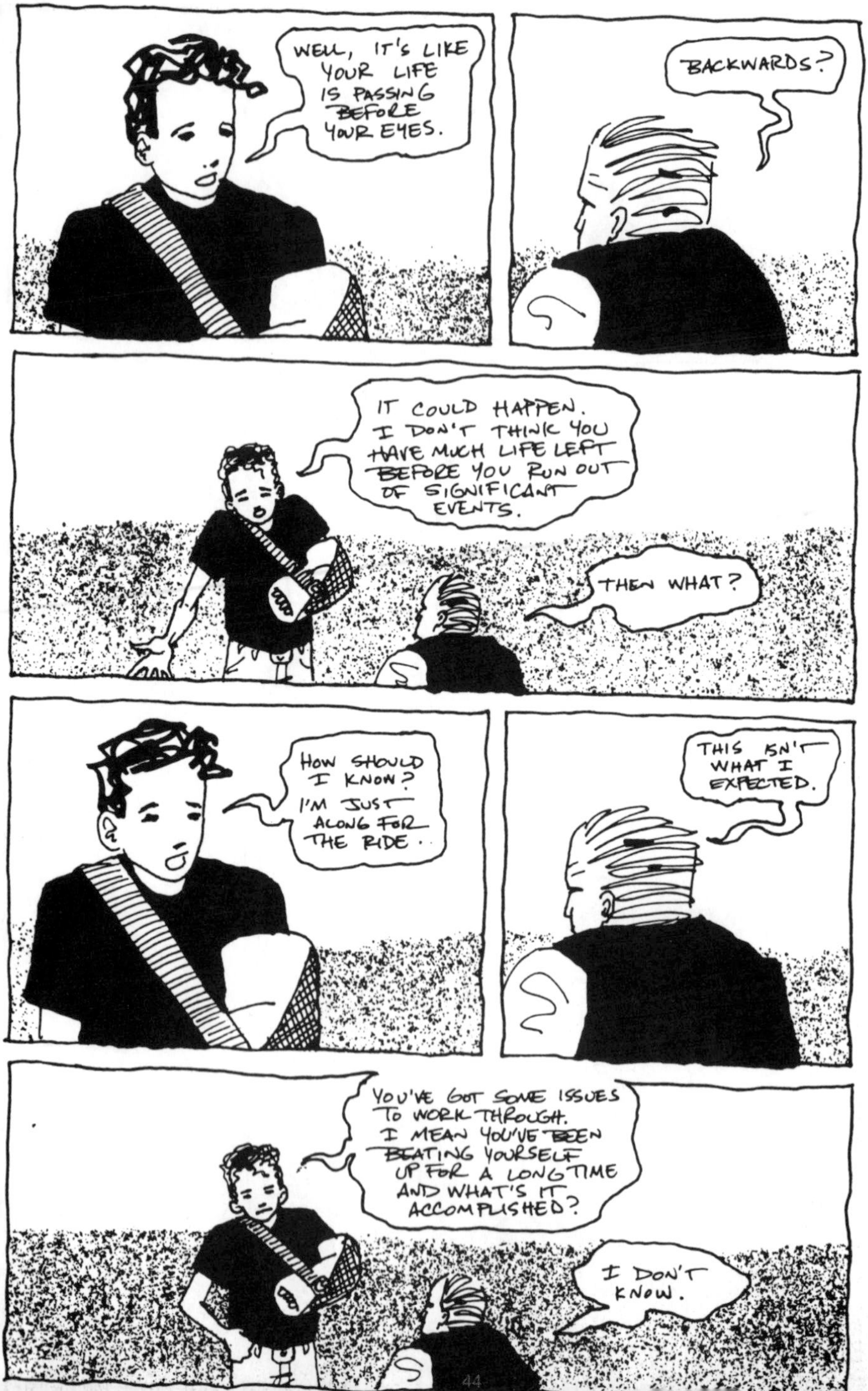
WELL, IT'S LIKE YOUR LIFE IS PASSING BEFORE YOUR EYES.
BACKWARDS?
IT COULD HAPPEN. I DON'T THINK YOU HAVE MUCH LIFE LEFT BEFORE YOU RUN OUT OF SIGNIFICANT EVENTS.
THEN WHAT?
HOW SHOULD I KNOW? I'M JUST ALONG FOR THE RIDE.
THIS ISN'T WHAT I EXPECTED.
YOU'VE GOT SOME ISSUES TO WORK THROUGH. I MEAN YOU'VE BEEN BEATING YOURSELF UP FOR A LONG TIME AND WHAT'S IT ACCOMPLISHED?
I DON'T KNOW.

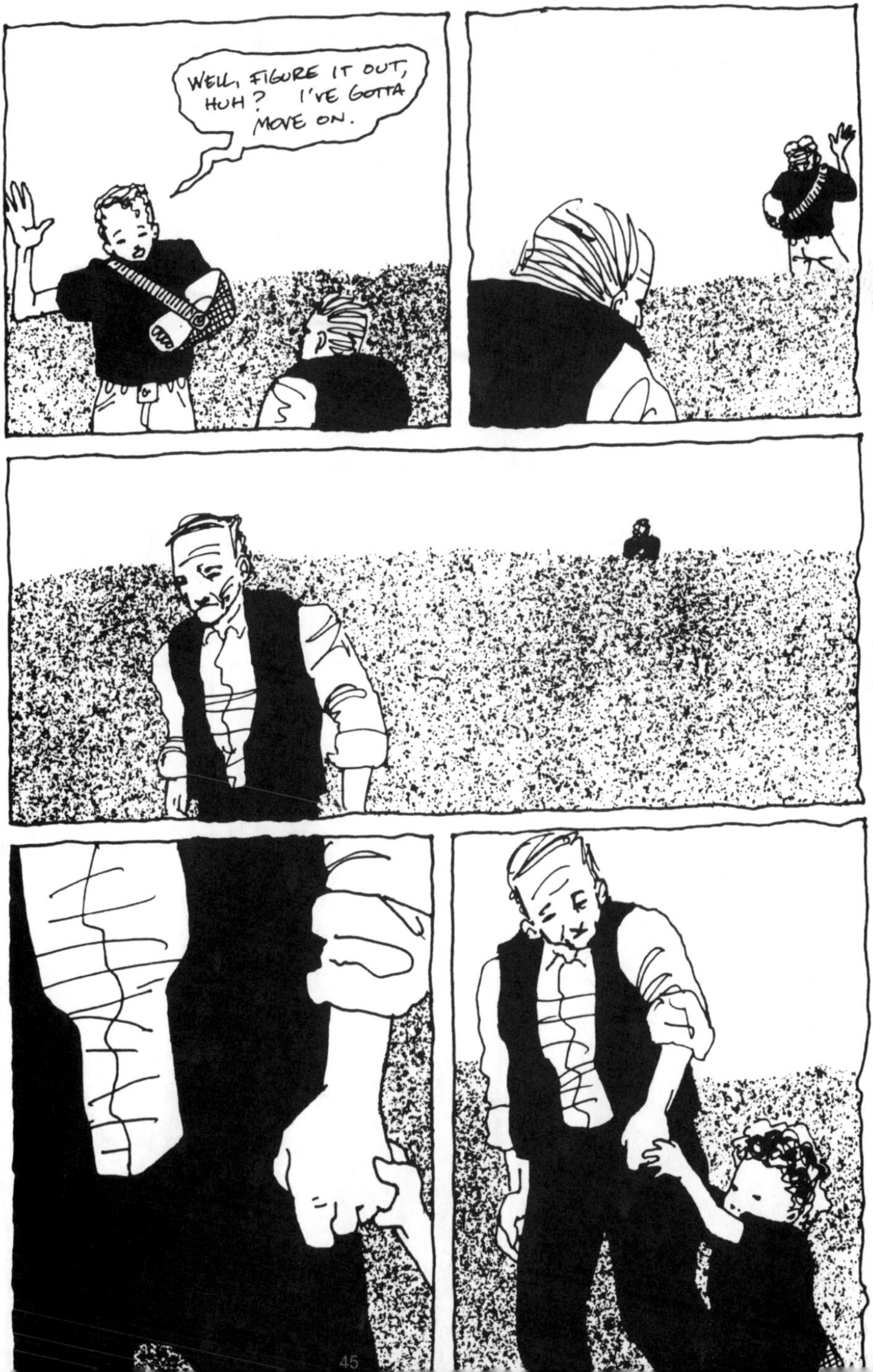
WELL, FIGURE IT OUT, HUH? I'VE GOTTA MOVE ON.

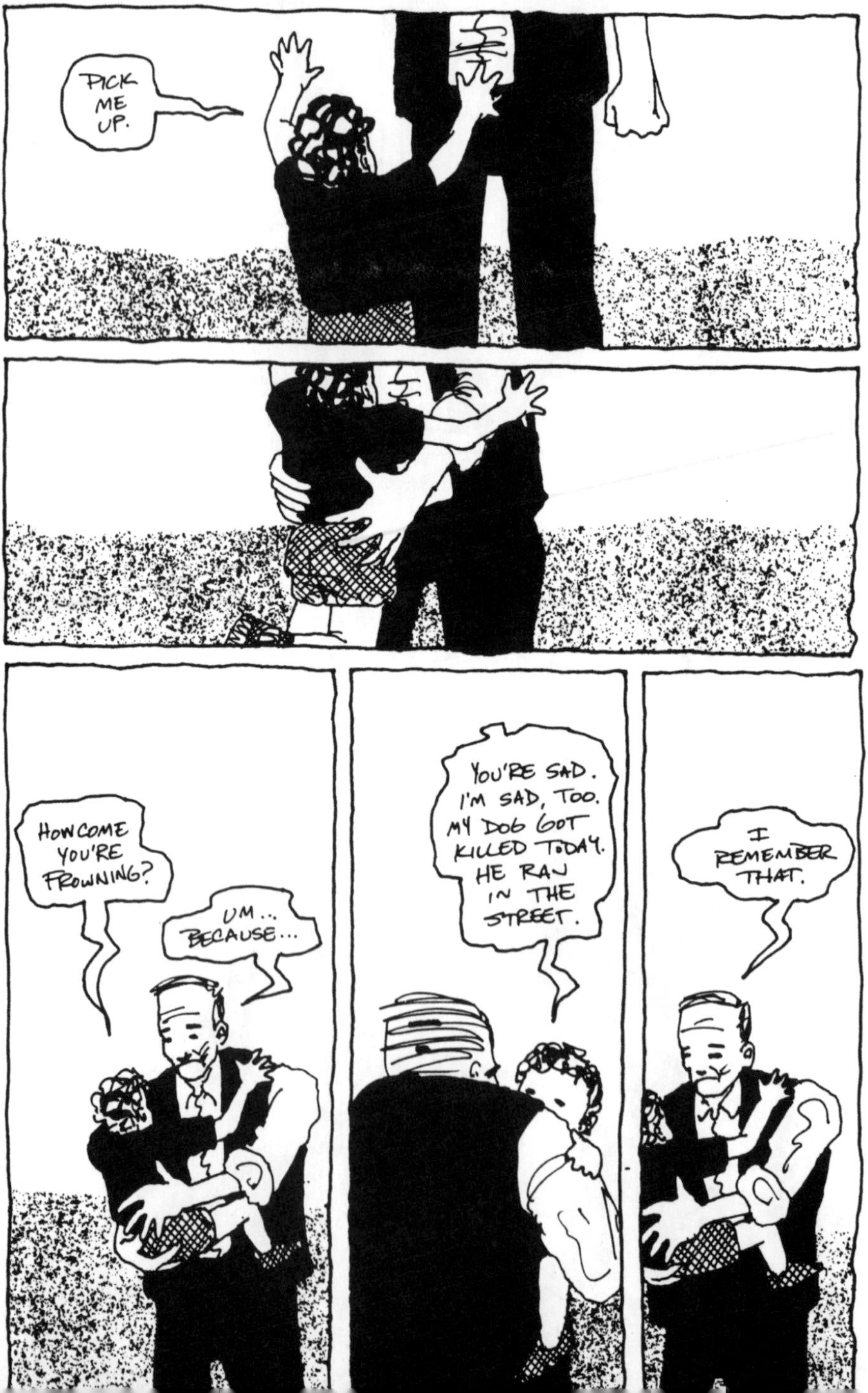
PICK ME UP.
HOW COME YOU'RE FROWNING?
UM... BECAUSE...
YOU'RE SAD. I'M SAD, TOO. MY DOG GOT KILLED TODAY. HE RAN IN THE STREET.
I REMEMBER THAT.

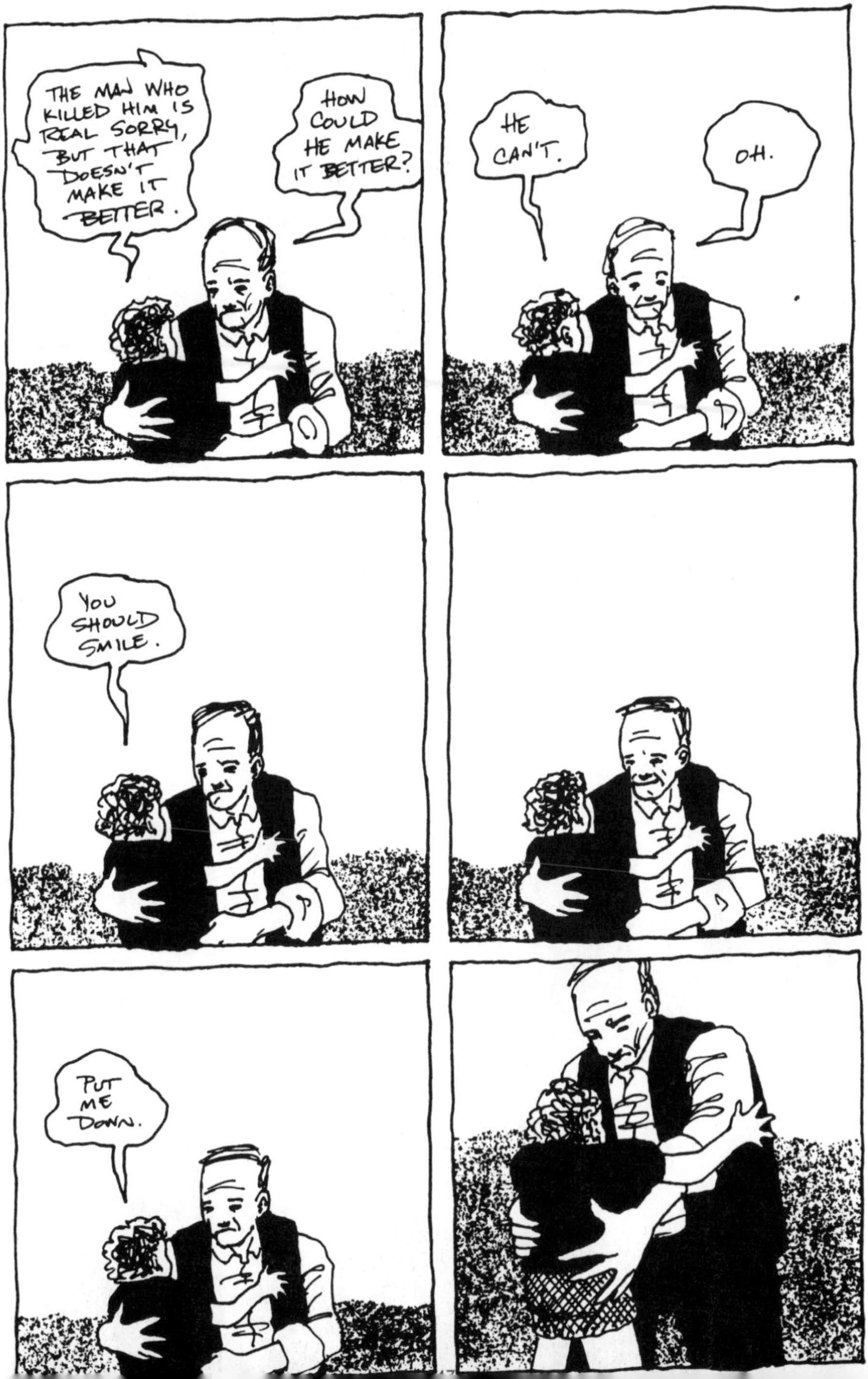
THE MAN WHO KILLED HIM IS REAL SORRY, BUT THAT DOESN'T MAKE IT BETTER.
HOW COULD HE MAKE IT BETTER?
HE CAN'T.
OH.
YOU SHOULD SMILE.
PUT ME DOWN.

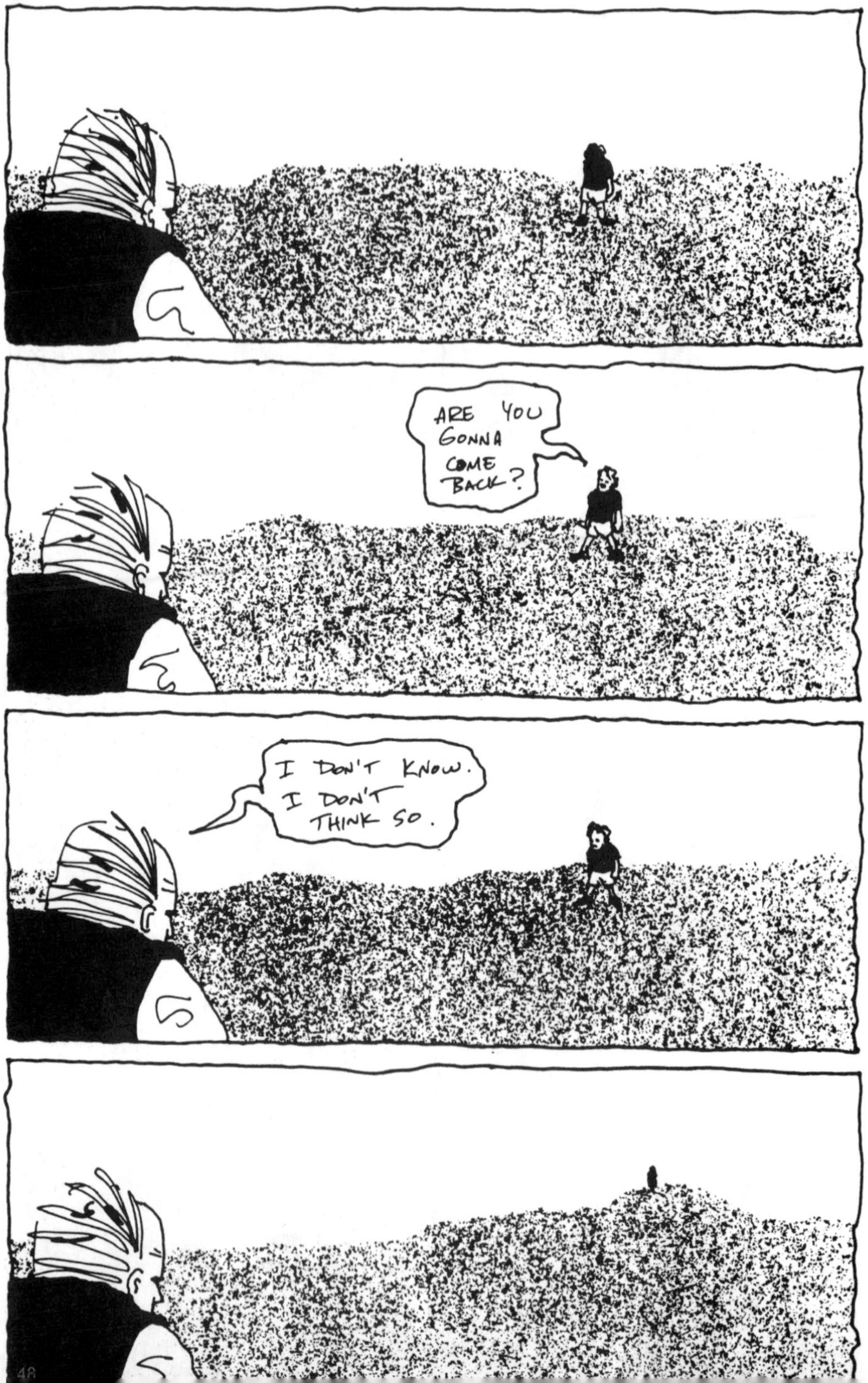
ARE YOU GONNA COME BACK?
I DON'T KNOW. I DON'T THINK SO.

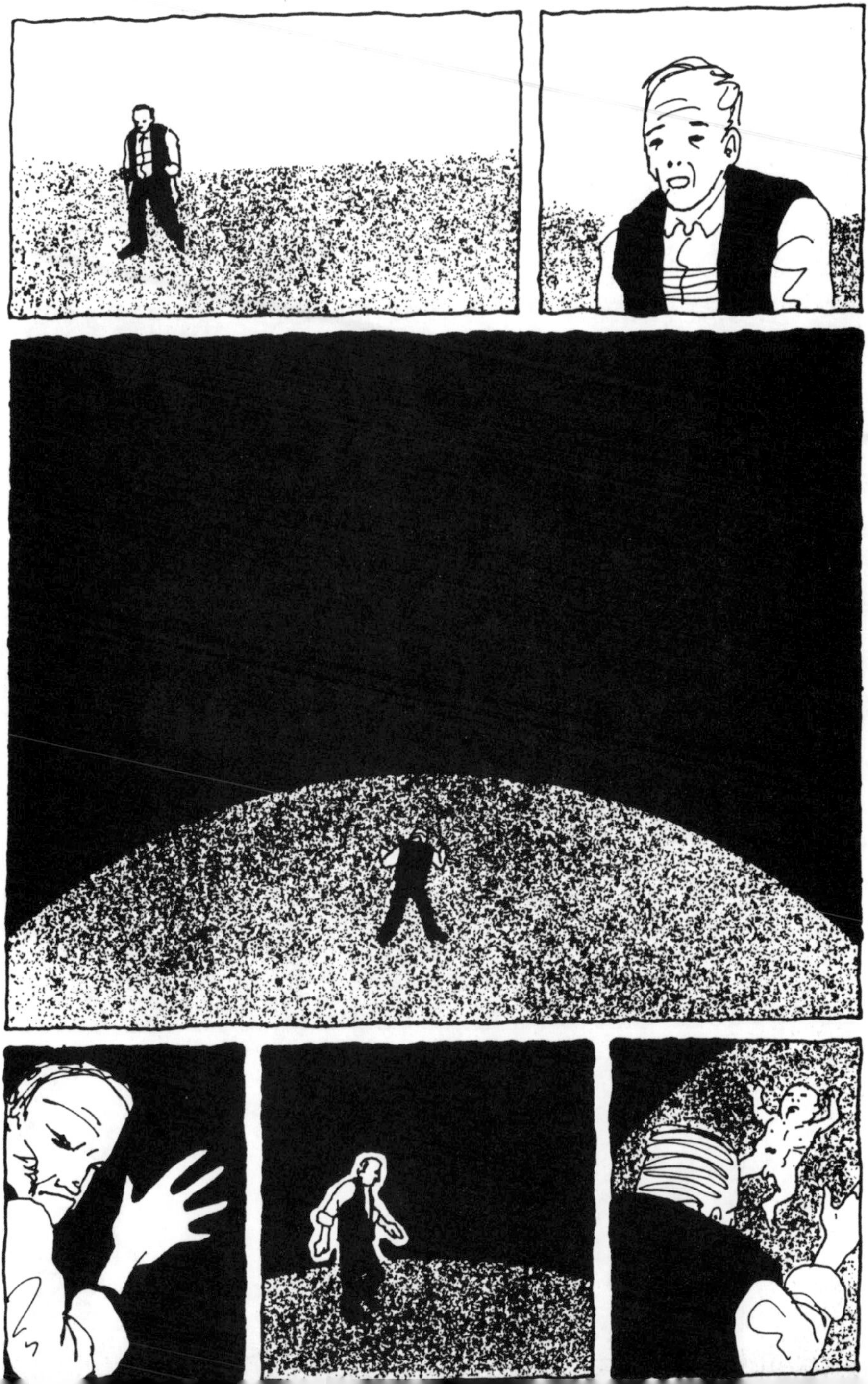

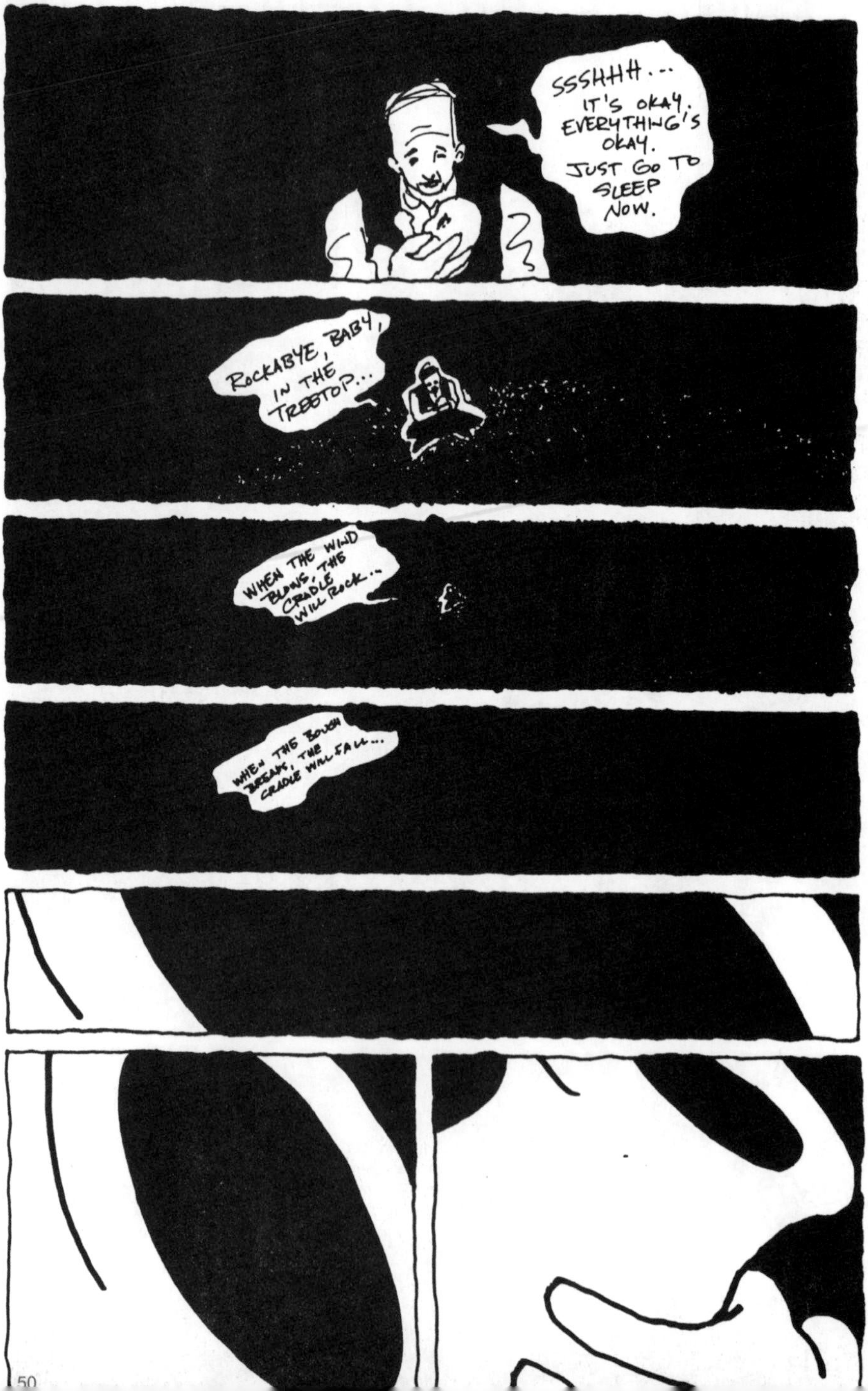
SSSHHH...
IT'S OKAY. EVERYTHING'S OKAY. JUST GO TO SLEEP NOW.
ROCKABYE, BABY, IN THE TREETOP...
WHEN THE WIND BLOWS, THE CRADLE WILL ROCK...
WHEN THE BOUGH BREAKS, THE CRADLE WILL FALL...

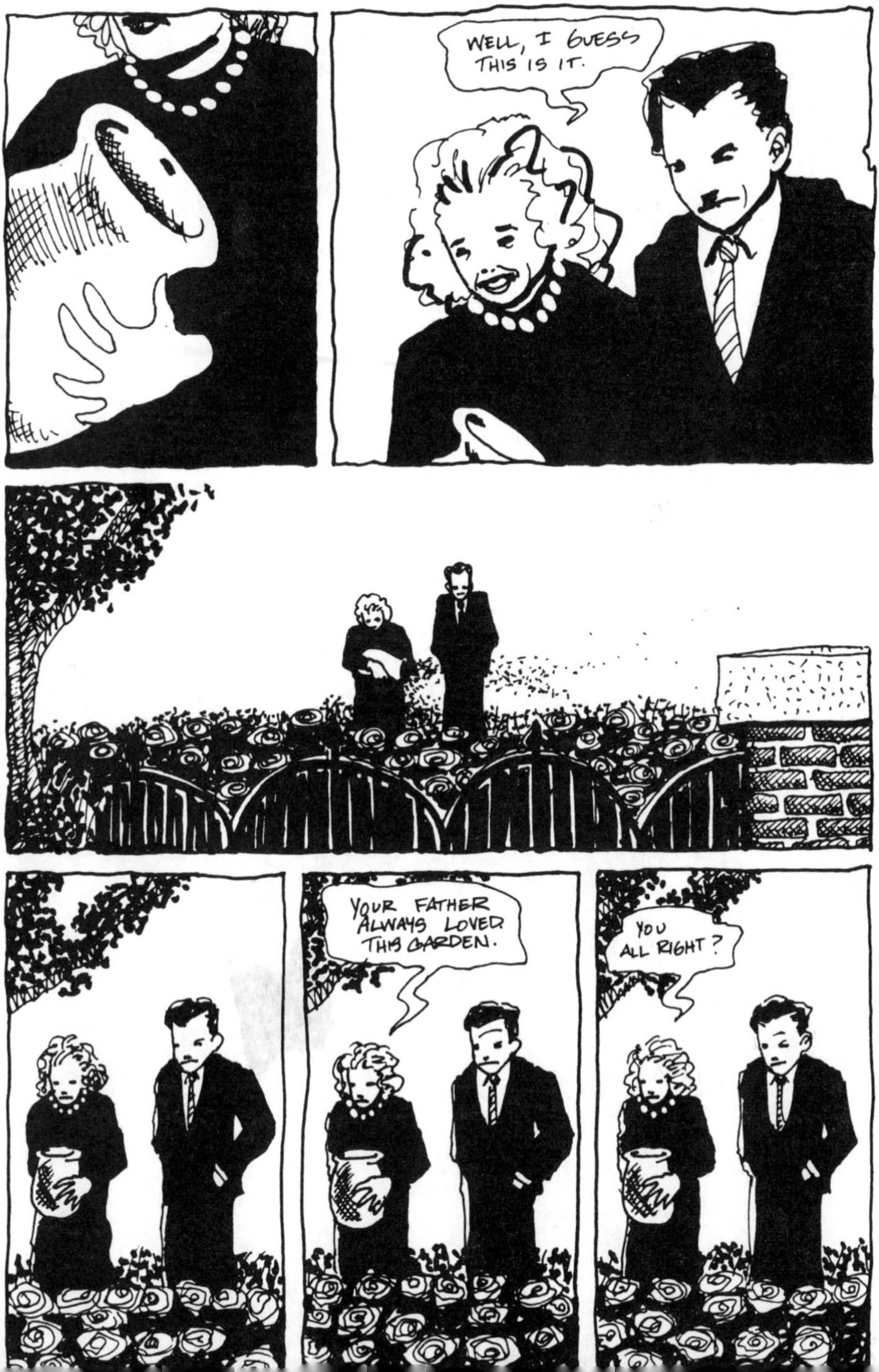
WELL, I GUESS THIS IS IT.
YOUR FATHER ALWAYS LOVED THIS GARDEN.
YOU ALL RIGHT?

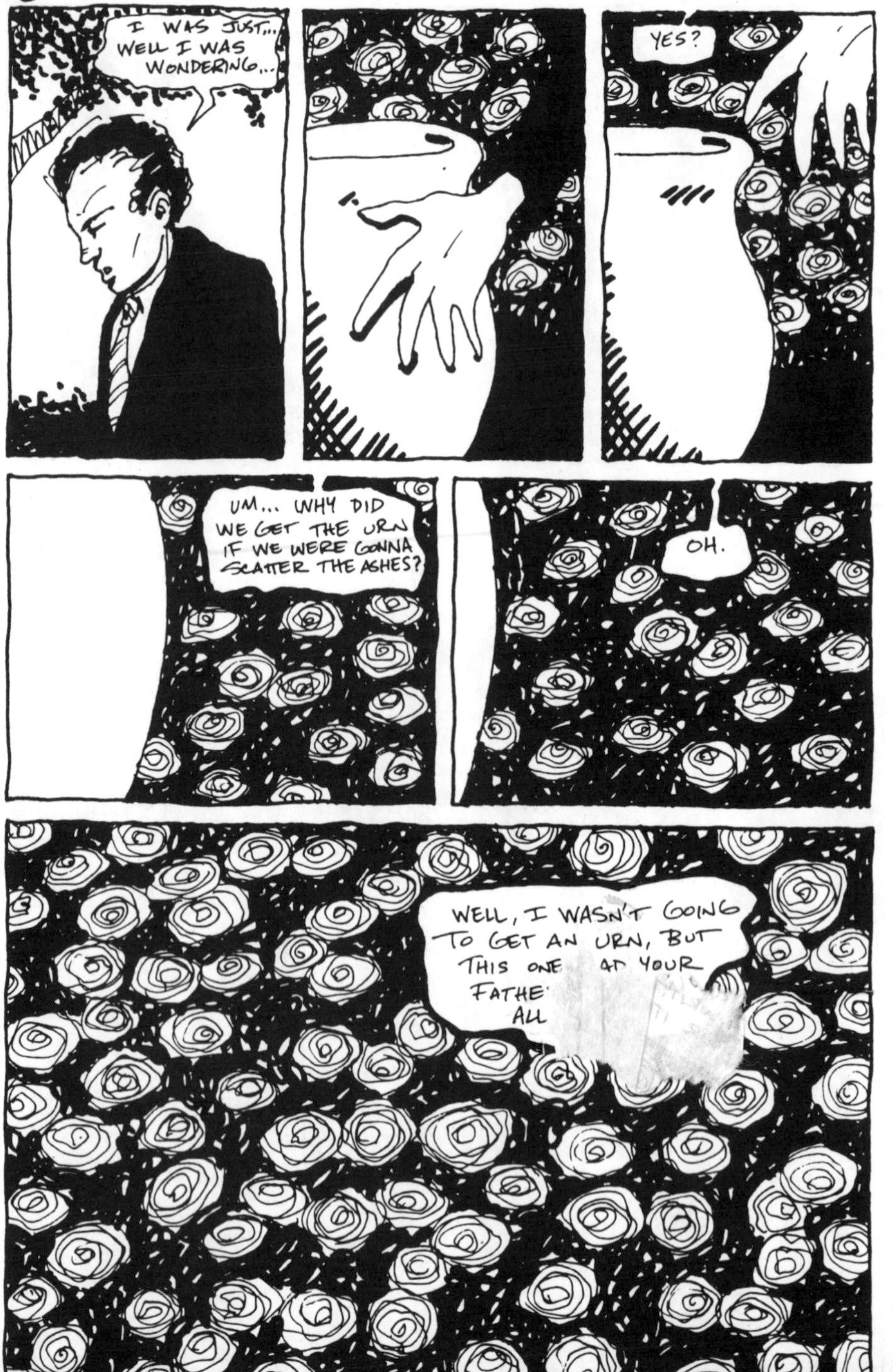
I WAS JUST... WELL I WAS WONDERING...
YES?
UM... WHY DID WE GET THE URN IF WE WERE GONNA SCATTER THE ASHES?
OH.
WELL, I WASN'T GOING TO GET AN URN, BUT THIS ONE AT YOUR FATHE ALL

PAUL WINKLER

Paul Winkler is *not* a professional comics artist. He tried his hand at them for a while, got distracted by other things (most notably music) and eventually moved on. And yet, his 24-hour comic was, for many years, a personal favorite of mine.

"Cat" is a wordless story, told from the point of view of a wandering house cat. The drawings are sketchy, yet strangely effective; the storytelling is masterful; and the environments and events depicted are vivid and memorable. It's also a deeply synaesthetic reading experience, conveying not just the sights confronted by our feline protagonist, but the sounds and sensations as well.

And Paul knows how to draw cats, which is a rarity.

I first met Paul in the mid-'80s at a monthly comic convention at the Roosevelt Hotel in Manhattan. A small, dedicated group of readers would sometimes congregate at my table and we'd often go out to eat at a nearby McDonalds or other fast food joint. Within a short span of time, everyone in "The McDonalds Club" knew each other on a first name basis. Paul was the tall, quiet one with the long hair.

Each was working on a comic of their own; each had dreams of what could be done in the medium, and nearly all of them would eventually try their hand at a 24-hour comic. In the end, only one of them—Jenn Manley Lee—would keep making comics to the present day (at jennworks.com) but the small tribe largely stayed in contact with one another over the years. In fact Jenn is "Manley Lee" instead of just "Lee" because she and fellow tribesman Kip Manley tied the knot just a few years ago.

Paul, though, is living his own life now; no longer connected to the scene. Like some Jazz legend, Paul just picked up a saxophone one night, stepped up to the mike, played a solo that brought down the house—and walked off the stage forever.

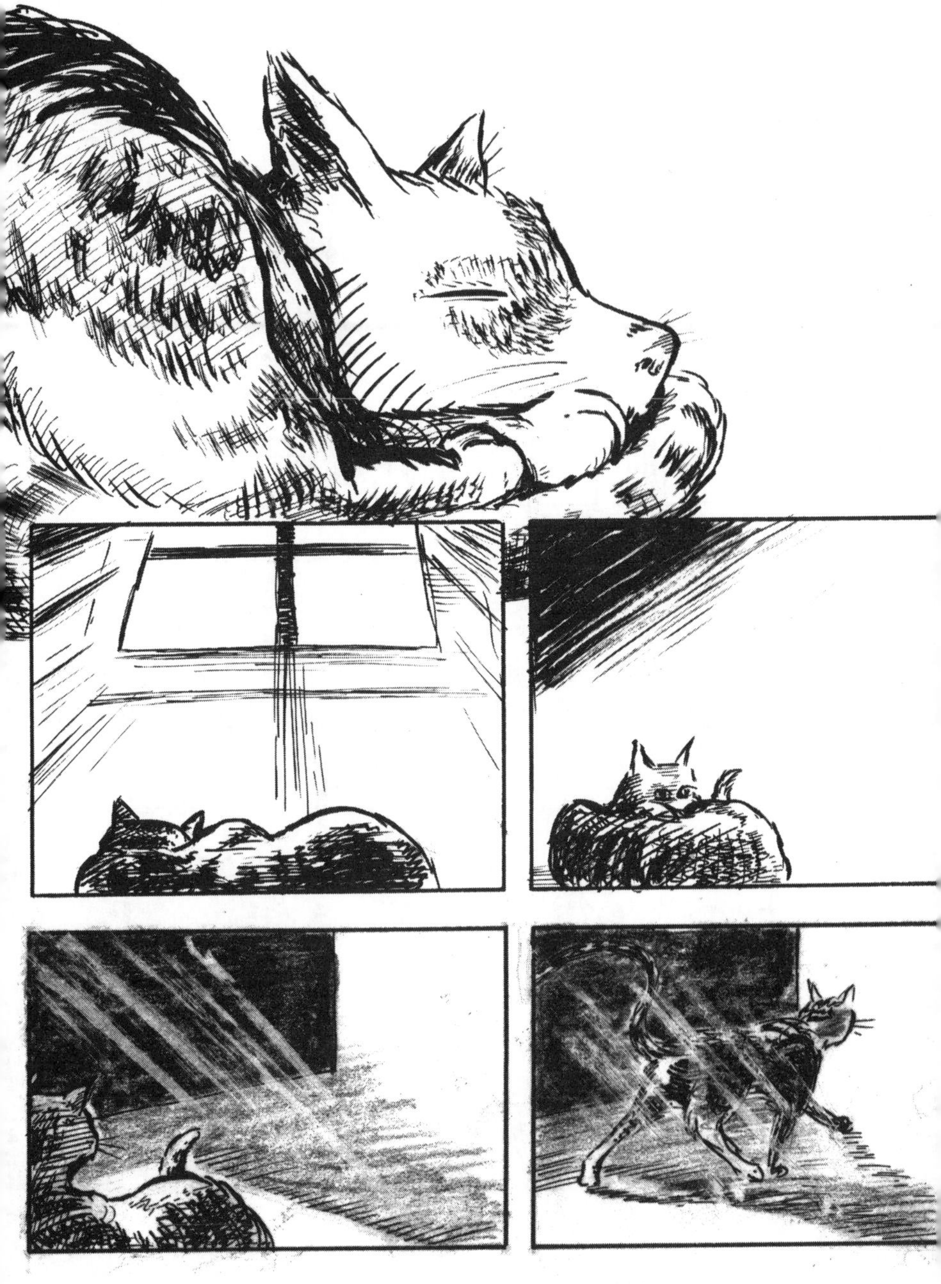

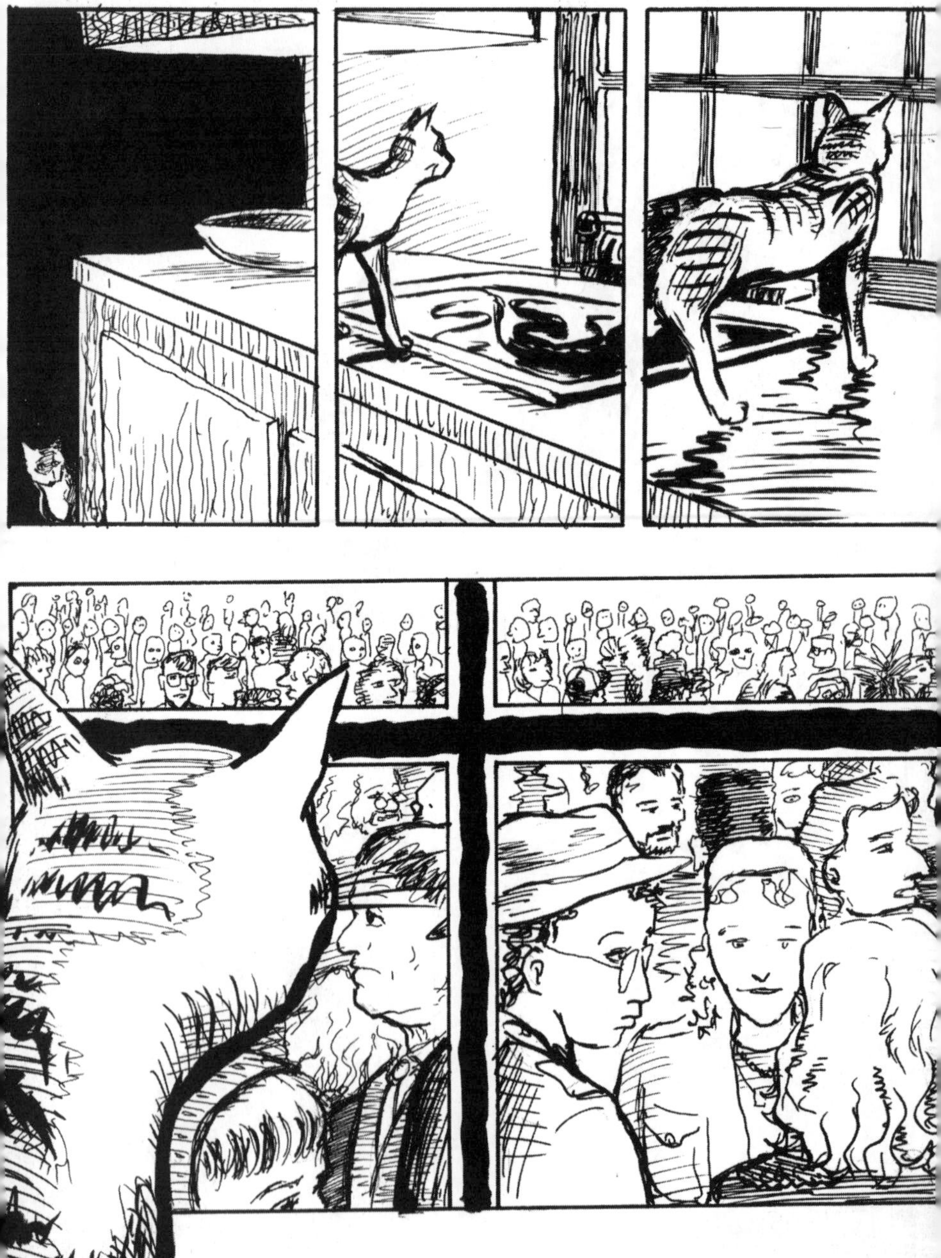

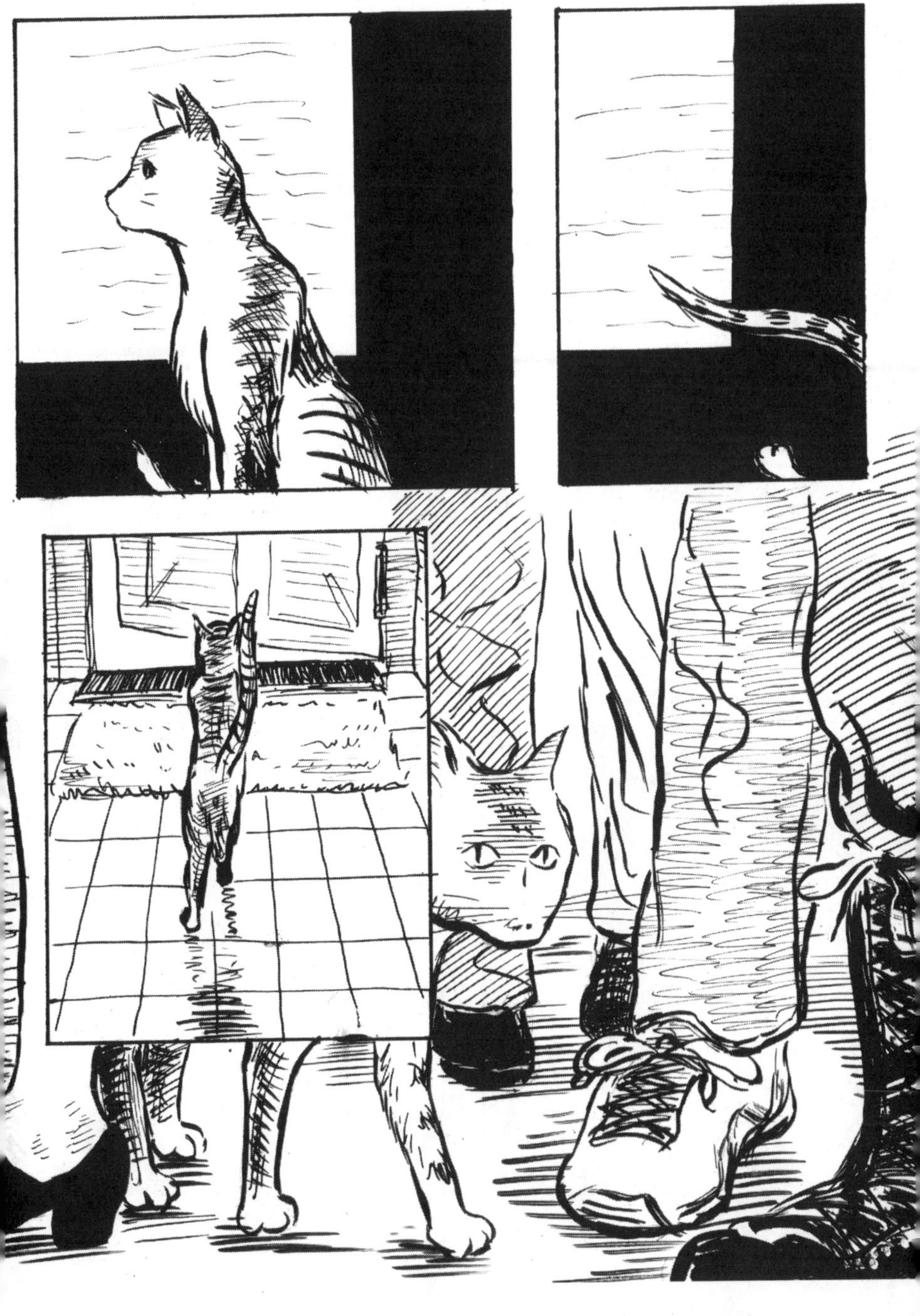

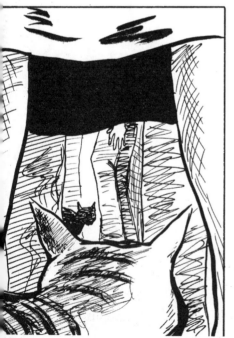

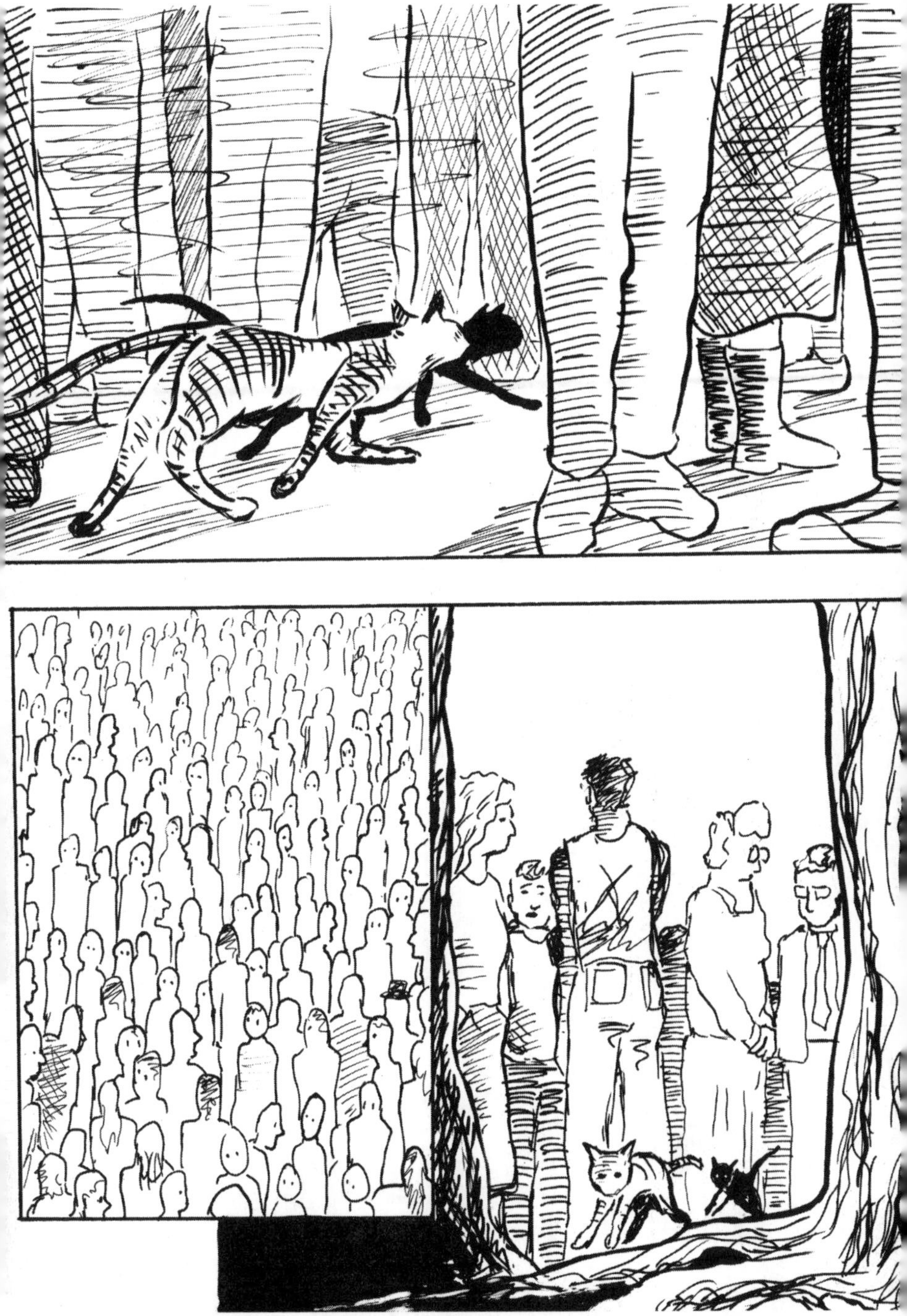

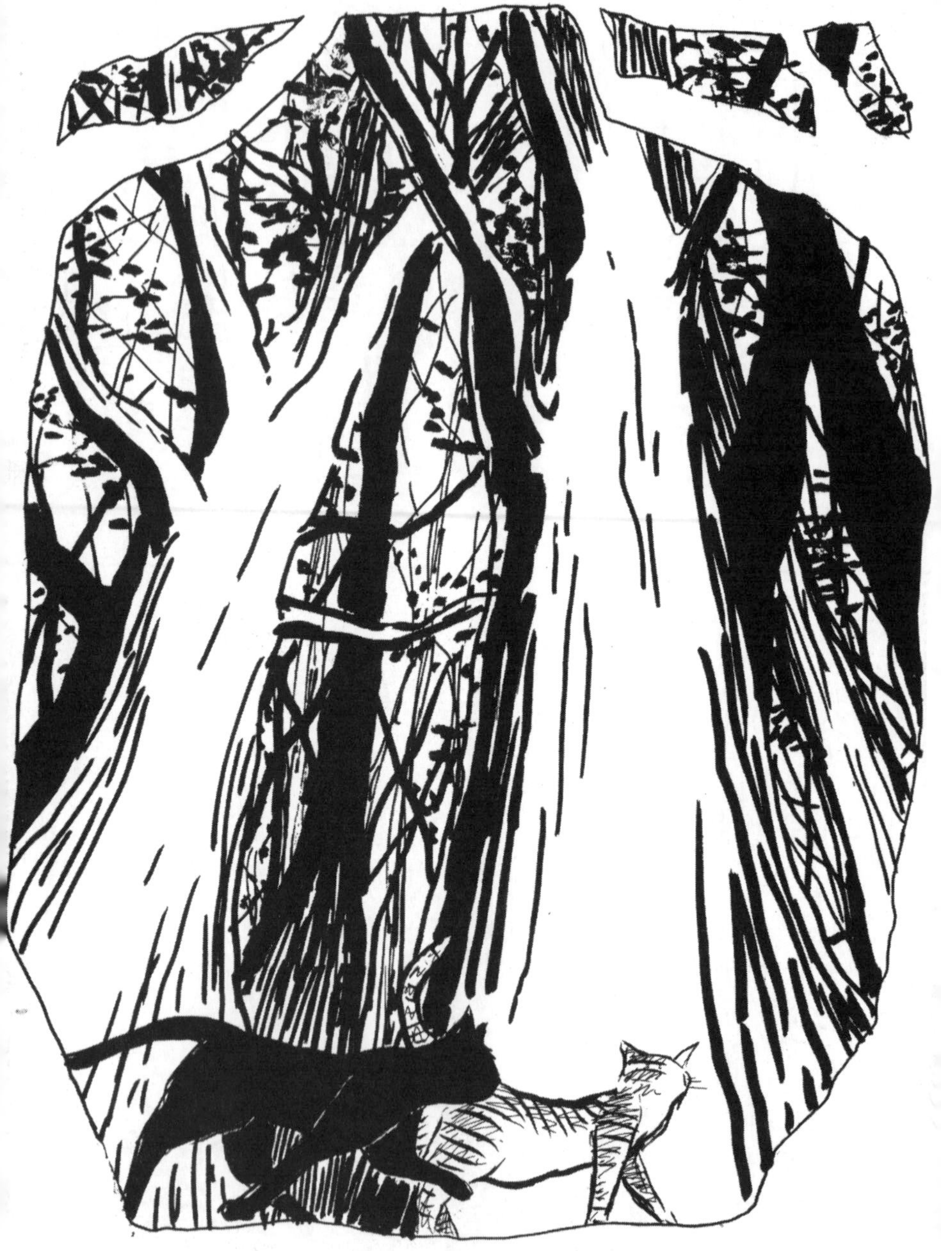

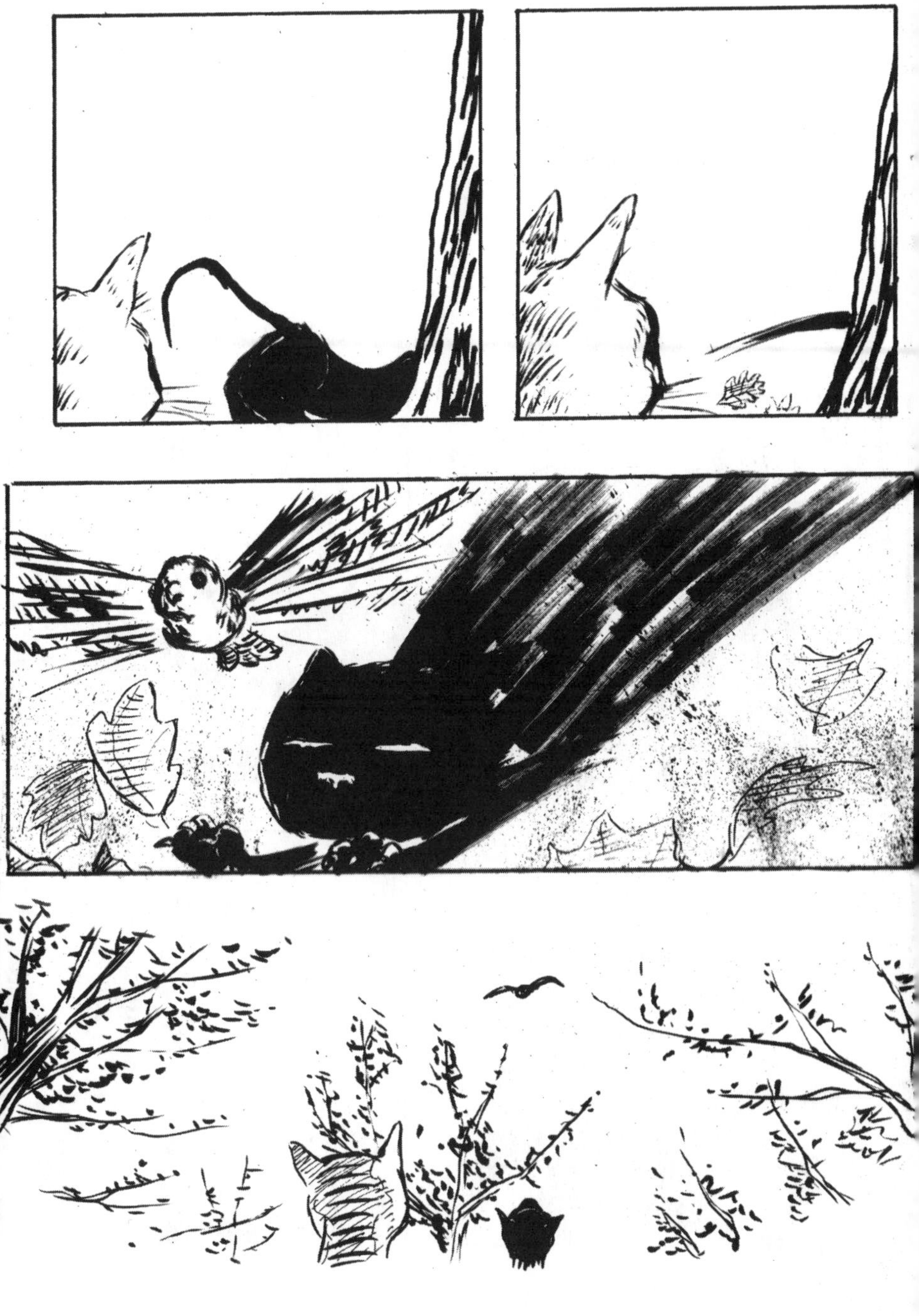

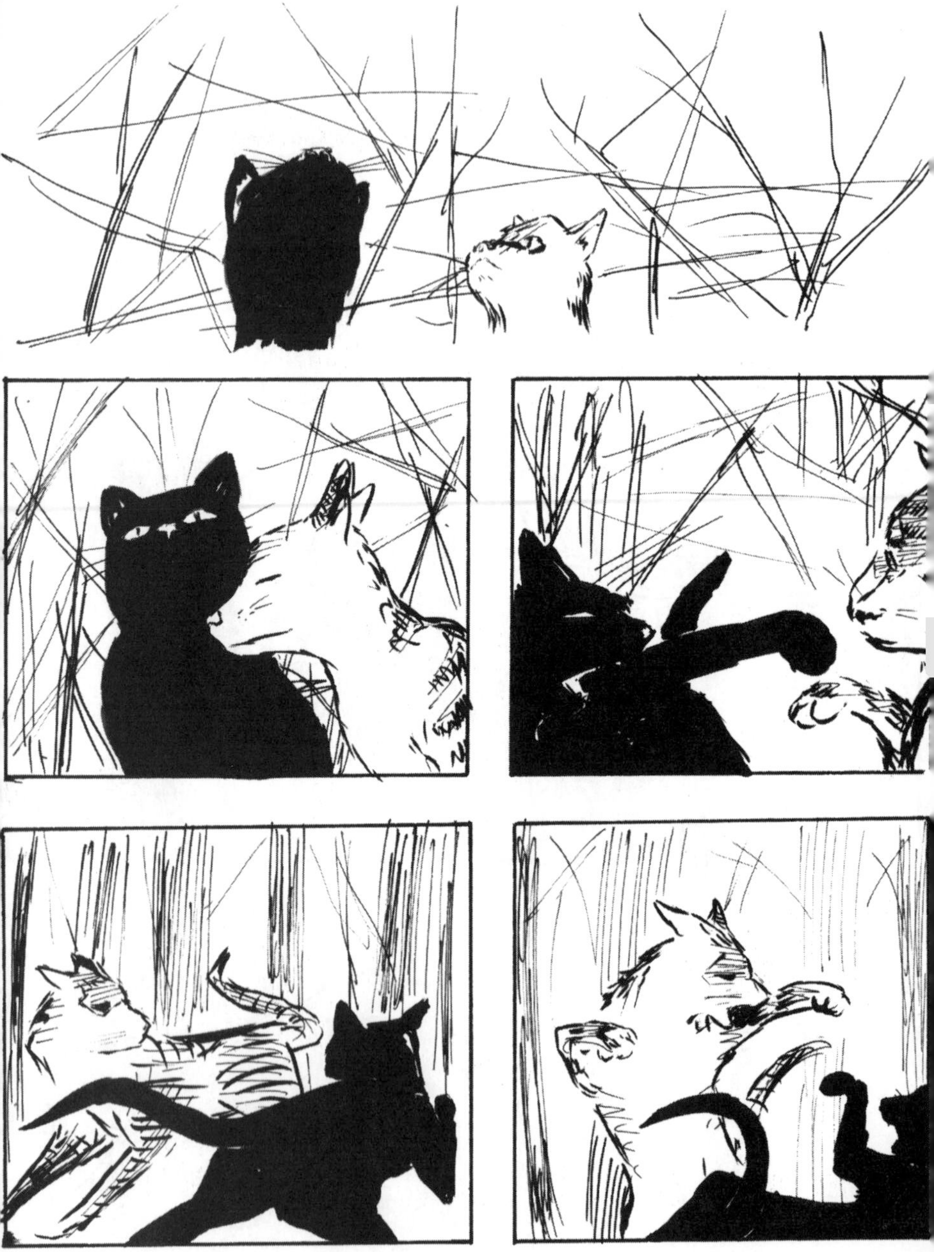

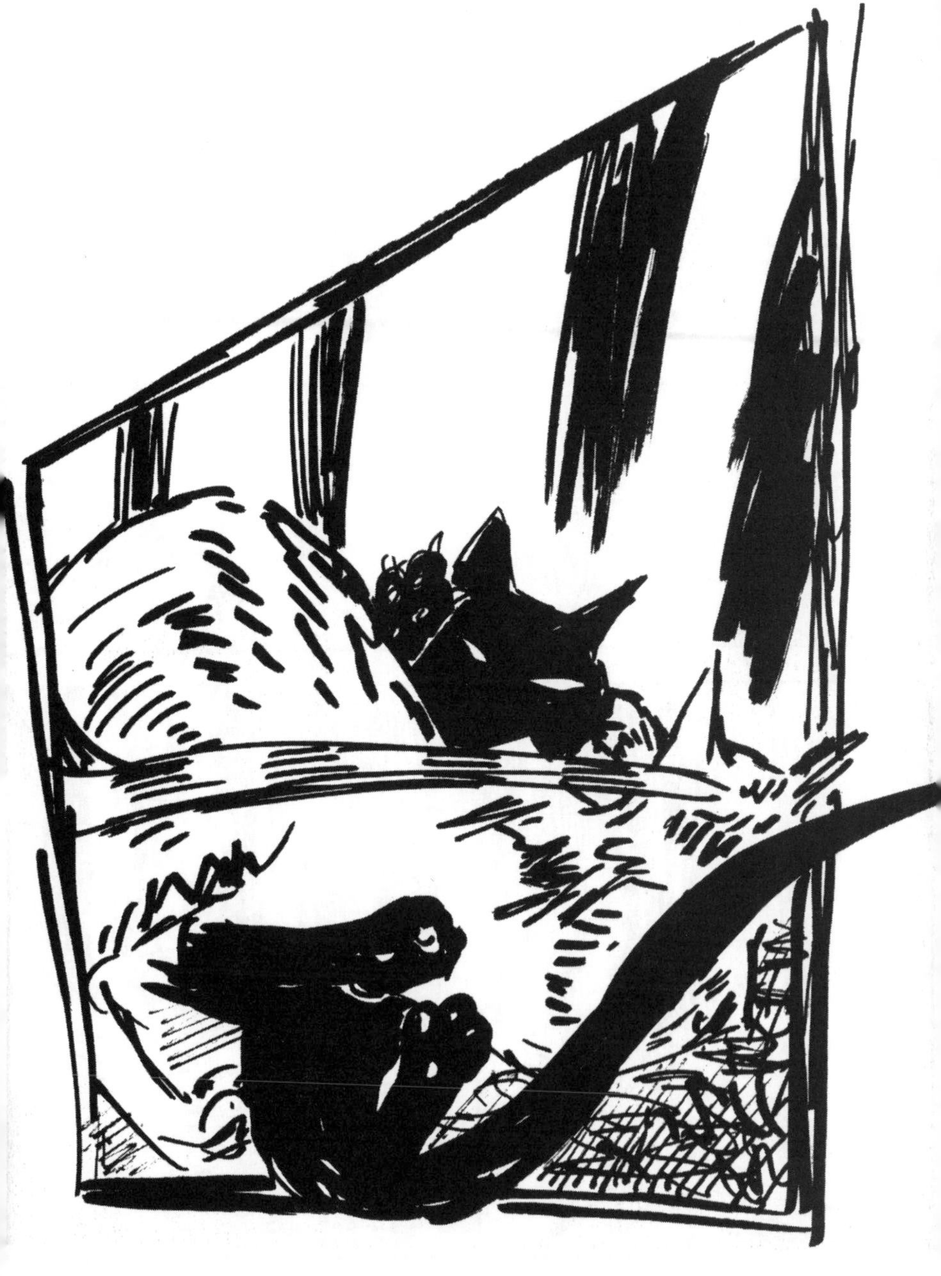

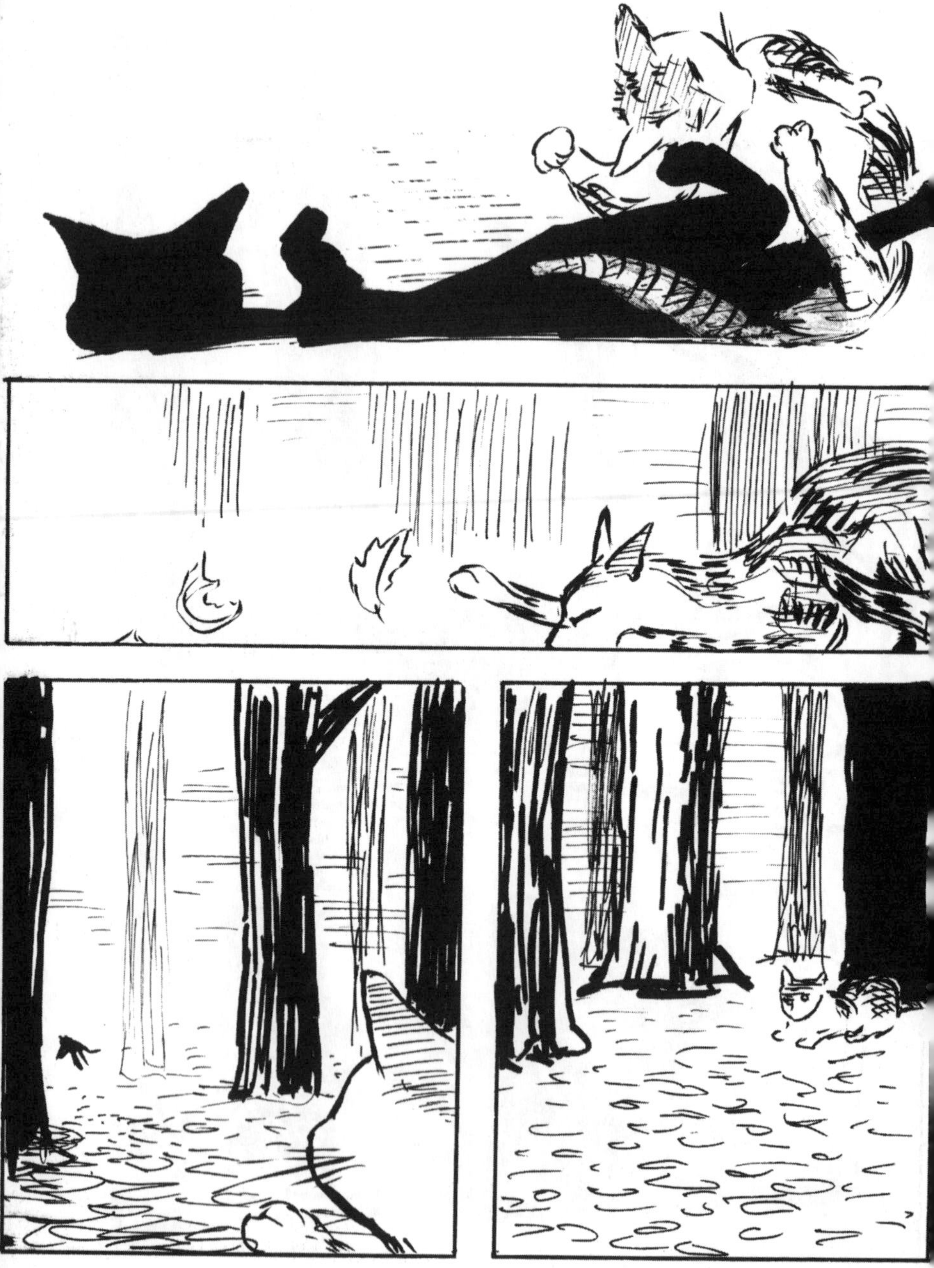

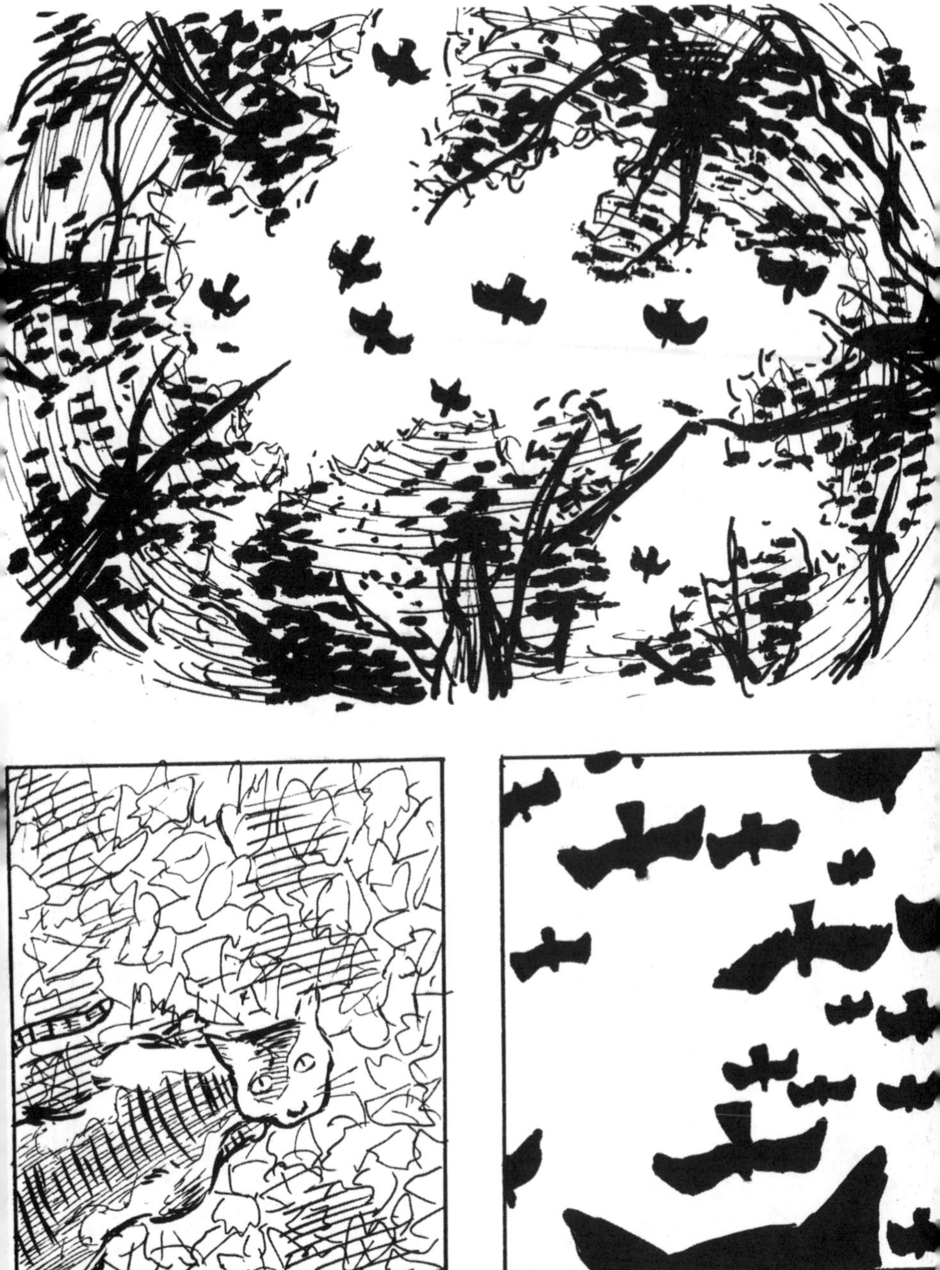

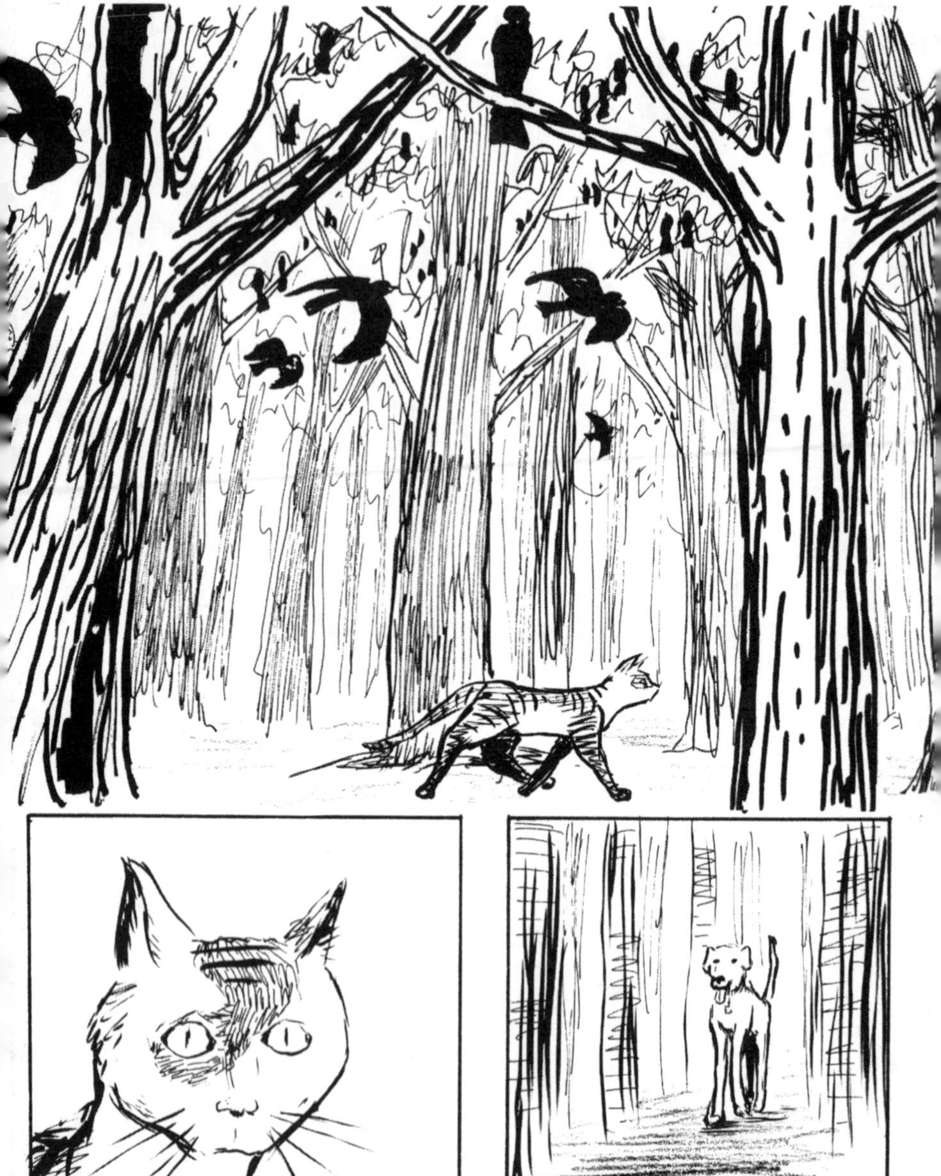

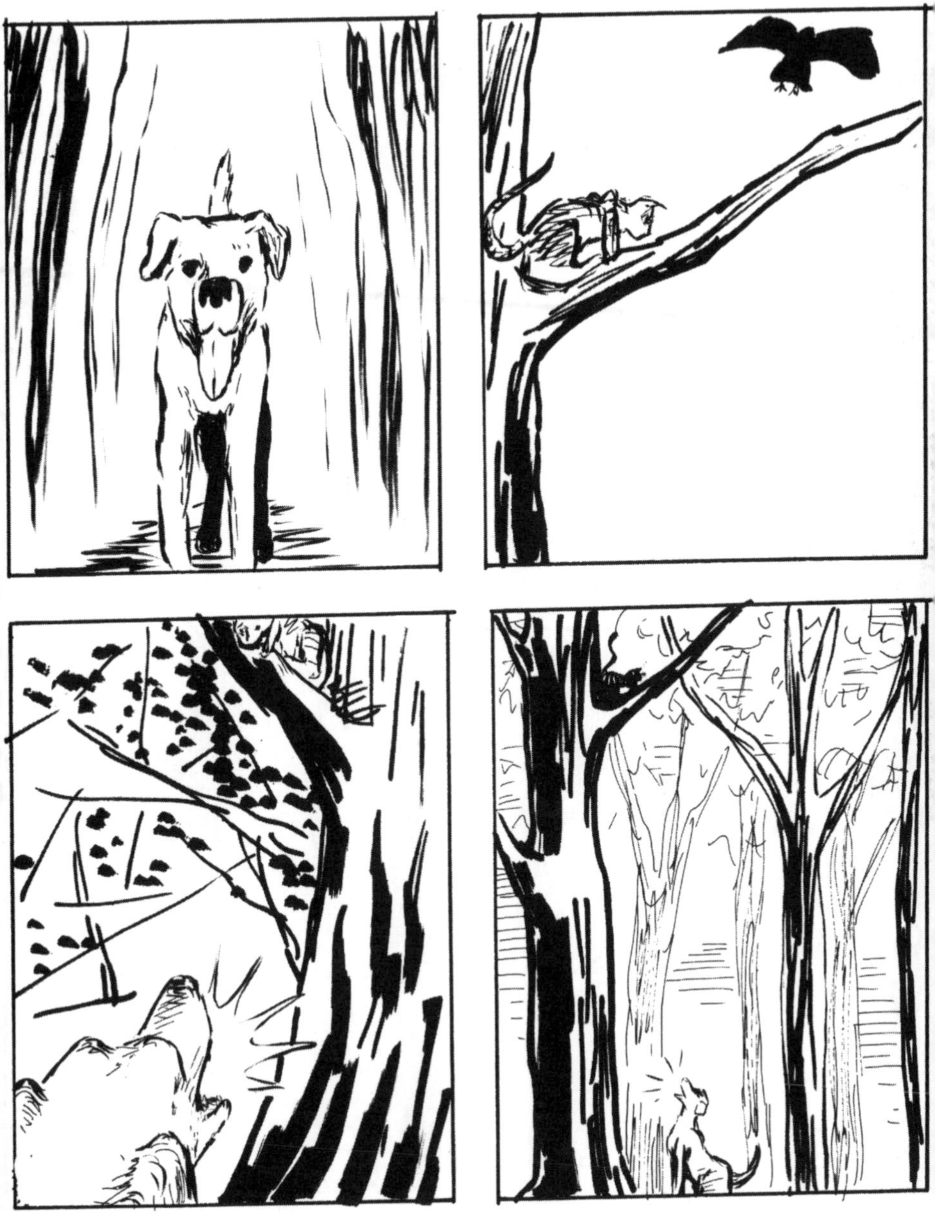

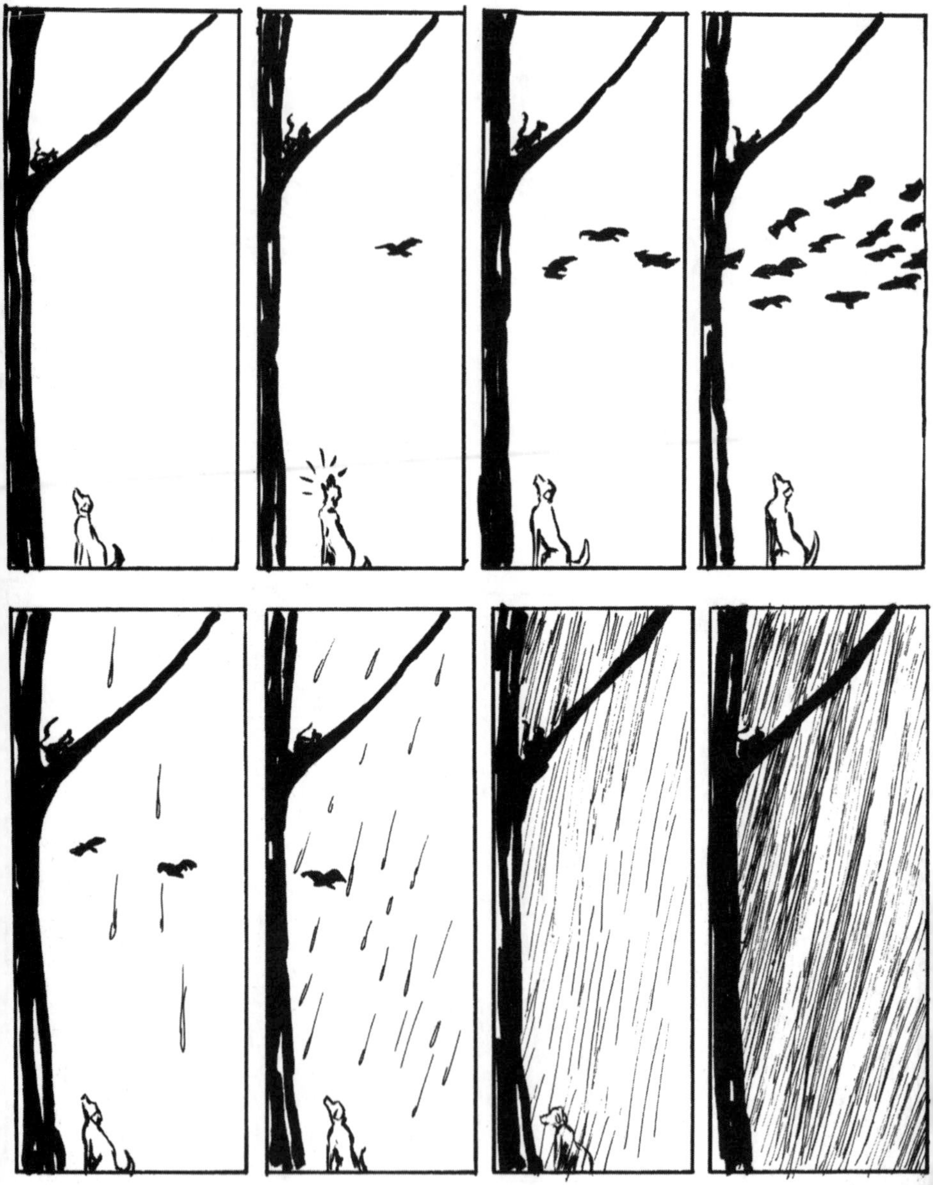

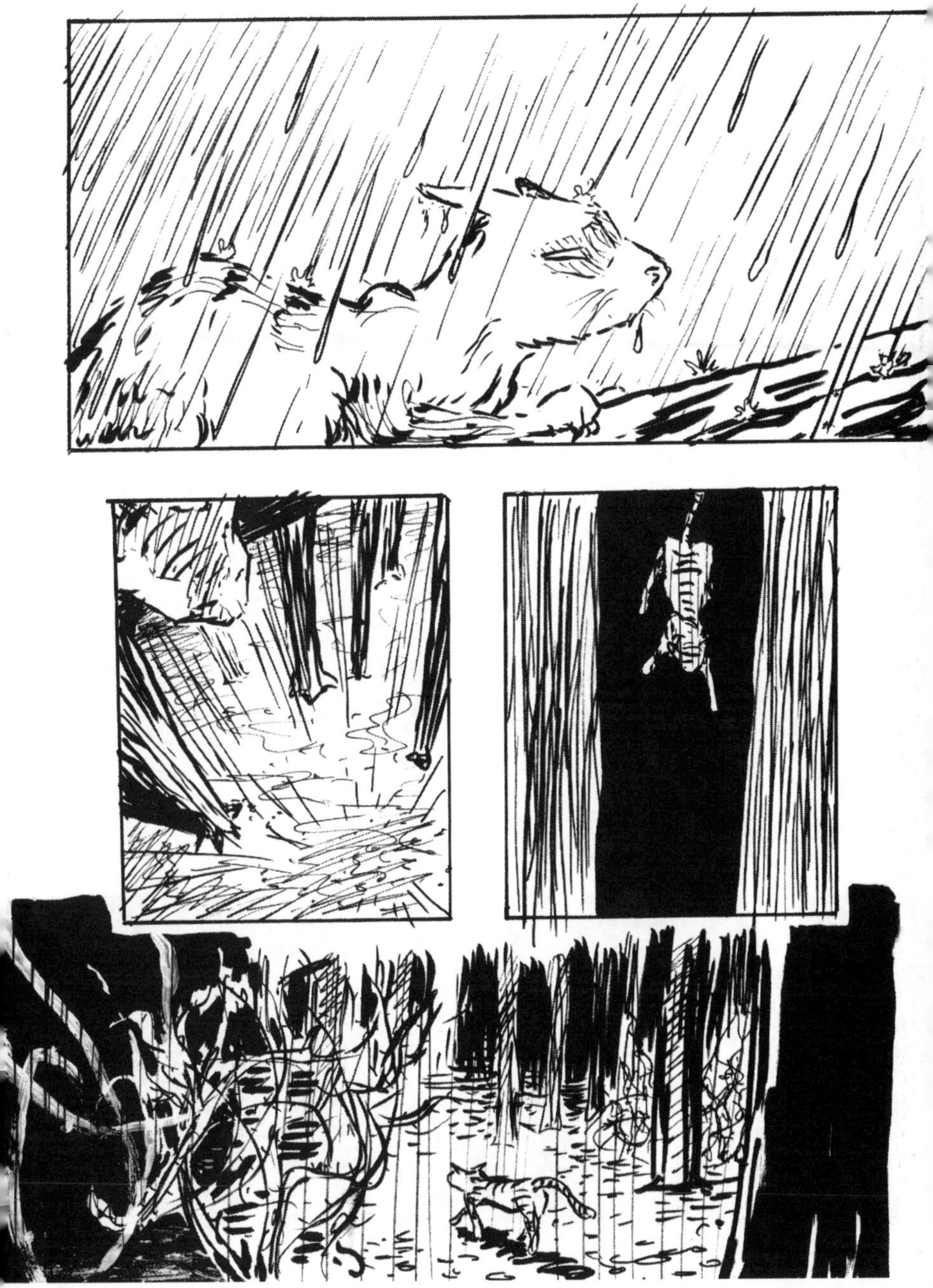

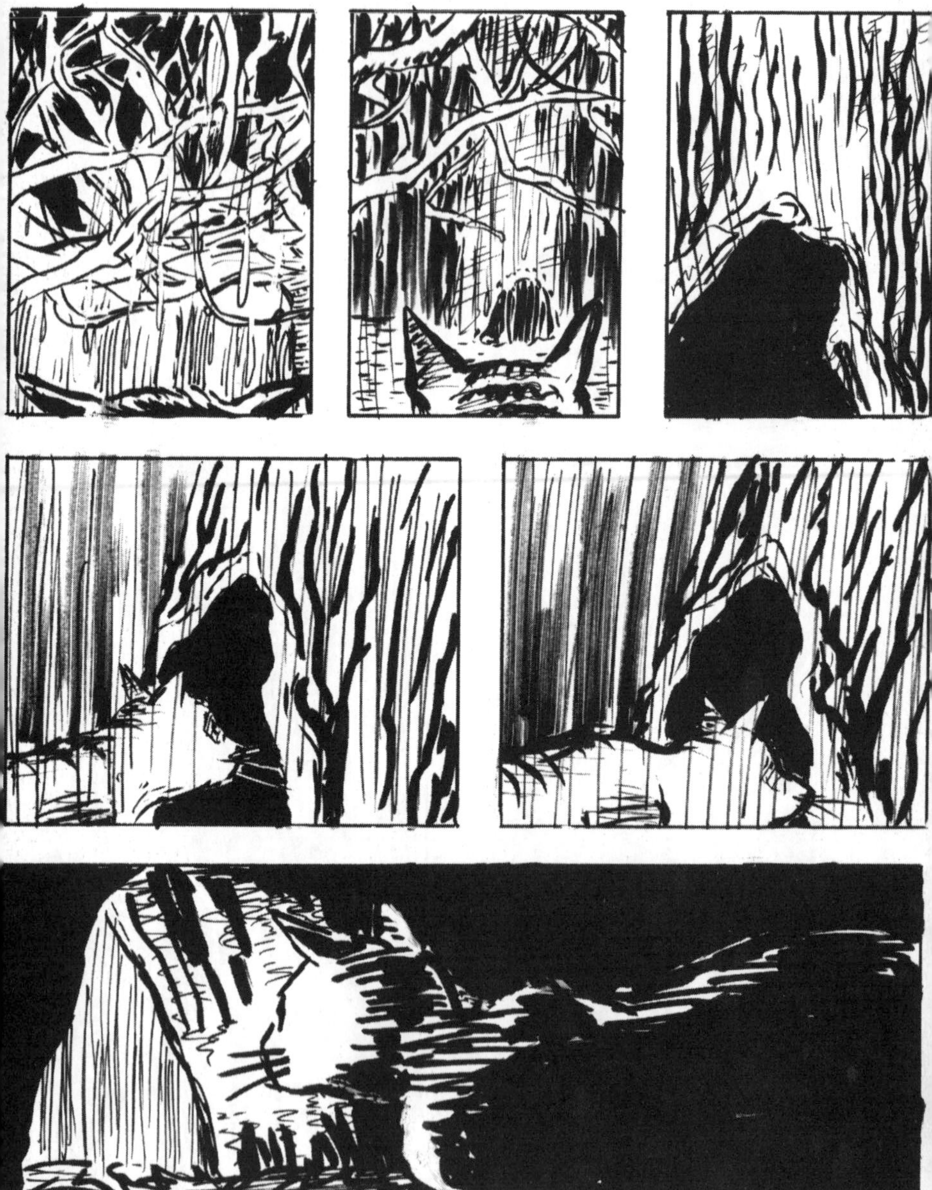

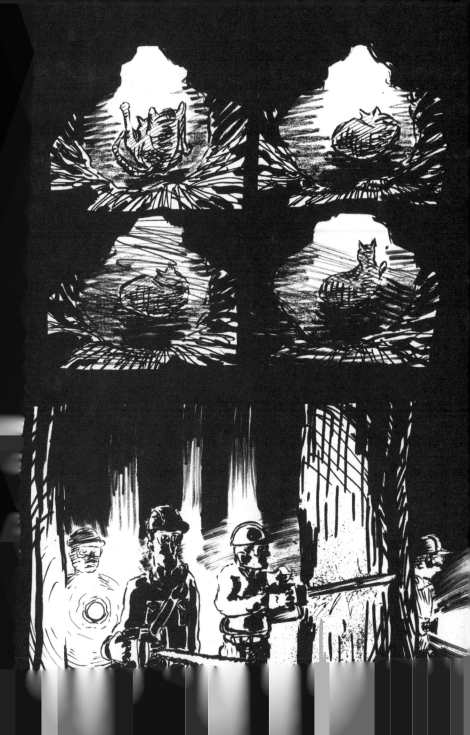

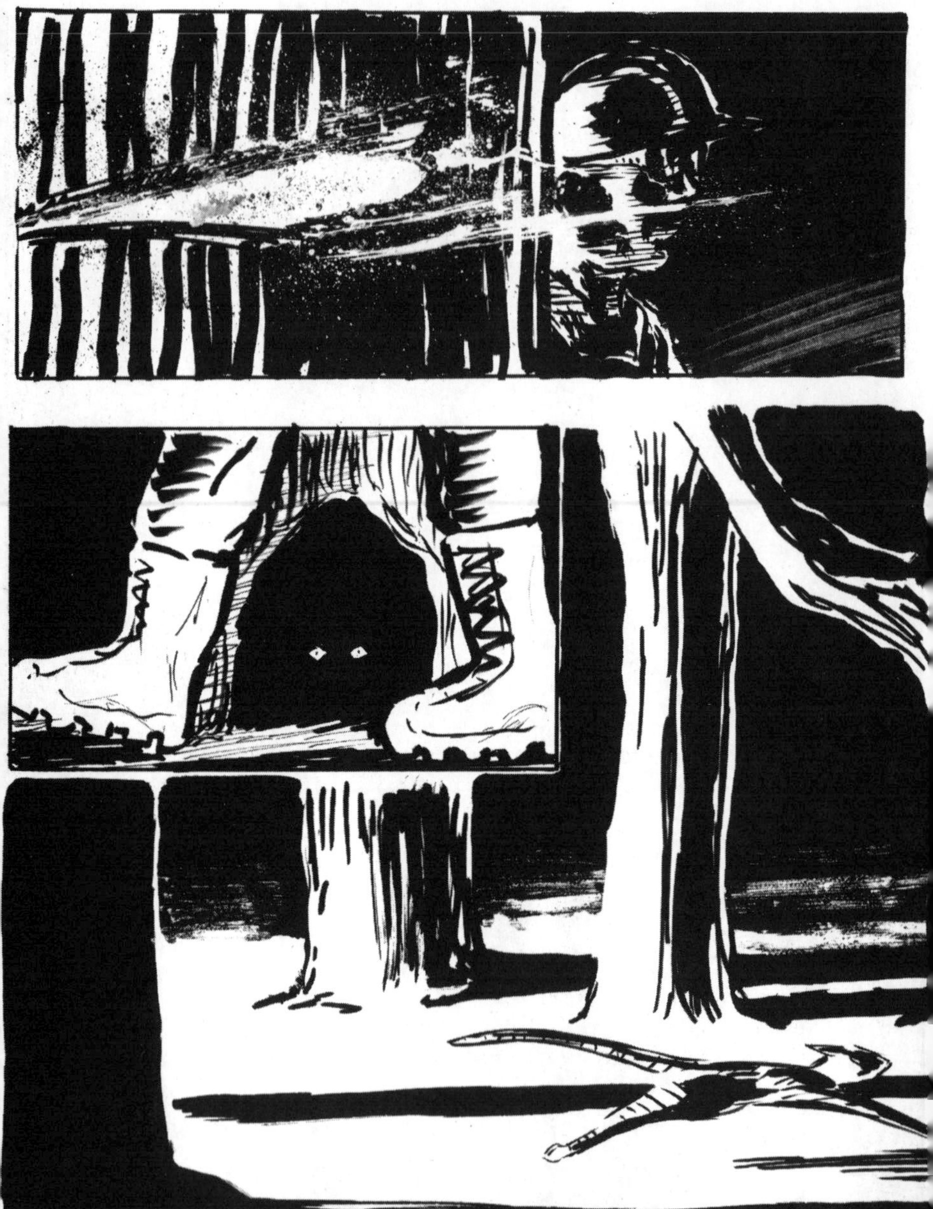

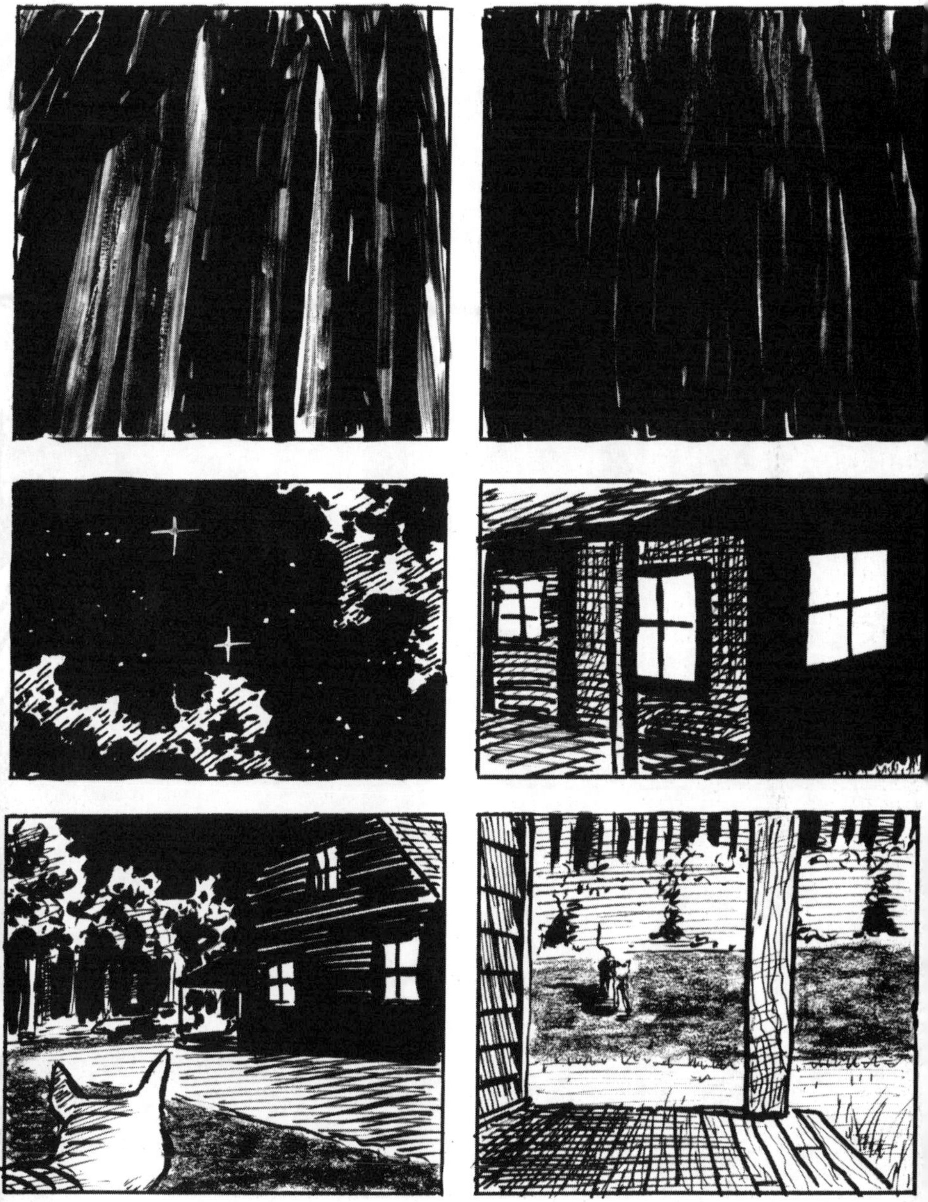

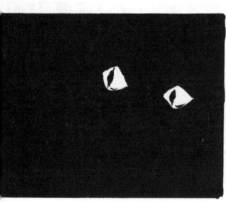

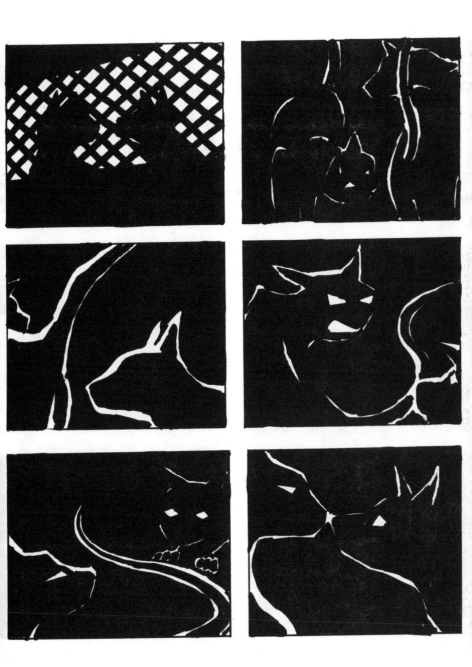

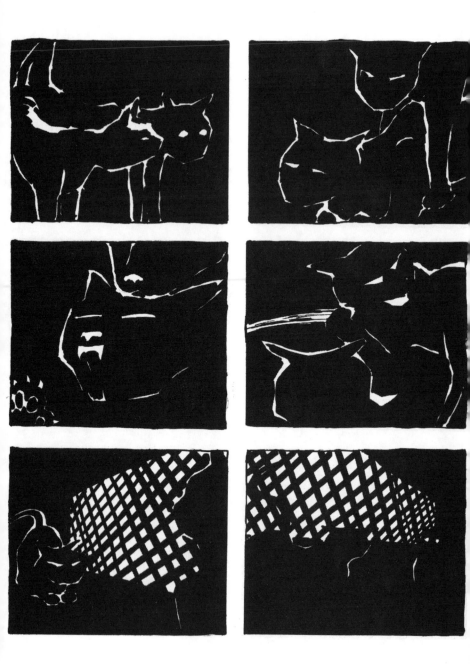

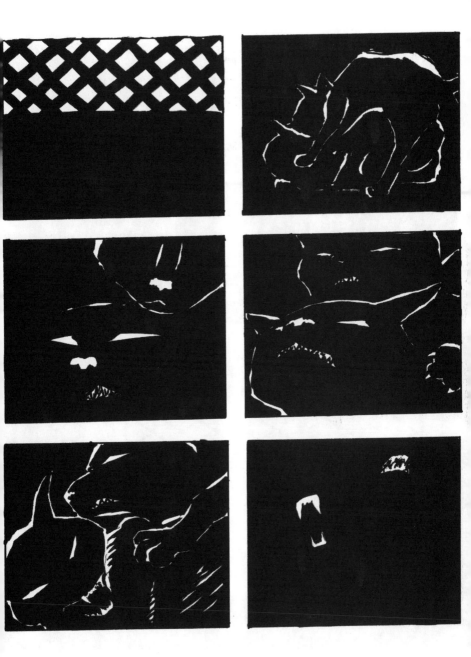

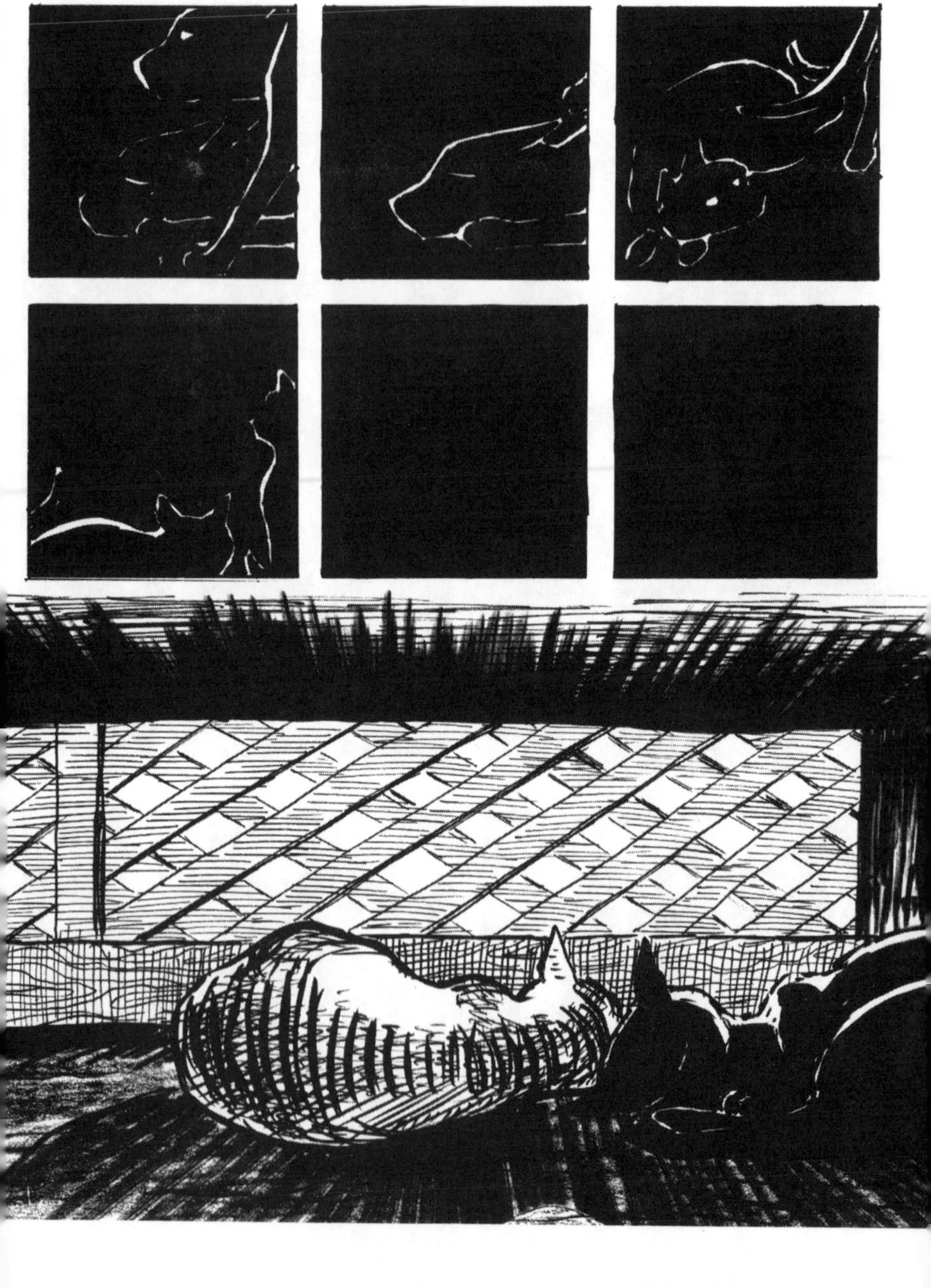

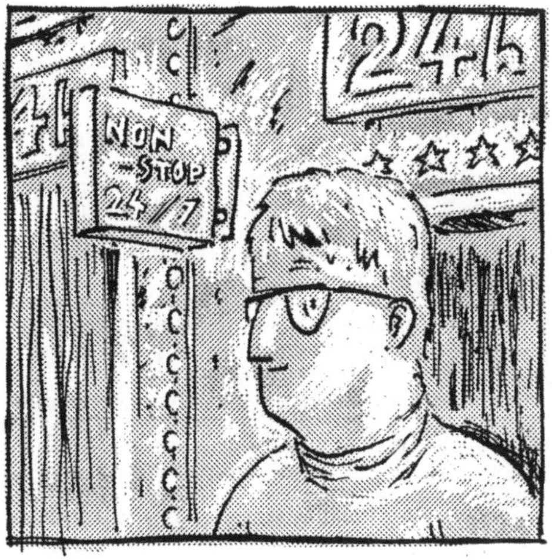
NON-STOP
24/7
24h

Jakob Klemenčič

Jakob Klemenčič's Untitled 24-hour comic perfectly captures the rootless, surreal existence sometimes faced by seasoned world travelers. A traveler himself, Jakob spent some time with my wife and I at the annual comics festival in Angouleme, France in early 2000. He walked me through an exhibit of comics art from his native Slovenia and other neighboring countries (an only half-cooled molten mass at the time, part of the recently transformed Eastern Europe). The talent in the region was formidable, Jakob's own not the least of it. I was reminded of what a vast and varied world of comics there was out there, and the 24-hour comics I've received from abroad over the years have continued to bolster that impression.

Sparseness is an inevitable quality to the artwork found in many 24-hour comics, and this one is no exception, but Jakob's panels nevertheless have a fullness to them that stems from his naturalistic drawing style, and an uncommon willingness to depict the details of his imaginary environments, not just its inhabitants. Far too many cartoonists in North America focus on the interplay of their favorite characters while ignoring the rest of the world they live in, but Jakob's storytelling displays a joy of world-building much like that found in many of the great European comics; comics from another world offering windows into still more worlds.

Finally, Jakob's entry effectively produces the feeling of jetlag that accompanies long-distance journeys. And what better way to express the sleep deprivation that every 24-hour cartoonist has to contend with?

Now boarding...

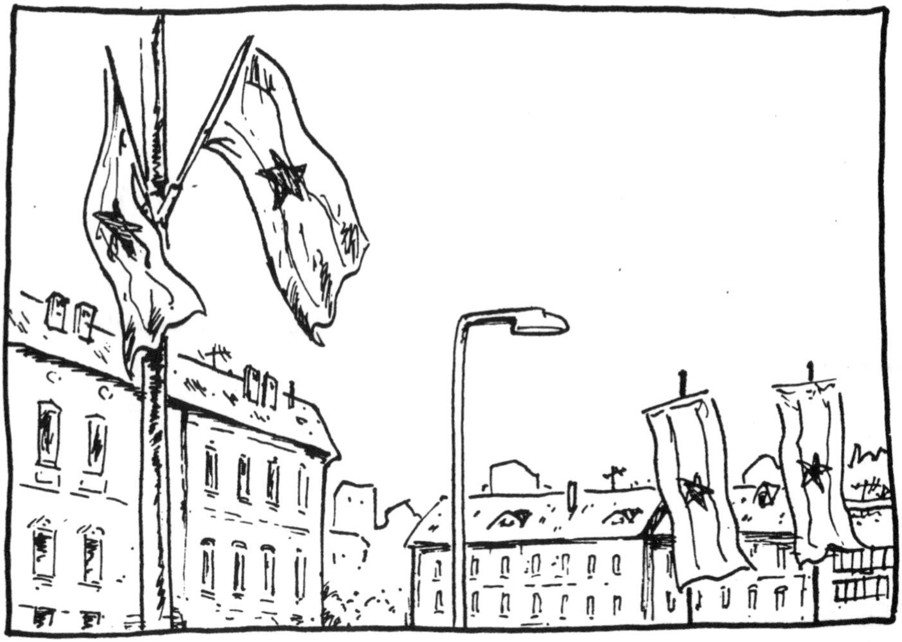
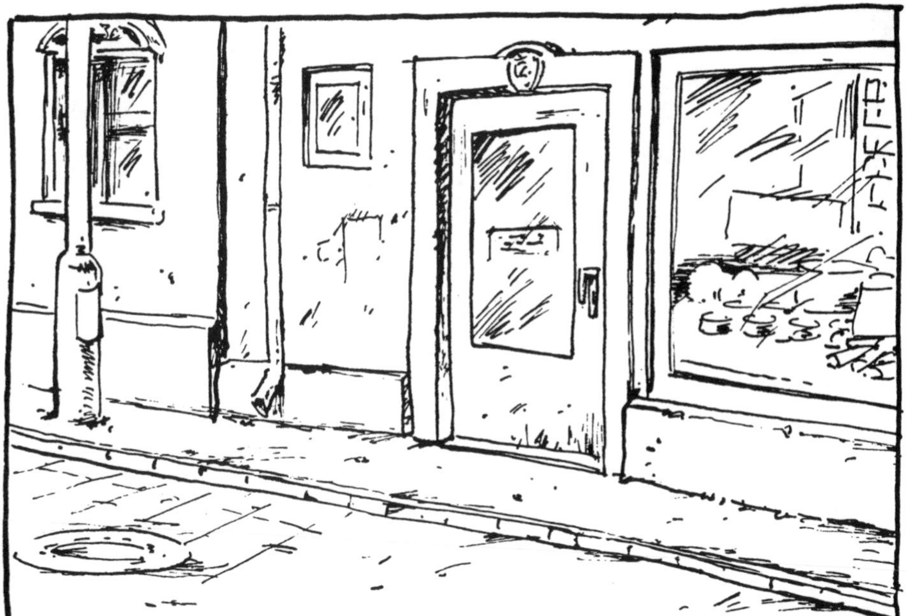

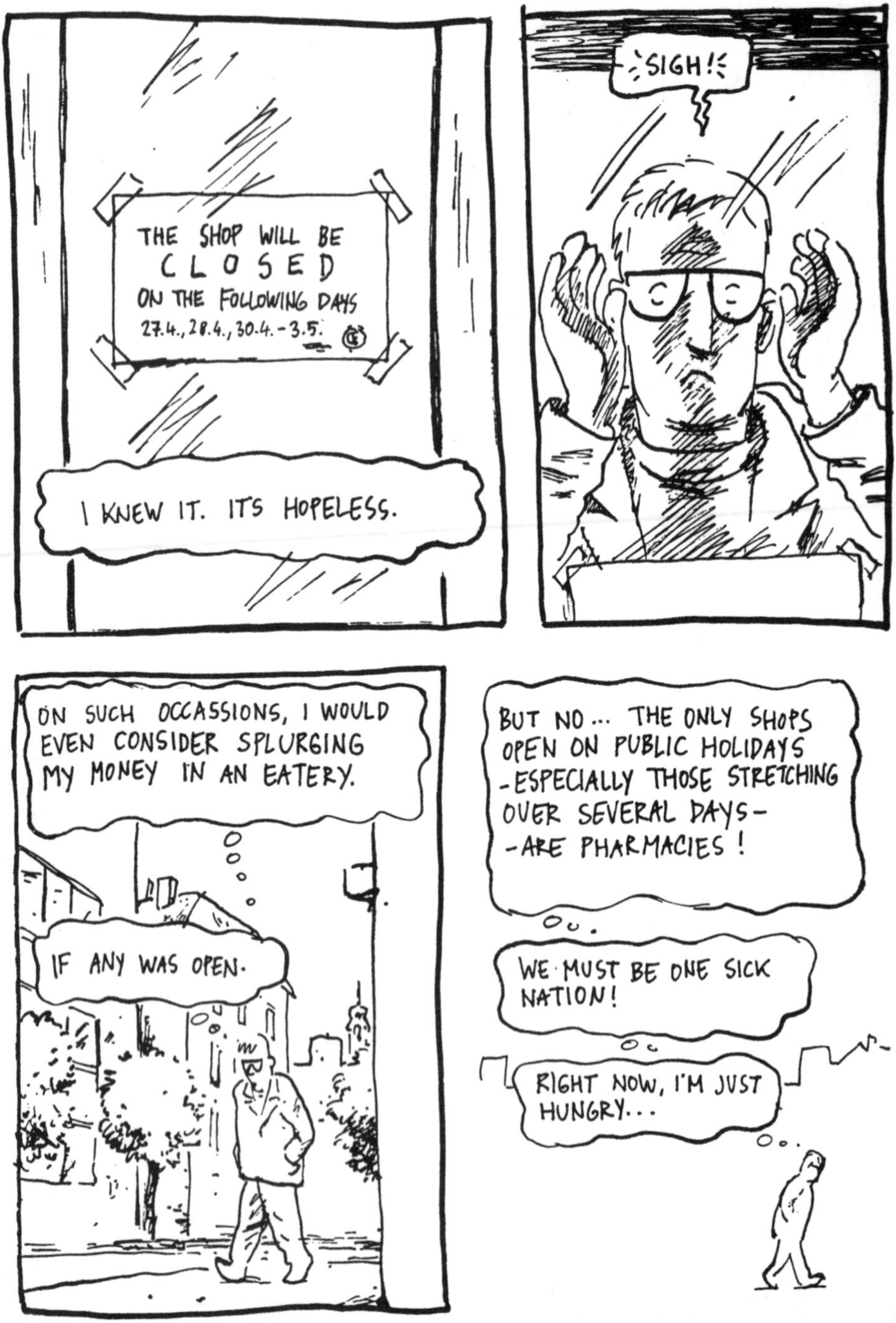
THE SHOP WILL BE CLOSED ON THE FOLLOWING DAYS 27.4., 28.4., 30.4.-3.5.
I KNEW IT. IT'S HOPELESS.
SIGH!
ON SUCH OCCASSIONS, I WOULD EVEN CONSIDER SPLURGING MY MONEY IN AN EATERY.
IF ANY WAS OPEN.
BUT NO... THE ONLY SHOPS OPEN ON PUBLIC HOLIDAYS -ESPECIALLY THOSE STRETCHING OVER SEVERAL DAYS- -ARE PHARMACIES!
WE MUST BE ONE SICK NATION!
RIGHT NOW, I'M JUST HUNGRY...

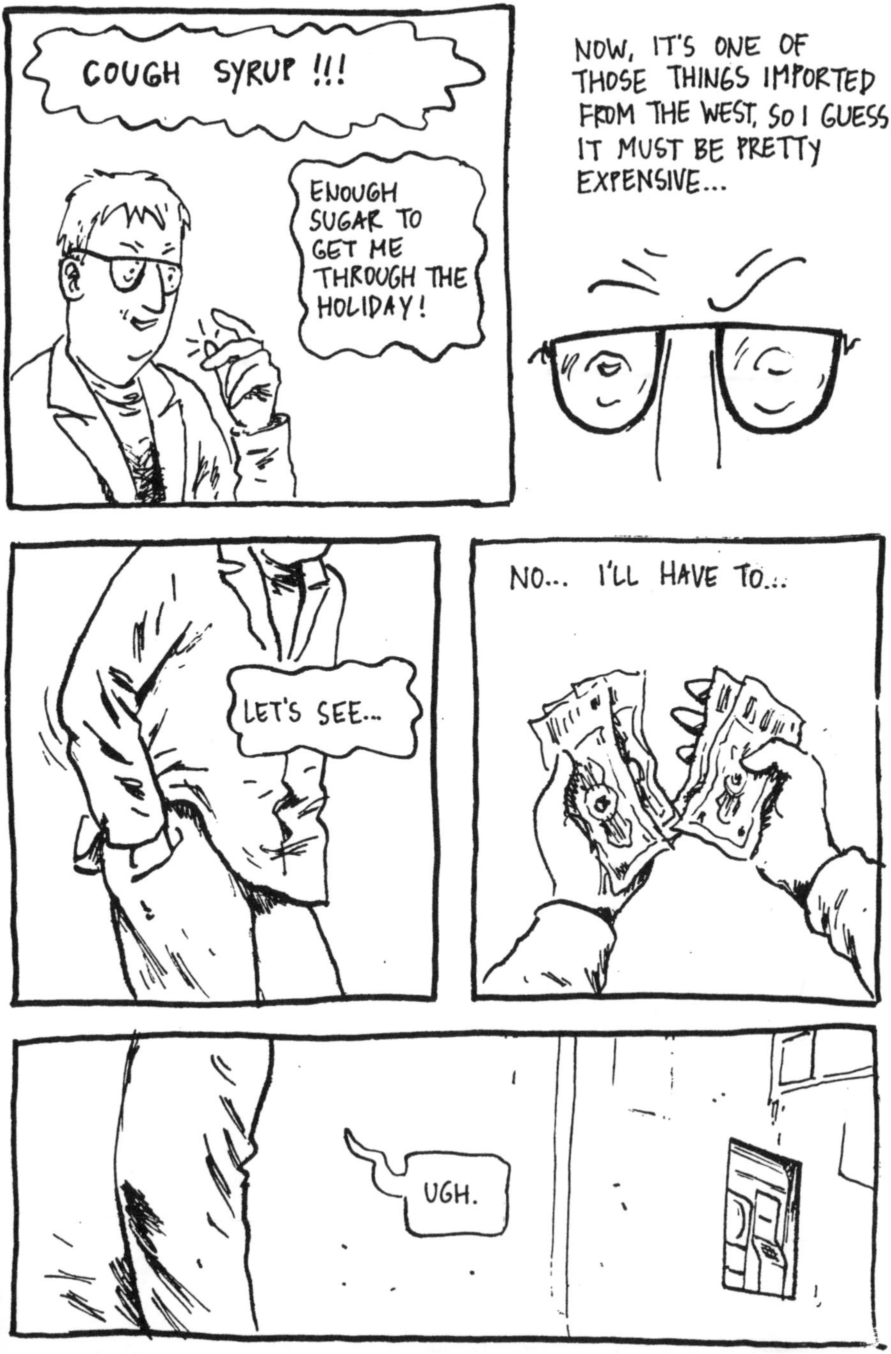
COUGH SYRUP !!!
ENOUGH SUGAR TO GET ME THROUGH THE HOLIDAY!
NOW, IT'S ONE OF THOSE THINGS IMPORTED FROM THE WEST, SO I GUESS IT MUST BE PRETTY EXPENSIVE...
LET'S SEE...
NO... I'LL HAVE TO...
UGH.

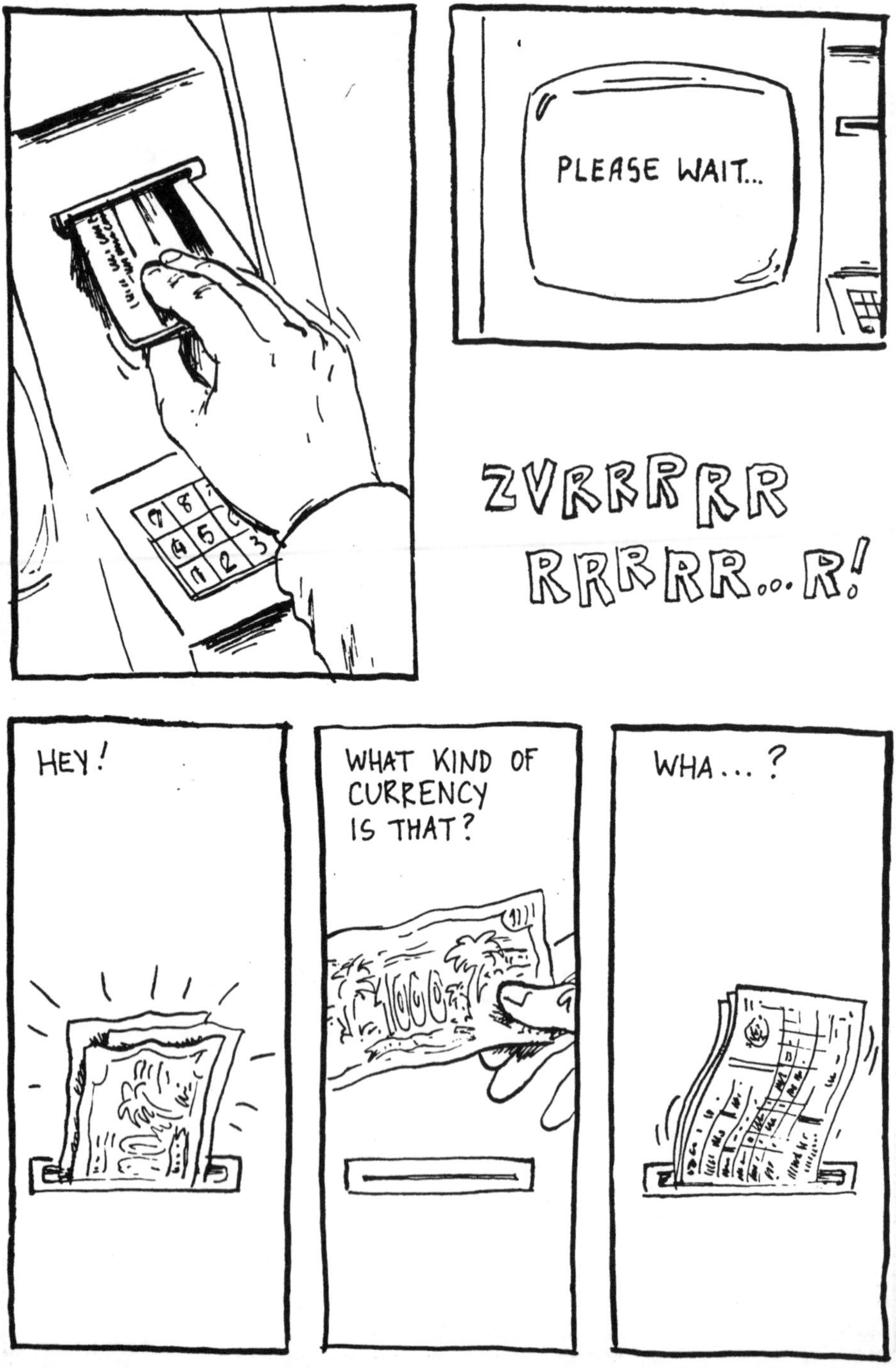
PLEASE WAIT...
ZVRRRRR
RRRRR...R!
HEY!
WHAT KIND OF CURRENCY IS THAT?
WHA...?

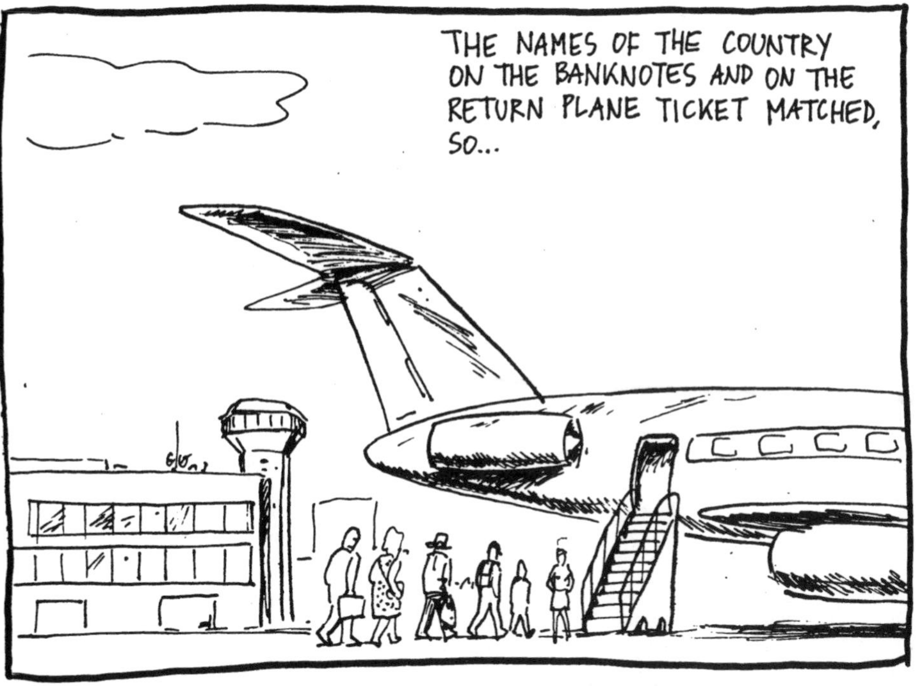
THE NAMES OF THE COUNTRY ON THE BANKNOTES AND ON THE RETURN PLANE TICKET MATCHED, SO...

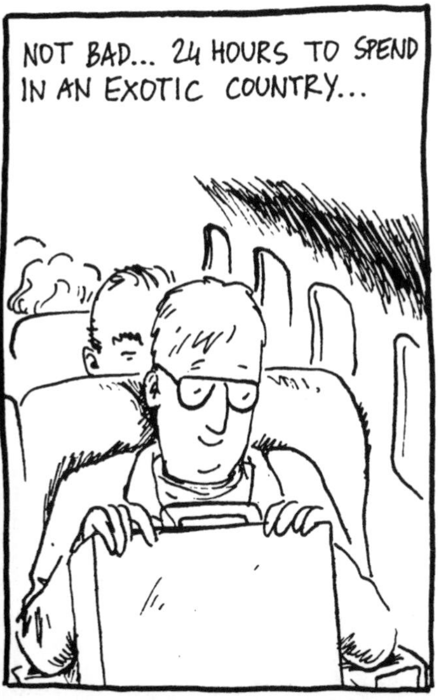
NOT BAD... 24 HOURS TO SPEND IN AN EXOTIC COUNTRY...

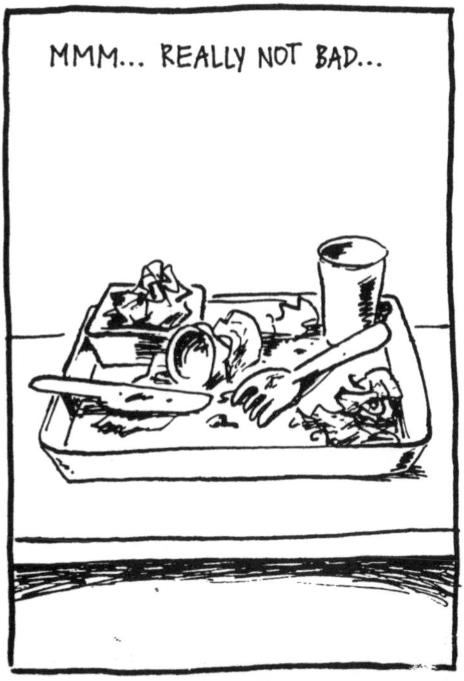
MMM... REALLY NOT BAD...

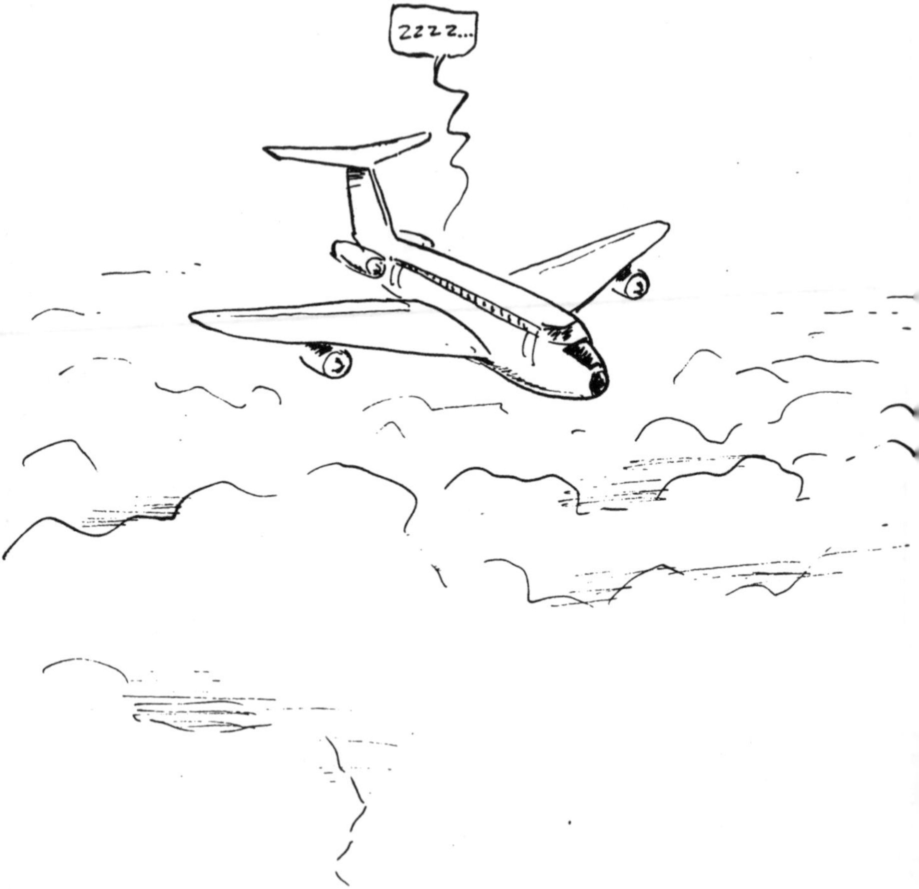
zzzz...

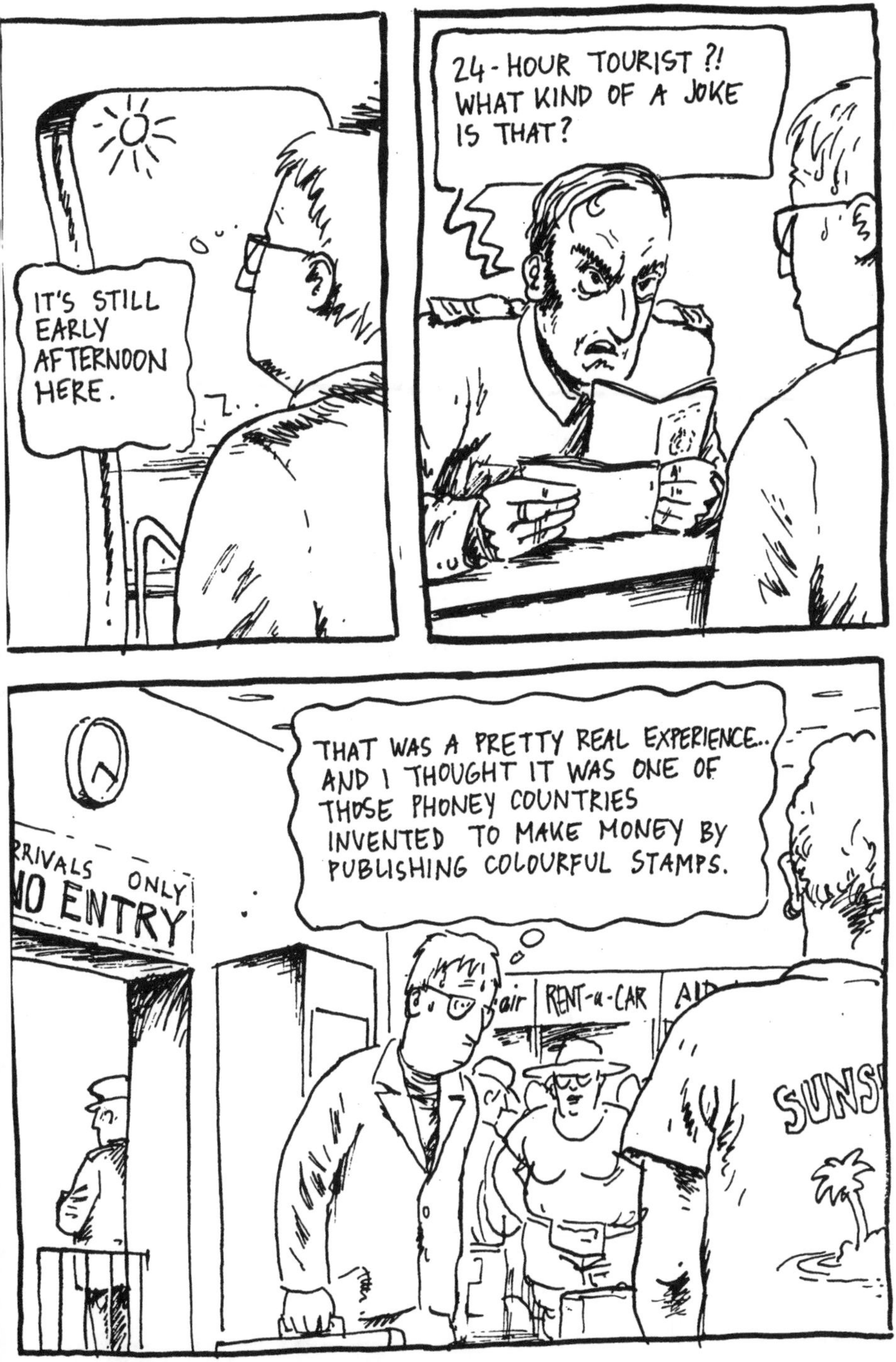
IT'S STILL EARLY AFTERNOON HERE.
24-HOUR TOURIST ?! WHAT KIND OF A JOKE IS THAT?
THAT WAS A PRETTY REAL EXPERIENCE.. AND I THOUGHT IT WAS ONE OF THOSE PHONEY COUNTRIES INVENTED TO MAKE MONEY BY PUBLISHING COLOURFUL STAMPS.
ARRIVALS ONLY
NO ENTRY
RENT-a-CAR
SUNS

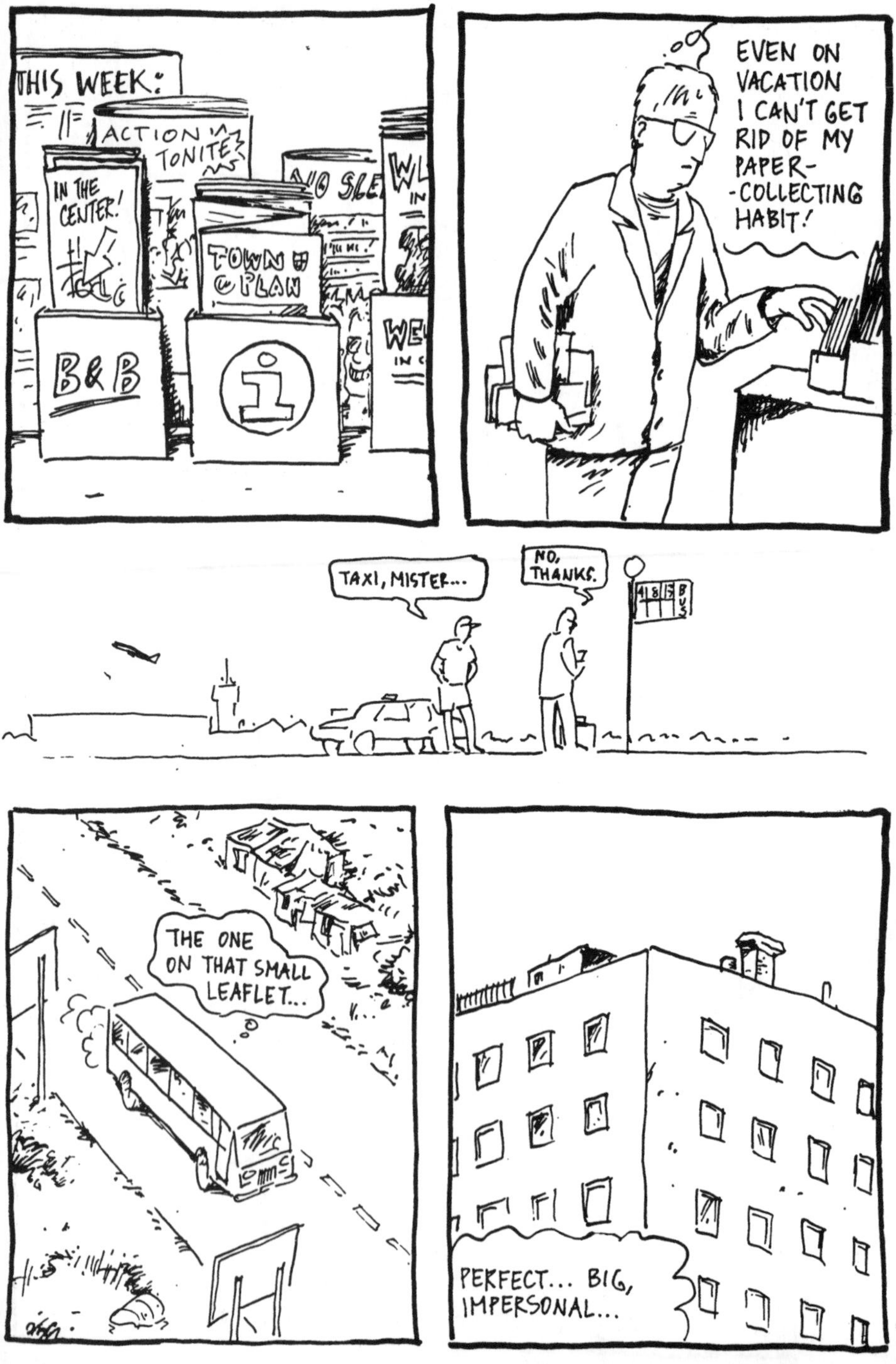
THIS WEEK:
ACTION TONITE
IN THE CENTER!
TOWN PLAN
B&B
EVEN ON VACATION I CAN'T GET RID OF MY PAPER-COLLECTING HABIT!
TAXI, MISTER...
NO, THANKS.
BUS
THE ONE ON THAT SMALL LEAFLET...
PERFECT... BIG, IMPERSONAL...

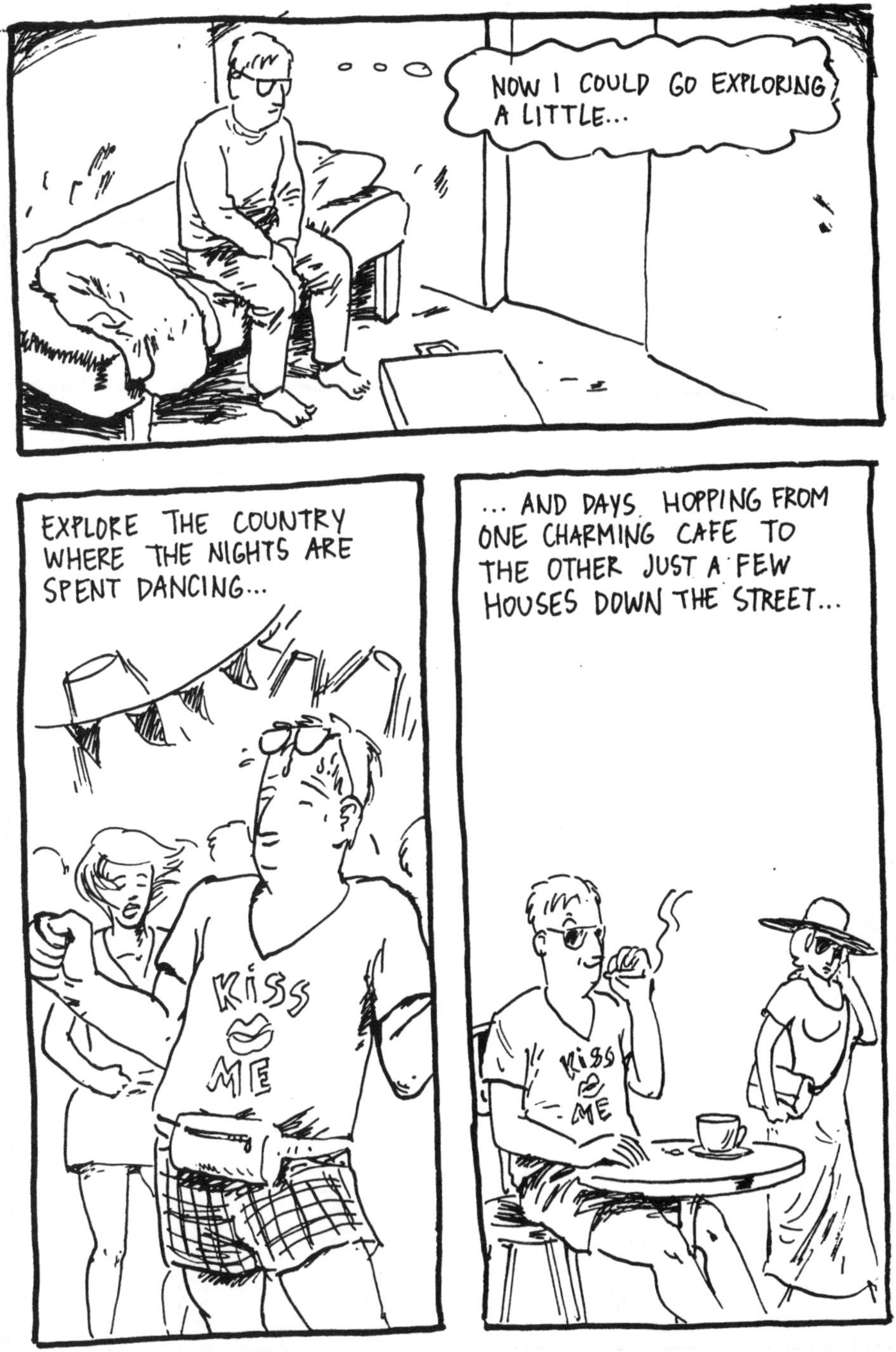
NOW I COULD GO EXPLORING A LITTLE...
EXPLORE THE COUNTRY WHERE THE NIGHTS ARE SPENT DANCING...
KISS ME
... AND DAYS HOPPING FROM ONE CHARMING CAFE TO THE OTHER JUST A FEW HOUSES DOWN THE STREET...
KISS ME

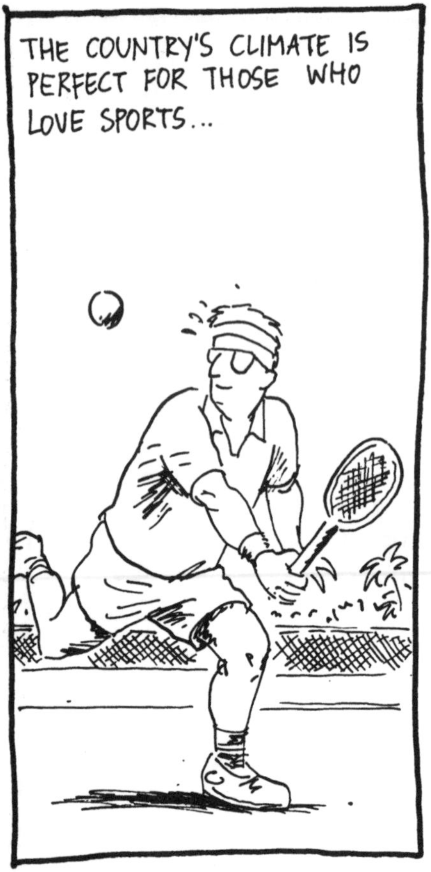
THE COUNTRY'S CLIMATE IS PERFECT FOR THOSE WHO LOVE SPORTS...

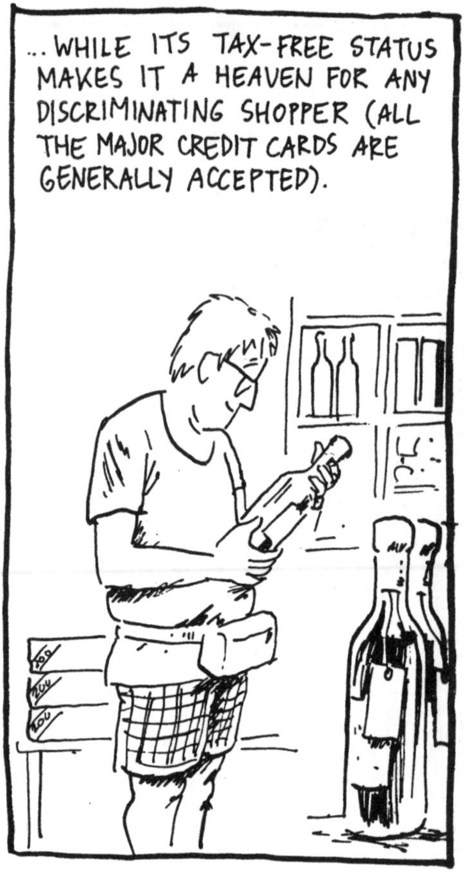
...WHILE ITS TAX-FREE STATUS MAKES IT A HEAVEN FOR ANY DISCRIMINATING SHOPPER (ALL THE MAJOR CREDIT CARDS ARE GENERALLY ACCEPTED).

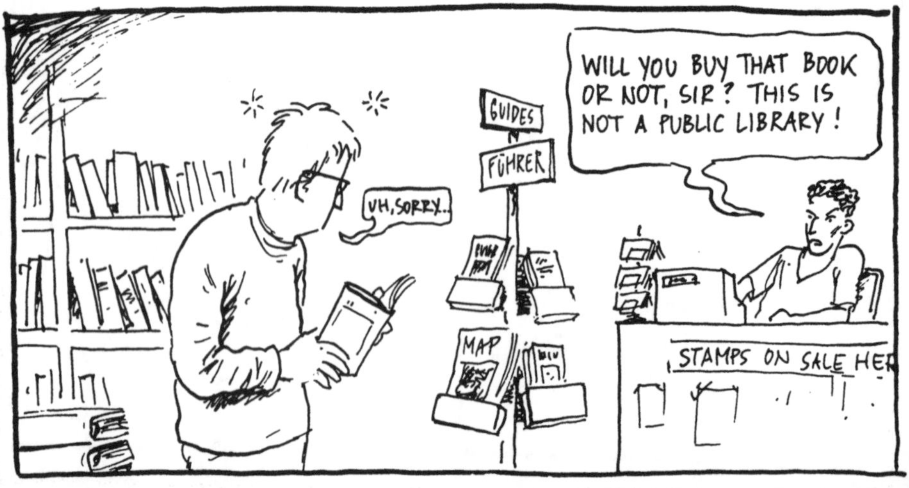
GUIDES
FÜHRER
MAP
UH, SORRY...
WILL YOU BUY THAT BOOK OR NOT, SIR? THIS IS NOT A PUBLIC LIBRARY!
STAMPS ON SALE HER

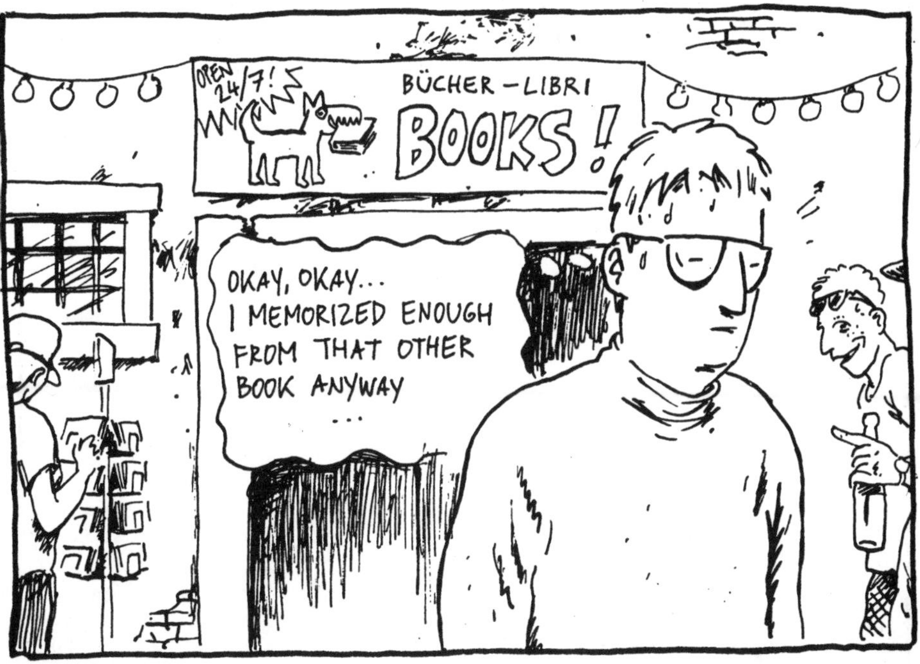
OPEN 24/7!
BÜCHER – LIBRI
BOOKS!
OKAY, OKAY...
I MEMORIZED ENOUGH FROM THAT OTHER BOOK ANYWAY
...

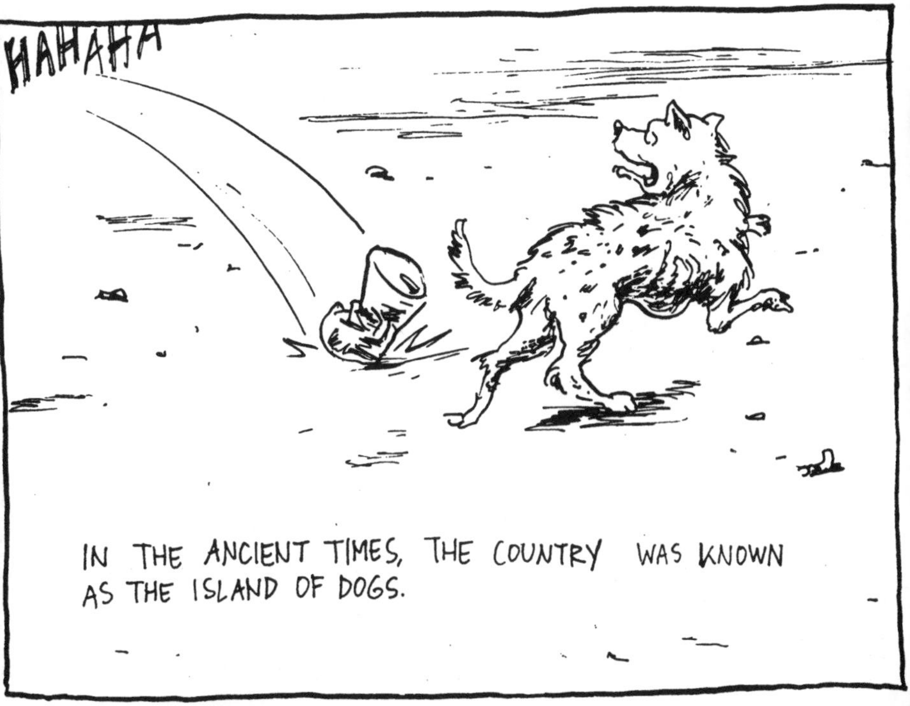
HAHAHA
IN THE ANCIENT TIMES, THE COUNTRY WAS KNOWN AS THE ISLAND OF DOGS.

APART FROM TOURISM, DOG-BREEDING IS STILL COUNTRY'S LEADING SOURCE OF INCOME.

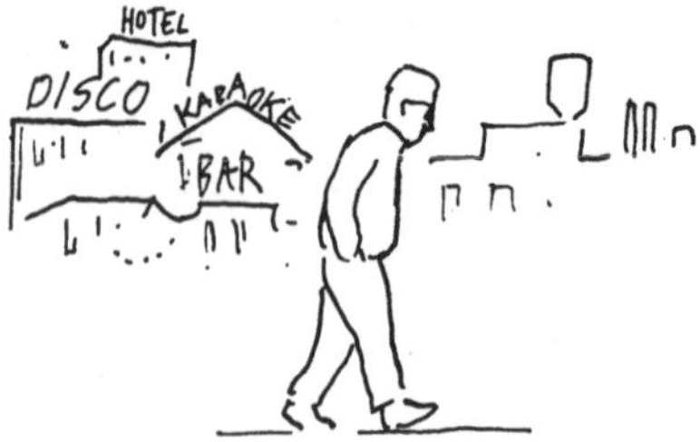
HOTEL
DISCO
KARAOKE
BAR

THE DOG FARMS ARE LOCATED JUST OUT OF THE TOWN CENTER.

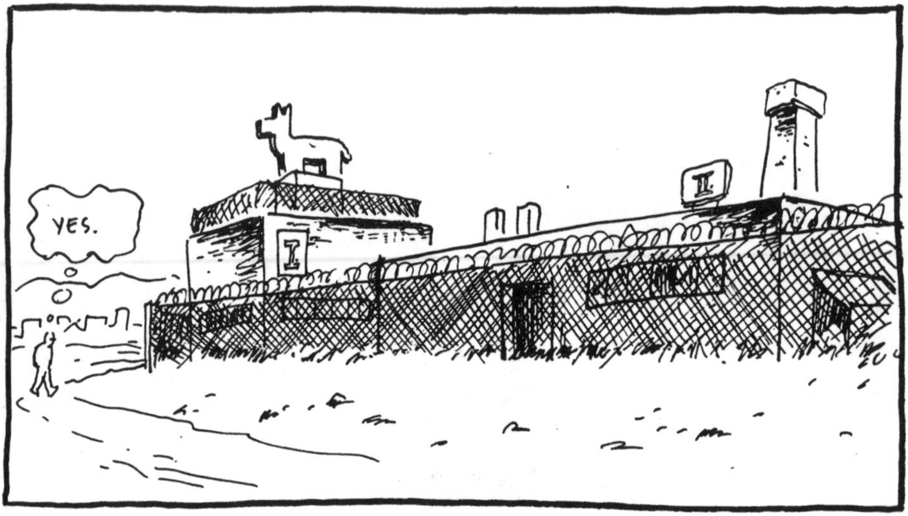
YES.
I
II

EXCELLENT QUALITY OF DOGS' SKIN IS USUALLY ATTRIBUTED TO COUNTRY'S WEATHER CONDITIONS.
THERE ARE TWO MAJOR TYPES OF DOGS BRED ON THE ISLAND. TYPE ONE, ALSO KNOWN AS PREMIUM QUALITY, IS SMALLER THAN SPECIALLY DEVELOPED TYPE TWO, A PRODUCT OF 19TH CENTURY DOGSKIN GLOVE MANIA, WHOSE SKIN'S QUALITY HAS DETERIORATED DUE TO TOO MUCH INBREEDING.

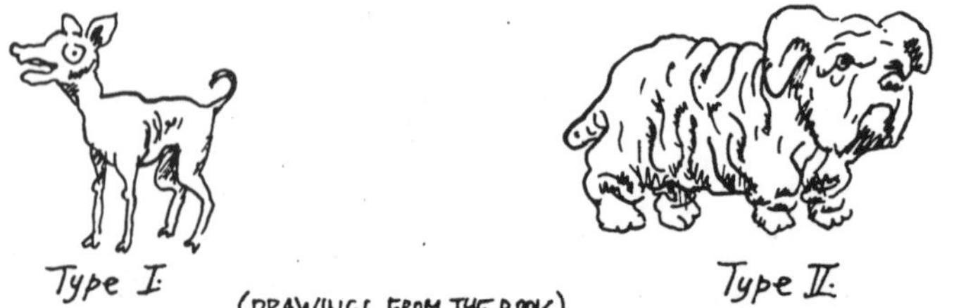
Type I.
Type II.

(DRAWINGS FROM THE BOOK)

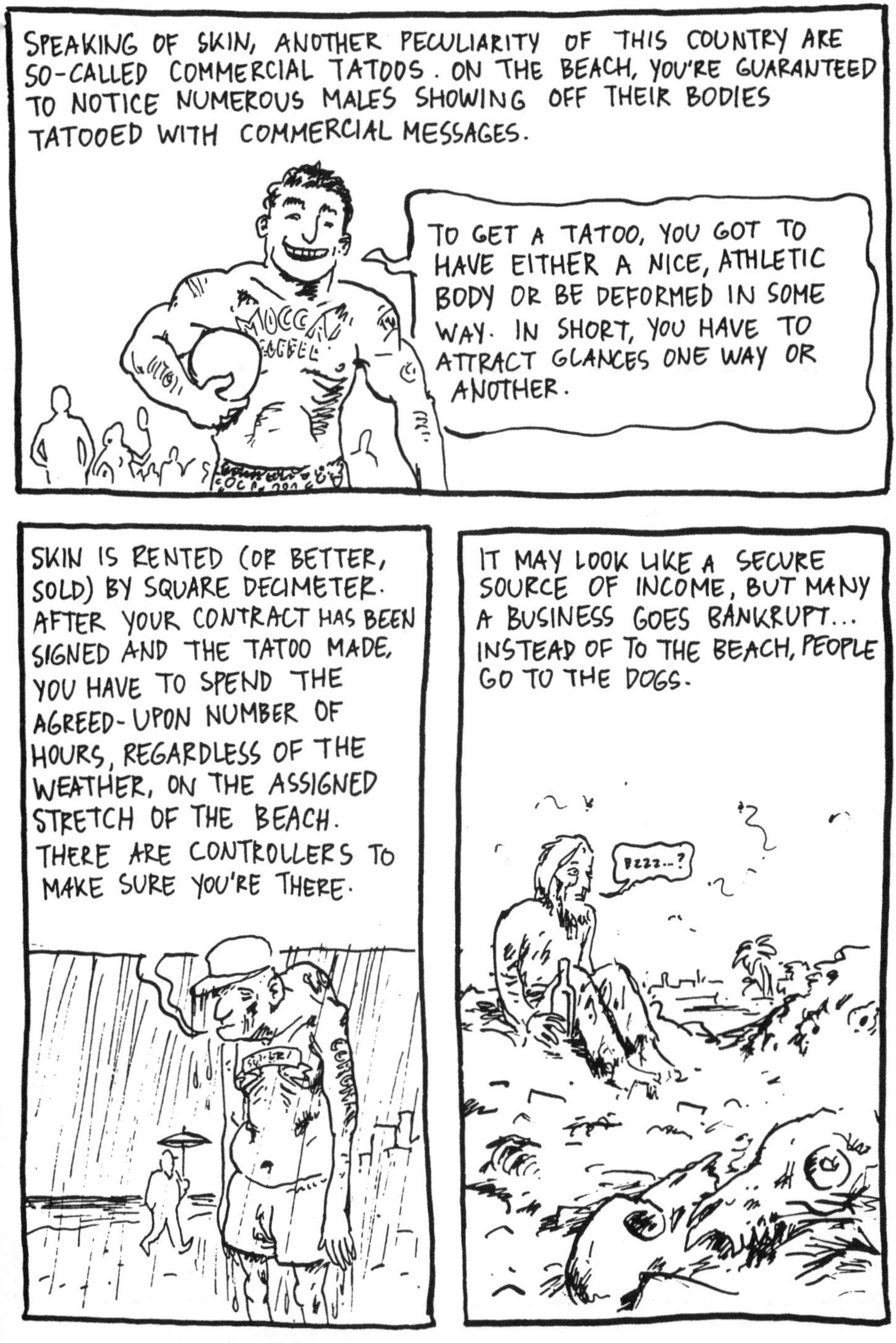
SPEAKING OF SKIN, ANOTHER PECULIARITY OF THIS COUNTRY ARE SO-CALLED COMMERCIAL TATOOS. ON THE BEACH, YOU'RE GUARANTEED TO NOTICE NUMEROUS MALES SHOWING OFF THEIR BODIES TATOOED WITH COMMERCIAL MESSAGES.
TO GET A TATOO, YOU GOT TO HAVE EITHER A NICE, ATHLETIC BODY OR BE DEFORMED IN SOME WAY. IN SHORT, YOU HAVE TO ATTRACT GLANCES ONE WAY OR ANOTHER.
SKIN IS RENTED (OR BETTER, SOLD) BY SQUARE DECIMETER. AFTER YOUR CONTRACT HAS BEEN SIGNED AND THE TATOO MADE, YOU HAVE TO SPEND THE AGREED-UPON NUMBER OF HOURS, REGARDLESS OF THE WEATHER, ON THE ASSIGNED STRETCH OF THE BEACH. THERE ARE CONTROLLERS TO MAKE SURE YOU'RE THERE.
IT MAY LOOK LIKE A SECURE SOURCE OF INCOME, BUT MANY A BUSINESS GOES BANKRUPT... INSTEAD OF TO THE BEACH, PEOPLE GO TO THE DOGS.
BZZZ...?

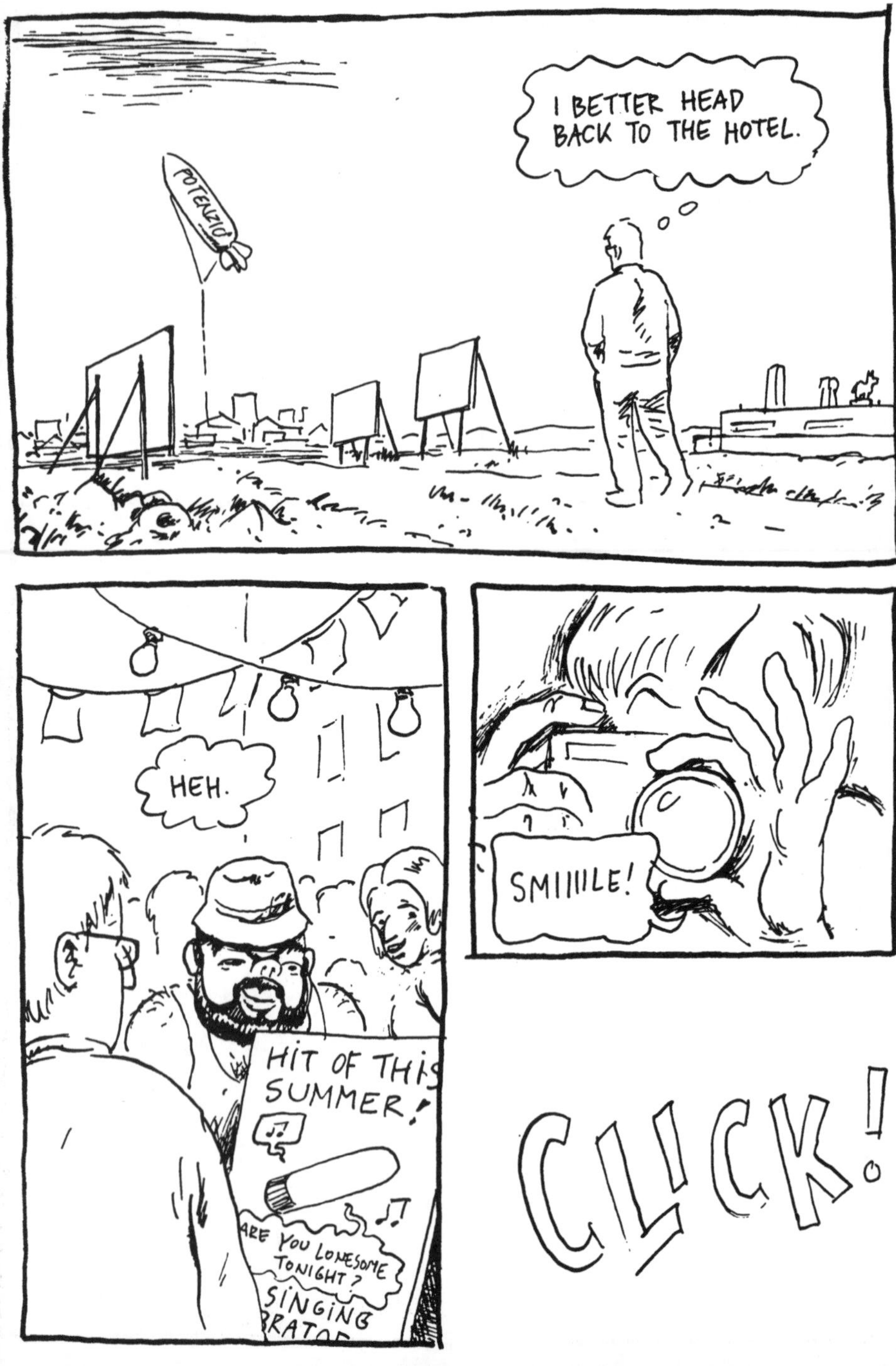
POTENZIO
I BETTER HEAD BACK TO THE HOTEL.
HEH.
HIT OF THIS SUMMER!
ARE YOU LONESOME TONIGHT?
SINGING
SMIIIILE!
CLICK!

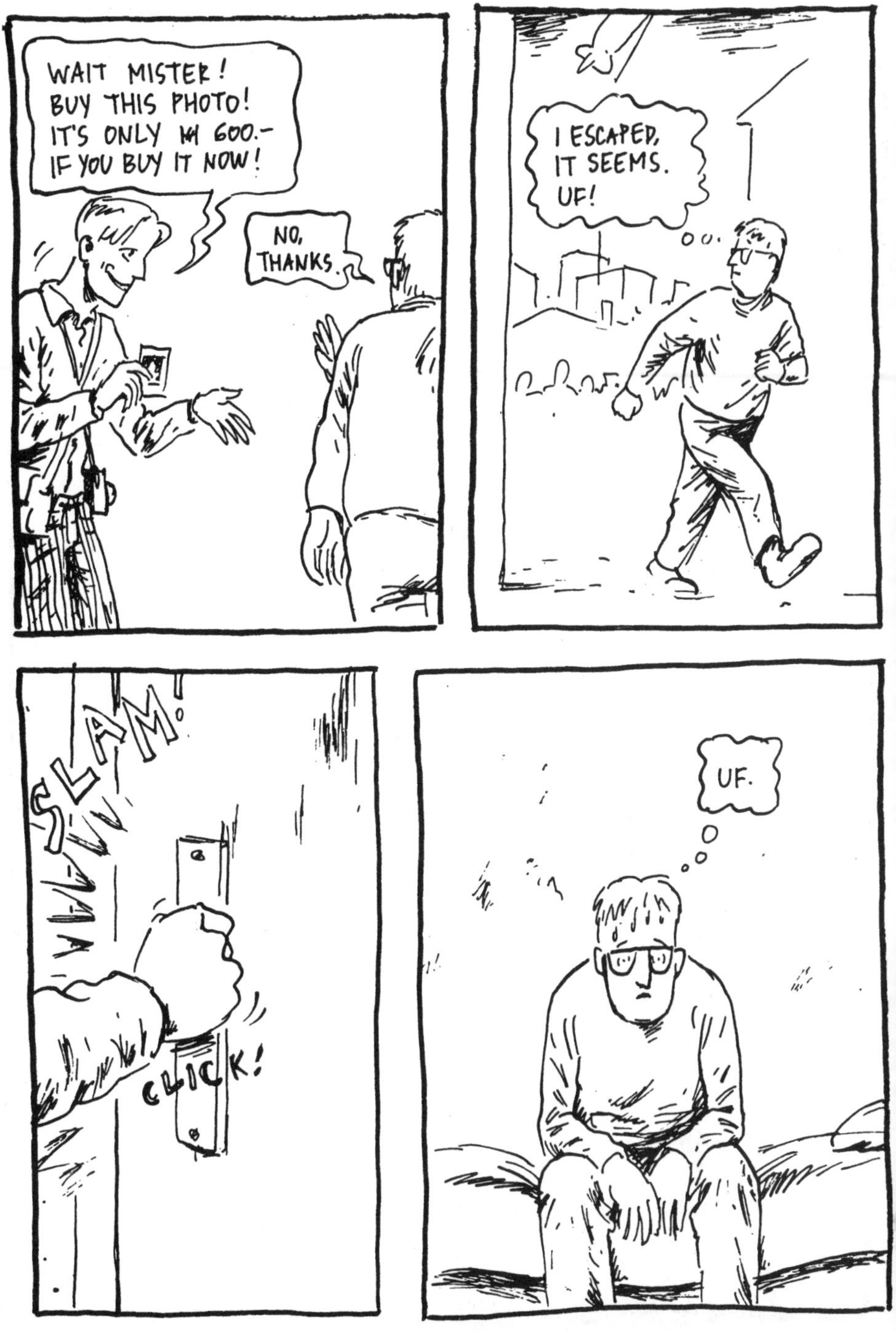
WAIT MISTER! BUY THIS PHOTO! IT'S ONLY 600.- IF YOU BUY IT NOW!
NO, THANKS.
I ESCAPED, IT SEEMS. UF!
SLAM!
CLICK!
UF.

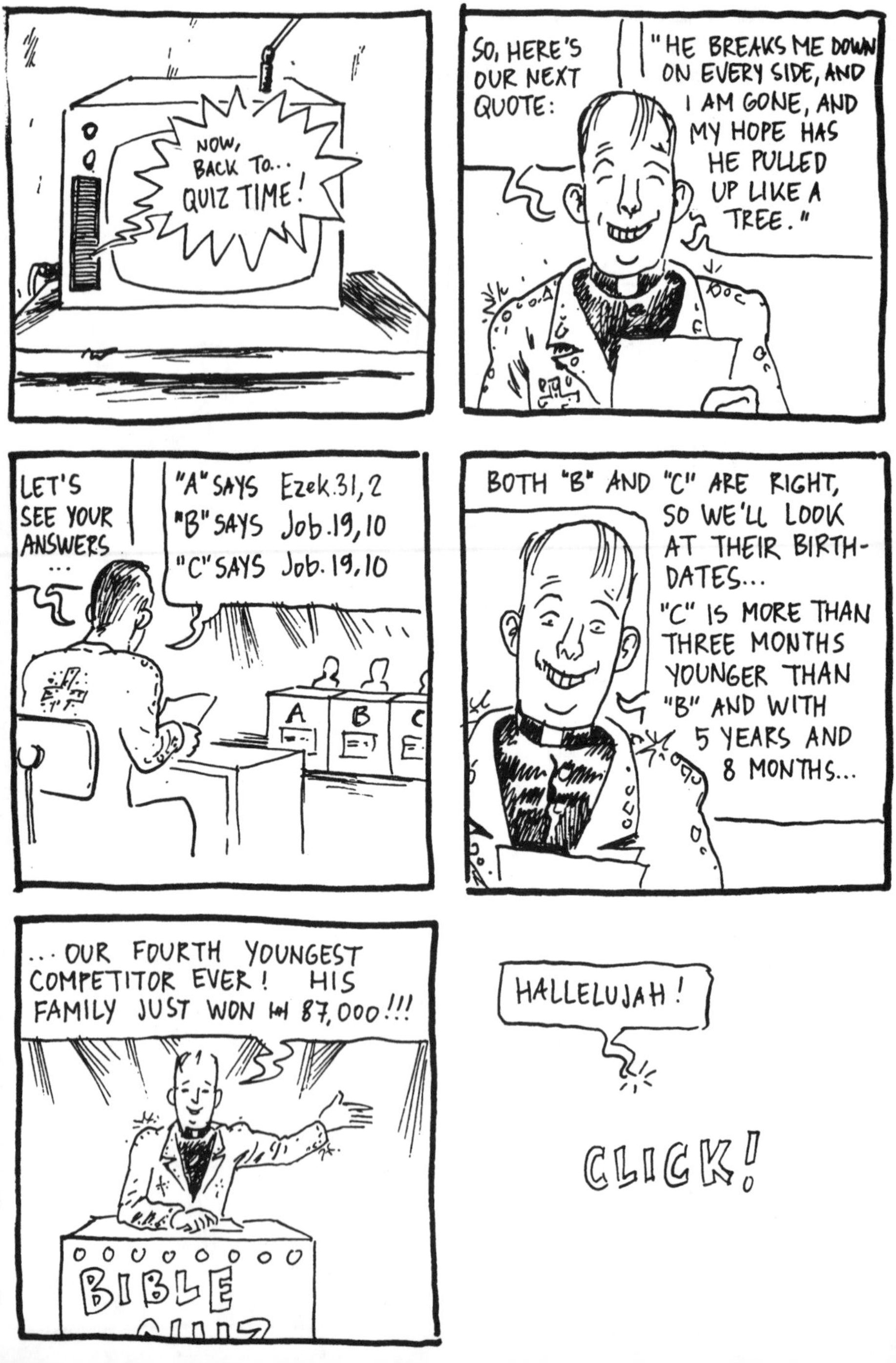
NOW, BACK TO... QUIZ TIME!
SO, HERE'S OUR NEXT QUOTE:
"HE BREAKS ME DOWN ON EVERY SIDE, AND I AM GONE, AND MY HOPE HAS HE PULLED UP LIKE A TREE."
LET'S SEE YOUR ANSWERS ...
"A" SAYS Ezek.31,2
"B" SAYS Job.19,10
"C" SAYS Job.19,10
A
B
C
BOTH "B" AND "C" ARE RIGHT, SO WE'LL LOOK AT THEIR BIRTH-DATES...
"C" IS MORE THAN THREE MONTHS YOUNGER THAN "B" AND WITH 5 YEARS AND 8 MONTHS...
...OUR FOURTH YOUNGEST COMPETITOR EVER! HIS FAMILY JUST WON 87,000!!!
BIBLE
HALLELUJAH!
CLICK!

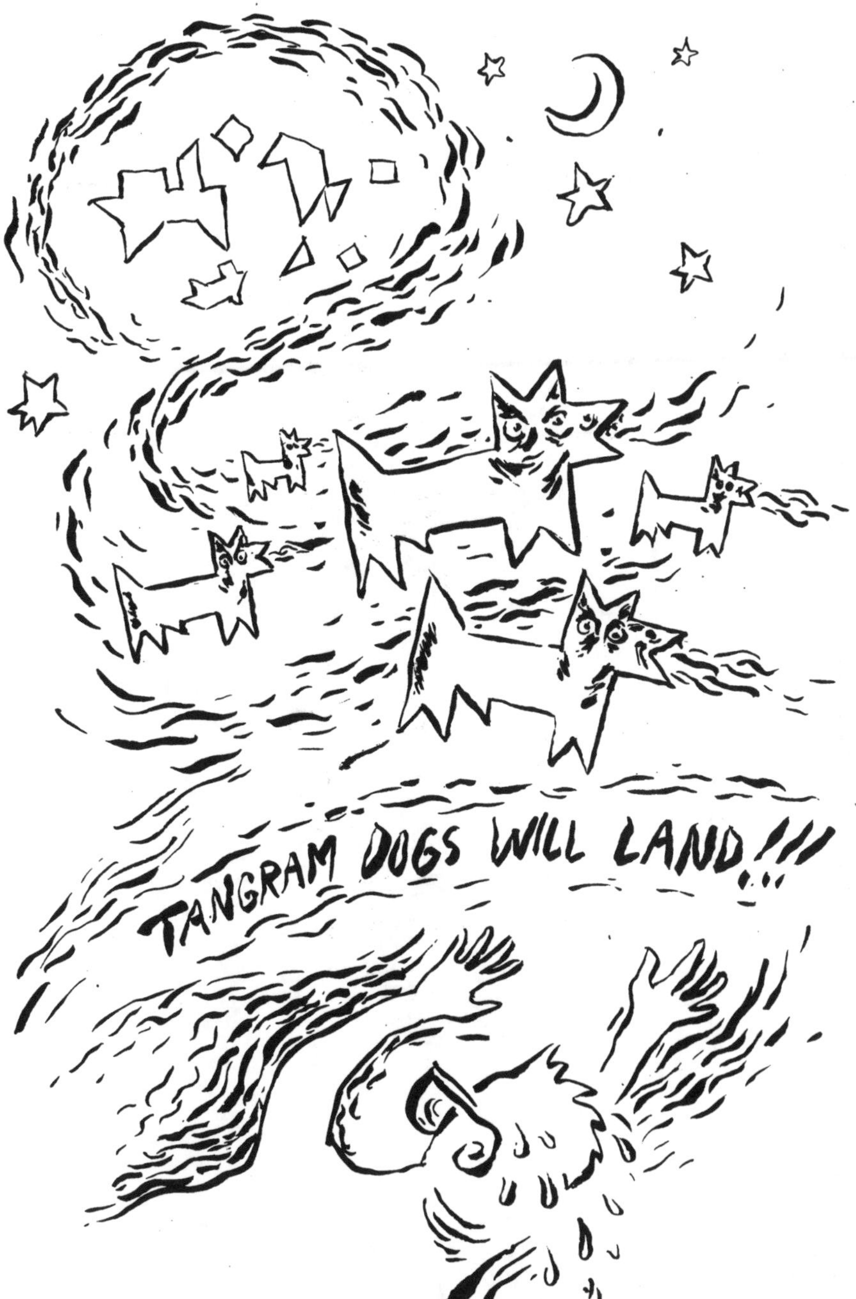
TANGRAM DOGS WILL LAND!!!

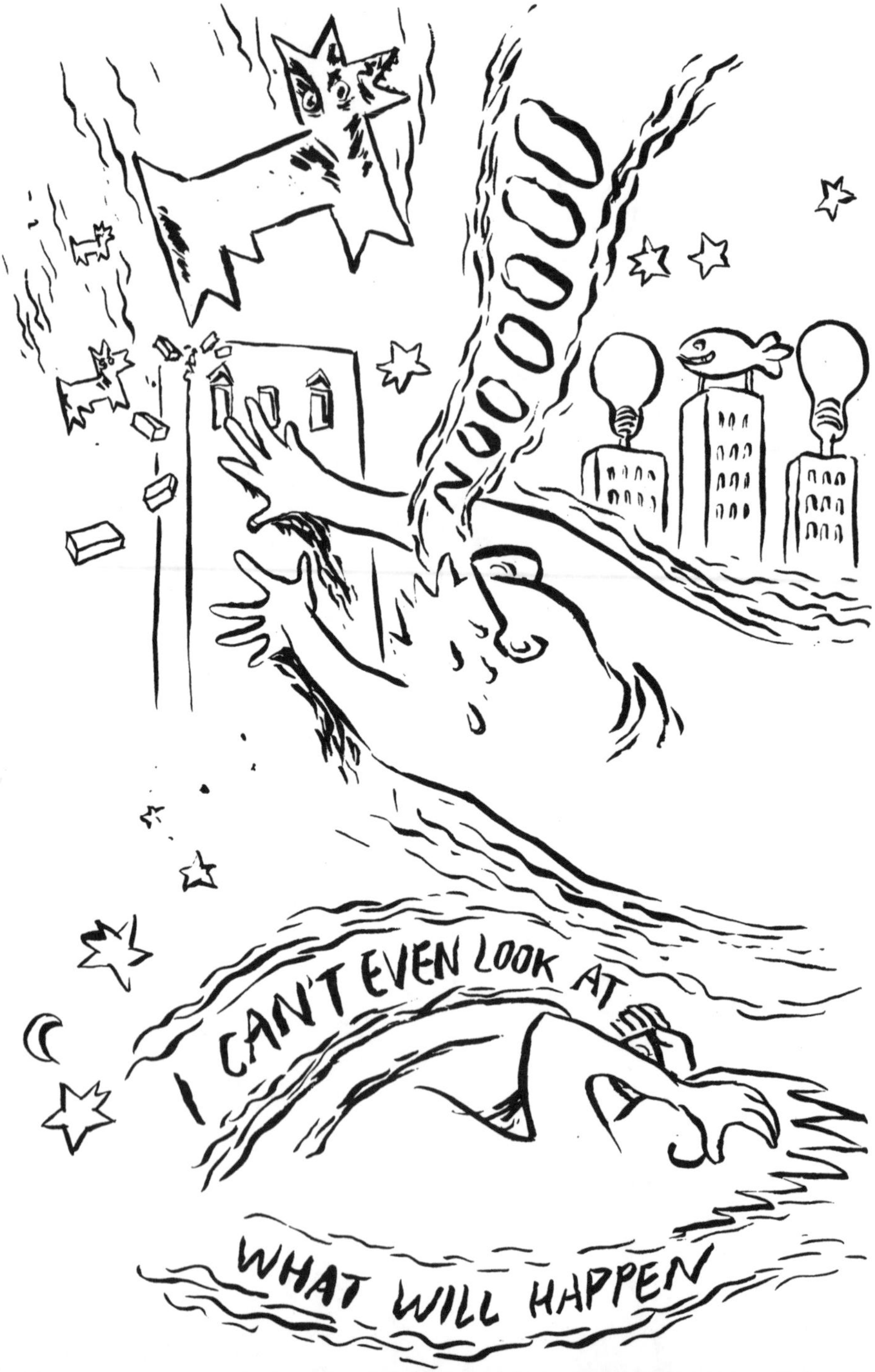
NOOOOOO
I CAN'T EVEN LOOK AT
WHAT WILL HAPPEN

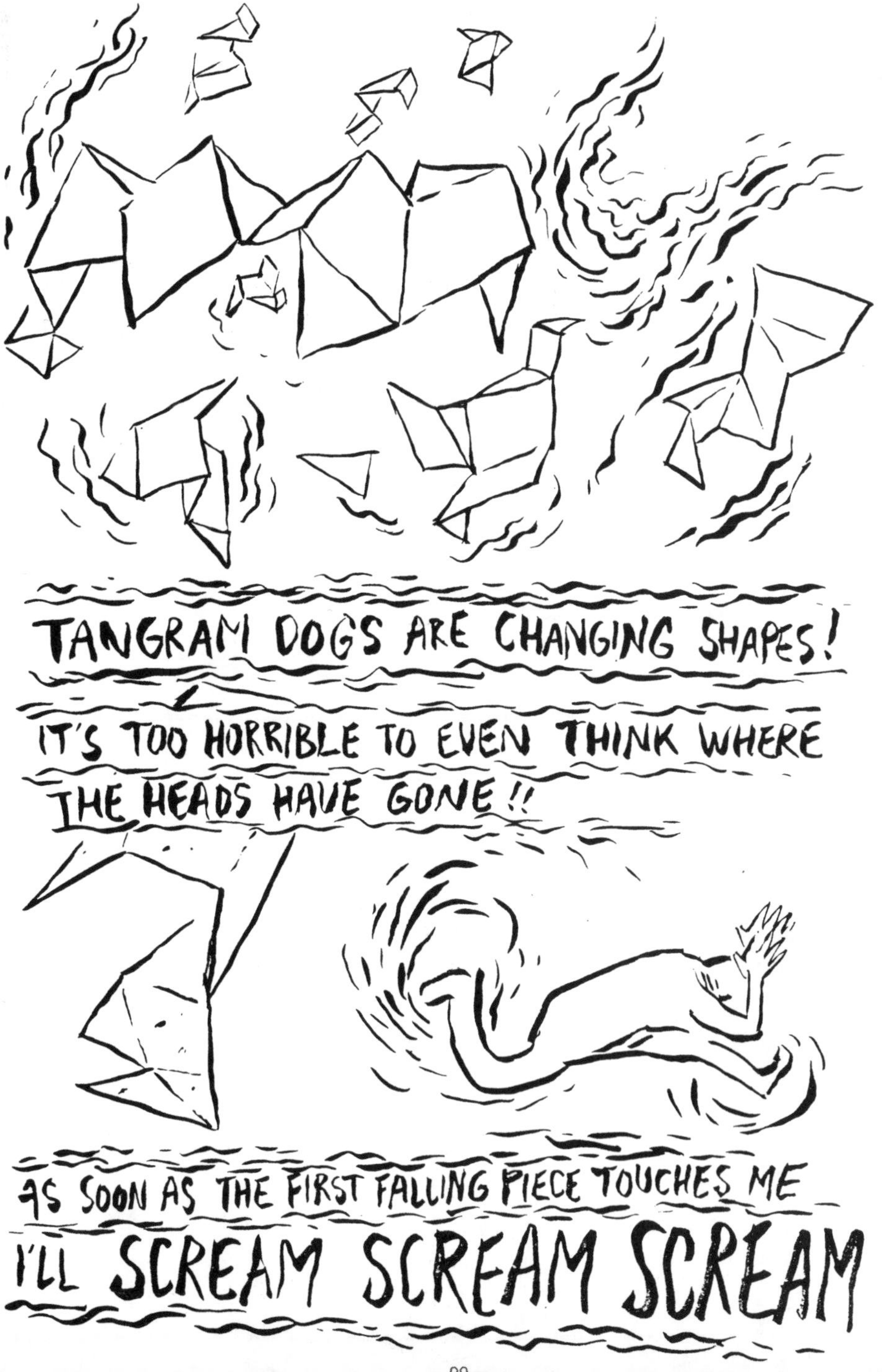
TANGRAM DOGS ARE CHANGING SHAPES!
IT'S TOO HORRIBLE TO EVEN THINK WHERE THE HEADS HAVE GONE!!
AS SOON AS THE FIRST FALLING PIECE TOUCHES ME
I'LL SCREAM SCREAM SCREAM

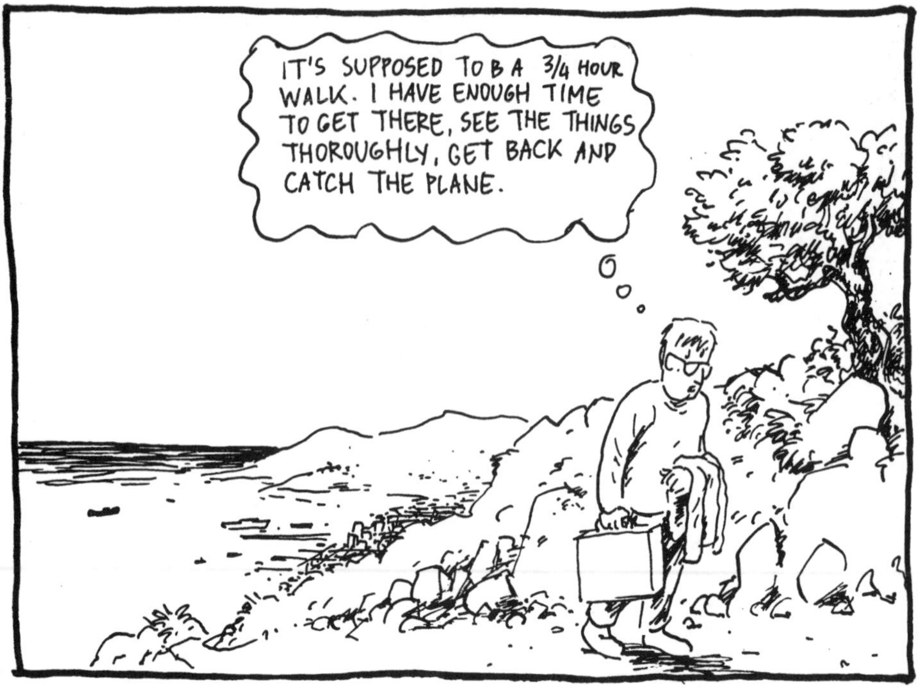
IT'S SUPPOSED TO B A 3/4 HOUR WALK. I HAVE ENOUGH TIME TO GET THERE, SEE THE THINGS THOROUGHLY, GET BACK AND CATCH THE PLANE.

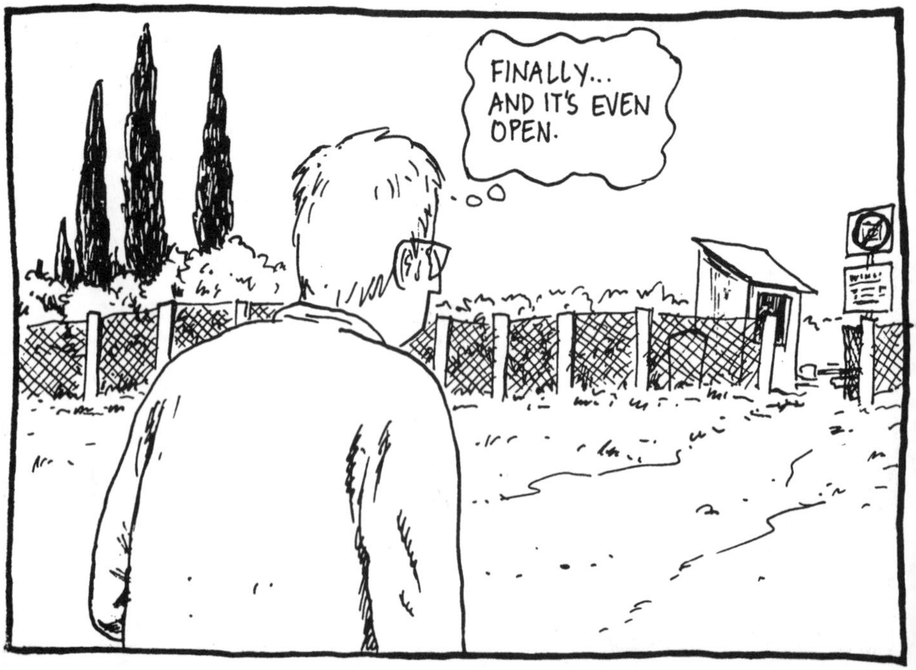
FINALLY... AND IT'S EVEN OPEN.

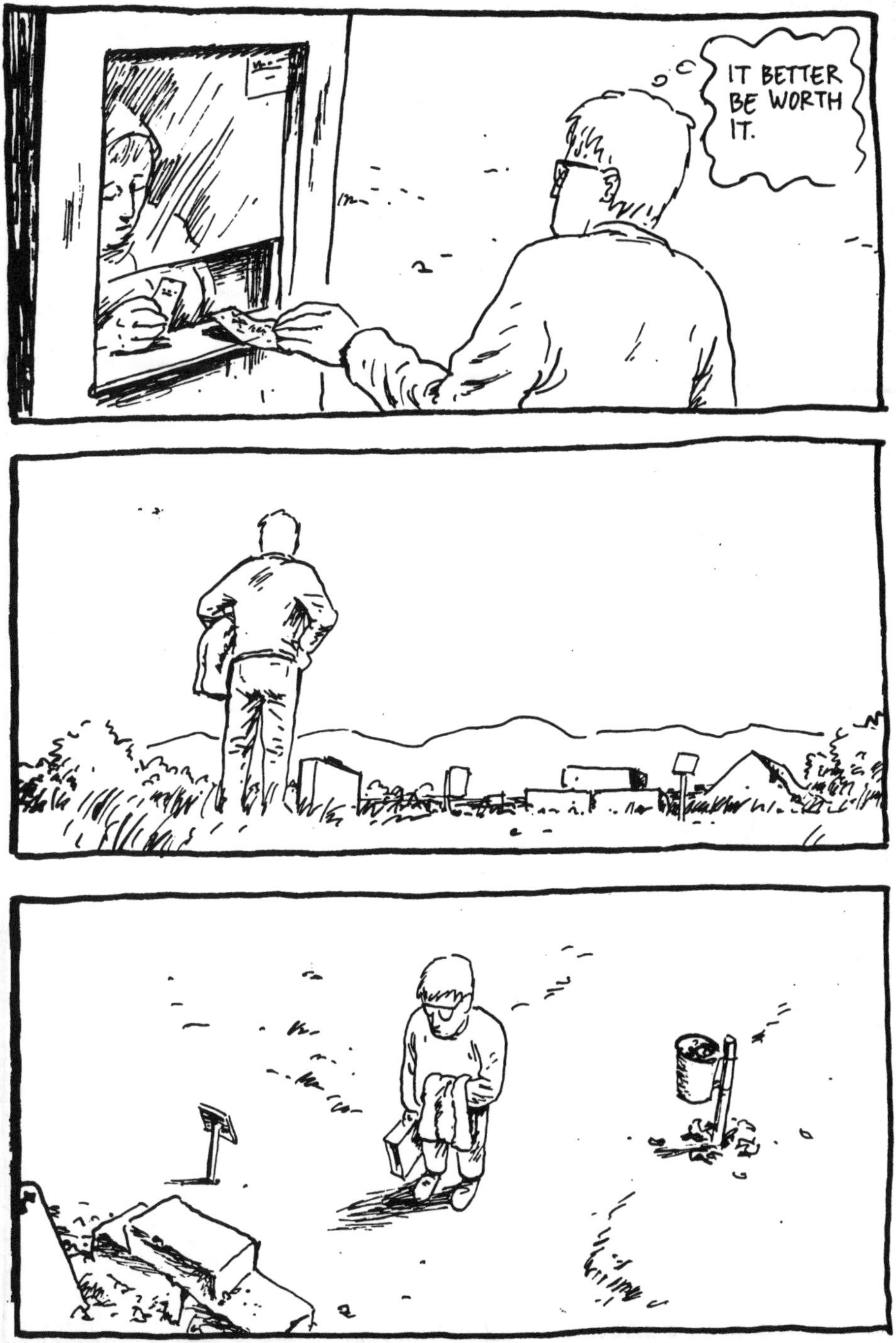
IT BETTER BE WORTH IT.

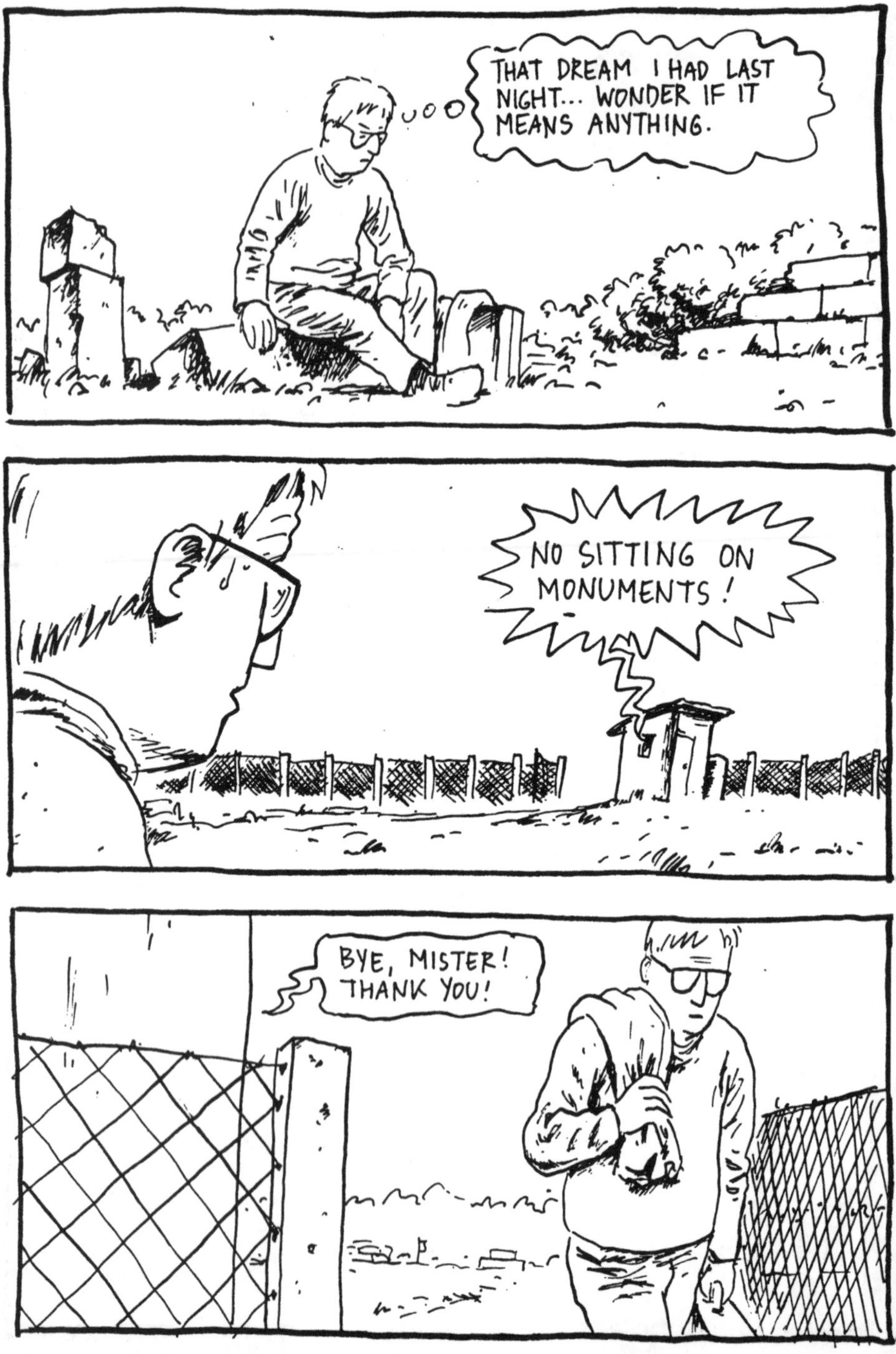
THAT DREAM I HAD LAST NIGHT... WONDER IF IT MEANS ANYTHING.
NO SITTING ON MONUMENTS!
BYE, MISTER! THANK YOU!

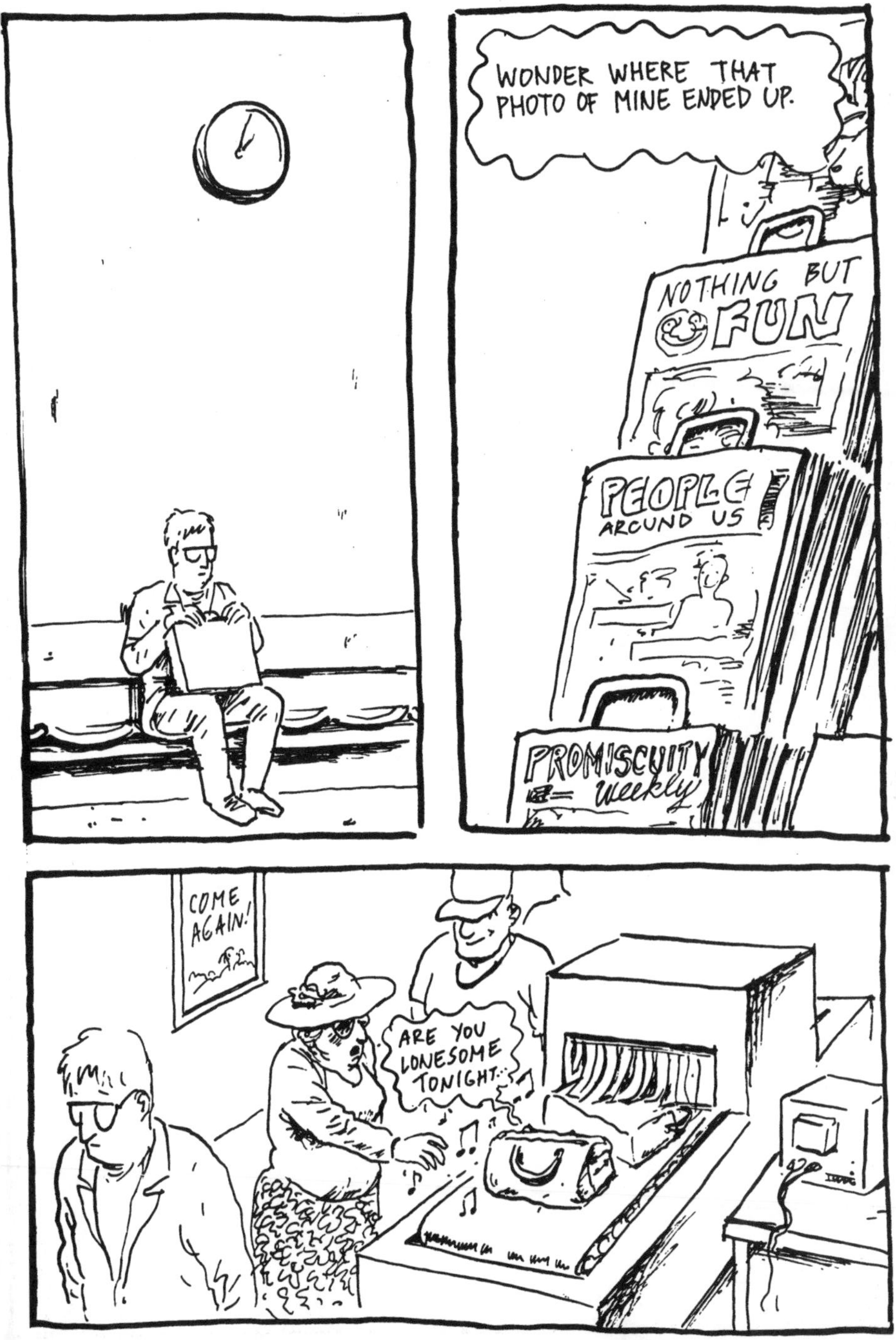
WONDER WHERE THAT PHOTO OF MINE ENDED UP.
NOTHING BUT FUN
PEOPLE AROUND US
PROMISCUITY Weekly
COME AGAIN!
ARE YOU LONESOME TONIGHT...

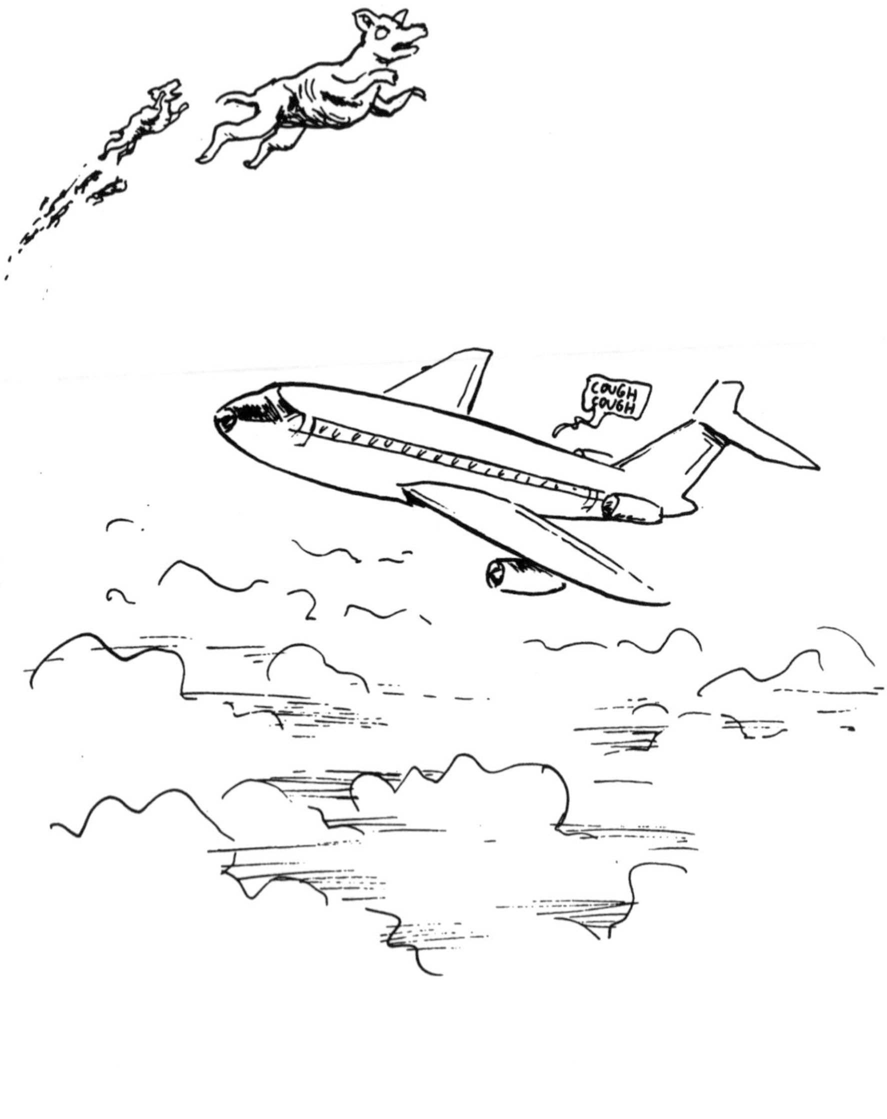
COUGH COUGH

FIRST
WARNING

A 24-HOUR COMIC BOOK

MATT MADDEN

So why are so many 24-hour comics so... dark? It's a tendency I didn't even notice until I began editing this anthology, and I can only guess at its cause.

The most obvious explanation would be sleep deprivation; dark thoughts have a way of creeping in the longer we go without rest. But then, one would expect that most 24-hour comics would start out sunny and only become grim at the end of the process, when in fact, many have been downright morbid from the get-go. The same goes for the influence of night, since most are begun in the morning.

I think the real reason may lie in the nature of improvisation itself. Both in the way it unleashes the monsters of the unconscious, and for the practical reason that getting things to feel just right might be too much to hope for in so short a time, while getting things to feel horribly horribly wrong is usually an attainable goal. Also, let's face it: Cartoonists are a morbid lot. (I've been doing a series improvisational comics at scottmccloud.com each morning for a few years and nearly two thirds of the stories end up in some form of death, destruction or despair!).

Matt Madden's "Storm Warning" is a great exploration of comics' ability to capture a mood. A tone-poem of oppressive foreboding and isolation. It features no demented murderous emperors, brutal dismemberings, or cremations, yet for my money, this one is the darkest of the lot.

Matt notes: "The bulk of this comic was written and drawn in the 24-hour period from 10 am 5/5/96 to 10 am 5/6/96." The remaining inks were finished up a few days later. So not a 24-hour comic in full, but very much in spirit.

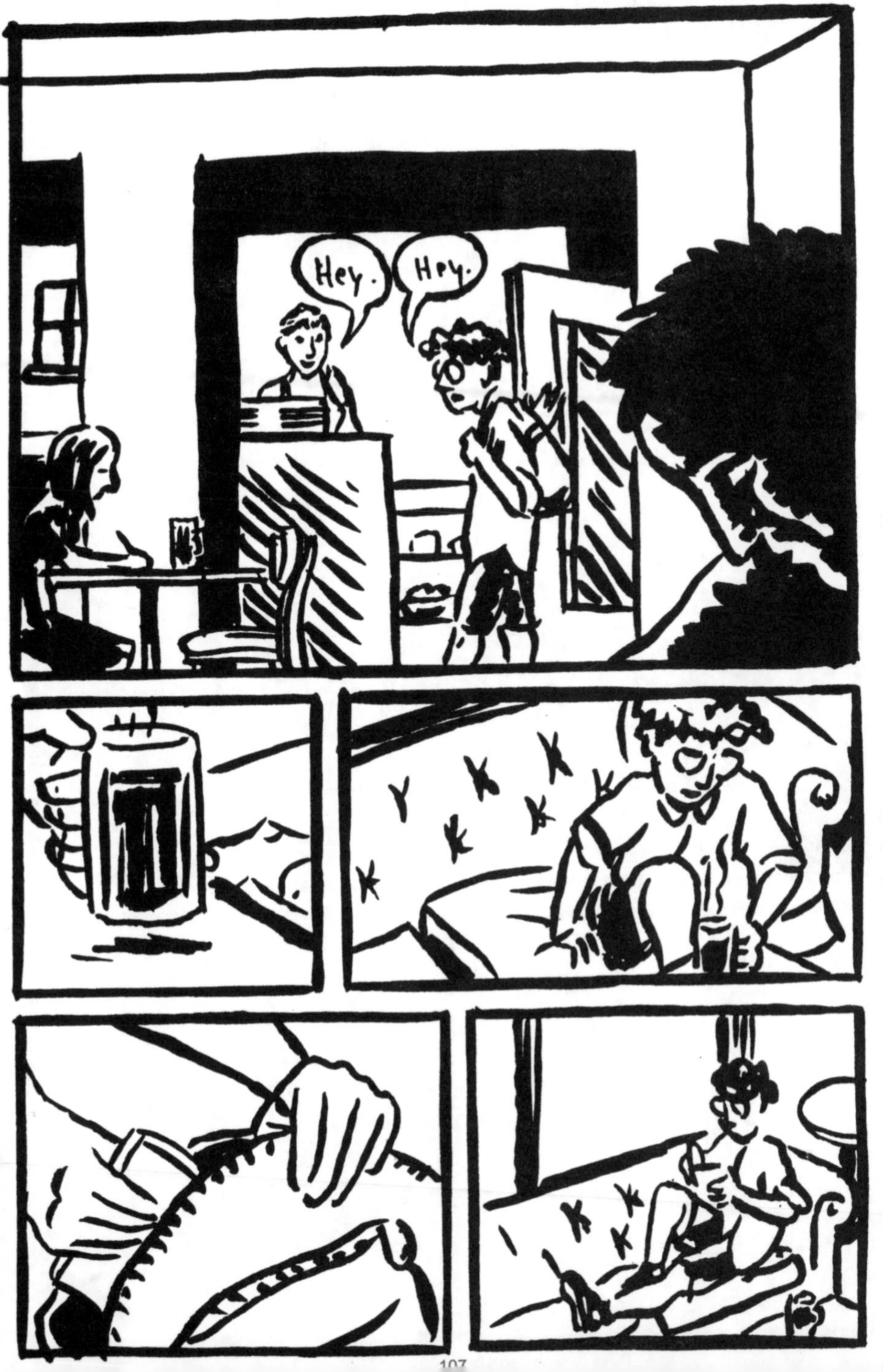
Hey.
Hey.

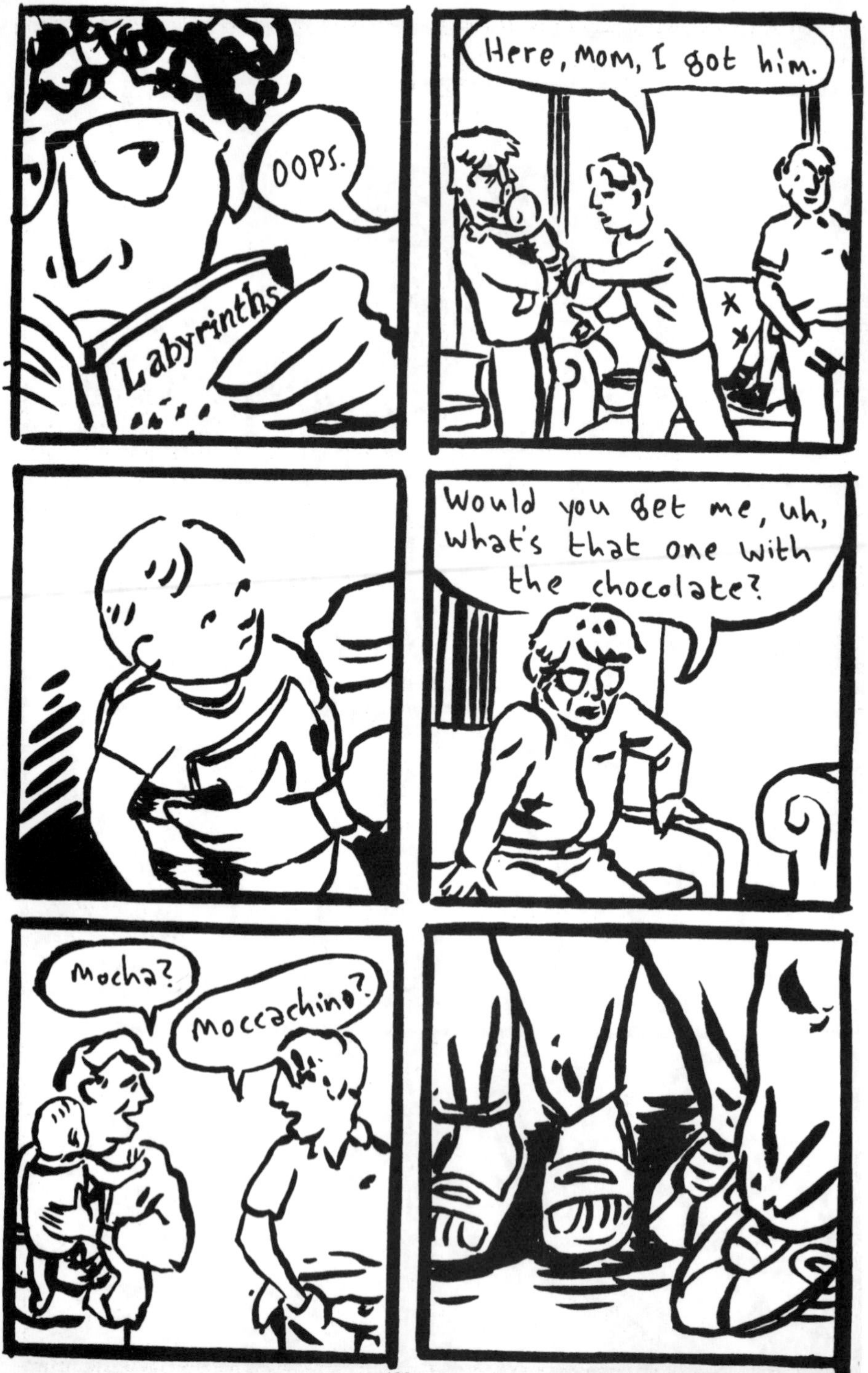
OOPS.
Labyrinths
Here, mom, I got him.
Would you get me, uh, what's that one with the chocolate?
Mocha?
Moccachino?

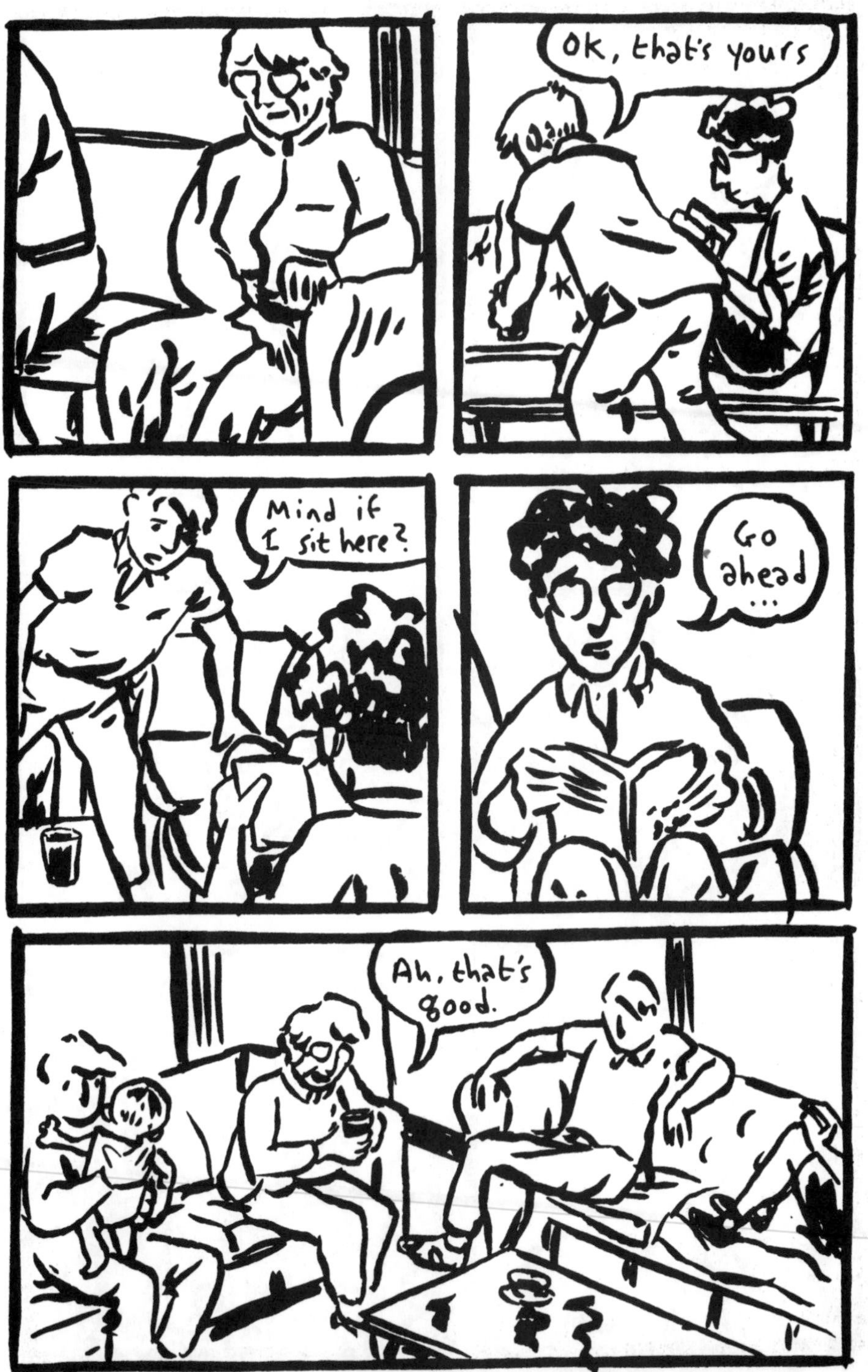
Ok, that's yours
Mind if I sit here?
Go ahead ...
Ah, that's good.

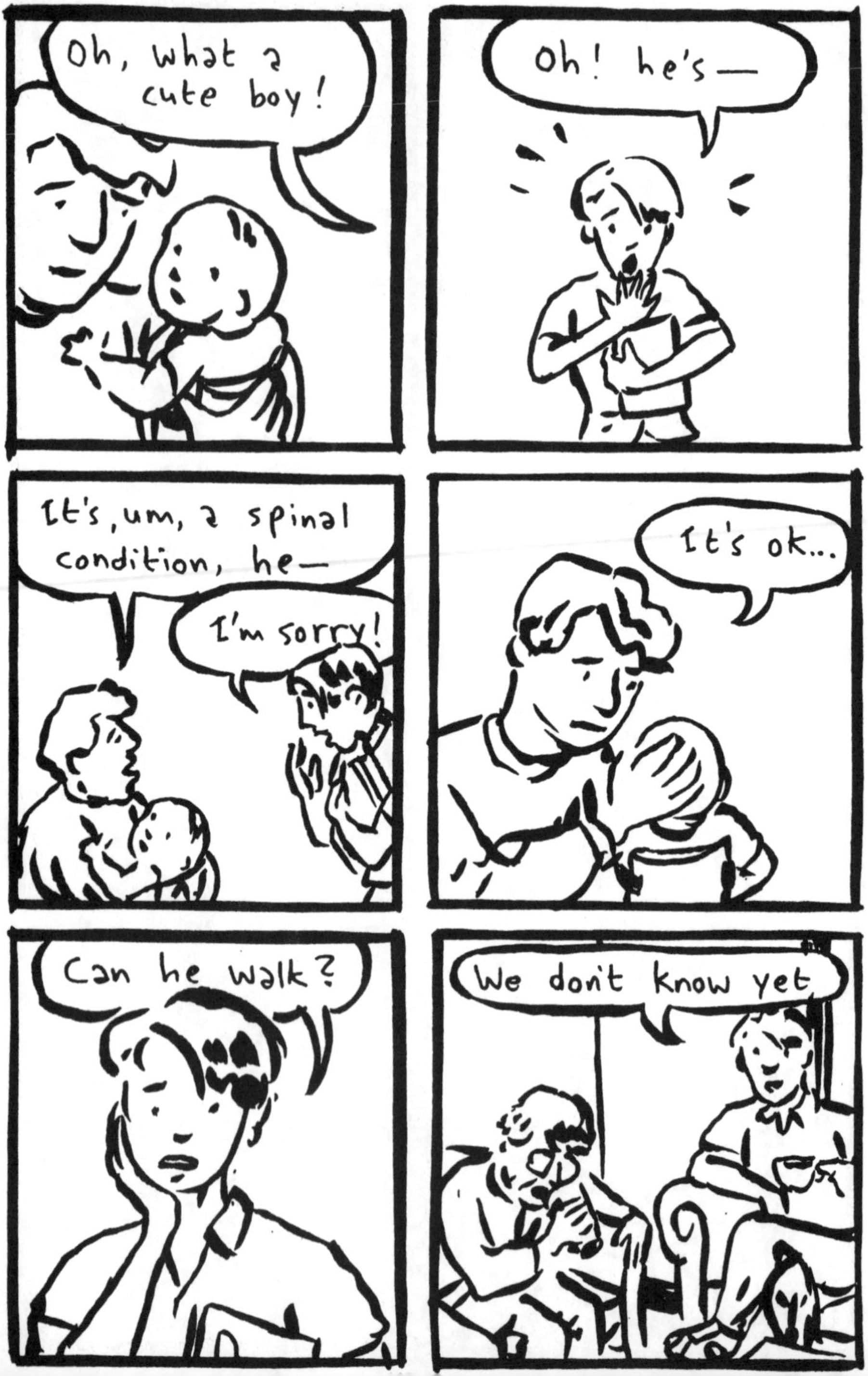
Oh, what a cute boy!
Oh! he's—
It's, um, a spinal condition, he—
I'm sorry!
It's ok...
Can he walk?
We don't know yet

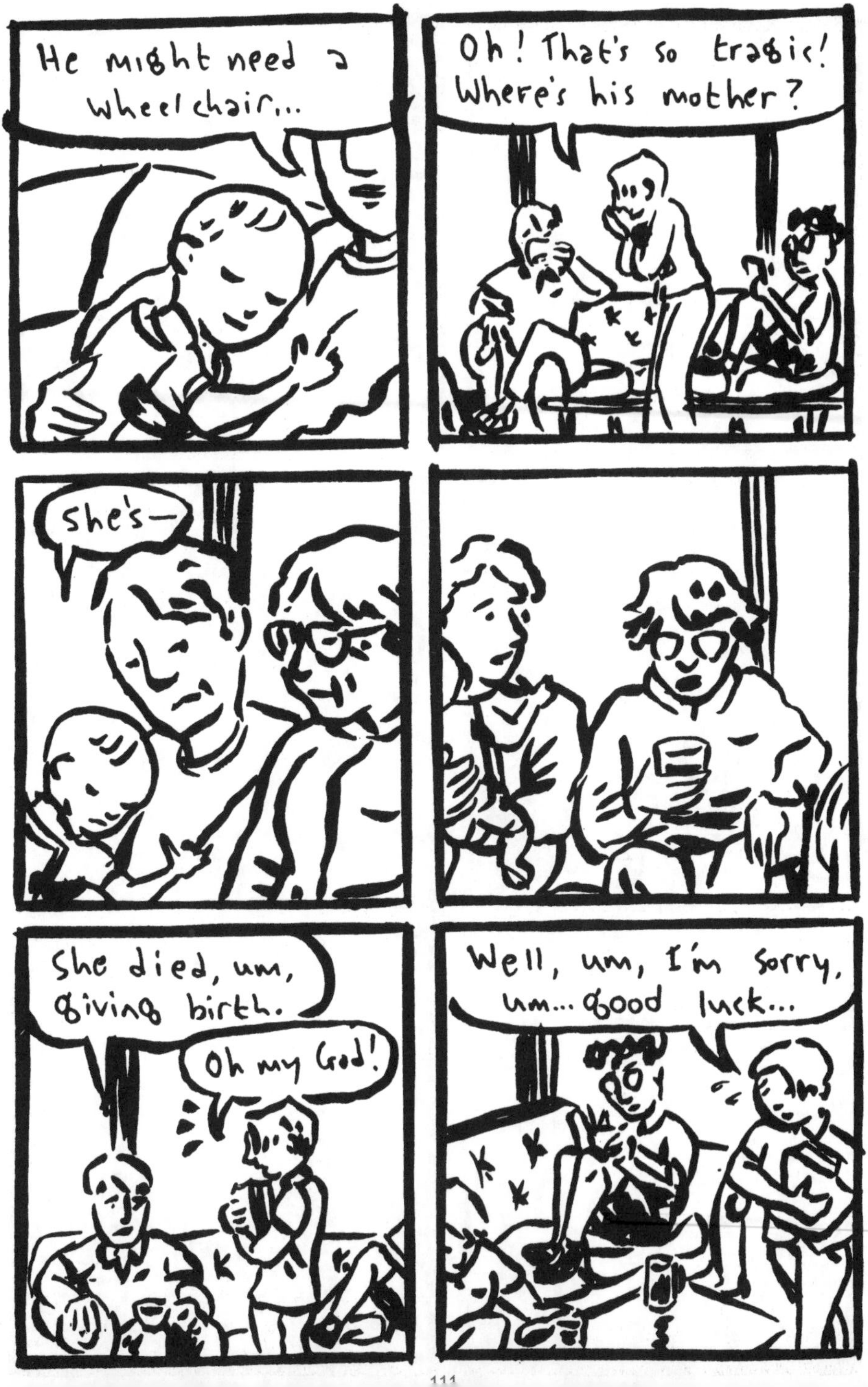
He might need a wheelchair...
Oh! That's so tragic! Where's his mother?
She's—
She died, um, giving birth.
Oh my God!
Well, um, I'm sorry, um... good luck...

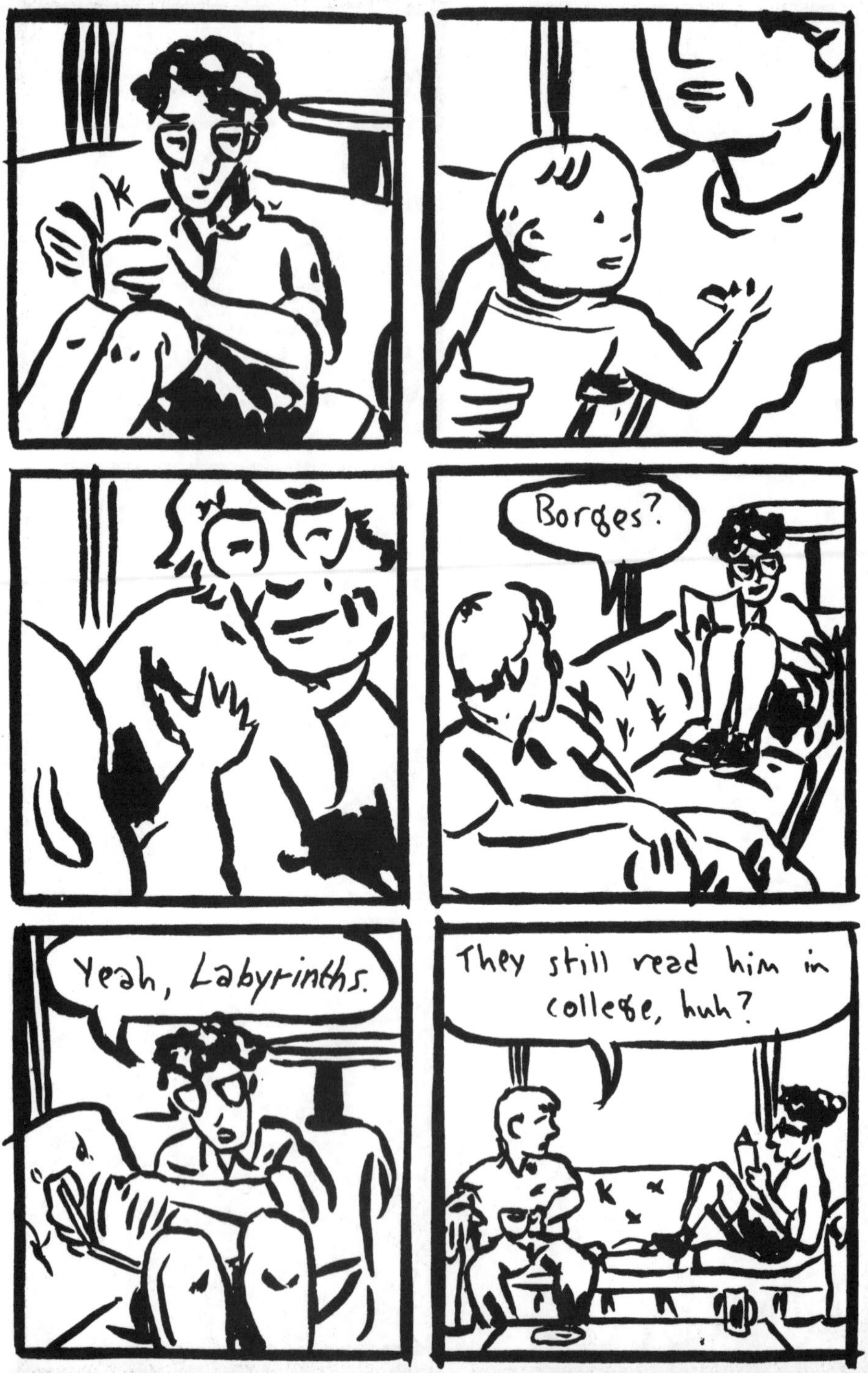
Borges?
Yeah, Labyrinths.
They still read him in college, huh?

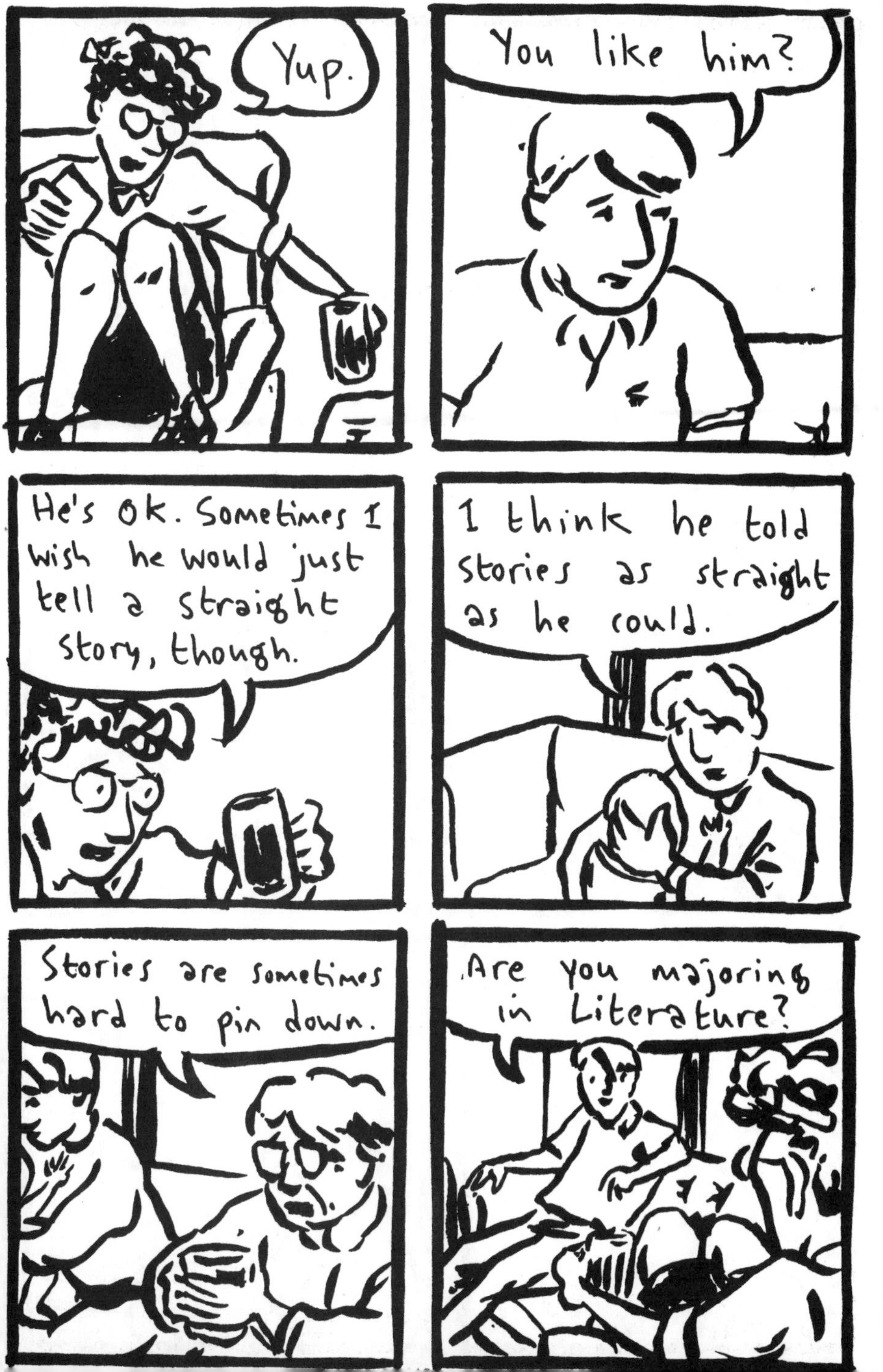
Yup.
You like him?
He's OK. Sometimes I wish he would just tell a straight story, though.
I think he told stories as straight as he could.
Stories are sometimes hard to pin down.
Are you majoring in Literature?

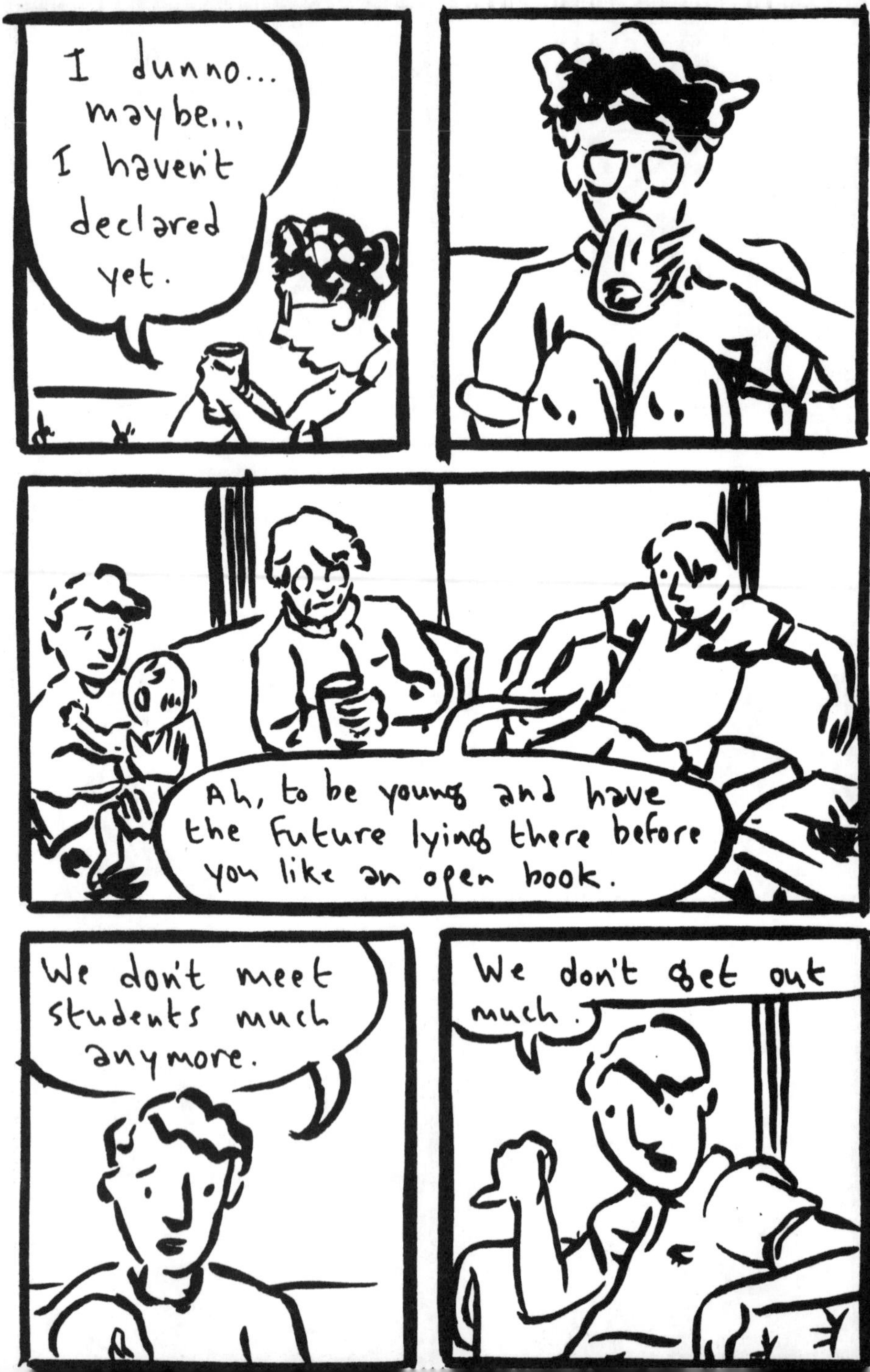
I dunno... maybe... I haven't declared yet.
Ah, to be young and have the future lying there before you like an open book.
We don't meet students much anymore.
We don't get out much.

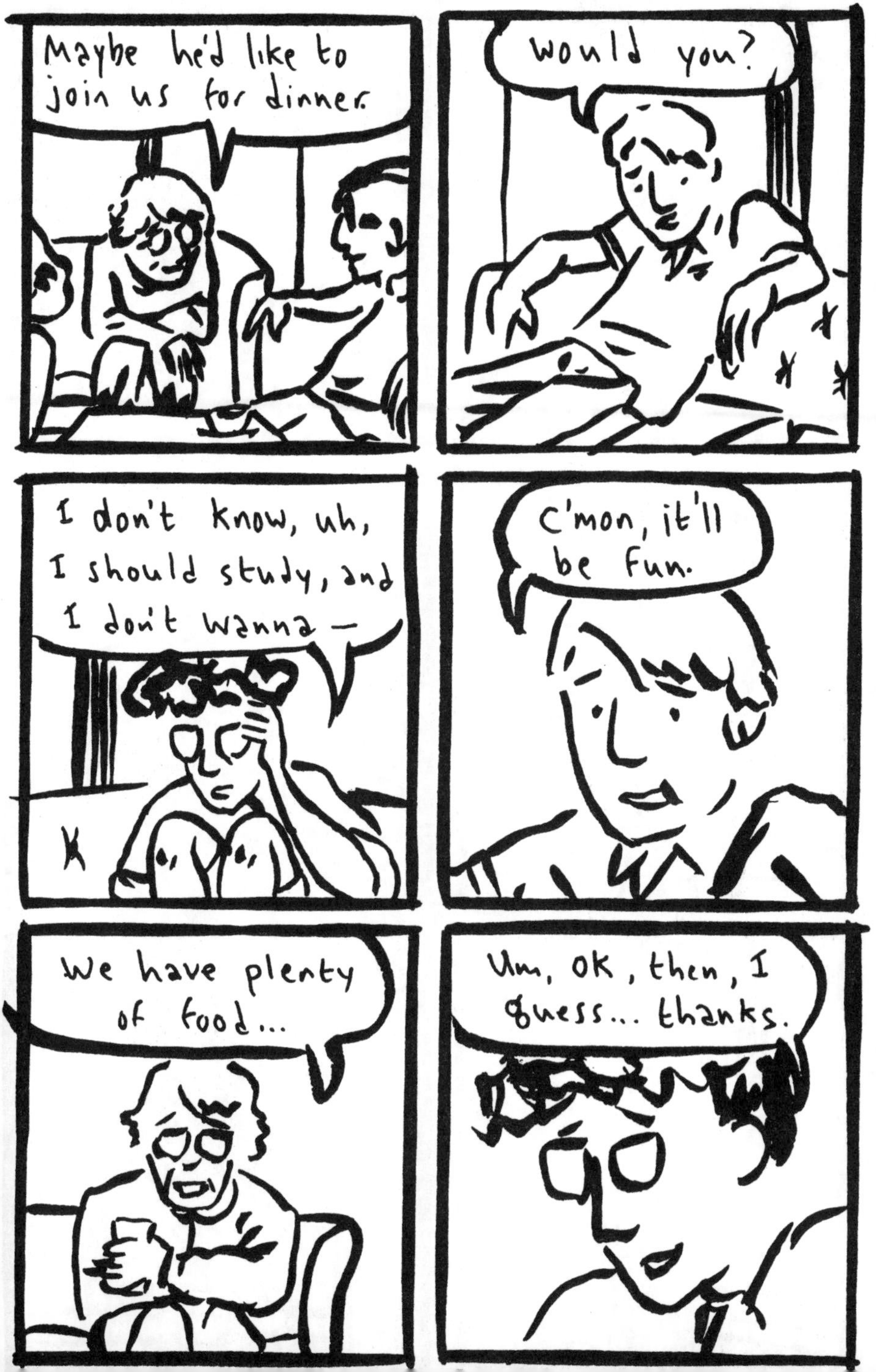
Maybe he'd like to join us for dinner.
Would you?
I don't know, uh, I should study, and I don't wanna —
C'mon, it'll be fun.
We have plenty of food...
Um, OK, then, I guess... thanks.

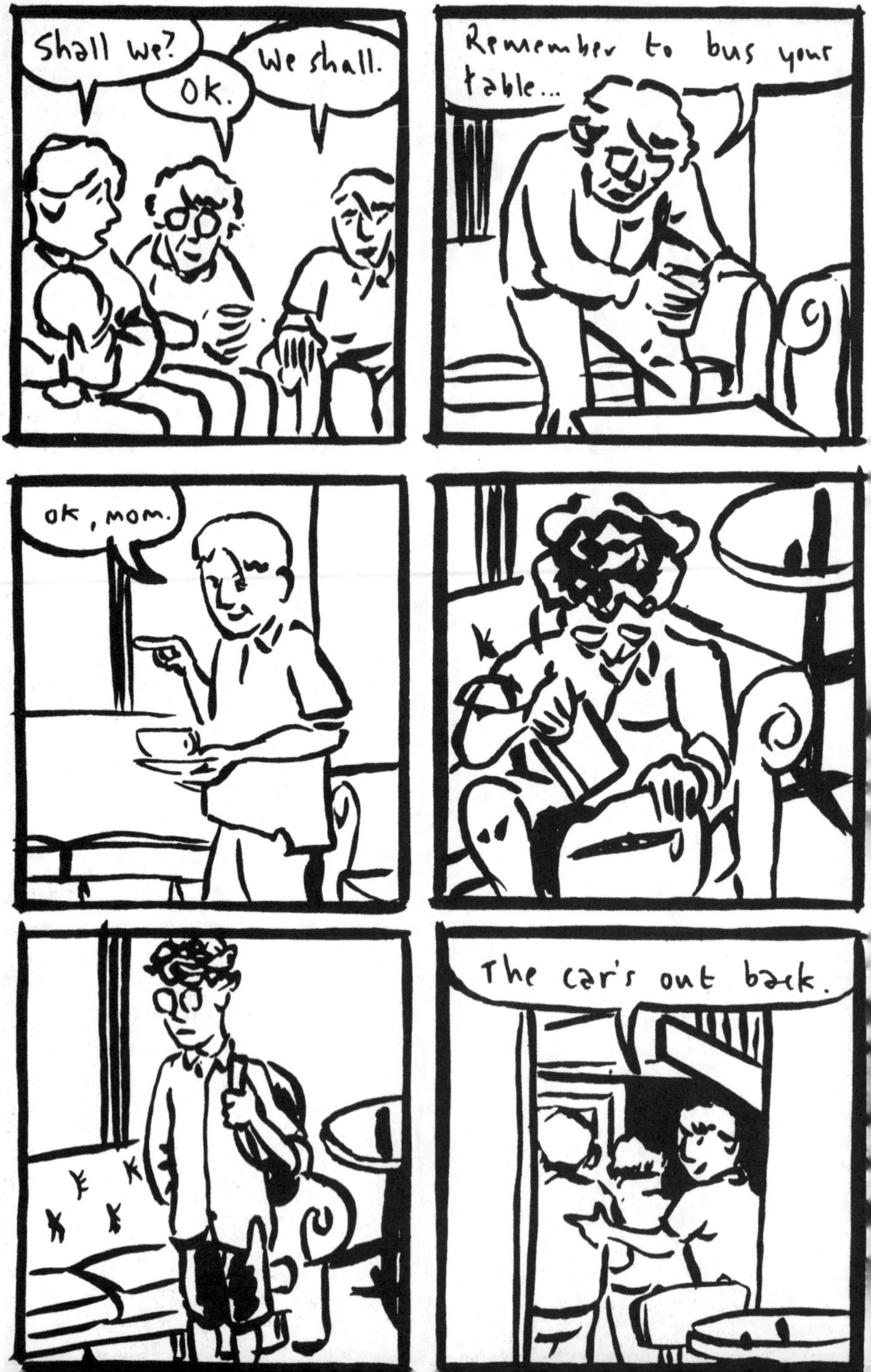
Shall we?
OK.
We shall.
Remember to bus your table...
ok, mom.
The car's out back.

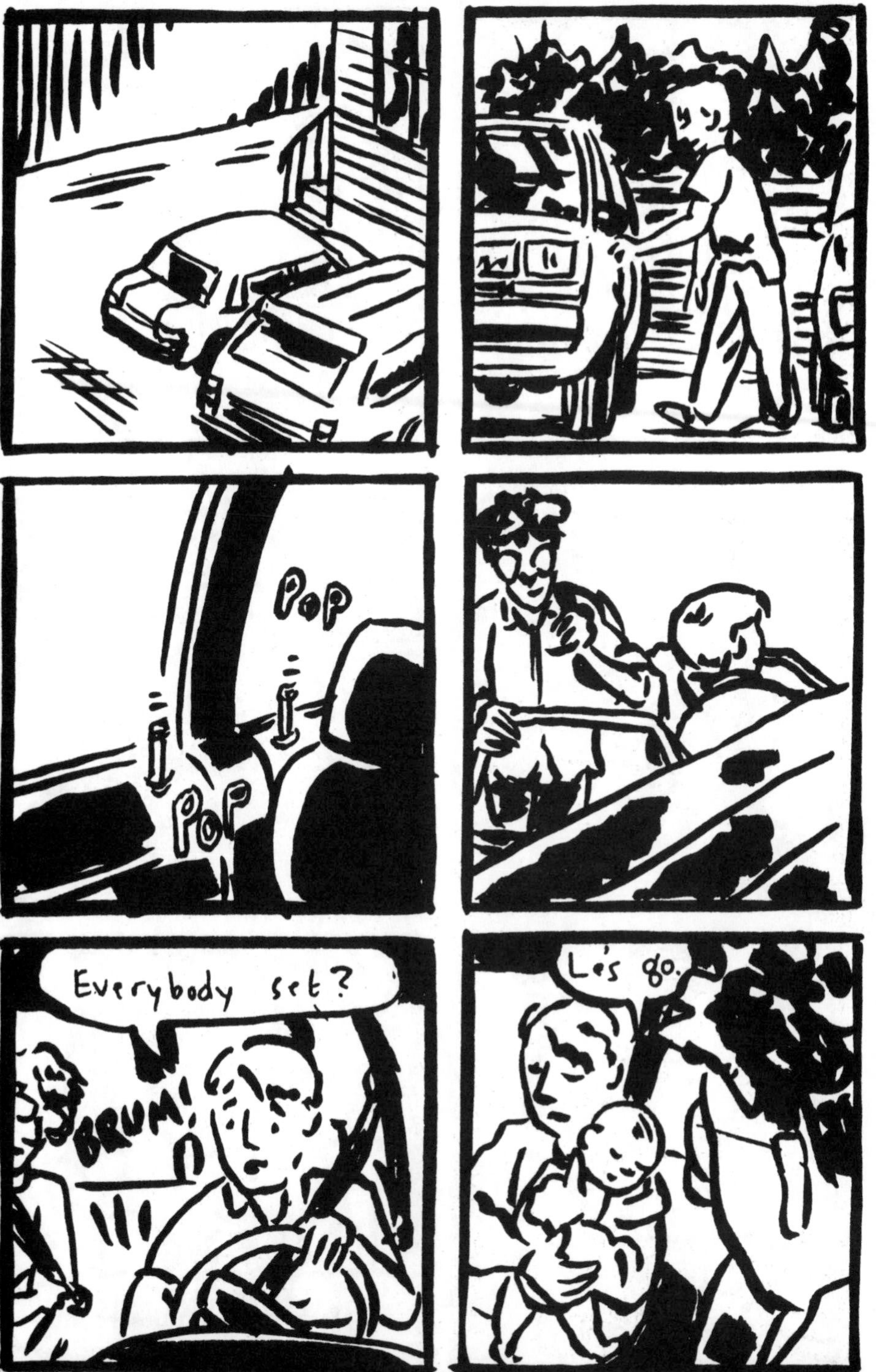

POP
POP
Everybody set?
BRUM!
L's go.

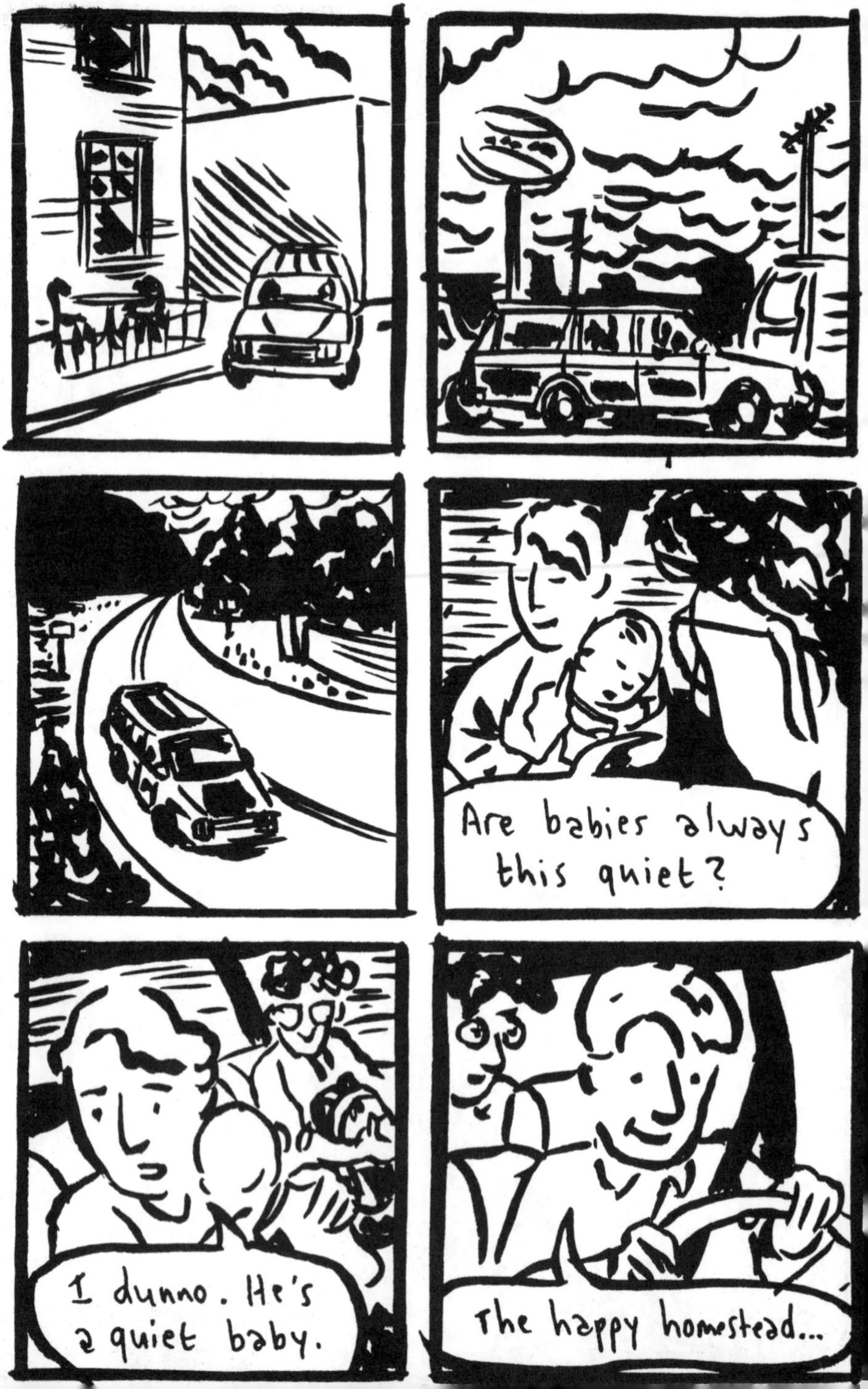
Are babies always this quiet?
I dunno. He's a quiet baby.
The happy homestead...

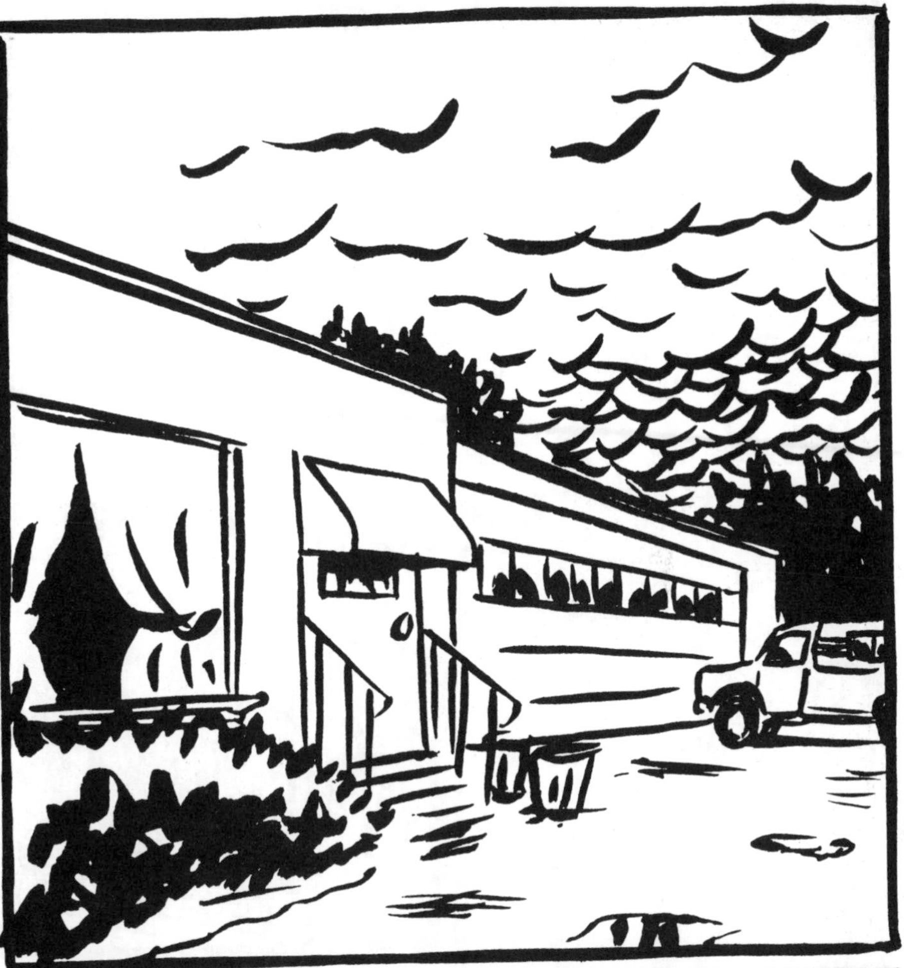

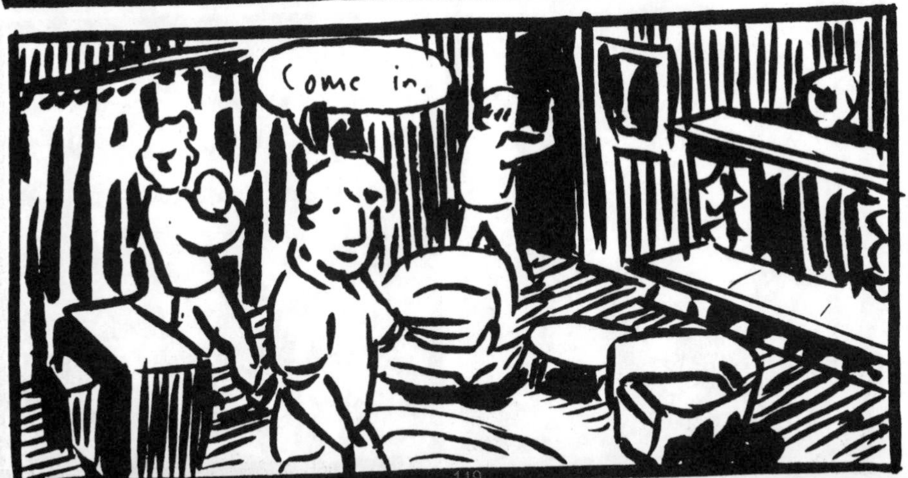
Come in.

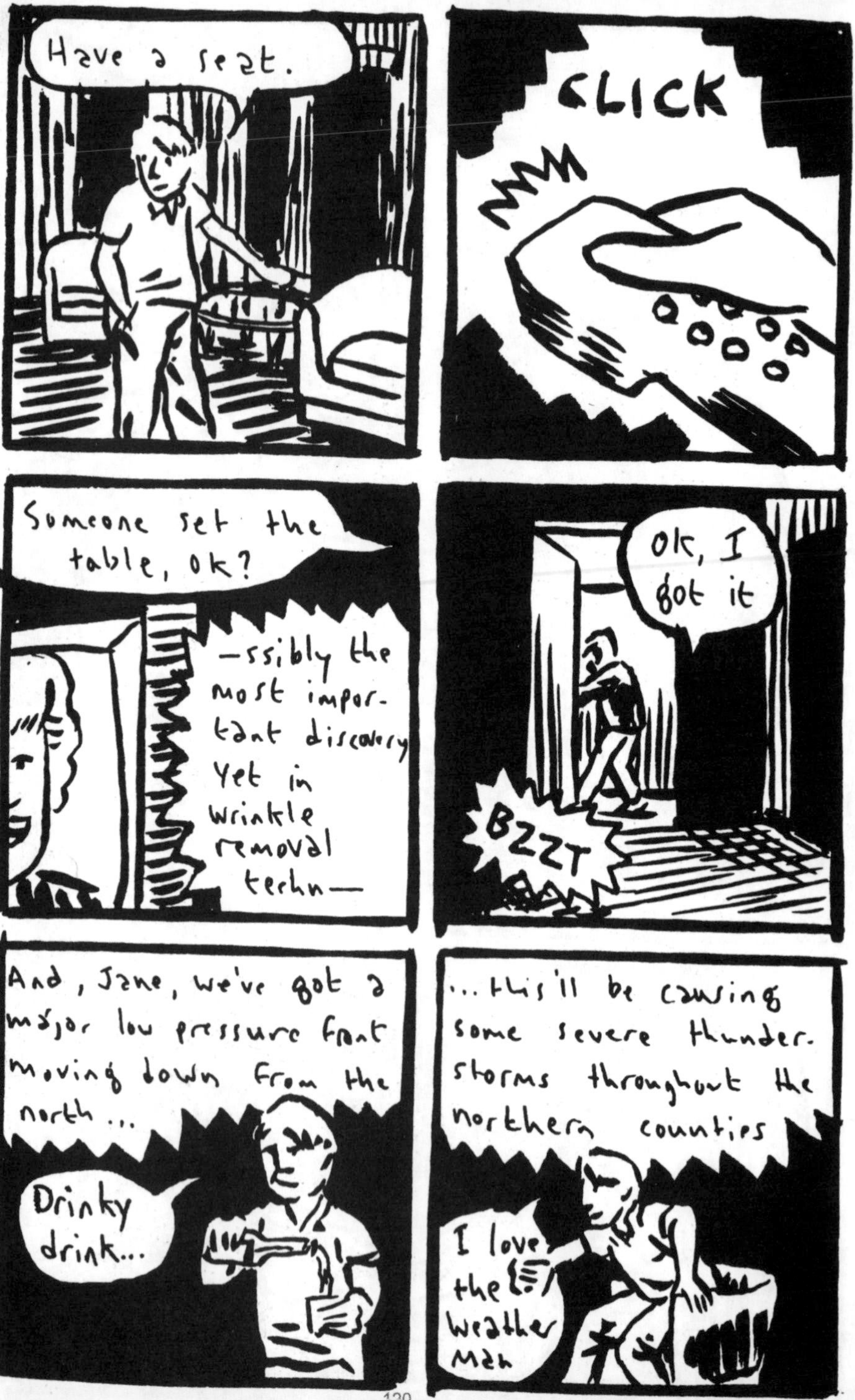
Have a seat.
CLICK
Someone set the table, ok?
—ssibly the most impor-tant discovery yet in wrinkle removal techn—
Ok, I got it
BZZT
And, Jane, we've got a major low pressure front moving down from the north...
Drinky drink...
...this'll be causing some severe thunder-storms throughout the northern counties
I love the weather man

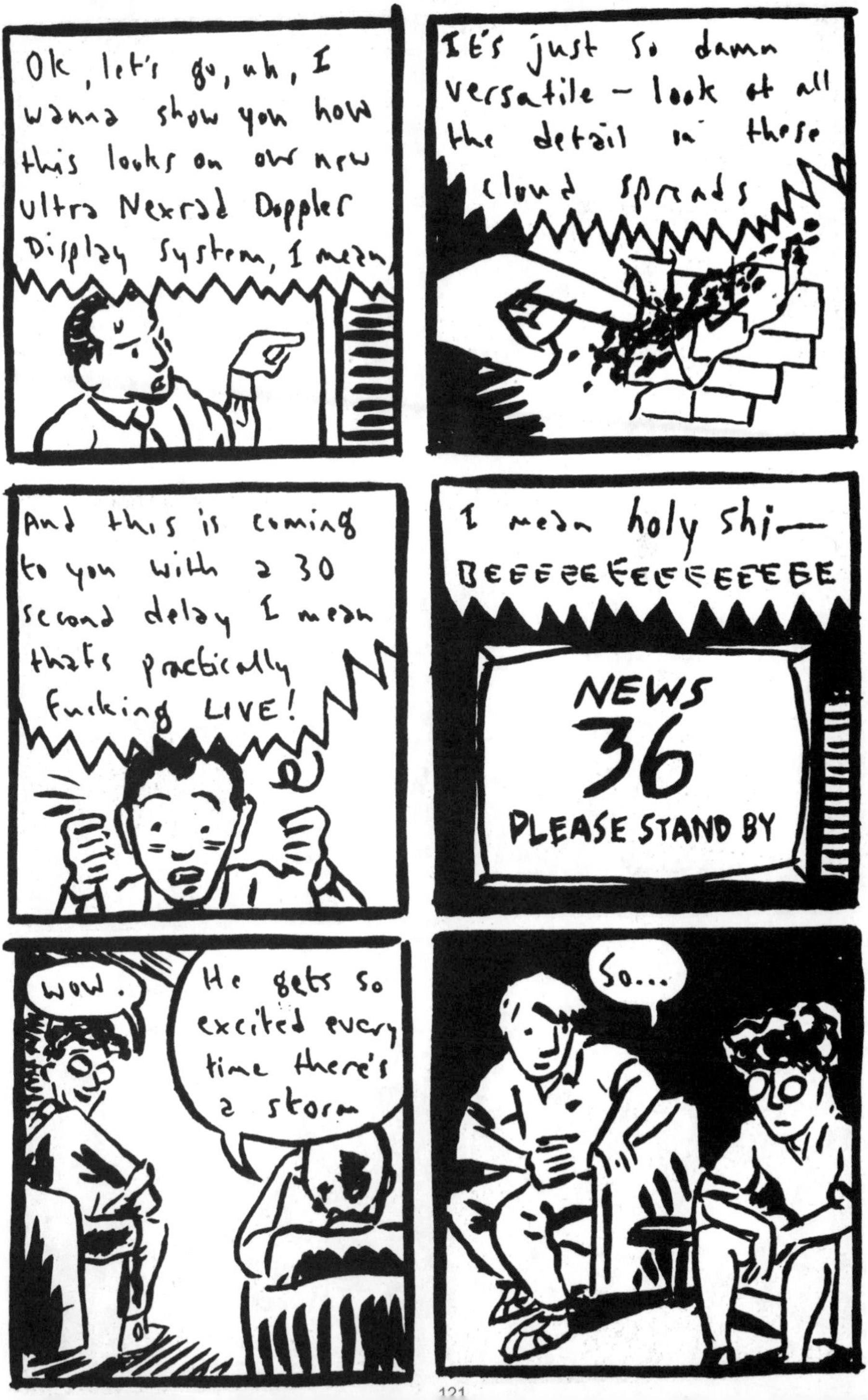
Ok, let's go, uh, I wanna show you how this looks on our new ultra Nexrad Doppler Display System, I mean
It's just so damn versatile - look at all the detail in these cloud spreads
And this is coming to you with a 30 second delay I mean that's practically fucking LIVE!
I mean holy shi—
BEEEEEEEEEEEEEEE
NEWS
36
PLEASE STAND BY
wow.
He gets so excited every time there's a storm
So...

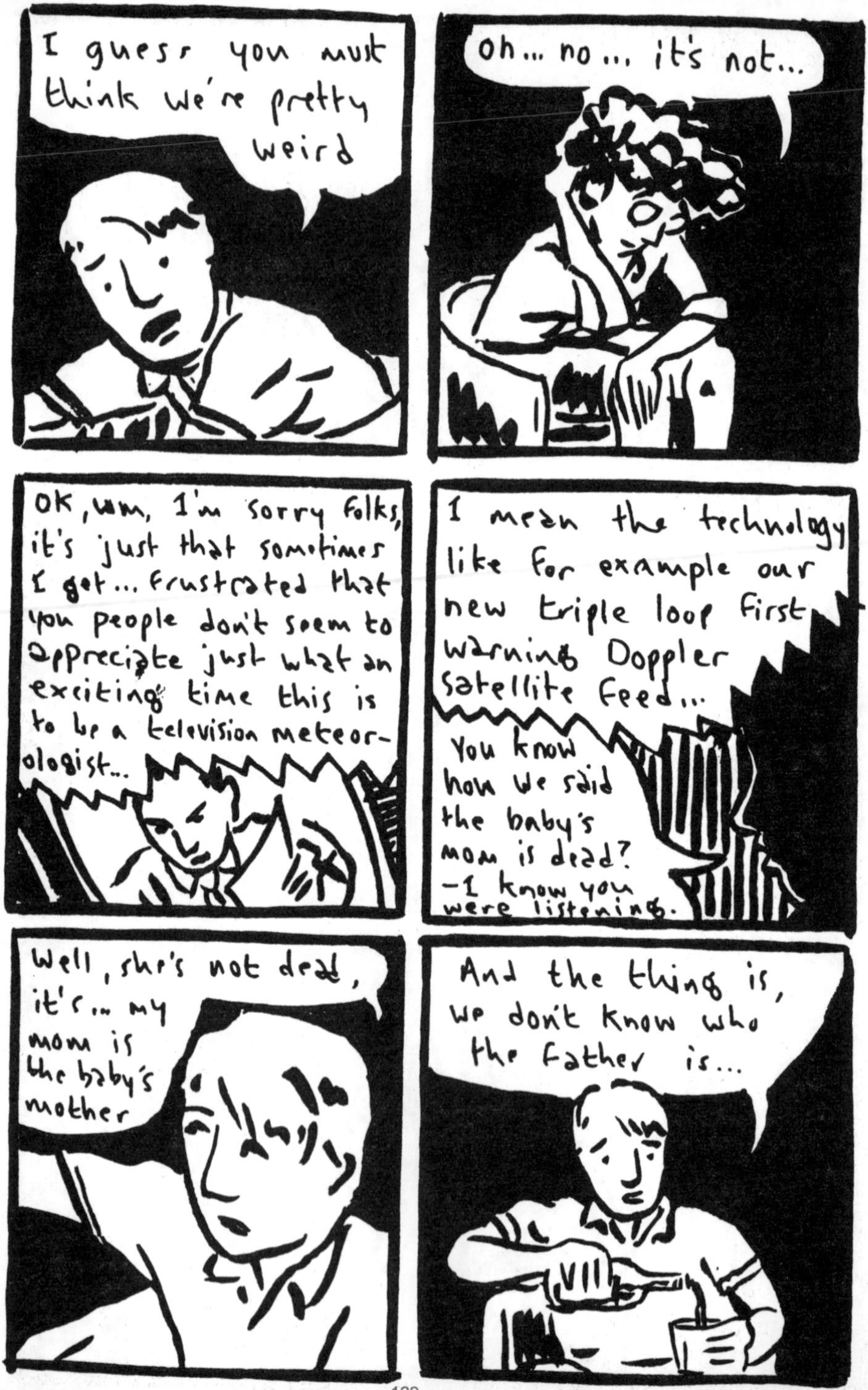
I guess you must think we're pretty weird
oh... no... it's not...
OK, um, I'm sorry folks, it's just that sometimes I get... frustrated that you people don't seem to appreciate just what an exciting time this is to be a television meteor-ologist...
I mean the technology like for example our new triple loop first warning Doppler satellite feed...
You know how we said the baby's mom is dead? —I know you were listening.
Well, she's not dead, it's... my mom is the baby's mother
And the thing is, we don't know who the father is...

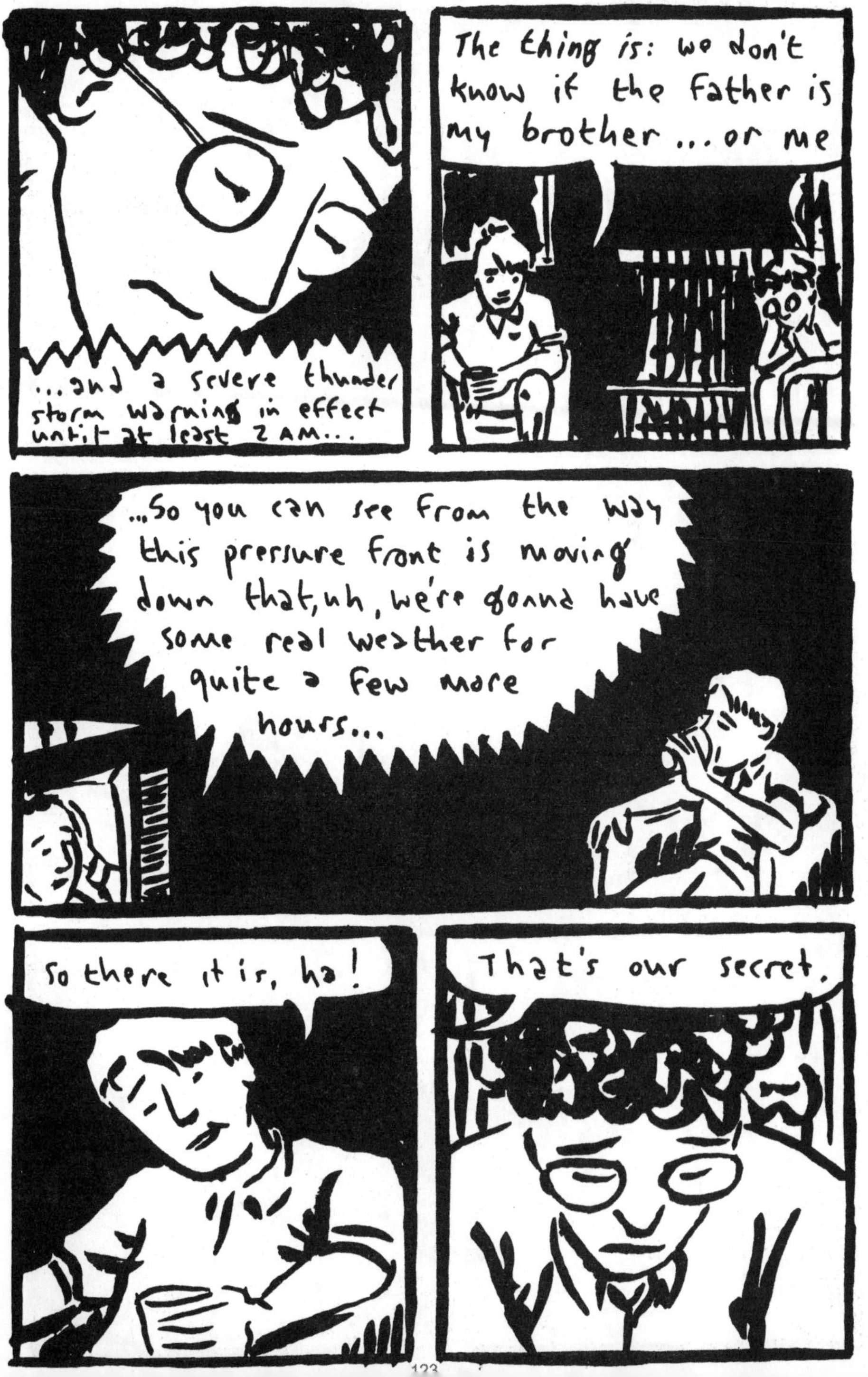
...and a severe thunder storm warning in effect until at least 2 AM...
The thing is: we don't know if the father is my brother... or me
...So you can see from the way this pressure front is moving down that, uh, we're gonna have some real weather for quite a few more hours...
So there it is, ha!
That's our secret.

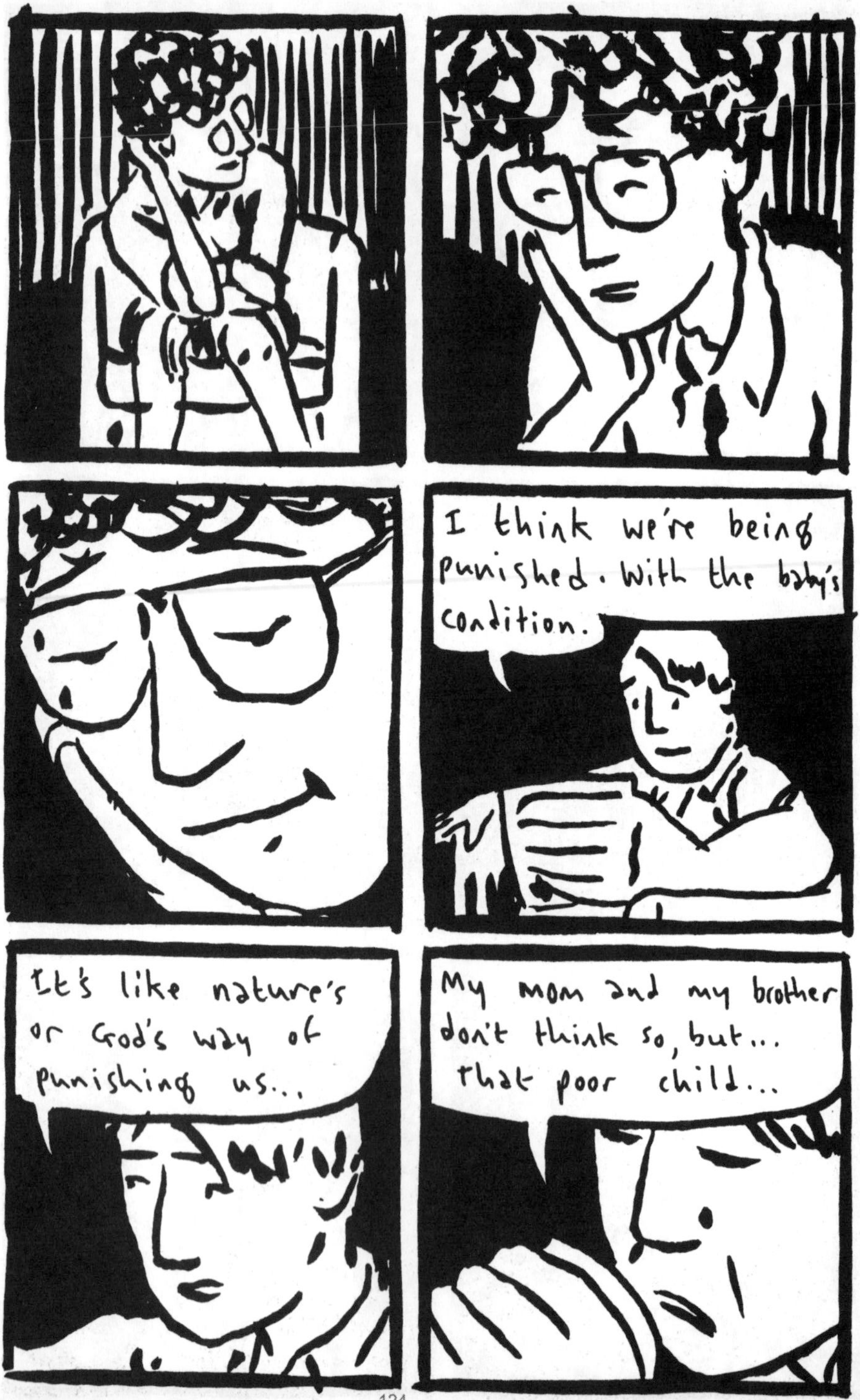
I think we're being punished. With the baby's condition.
It's like nature's or God's way of punishing us...
My mom and my brother don't think so, but... that poor child...

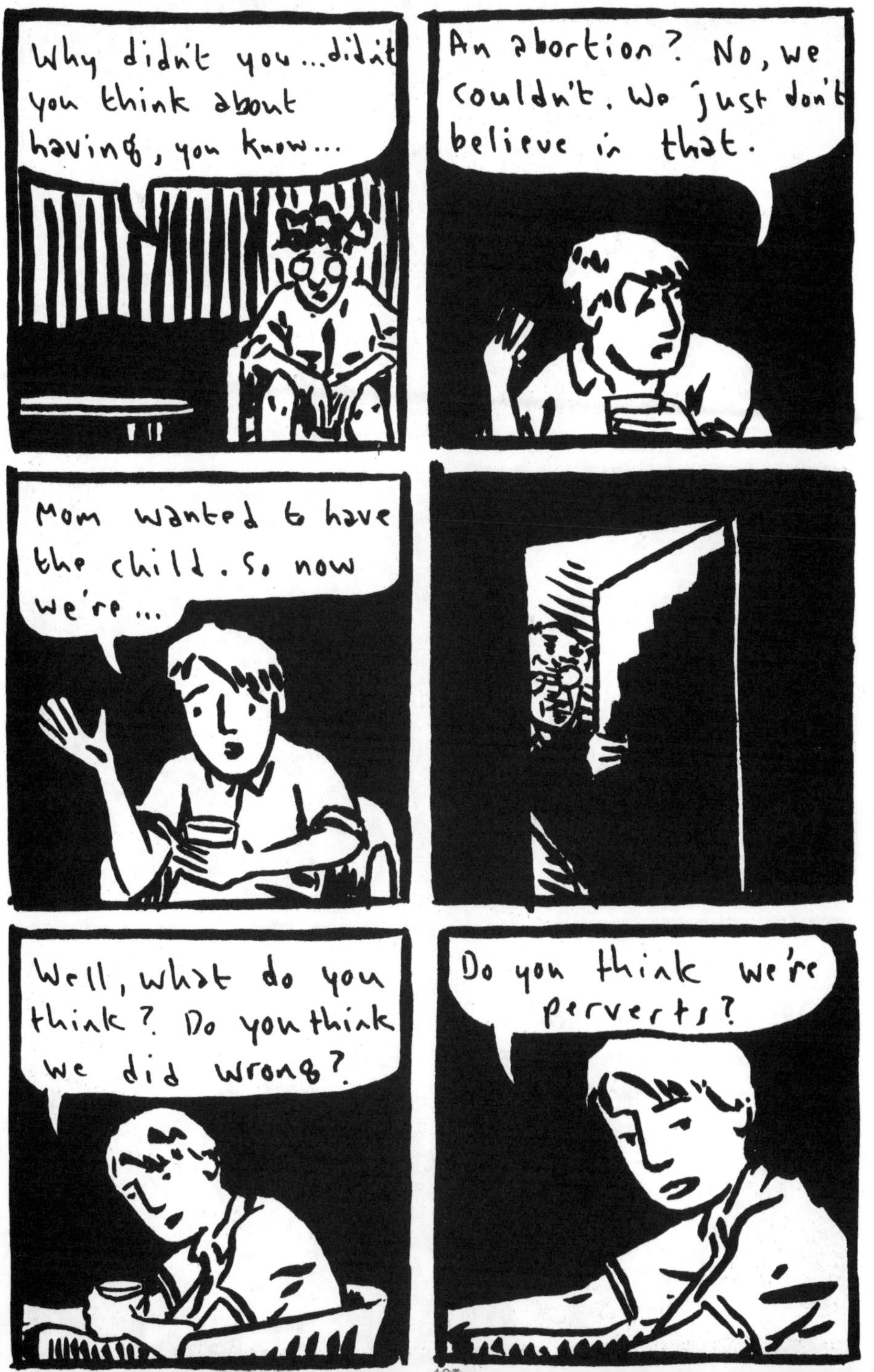
Why didn't you...didn't you think about having, you know...
An abortion? No, we couldn't. We just don't believe in that.
Mom wanted to have the child. So now we're...
Well, what do you think? Do you think we did wrong?
Do you think we're perverts?

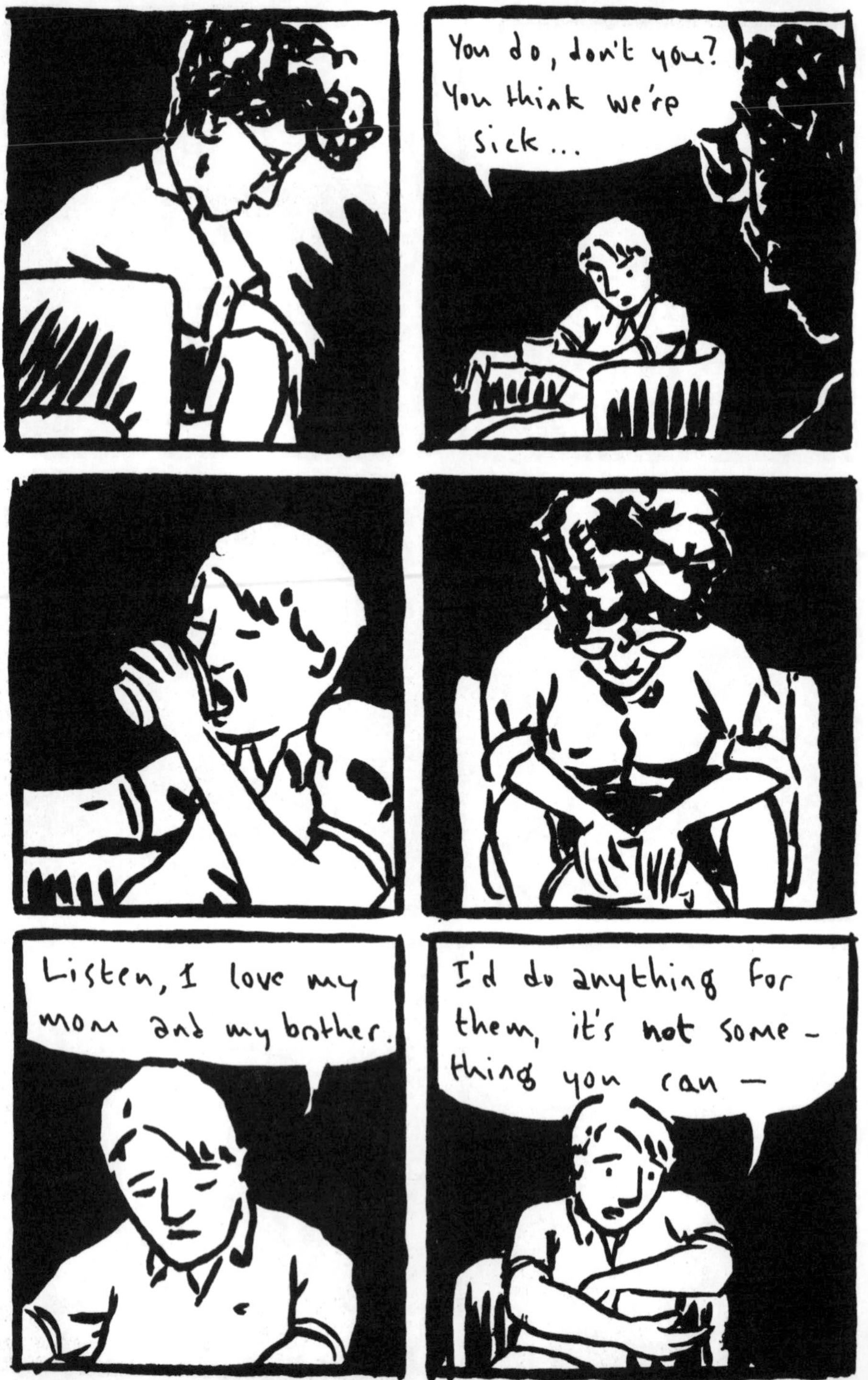
You do, don't you? You think we're sick...
Listen, I love my mom and my brother.
I'd do anything for them, it's not some-thing you can —

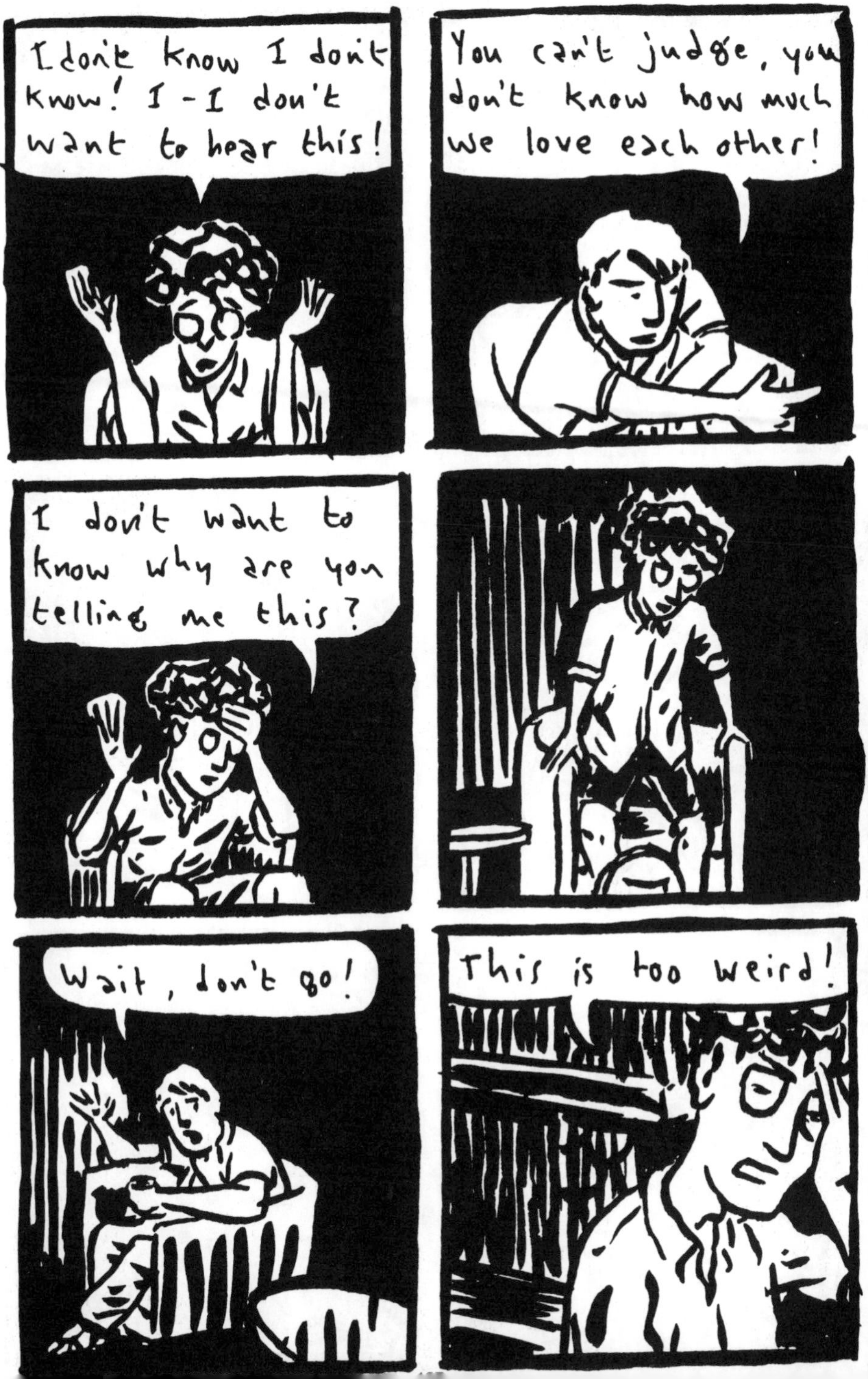
I don't know I don't know! I-I don't want to hear this!
You can't judge, you don't know how much we love each other!
I don't want to know why are you telling me this?
Wait, don't go!
This is too weird!

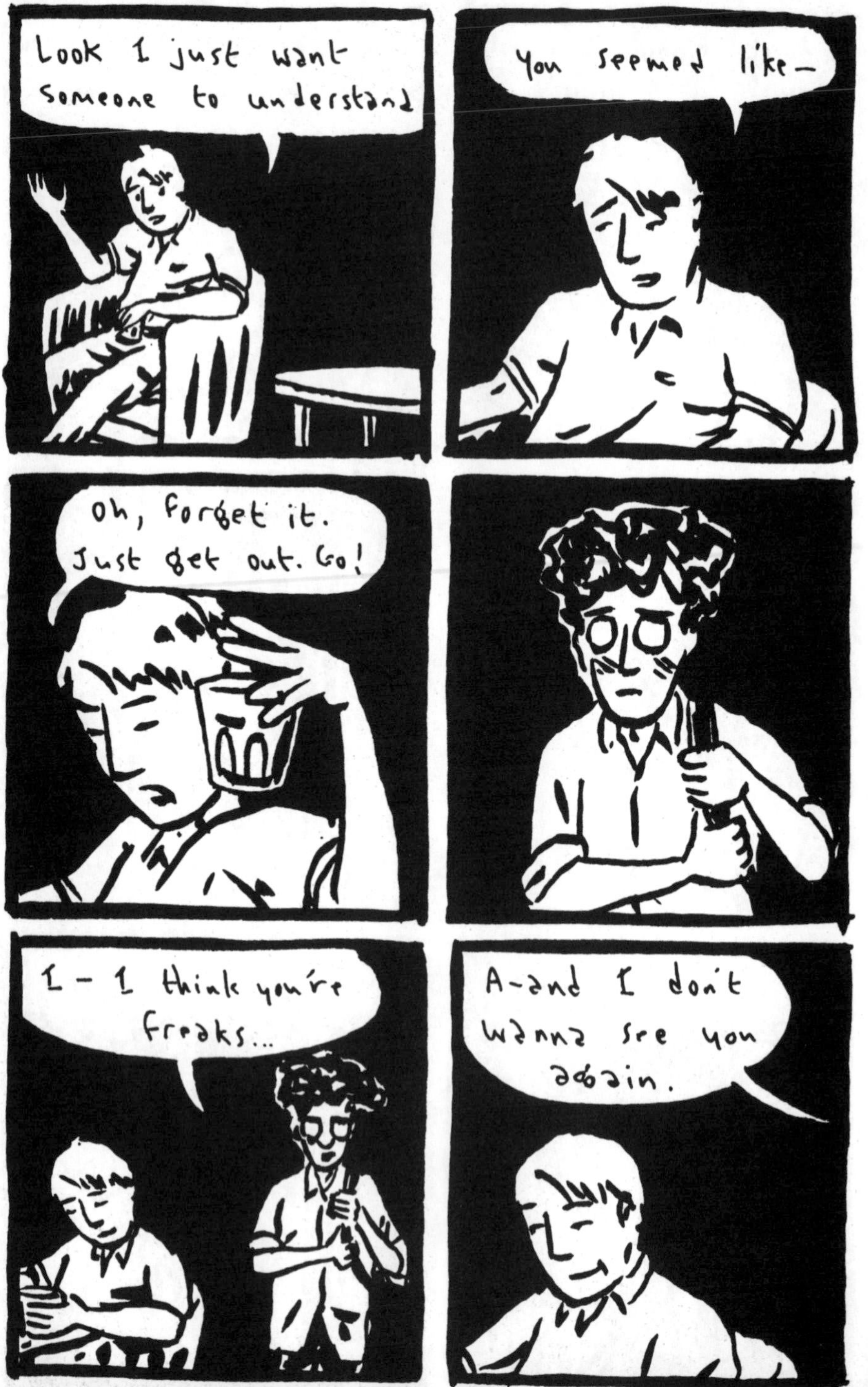
Look I just want someone to understand
You seemed like—
Oh, forget it. Just get out. Go!
I - I think you're freaks...
A-and I don't wanna see you again.

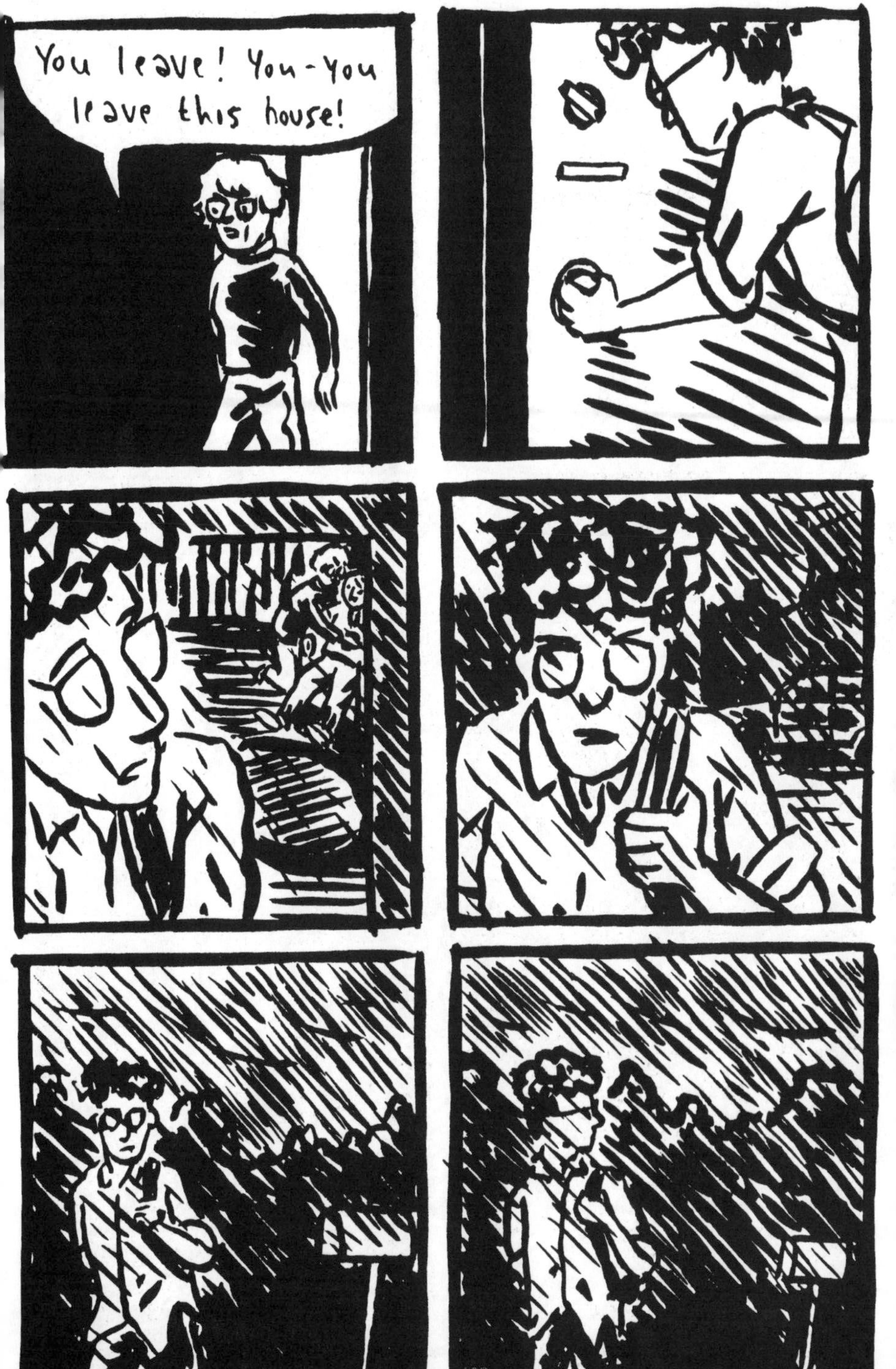
You leave! You-you leave this house!

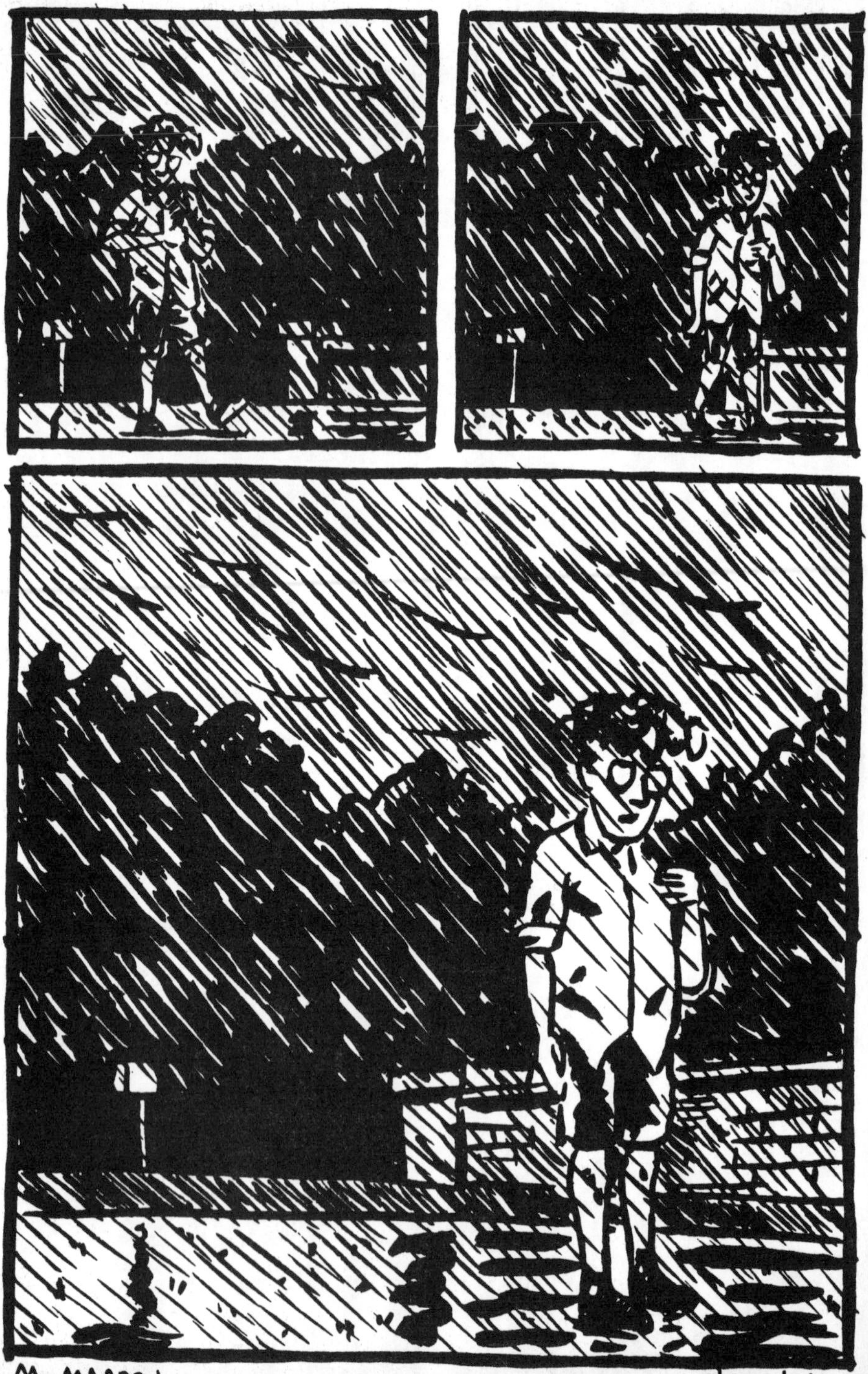
M. MADDEN

BEING AN ACCOUNT OF THE LIFE AND DEATH OF THE EMPEROR HELIOGABOLUS

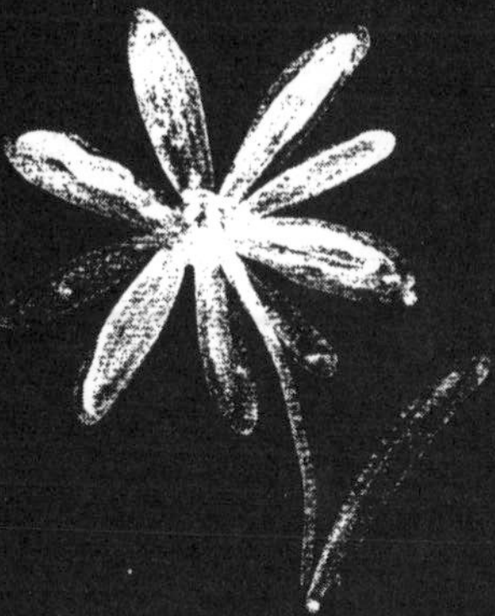

by Neil Gaiman.

A 24 hour Comic

NEIL GAIMAN

[First of all, it's pronounced "He'll-Leo-Gabble-Us." Got it? Good.]

Reading Neil Gaiman's 24-Hour comic is a lot like spending a pleasant evening with the man himself (Neil, that is, not the crazy Roman emperor it depicts). The stream of words ramble, digress, stop and careen, but they're always entertaining and informative. I know hundreds of cartoonists personally, but this is one of the few cases where I hear the author's voice clearly in my head while reading (despite the teeny tiny lettering—yeesh!; get out your magnifying glasses).

Word for word, "Heliogabolus" is probably the best written of the 24-hour comics. This will surprise no one, considering the author. What's particularly interesting though is the way it's forever losing and then rediscovering its structure—as if Neil was continually forgetting where he was, until every few pages, he surfaced, groundhog-like, took it all in and then burrowed back down.

Like our friend Bissette, Neil relies on a few big black pages as pit-stops, but considering how labor intensive lettering can be, it's remarkable that he was able to get as far as he did while still cramming each page with his irresistible prose.

Most remarkable of all is the simple fact that he drew it at all, of course. The first comic drawn by comics' most celebrated writer in over 14 years. And the last, as far as I know.

Neil was unable to finish the full 24 pages, but created as much as possible within a full 24 hour session. Luckily, he saw it coming and still managed to wrap it up nicely. Having gone the distance, at least where time and physical endurance were concerned, we christened it Noble Failure Variant #1 - The Gaiman Variation.

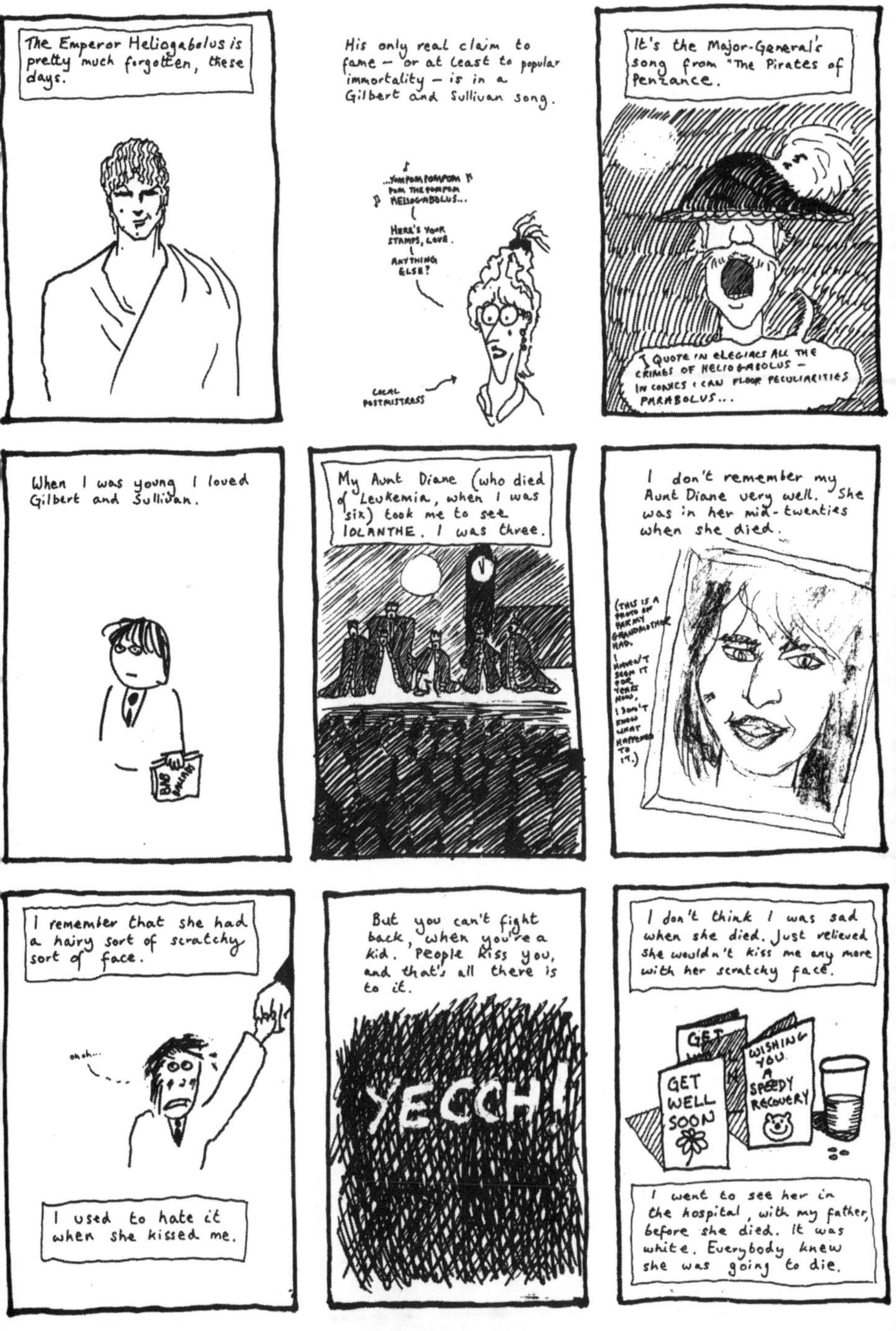

The Emperor Heliogabolus is pretty much forgotten, these days.
His only real claim to fame — or at least to popular immortality — is in a Gilbert and Sullivan song.
...YOM POM POMPOM POM THE POMPOM HELIOGABOLUS...
HERE'S YOUR STAMPS, LOVE.
ANYTHING ELSE?
LOCAL POSTMISTRESS
It's the Major-General's song from "The Pirates of Penzance.
I QUOTE IN ELEGIACS ALL THE CRIMES OF HELIOGABOLUS — IN CONICS I CAN FLOOR PECULIARITIES PARABOLUS...
When I was young I loved Gilbert and Sullivan.
My Aunt Diane (who died of Leukemia, when I was six) took me to see IOLANTHE. I was three.
I don't remember my Aunt Diane very well. She was in her mid-twenties when she died.
(THIS IS A PHOTO OF HER MY GRANDMOTHER HAD. I HAVEN'T SEEN IT FOR YEARS NOW, I DON'T KNOW WHAT HAPPENED TO IT.)
I remember that she had a hairy sort of scratchy sort of face.
ohoh...
I used to hate it when she kissed me.
But you can't fight back, when you're a kid. People kiss you, and that's all there is to it.
YECCH!
I don't think I was sad when she died. Just relieved she wouldn't kiss me any more with her scratchy face.
GET WELL SOON
WISHING YOU A SPEEDY RECOVERY
I went to see her in the hospital, with my father, before she died. It was white. Everybody knew she was going to die.

But this isn't about me. This is about the life and crimes of the Emperor Heliogabolus (204 AD – 222 AD). He was fourteen when he ascended to the throne of Rome; eighteen when he was assassinated. No-one knows quite how he came to be in line for the throne.

Right. It's like this. You're Emperor.

I dunno. Me and the lads just liked the sound of you...

Well, the name. It was the name, really...

He was named Marcus Aurelius Antoninus — and it is said that the army put him into office, because they liked his name.

He was called Heliogabolus, because he was High Priest of Heliogabolus – a minor Syrian Sun-God.

He was also called Varius.

He was called Varius, because his mother, Symiamira, was unsure of his parentage. His schoolfellows rechristened him 'Varius' because he was the son of "various" people.

OY! YOU! WHO'S YOUR FATHER? EH? EH?

Yeah, Varius... who's today's candidate?

I don't know if this is true or not.

?

None of the ancient writers have a kind word to say about him, though.

Lessee... He was a creep? No. (Too nice.) Bastard? Prat? Pillock?

But then, he was dead, and they weren't.

KNOCK-KNEED, PERVERTED, SPINELESS LITTLE... ...LITTLE...

UT...

Not then, at any rate.

THUD!

They died later I expect...

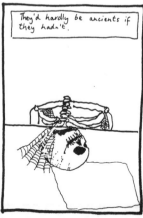

They'd hardly be ancients if they hadn't.

3

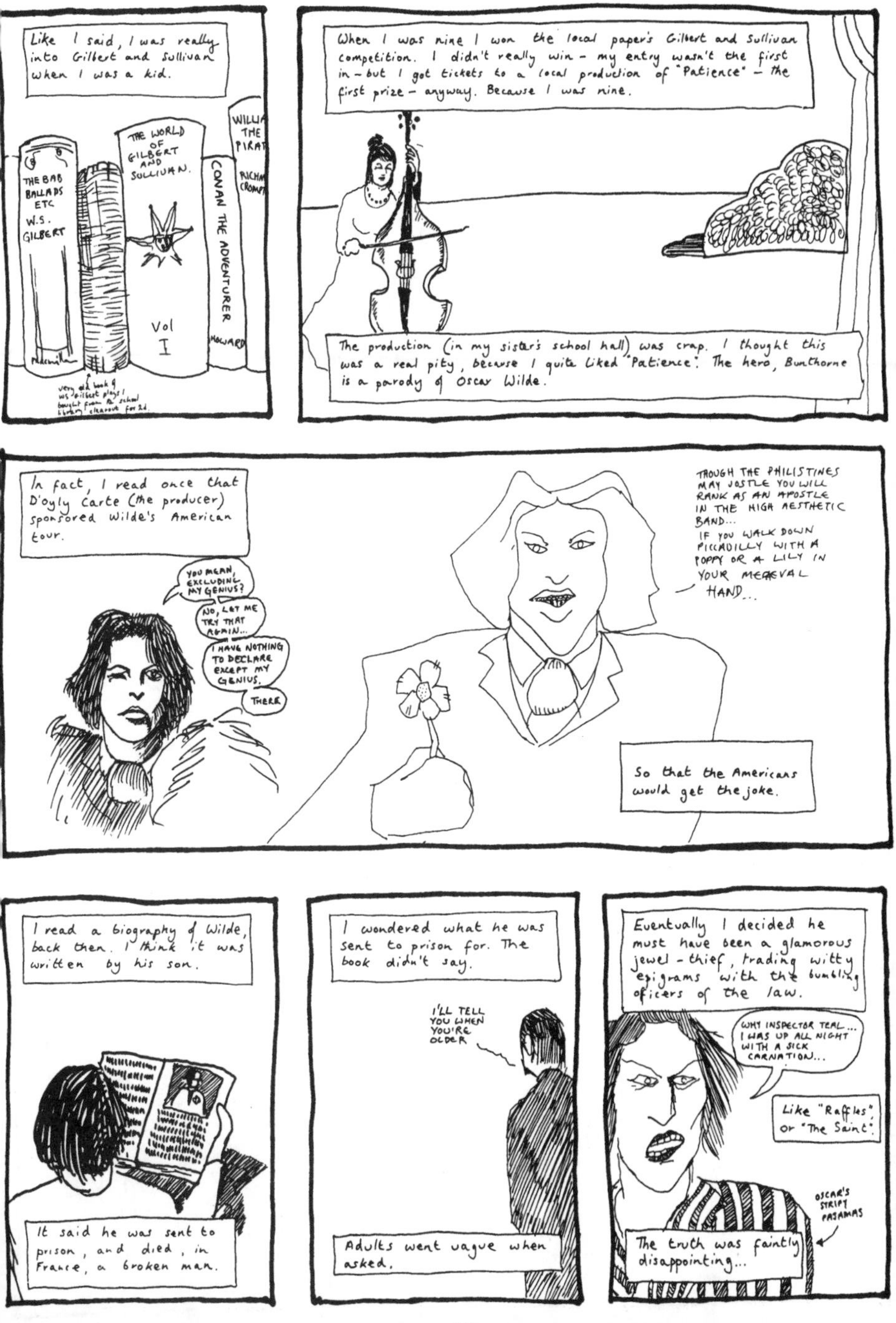
Like I said, I was really into Gilbert and Sullivan when I was a kid.
THE BAB BALLADS ETC W.S. GILBERT
THE WORLD OF GILBERT AND SULLIVAN. Vol I
CONAN THE ADVENTURER
HOWARD
very old book of WS Gilbert plays I bought from the school library clearout for 2d.
When I was nine I won the local paper's Gilbert and Sullivan competition. I didn't really win - my entry wasn't the first in - but I got tickets to a local production of "Patience" - the first prize - anyway. Because I was nine.
The production (in my sister's school hall) was crap. I thought this was a real pity, because I quite liked "Patience". The hero, Bunthorne is a parody of Oscar Wilde.
In fact, I read once that D'oyly Carte (the producer) sponsored Wilde's American tour.
YOU MEAN, EXCLUDING MY GENIUS?
NO, LET ME TRY THAT AGAIN...
I HAVE NOTHING TO DECLARE EXCEPT MY GENIUS.
THERE
THOUGH THE PHILISTINES MAY JOSTLE YOU WILL RANK AS AN APOSTLE IN THE HIGH AESTHETIC BAND... IF YOU WALK DOWN PICCADILLY WITH A POPPY OR A LILY IN YOUR MEDIEVAL HAND...
So that the Americans would get the joke.
I read a biography of Wilde, back then. I think it was written by his son.
It said he was sent to prison, and died, in France, a broken man.
I wondered what he was sent to prison for. The book didn't say.
I'LL TELL YOU WHEN YOU'RE OLDER
Adults went vague when asked.
Eventually I decided he must have been a glamorous jewel-thief, trading witty epigrams with the bumbling officers of the law.
WHY INSPECTOR TEAL... I WAS UP ALL NIGHT WITH A SICK CARNATION...
Like "Raffles" or "The Saint".
OSCAR'S STRIPY PAJAMAS
The truth was faintly disappointing...

Of course, Wilde's crime was essentially that of Heliogabolus.

IF THIS IS HOW HER MAJESTY TREATS HER PRISONERS, SHE DOESN'T DESERVE TO HAVE ANY.

Or I should say, one of ↑ Heliogabolus's, anyway.

To wit, having sex with someone of your own gender.

Not suffocating people, or having them eaten by animals, or...

or any of the interesting things Heliogabolus did.

For example:

A banquet. Food consisting of flamingoes' brains, the heads of parrots, peacocks, and pheasants! Sows' udders. Peas with gold pieces, lentils with onyx, and ground pearls sprinkled (instead of pepper) over mushrooms and fish.

And, as the banquet ends, the petals begin to fall.

Violets and rose petals rain down from the ceiling.

The people marvel.

The flowers continue to fall.

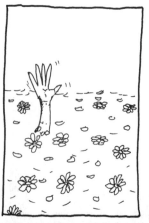

Heliogabolus thought this was very funny.

He even let the ones who succeeded in crawling to the surface of the petals live...

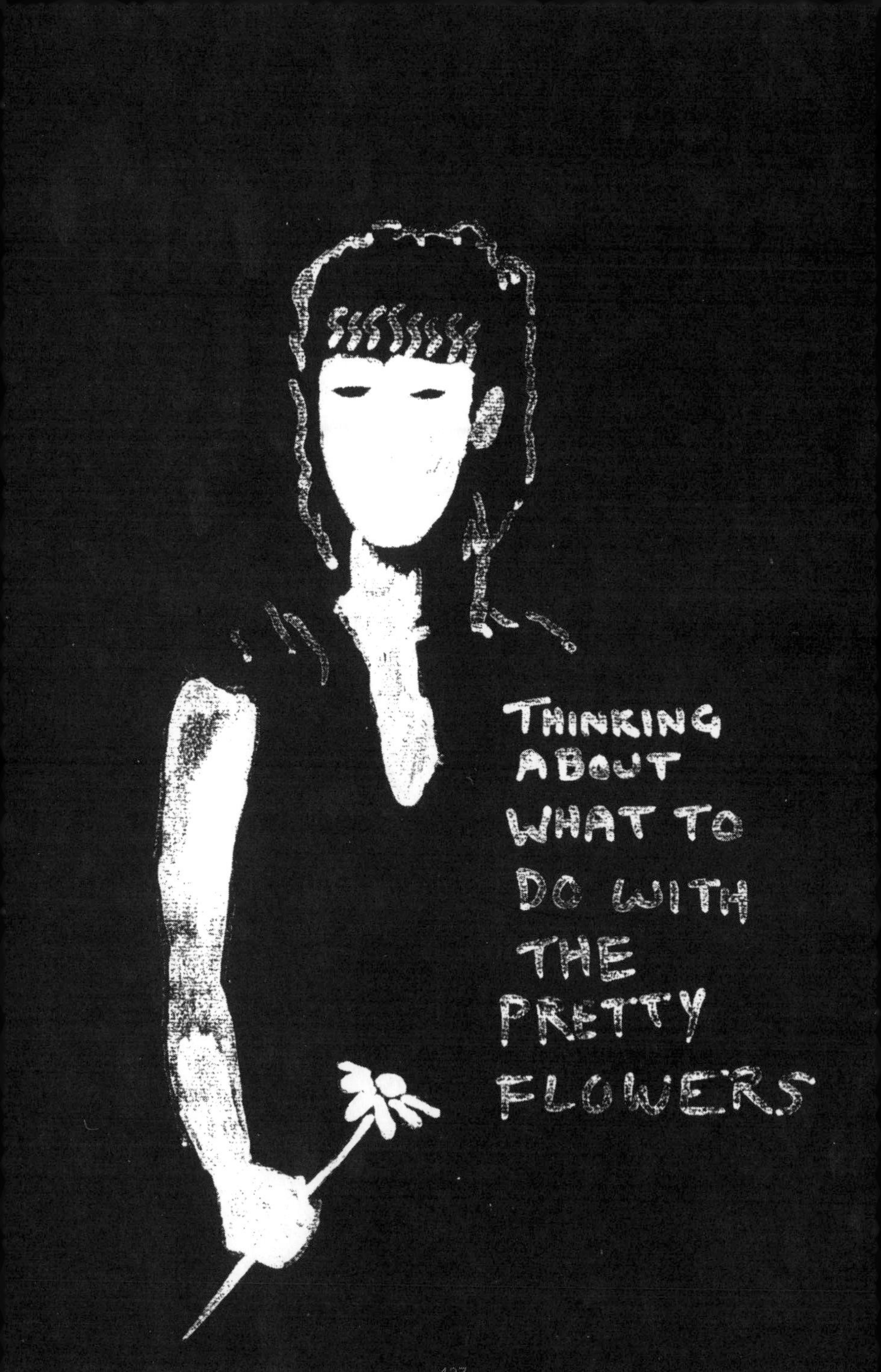
THINKING ABOUT WHAT TO DO WITH THE PRETTY FLOWERS

6.

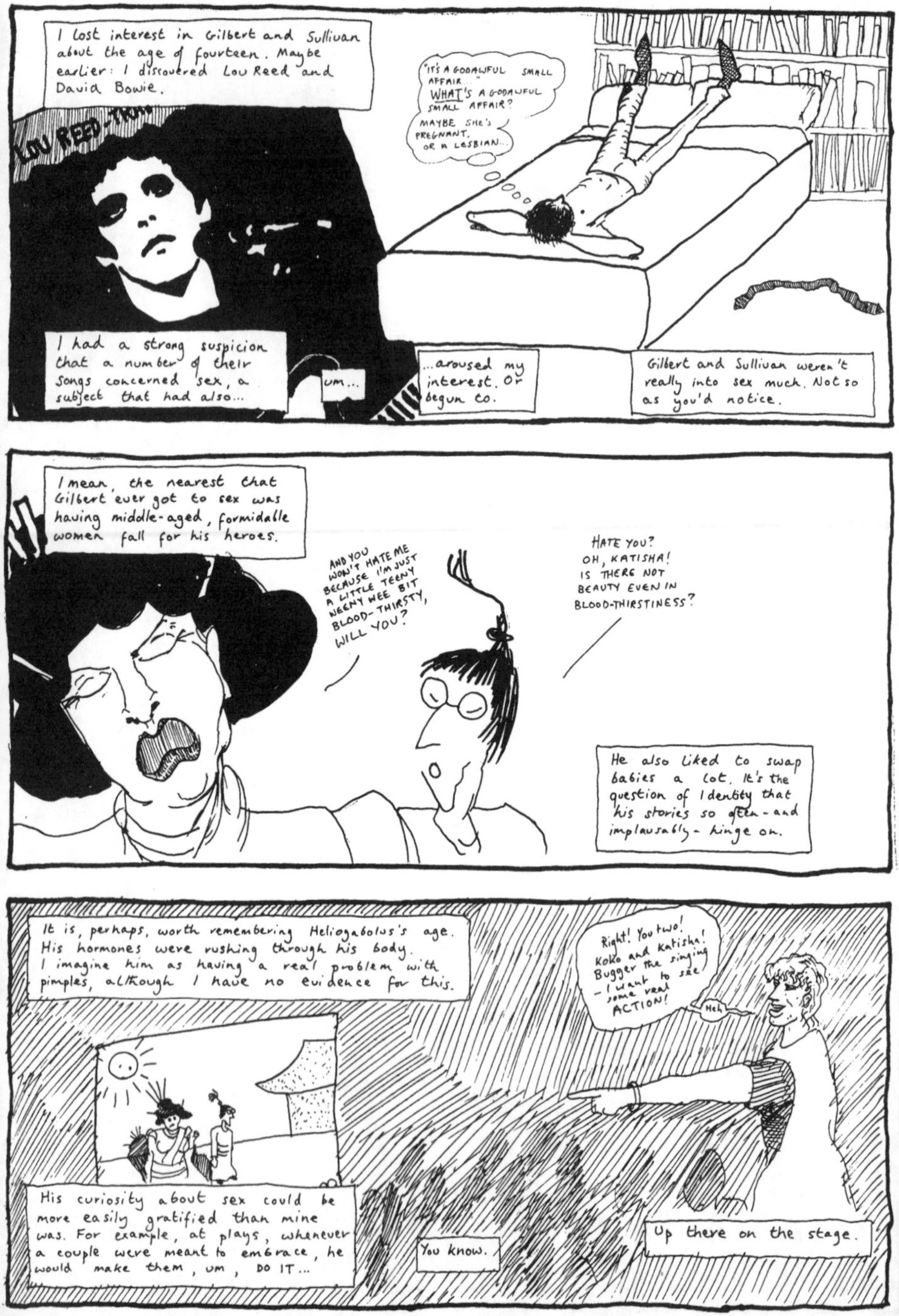

I lost interest in Gilbert and Sullivan about the age of fourteen. Maybe earlier: I discovered Lou Reed and David Bowie.
LOU REED-TRAN
I had a strong suspicion that a number of their songs concerned sex, a subject that had also...
um...
...aroused my interest. Or begun to.
"IT'S A GODAWFUL SMALL AFFAIR..." WHAT'S A GODAWFUL SMALL AFFAIR? MAYBE SHE'S PREGNANT. OR A LESBIAN...
Gilbert and Sullivan weren't really into sex much. Not so as you'd notice.
I mean, the nearest that Gilbert ever got to sex was having middle-aged, formidable women fall for his heroes.
AND YOU WON'T HATE ME BECAUSE I'M JUST A LITTLE TEENY WEENY WEE BIT BLOOD-THIRSTY, WILL YOU?
HATE YOU? OH, KATISHA! IS THERE NOT BEAUTY EVEN IN BLOOD-THIRSTINESS?
He also liked to swap babies a lot. It's the question of Identity that his stories so often - and implausably - hinge on.
It is, perhaps, worth remembering Heliogabolus's age. His hormones were rushing through his body. I imagine him as having a real problem with pimples, although I have no evidence for this.
Right! You two! Koko and Katisha! Bugger the singing - I want to see some real ACTION!
Heh
His curiosity about sex could be more easily gratified than mine was. For example, at plays, whenever a couple were meant to embrace, he would make them, um, DO IT...
You know.
Up there on the stage.

He did other things at the theatre. He used to kiss his boyfriends "in the groin" - claiming he was celebrating the festival of the Goddess Flora.

He would harness a number of naked women to his chariot and have them pull him around

He would normally be naked on these occasions.

Other things that pulled his chariot, at one time or another, include:

Four dogs.

Four stags.

Lions (calling himself "The Mother of all Gods").

Tigers (calling himself "Liber" - a name for Bacchus).

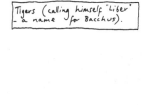

Someone once told me that Heligabolus's chariot was pulled by crocodiles.

However, I can find no reference to this anywhere

And he would invite groups of eight men to dinner.

Eight bald

or fat

or one-eyed

or deaf

or tall

or blind men to dinner. I don't know why he did this either.

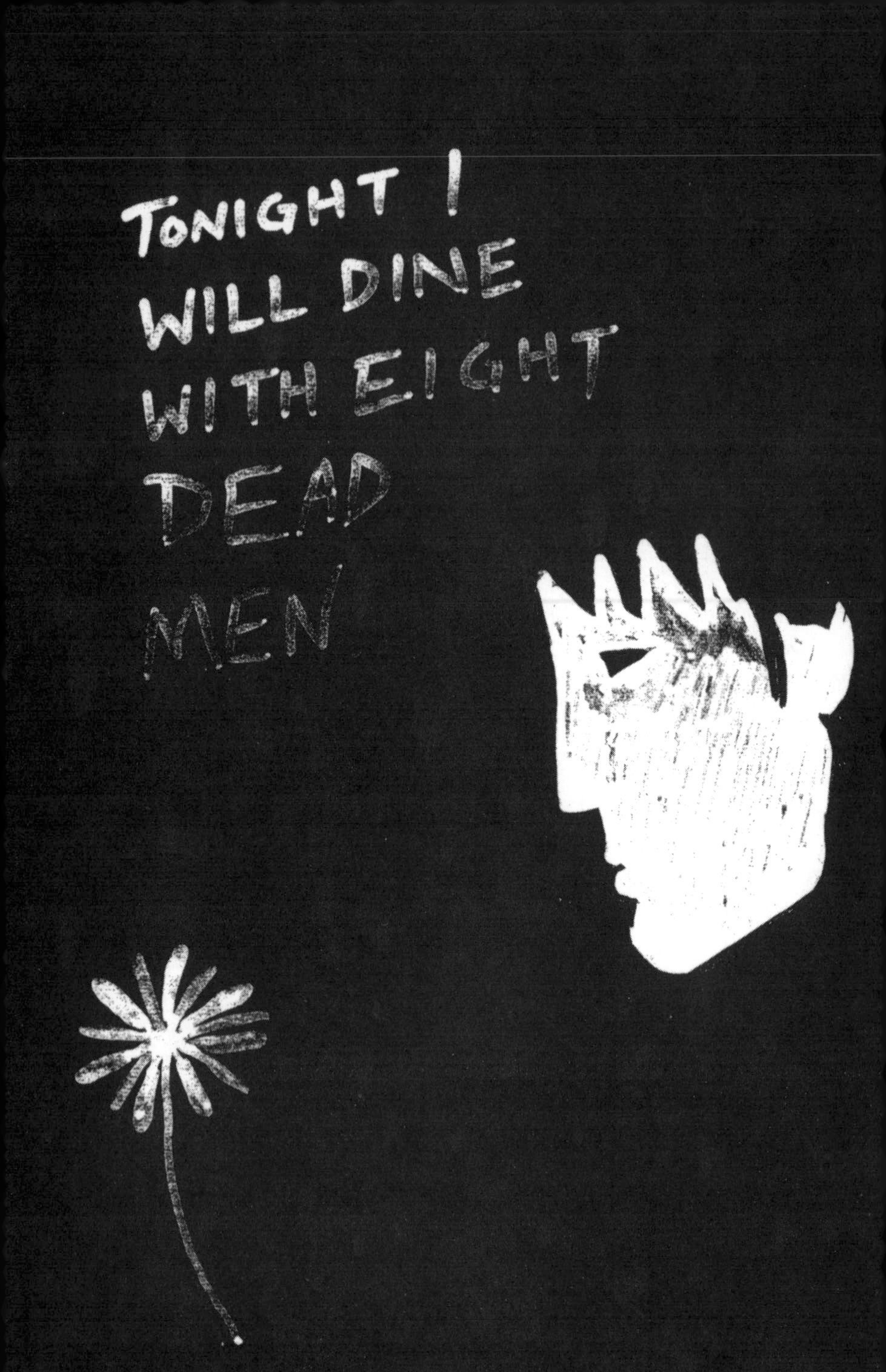
TONIGHT I
WILL DINE
WITH EIGHT
DEAD
MEN

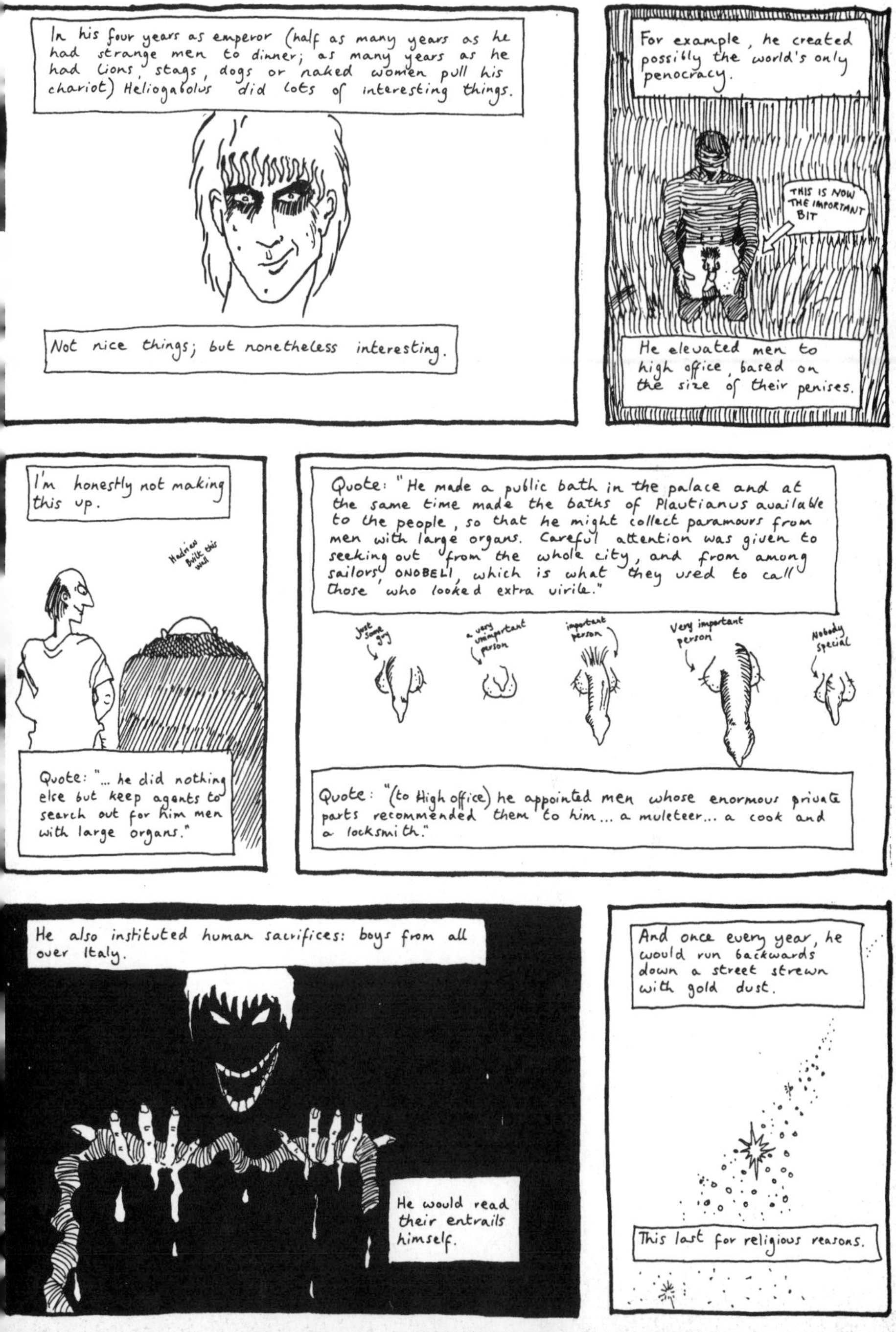
In his four years as emperor (half as many years as he had strange men to dinner; as many years as he had lions, stags, dogs or naked women pull his chariot) Heliogabolus did lots of interesting things.
Not nice things; but nonetheless interesting.
For example, he created possibly the world's only penocracy.
THIS IS NOW THE IMPORTANT BIT
He elevated men to high office, based on the size of their penises.
I'm honestly not making this up.
Hadrian Built this Wall
Quote: "... he did nothing else but keep agents to search out for him men with large organs."
Quote: "He made a public bath in the palace and at the same time made the baths of Plautianus available to the people, so that he might collect paramours from men with large organs. Careful attention was given to seeking out from the whole city, and from among sailors, ONOBELI, which is what they used to call those who looked extra virile."
just some guy
a very unimportant person
important person
Very important person
Nobody special
Quote: "(to High office) he appointed men whose enormous private parts recommended them to him... a muleteer... a cook and a locksmith."
He also instituted human sacrifices: boys from all over Italy.
He would read their entrails himself.
And once every year, he would run backwards down a street strewn with gold dust.
This last for religious reasons.

Sometimes I think it peculiar that Heliogabolus is so little known. I mean, everyone knows that Caligula made his horse, Incitatus, a senator.

This is not a already horse. I've already drawn—or tried to draw—or crocodiles and I don't want to draw a horse. However, if you wish you may pretend it's a horse. But it's ME.

Only he didn't. According to Seutonius, Caligula was only said to be planning to make the horse a consul.

This is also not a horse. It's a rotting zombie especially for Steve Bissette.

Heliogabolus, on the other hand, did make his horse a consul.

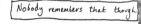

Nobody remembers that though.

I mean, did you know that?

Personally, I think it's because the histories of Heliogabolus's reign are so appalingly written.

Do my homework! Are you kidding? Have you tried reading this guy?

Also, of course, because Caligula got there first.

UNCLE CLAUDIUS? THERE'S BEEN A... TERRIBLE ACCIDENT...

I mean, he was seriously fractured.

YECH!

Heliogabolus was just a weird kid with a thing about animals and big dicks.

Heliogabolus was married four times (once to a Vestal Virgin. This was technically incest; also blasphemy). Four times to women.

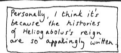

He never... from filthy word... used to make indecen... had no sense of shame... even when the people cou... hear.

Once, at least, to a man, Zoticus.

"Aelius Lampridius", the author of the main biography of Heliogabolus, was one of six slap-dash pen-names adopted by an untrustworthy historian with a hellish prose style.

I mean, when your only real source for somebody was written by an unreliable biographer, pretending to be a 'team of six biographers', writing about ninety years later than the manuscript claims...

I mean...

—well? Where are you?

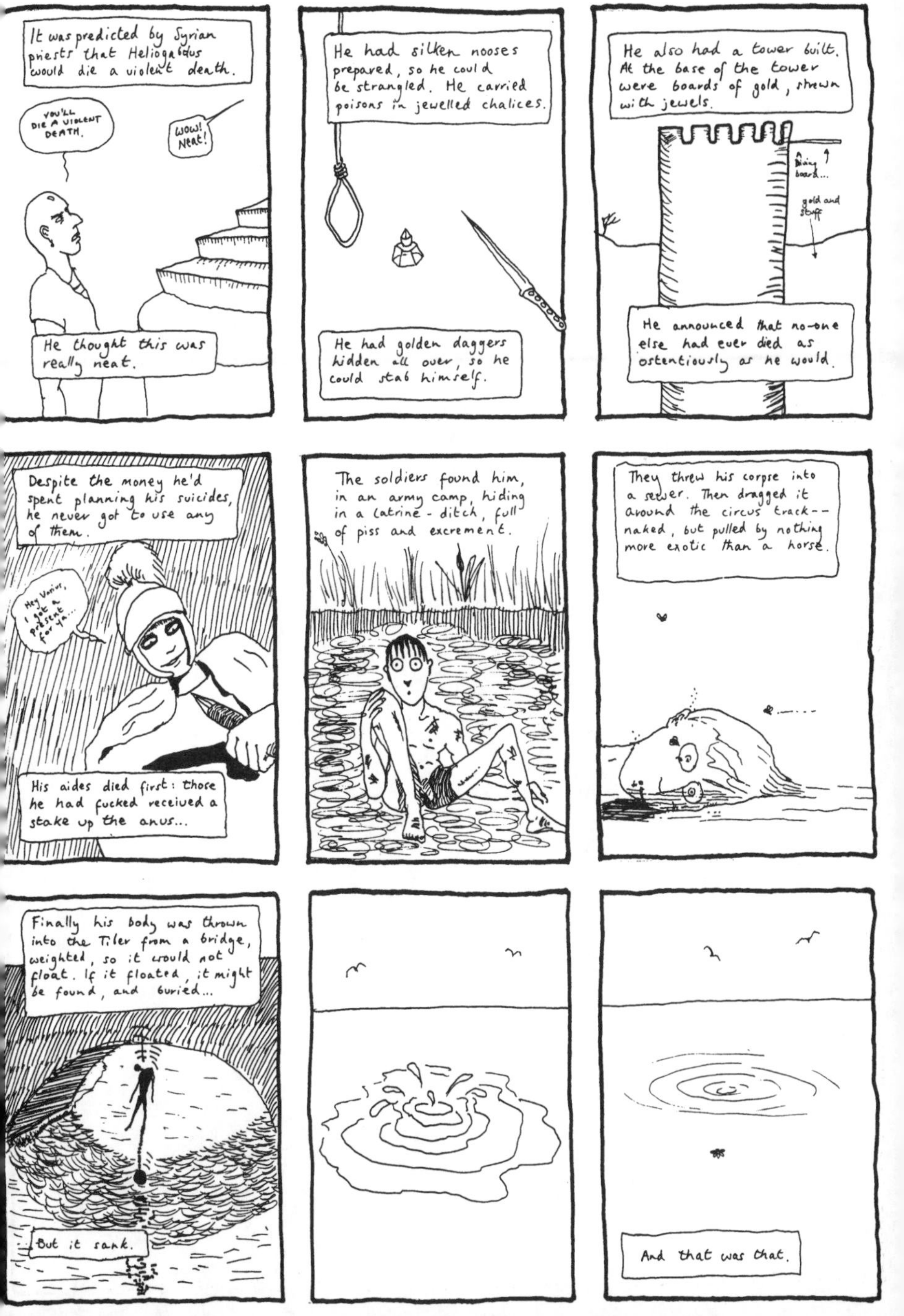
It was predicted by Syrian priests that Heliogabalus would die a violent death.
YOU'LL DIE A VIOLENT DEATH.
WOW! Neat!
He thought this was really neat.
He had silken nooses prepared, so he could be strangled. He carried poisons in jewelled chalices.
He had golden daggers hidden all over, so he could stab himself.
He also had a tower built. At the base of the tower were boards of gold, strewn with jewels.
Diving board...
gold and stuff
He announced that no-one else had ever died as ostentiously as he would.
Despite the money he'd spent planning his suicides, he never got to use any of them.
Hey Varius, I got a present for ya...
His aides died first: those he had fucked received a stake up the anus...
The soldiers found him, in an army camp, hiding in a latrine-ditch, full of piss and excrement.
They threw his corpse into a sewer. Then dragged it around the circus track-- naked, but pulled by nothing more exotic than a horse.
Finally his body was thrown into the Tiber from a bridge, weighted, so it would not float. If it floated, it might be found, and buried...
But it sank.
And that was that.

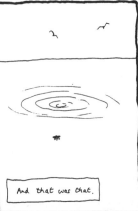

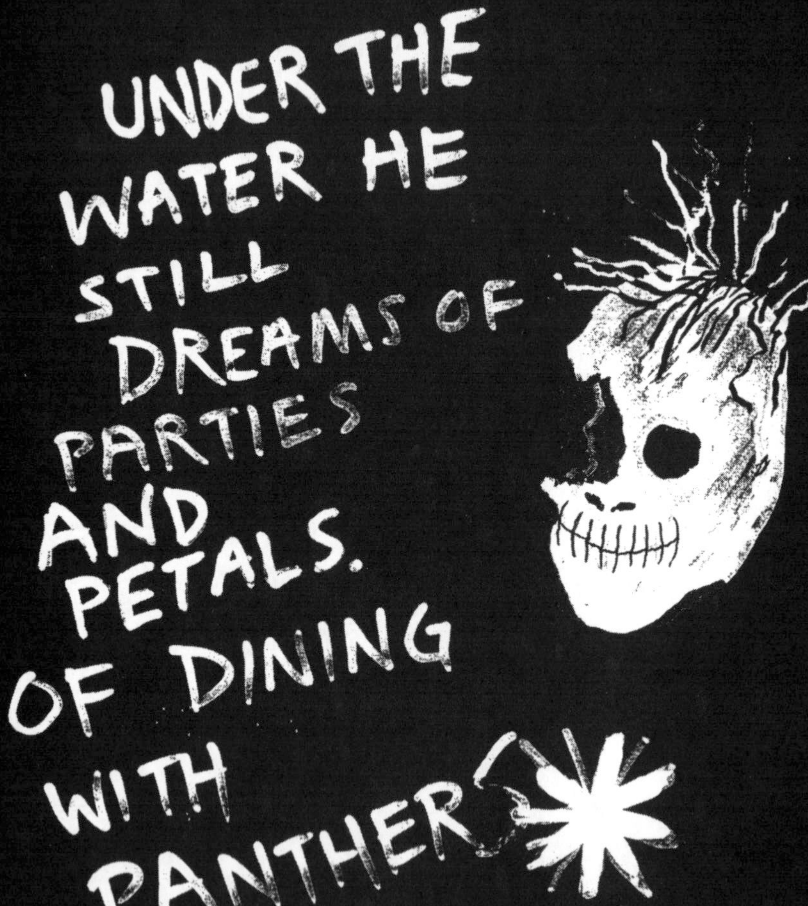
UNDER THE
WATER HE
STILL
DREAMS OF
PARTIES
AND
PETALS.
OF DINING
WITH
PANTHERS

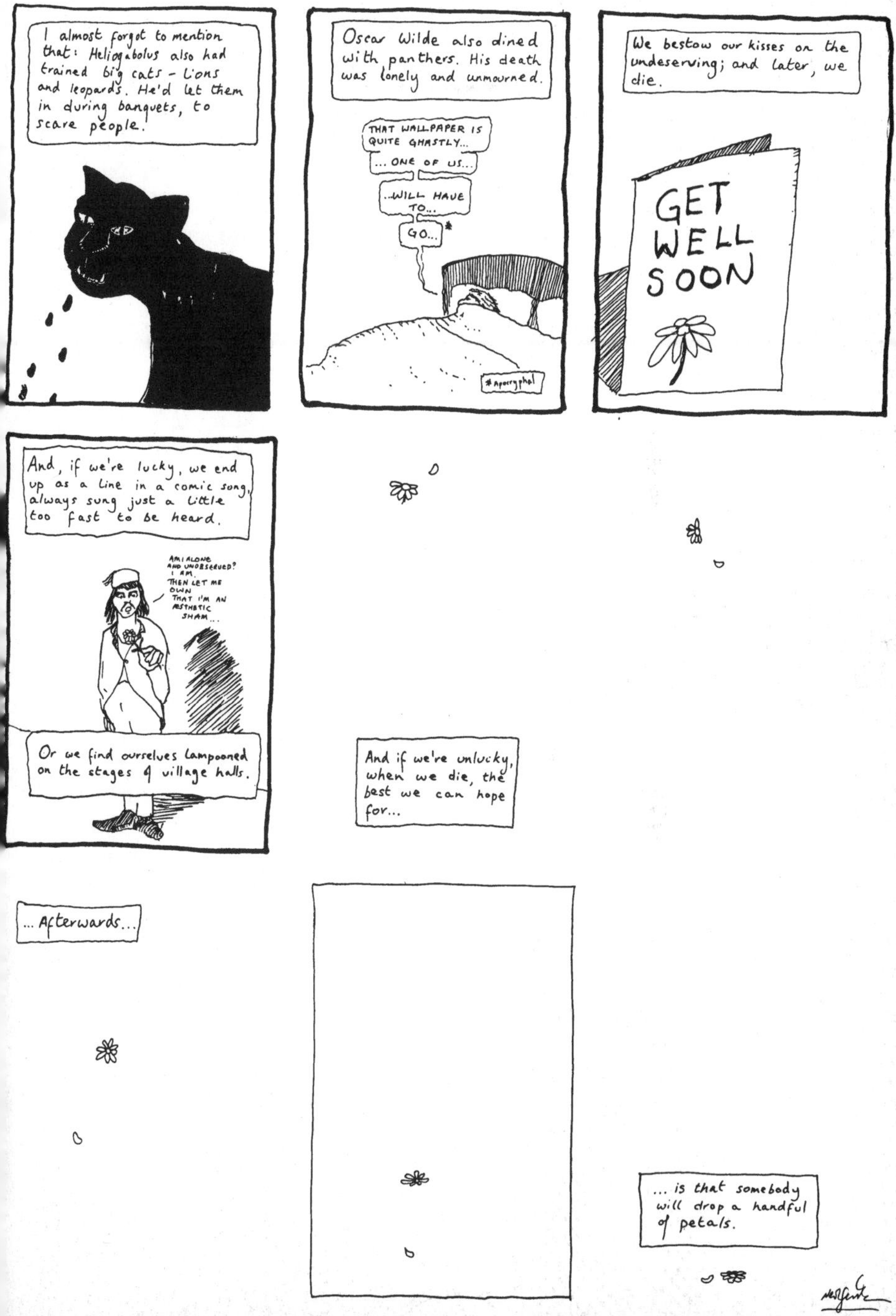
I almost forgot to mention that: Heliogabolus also had trained big cats – lions and leopards. He'd let them in during banquets, to scare people.
Oscar Wilde also dined with panthers. His death was lonely and unmourned.
THAT WALLPAPER IS QUITE GHASTLY...
... ONE OF US...
...WILL HAVE TO...
GO...*
*Apocryphal
We bestow our kisses on the undeserving; and later, we die.
GET WELL SOON
And, if we're lucky, we end up as a line in a comic song, always sung just a little too fast to be heard.
AM I ALONE AND UNOBSERVED? I AM. THEN LET ME OWN THAT I'M AN ÆSTHETIC SHAM...
Or we find ourselves lampooned on the stages of village halls.
And if we're unlucky, when we die, the best we can hope for...
... Afterwards...
... is that somebody will drop a handful of petals.

DAVID LASKY

Sophisticated character development isn't a hallmark of many 24-hour comics, but David Lasky's Minutiae is one happy exception to the rule. His protagonist's bizarre predicament and subsequent journey into voyeurism and self-examination are handled with subtlety and depth. You'll feel for the guy, even as you shake your head in disbelief at his actions.

Cartoonists like David were rare when I started getting published in '84. My generation had some major talents like Dan Clowes and the Hernandez Brothers but they were few and far between. The generation that followed us in the mid '90s had a lot more on the ball when it came to naturalistic characterization and their command of comics iconography and storytelling. They were also utterly disinterested in either celebrating or rebelling against mainstream genre/superhero comics, to their credit. When given a challenge like the 24-hour comic, they took it up with grace and good humor and turned out refreshing, readable stories about ordinary people.

The proliferation of 24-hour comics accelerated in the '90s as formalist comics games became increasingly popular—a trend I've been blamed for as often as not (though there were other factors). Artists like David, as well as Tom Hart, Nick Bertozzi, Jason Little, Matt Madden and many others took to the challenge like ducks to water. For artists more interested in storytelling and narrative composition than in surface details and anatomy, speed drawing was the perfect excuse to cut out the drudgery and go straight to the "good stuff." In fact, many artists of David's tribe were content to leave their artwork looking a bit rough even when they *weren't* rushing, so what did they have to lose?

When cartoonists like David are driving the bus, characterization moves to the front seats and everybody has something to say.

Even the sperm.

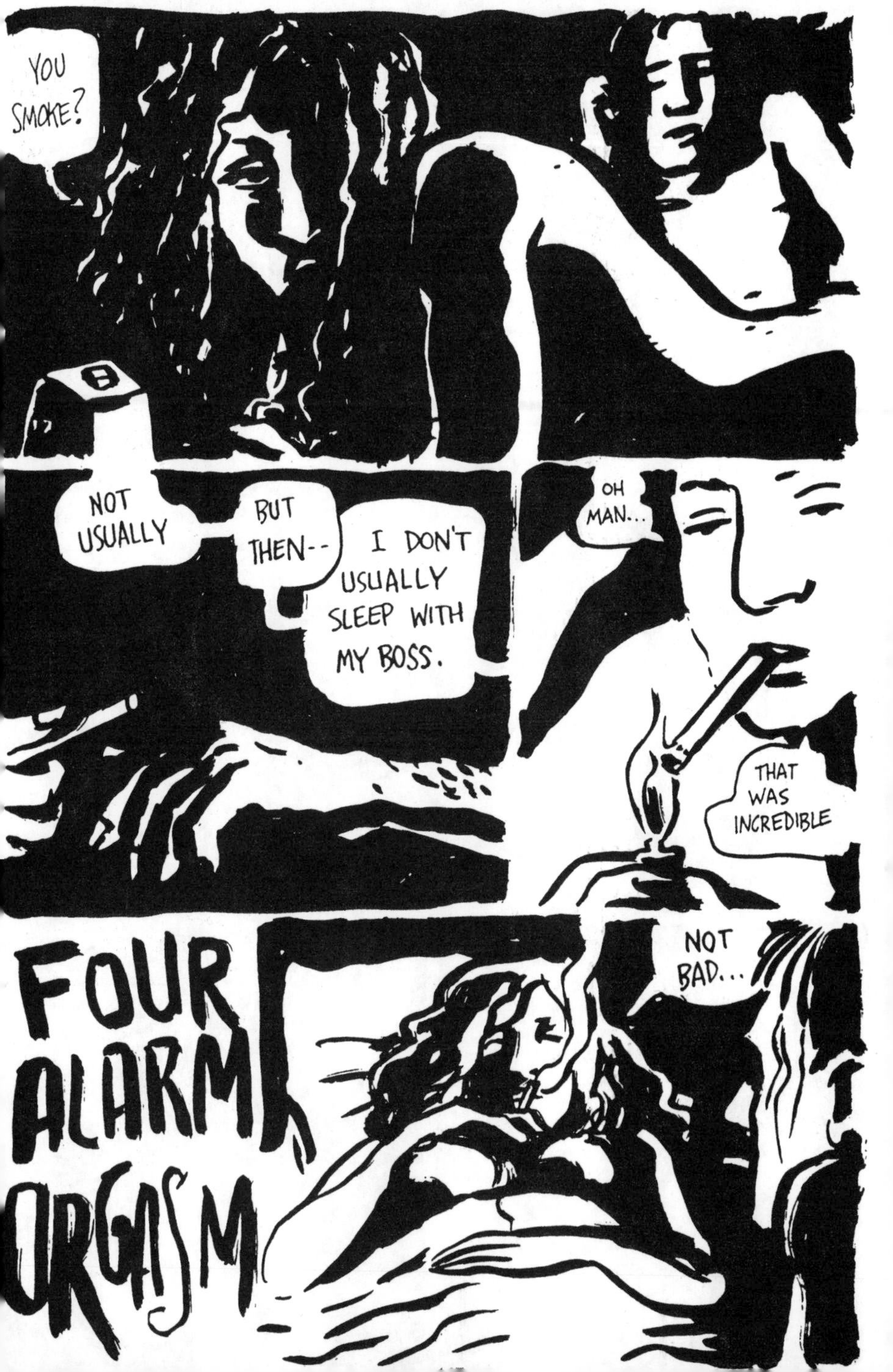
YOU SMOKE?
NOT USUALLY
BUT THEN--
I DON'T USUALLY SLEEP WITH MY BOSS.
OH MAN...
THAT WAS INCREDIBLE
FOUR ALARM ORGASM
NOT BAD...

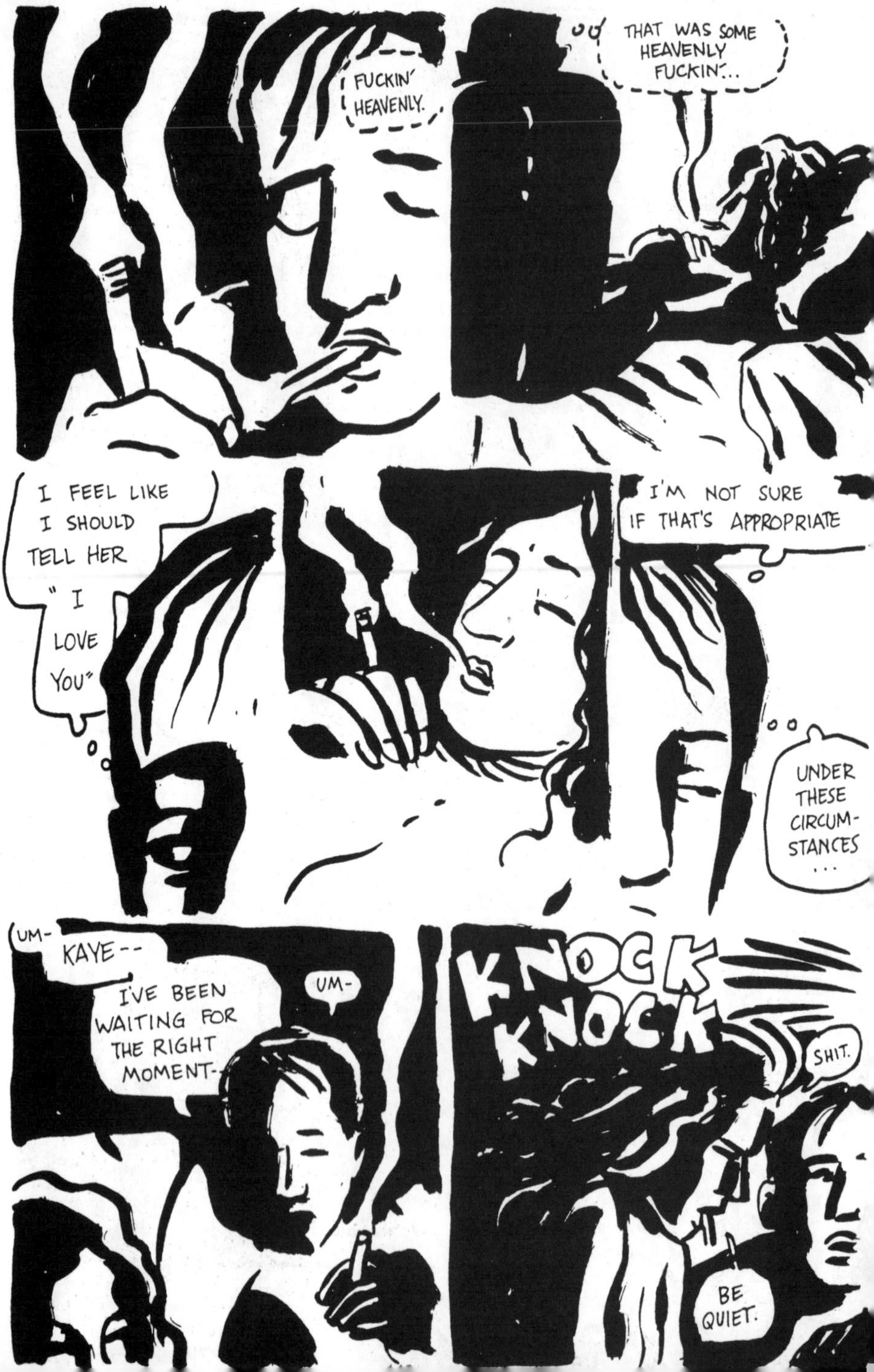
FUCKIN' HEAVENLY.
THAT WAS SOME HEAVENLY FUCKIN'...
I FEEL LIKE I SHOULD TELL HER "I LOVE YOU"
I'M NOT SURE IF THAT'S APPROPRIATE
UNDER THESE CIRCUM-STANCES ...
UM- KAYE--
I'VE BEEN WAITING FOR THE RIGHT MOMENT--
UM-
KNOCK KNOCK
SHIT.
BE QUIET.

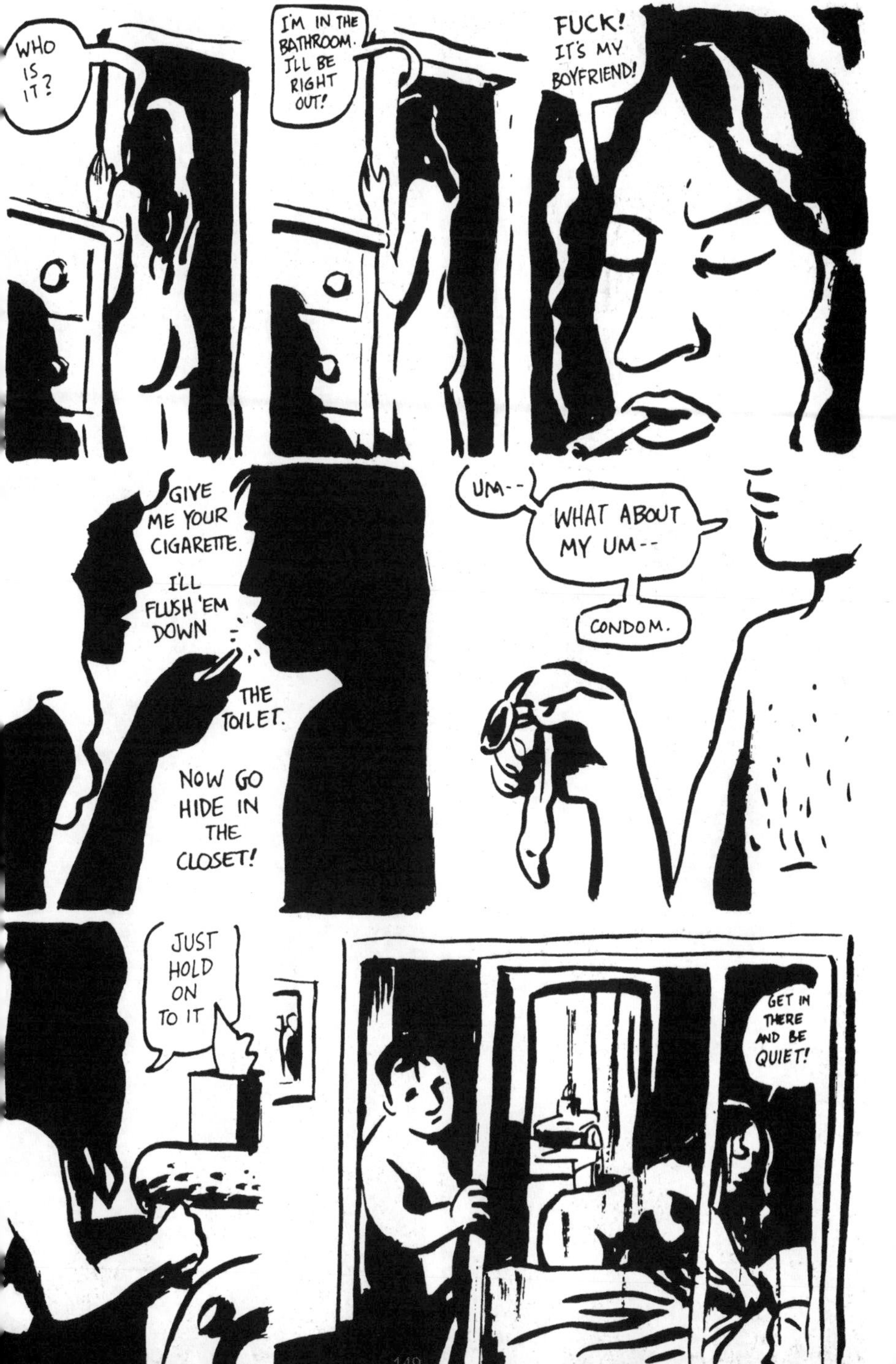
WHO IS IT?
I'M IN THE BATHROOM. I'LL BE RIGHT OUT!
FUCK! IT'S MY BOYFRIEND!
GIVE ME YOUR CIGARETTE.
I'LL FLUSH 'EM DOWN
THE TOILET.
NOW GO HIDE IN THE CLOSET!
UM--
WHAT ABOUT MY UM--
CONDOM.
JUST HOLD ON TO IT
GET IN THERE AND BE QUIET!

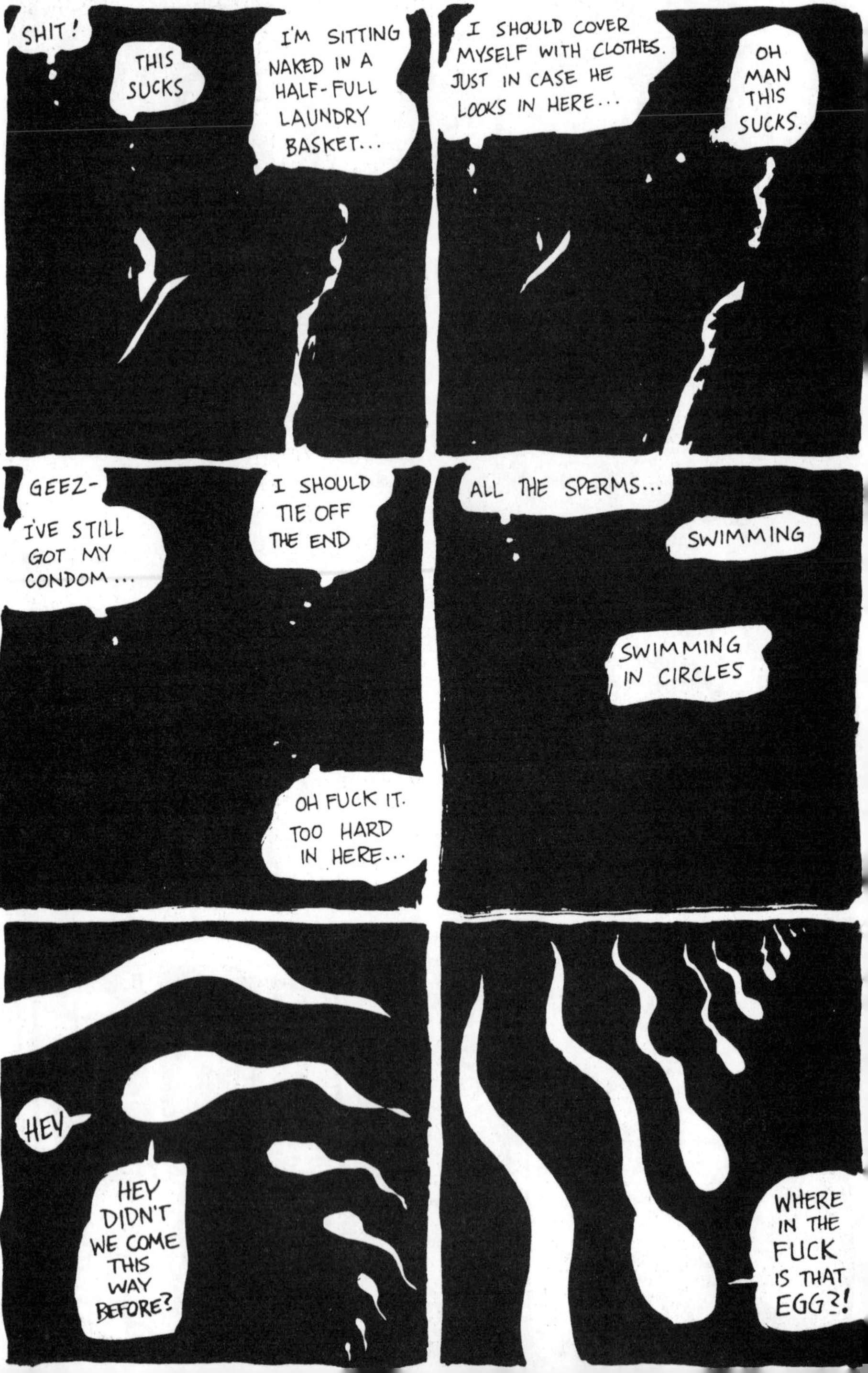

SHIT!
THIS SUCKS
I'M SITTING NAKED IN A HALF-FULL LAUNDRY BASKET...
I SHOULD COVER MYSELF WITH CLOTHES. JUST IN CASE HE LOOKS IN HERE...
OH MAN THIS SUCKS.
GEEZ-
I'VE STILL GOT MY CONDOM...
I SHOULD TIE OFF THE END
OH FUCK IT. TOO HARD IN HERE...
ALL THE SPERMS...
SWIMMING
SWIMMING IN CIRCLES
HEY
HEY DIDN'T WE COME THIS WAY BEFORE?
WHERE IN THE FUCK IS THAT EGG?!

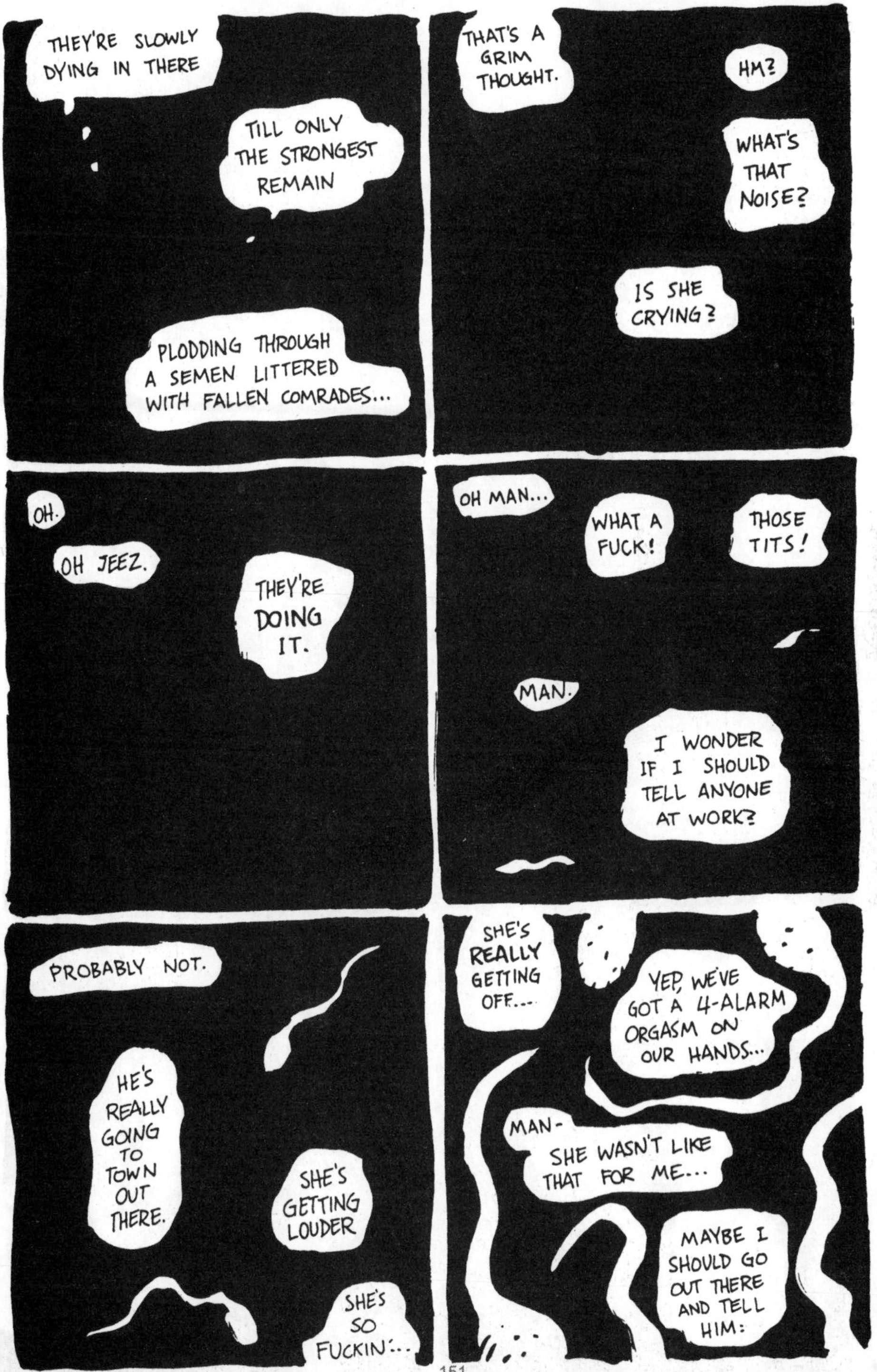
THEY'RE SLOWLY DYING IN THERE
TILL ONLY THE STRONGEST REMAIN
PLODDING THROUGH A SEMEN LITTERED WITH FALLEN COMRADES...
THAT'S A GRIM THOUGHT.
HM?
WHAT'S THAT NOISE?
IS SHE CRYING?
OH.
OH JEEZ.
THEY'RE DOING IT.
OH MAN...
WHAT A FUCK!
THOSE TITS!
MAN.
I WONDER IF I SHOULD TELL ANYONE AT WORK?
PROBABLY NOT.
HE'S REALLY GOING TO TOWN OUT THERE.
SHE'S GETTING LOUDER
SHE'S SO FUCKIN'...
SHE'S REALLY GETTING OFF...
YEP, WE'VE GOT A 4-ALARM ORGASM ON OUR HANDS...
MAN-
SHE WASN'T LIKE THAT FOR ME...
MAYBE I SHOULD GO OUT THERE AND TELL HIM:

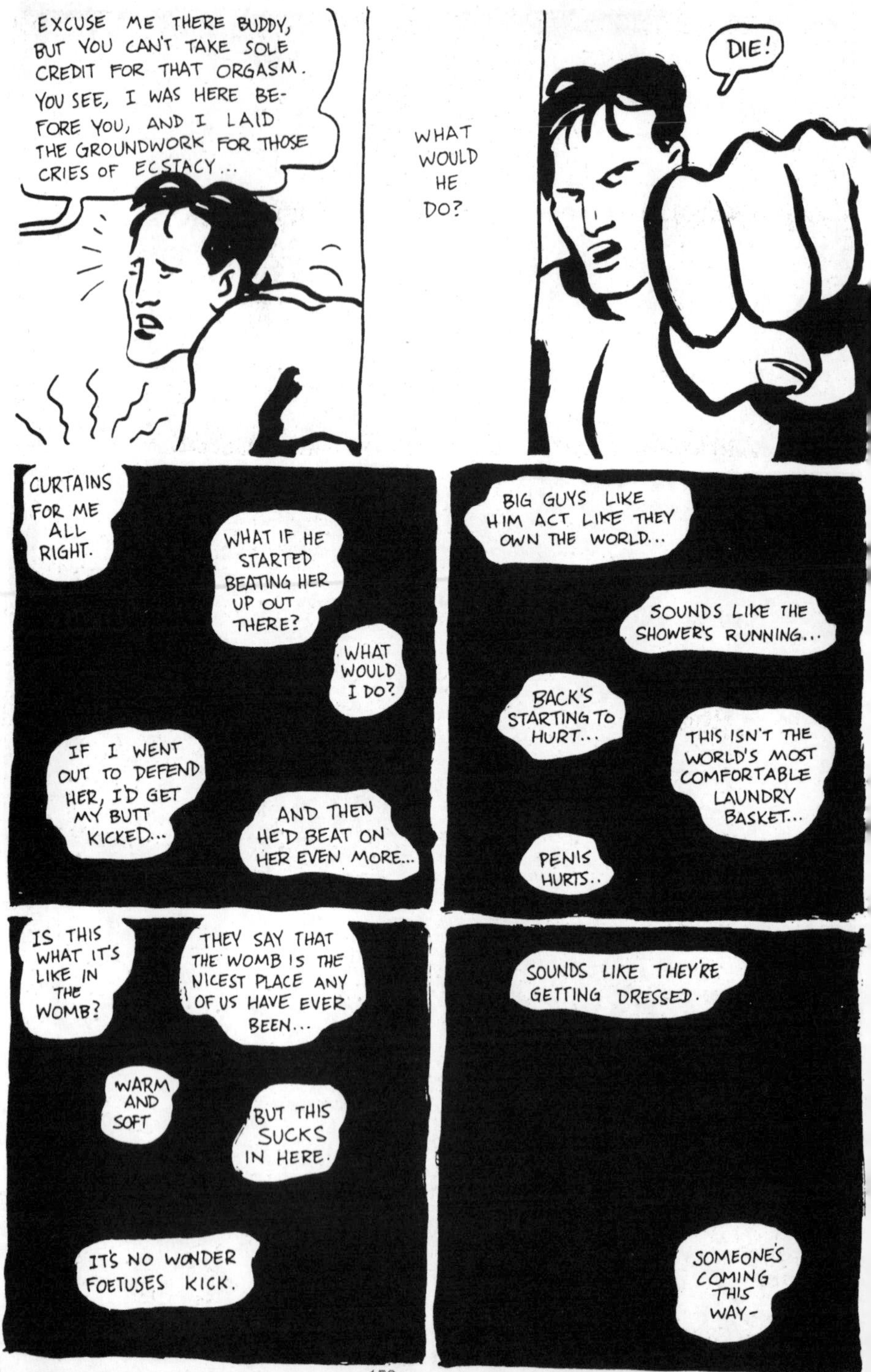
EXCUSE ME THERE BUDDY, BUT YOU CAN'T TAKE SOLE CREDIT FOR THAT ORGASM. YOU SEE, I WAS HERE BEFORE YOU, AND I LAID THE GROUNDWORK FOR THOSE CRIES OF ECSTACY...
WHAT WOULD HE DO?
DIE!
CURTAINS FOR ME ALL RIGHT.
WHAT IF HE STARTED BEATING HER UP OUT THERE?
WHAT WOULD I DO?
IF I WENT OUT TO DEFEND HER, I'D GET MY BUTT KICKED...
AND THEN HE'D BEAT ON HER EVEN MORE...
BIG GUYS LIKE HIM ACT LIKE THEY OWN THE WORLD...
SOUNDS LIKE THE SHOWER'S RUNNING...
BACK'S STARTING TO HURT...
THIS ISN'T THE WORLD'S MOST COMFORTABLE LAUNDRY BASKET...
PENIS HURTS..
IS THIS WHAT IT'S LIKE IN THE WOMB?
THEY SAY THAT THE WOMB IS THE NICEST PLACE ANY OF US HAVE EVER BEEN...
WARM AND SOFT
BUT THIS SUCKS IN HERE.
IT'S NO WONDER FOETUSES KICK.
SOUNDS LIKE THEY'RE GETTING DRESSED.
SOMEONE'S COMING THIS WAY-

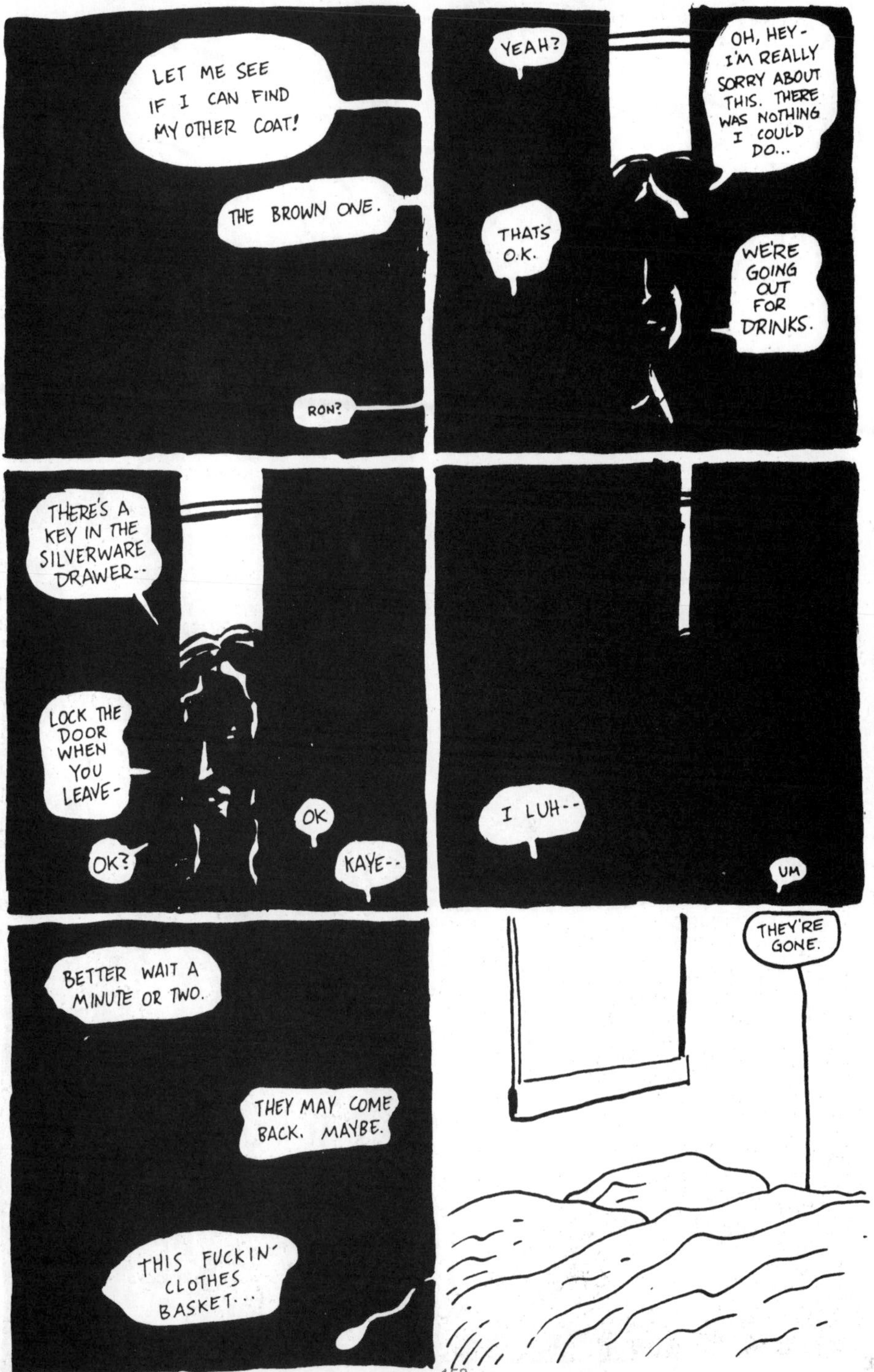
LET ME SEE IF I CAN FIND MY OTHER COAT!
THE BROWN ONE.
RON?
YEAH?
OH, HEY - I'M REALLY SORRY ABOUT THIS. THERE WAS NOTHING I COULD DO...
THAT'S O.K.
WE'RE GOING OUT FOR DRINKS.
THERE'S A KEY IN THE SILVERWARE DRAWER--
LOCK THE DOOR WHEN YOU LEAVE-
OK?
OK
KAYE--
I LUH--
UM
BETTER WAIT A MINUTE OR TWO.
THEY MAY COME BACK. MAYBE.
THIS FUCKIN' CLOTHES BASKET...
THEY'RE GONE.

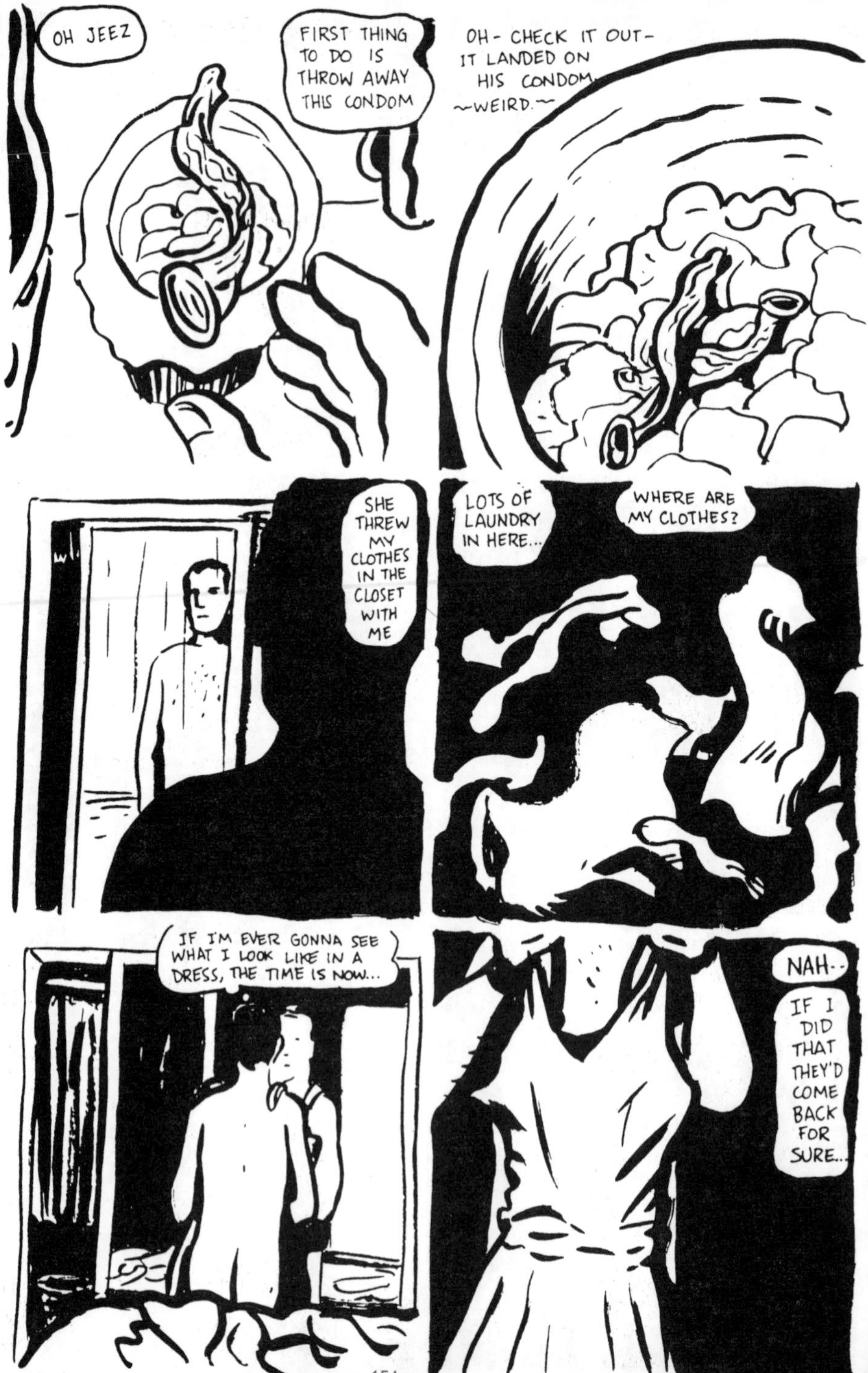
OH JEEZ
FIRST THING TO DO IS THROW AWAY THIS CONDOM
OH - CHECK IT OUT - IT LANDED ON HIS CONDOM ~WEIRD.~
SHE THREW MY CLOTHES IN THE CLOSET WITH ME
LOTS OF LAUNDRY IN HERE...
WHERE ARE MY CLOTHES?
IF I'M EVER GONNA SEE WHAT I LOOK LIKE IN A DRESS, THE TIME IS NOW...
NAH..
IF I DID THAT THEY'D COME BACK FOR SURE...

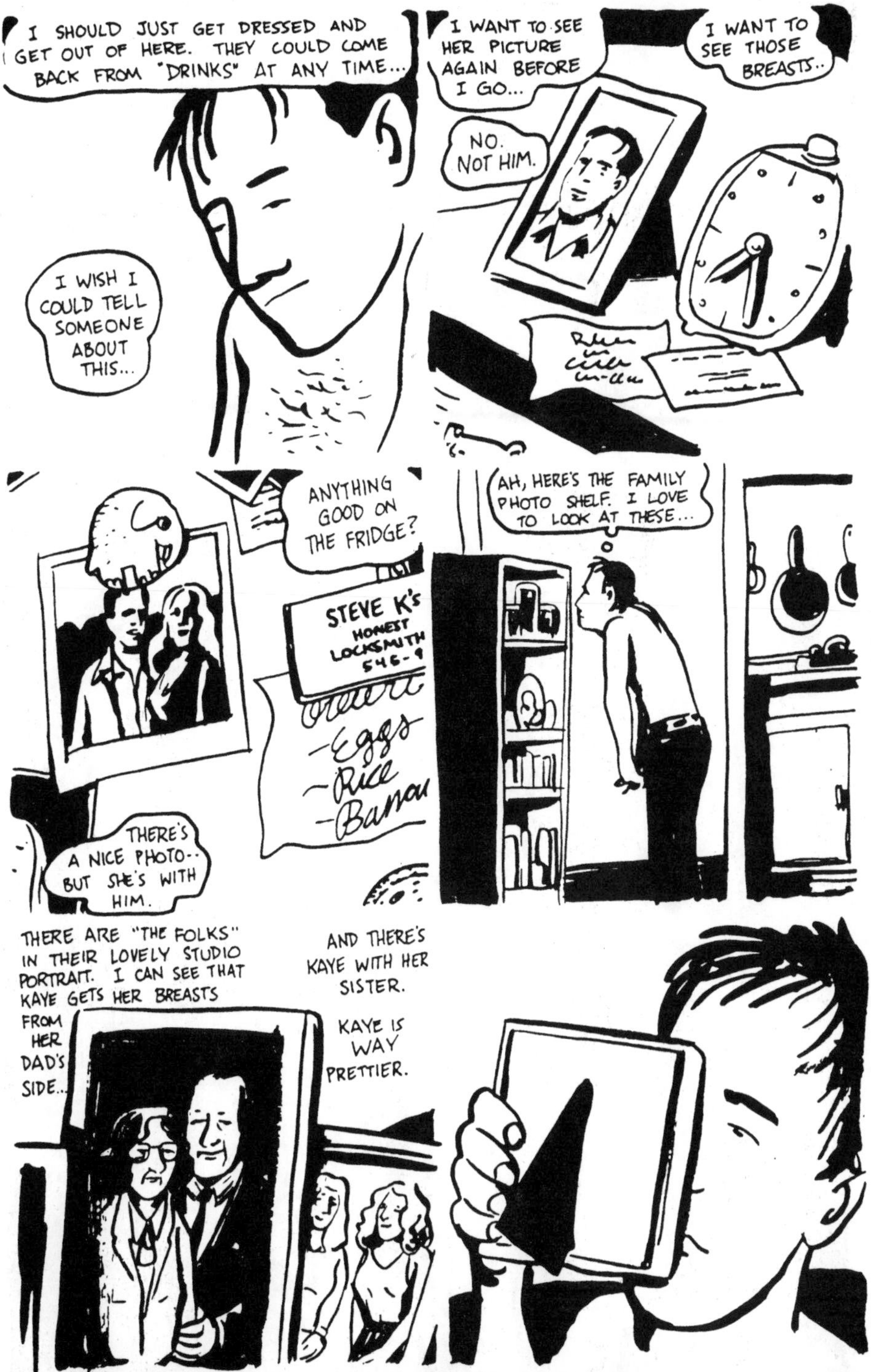

I SHOULD JUST GET DRESSED AND GET OUT OF HERE. THEY COULD COME BACK FROM "DRINKS" AT ANY TIME...
I WISH I COULD TELL SOMEONE ABOUT THIS...
I WANT TO SEE HER PICTURE AGAIN BEFORE I GO...
I WANT TO SEE THOSE BREASTS..
NO. NOT HIM.
ANYTHING GOOD ON THE FRIDGE?
STEVE K's HONEST LOCKSMITH 546-9
-Eggs
-Rice
THERE'S A NICE PHOTO-- BUT SHE'S WITH HIM.
AH, HERE'S THE FAMILY PHOTO SHELF. I LOVE TO LOOK AT THESE...
THERE ARE "THE FOLKS" IN THEIR LOVELY STUDIO PORTRAIT. I CAN SEE THAT KAYE GETS HER BREASTS FROM HER DAD'S SIDE...
AND THERE'S KAYE WITH HER SISTER.
KAYE IS WAY PRETTIER.

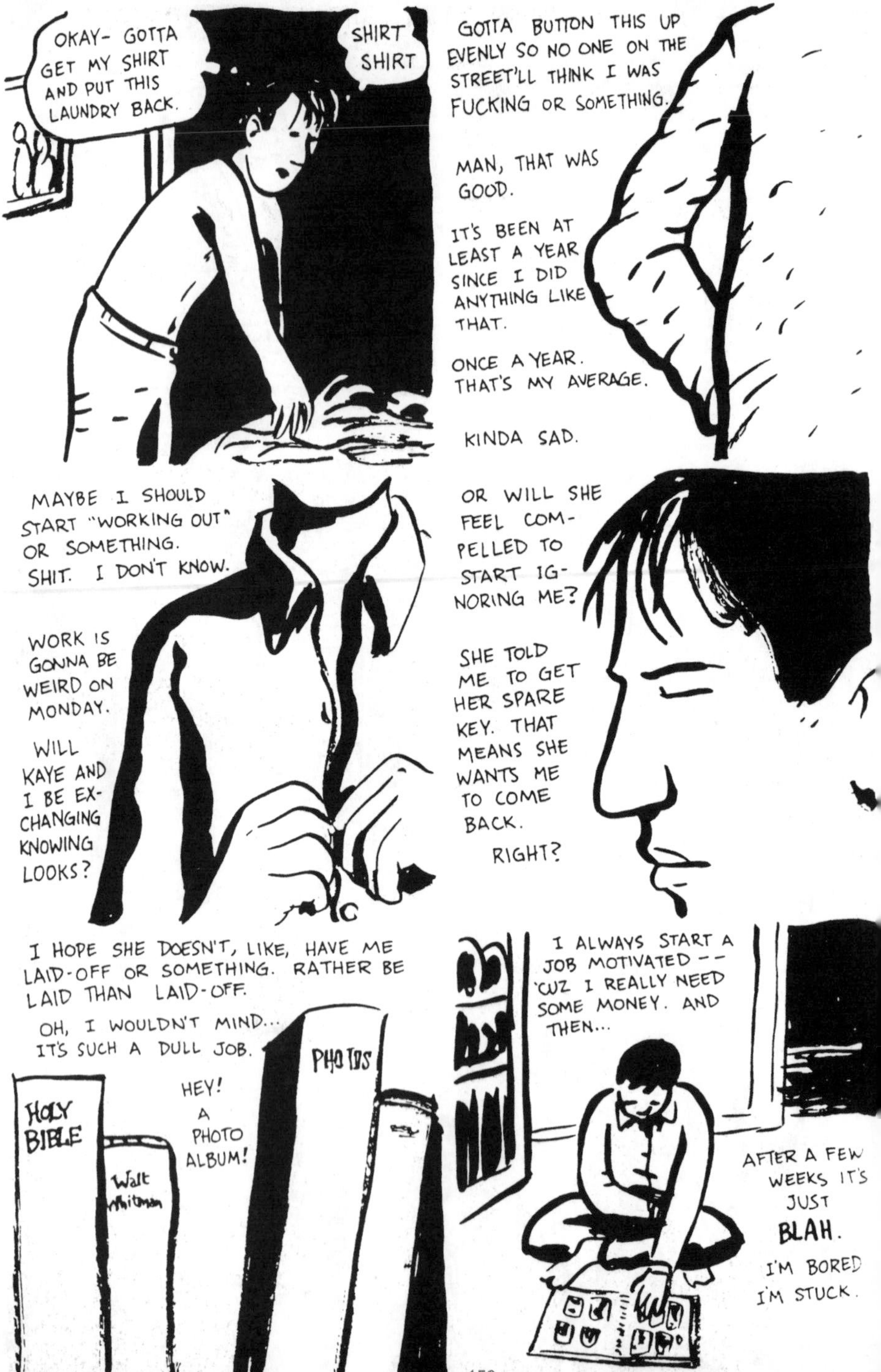
OKAY- GOTTA GET MY SHIRT AND PUT THIS LAUNDRY BACK.
SHIRT SHIRT
GOTTA BUTTON THIS UP EVENLY SO NO ONE ON THE STREET'LL THINK I WAS FUCKING OR SOMETHING.
MAN, THAT WAS GOOD.
IT'S BEEN AT LEAST A YEAR SINCE I DID ANYTHING LIKE THAT.
ONCE A YEAR. THAT'S MY AVERAGE.
KINDA SAD.
MAYBE I SHOULD START "WORKING OUT" OR SOMETHING. SHIT. I DON'T KNOW.
WORK IS GONNA BE WEIRD ON MONDAY.
WILL KAYE AND I BE EX-CHANGING KNOWING LOOKS?
OR WILL SHE FEEL COM-PELLED TO START IG-NORING ME?
SHE TOLD ME TO GET HER SPARE KEY. THAT MEANS SHE WANTS ME TO COME BACK.
RIGHT?
I HOPE SHE DOESN'T, LIKE, HAVE ME LAID-OFF OR SOMETHING. RATHER BE LAID THAN LAID-OFF.
OH, I WOULDN'T MIND... IT'S SUCH A DULL JOB.
HOLY BIBLE
Walt Whitman
HEY! A PHOTO ALBUM!
PHOTOS
I ALWAYS START A JOB MOTIVATED -- 'CUZ I REALLY NEED SOME MONEY. AND THEN...
AFTER A FEW WEEKS IT'S JUST **BLAH**.
I'M BORED I'M STUCK.

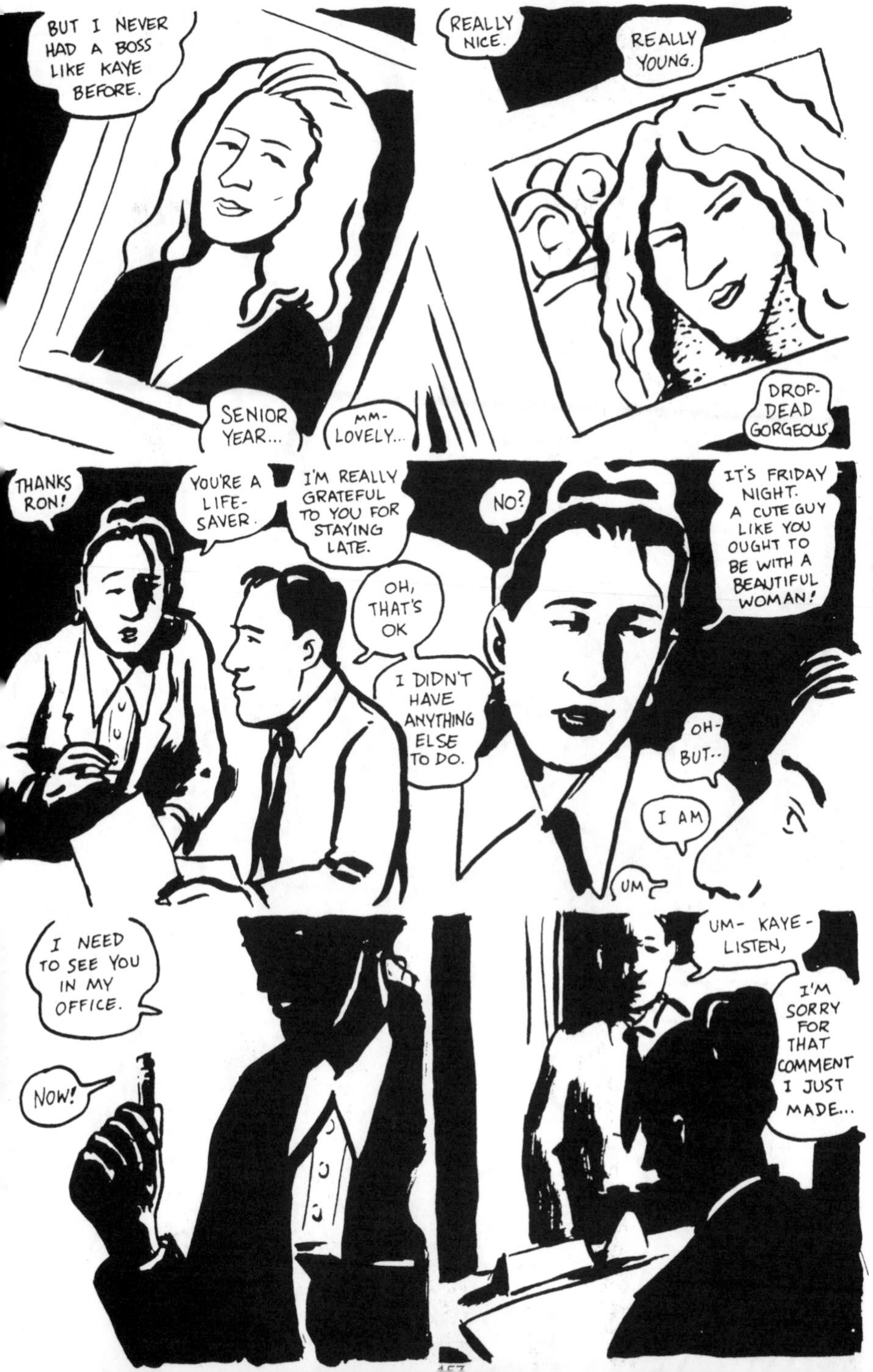
BUT I NEVER HAD A BOSS LIKE KAYE BEFORE.
SENIOR YEAR...
MM-LOVELY...
REALLY NICE.
REALLY YOUNG.
DROP-DEAD GORGEOUS.
THANKS RON!
YOU'RE A LIFE-SAVER.
I'M REALLY GRATEFUL TO YOU FOR STAYING LATE.
OH, THAT'S OK
I DIDN'T HAVE ANYTHING ELSE TO DO.
NO?
IT'S FRIDAY NIGHT. A CUTE GUY LIKE YOU OUGHT TO BE WITH A BEAUTIFUL WOMAN!
OH-BUT..
I AM
UM
I NEED TO SEE YOU IN MY OFFICE.
NOW!
UM- KAYE- LISTEN,
I'M SORRY FOR THAT COMMENT I JUST MADE...

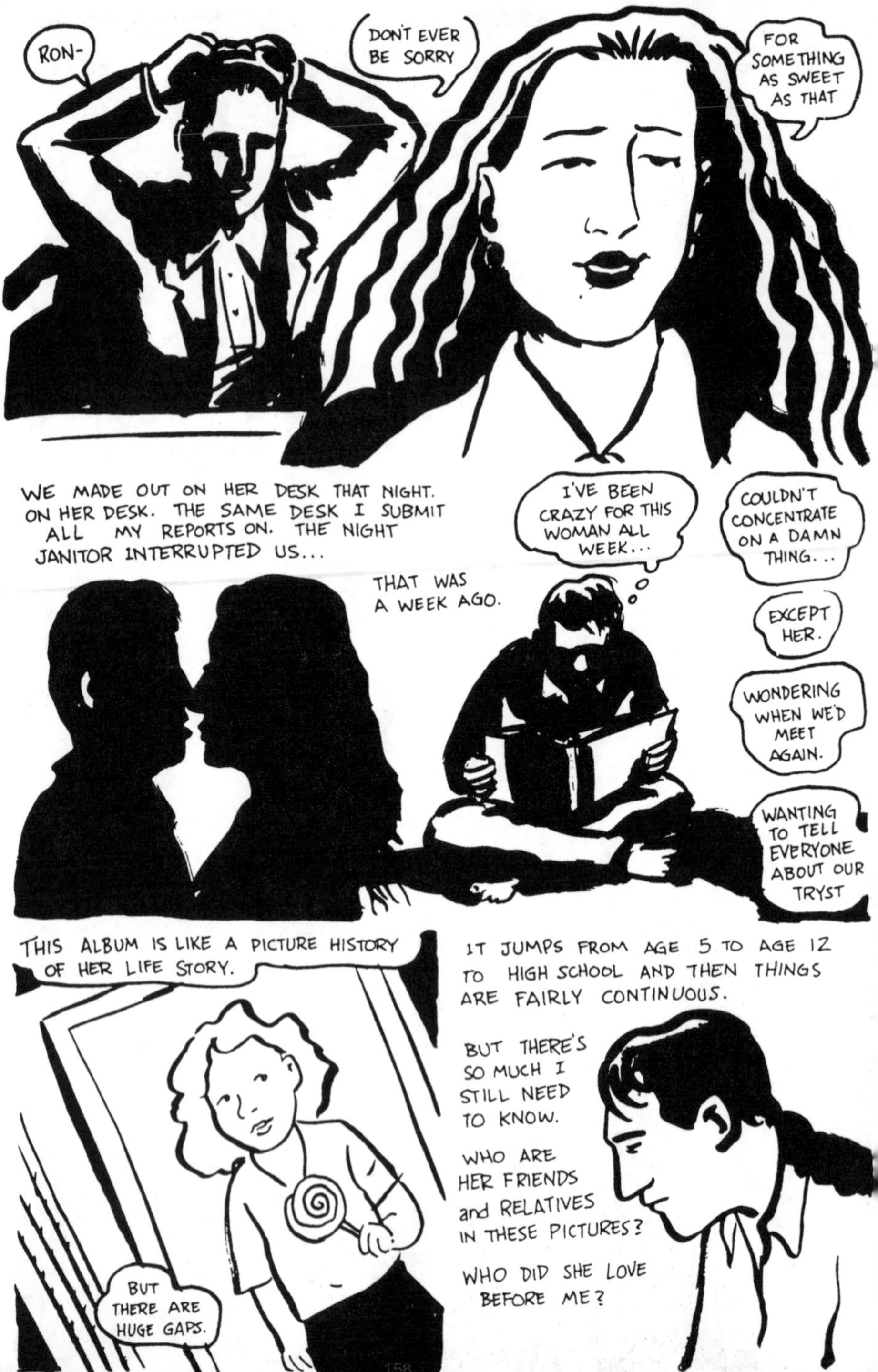

RON-
DON'T EVER BE SORRY
FOR SOMETHING AS SWEET AS THAT
WE MADE OUT ON HER DESK THAT NIGHT. ON HER DESK. THE SAME DESK I SUBMIT ALL MY REPORTS ON. THE NIGHT JANITOR INTERRUPTED US...
THAT WAS A WEEK AGO.
I'VE BEEN CRAZY FOR THIS WOMAN ALL WEEK...
COULDN'T CONCENTRATE ON A DAMN THING...
EXCEPT HER.
WONDERING WHEN WE'D MEET AGAIN.
WANTING TO TELL EVERYONE ABOUT OUR TRYST
THIS ALBUM IS LIKE A PICTURE HISTORY OF HER LIFE STORY.
BUT THERE ARE HUGE GAPS.
IT JUMPS FROM AGE 5 TO AGE 12 TO HIGH SCHOOL AND THEN THINGS ARE FAIRLY CONTINUOUS.
BUT THERE'S SO MUCH I STILL NEED TO KNOW.
WHO ARE HER FRIENDS and RELATIVES IN THESE PICTURES?
WHO DID SHE LOVE BEFORE ME?

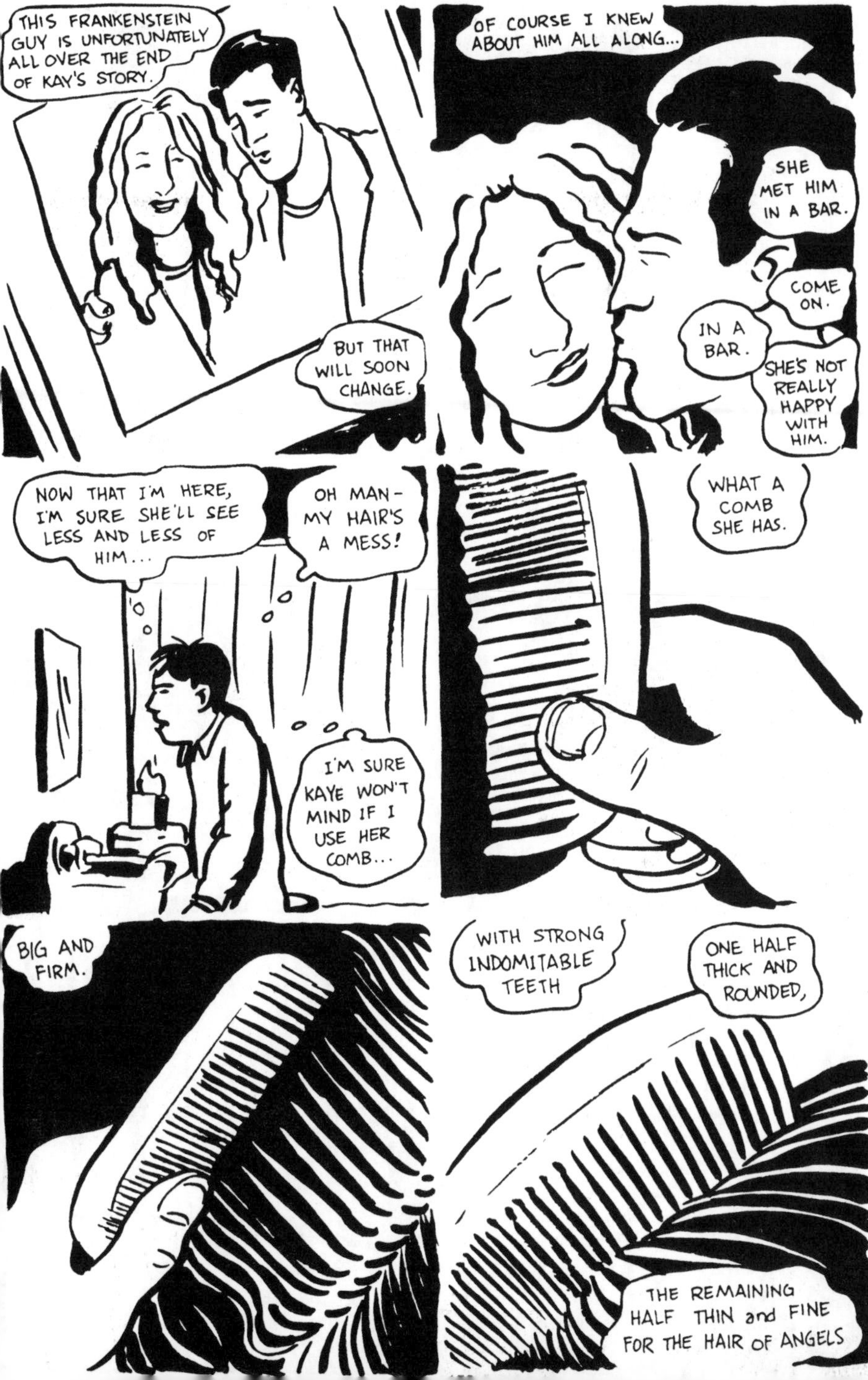
THIS FRANKENSTEIN GUY IS UNFORTUNATELY ALL OVER THE END OF KAY'S STORY.
BUT THAT WILL SOON CHANGE.
OF COURSE I KNEW ABOUT HIM ALL ALONG...
SHE MET HIM IN A BAR.
COME ON.
IN A BAR.
SHE'S NOT REALLY HAPPY WITH HIM.
NOW THAT I'M HERE, I'M SURE SHE'LL SEE LESS AND LESS OF HIM...
OH MAN - MY HAIR'S A MESS!
I'M SURE KAYE WON'T MIND IF I USE HER COMB...
WHAT A COMB SHE HAS.
BIG AND FIRM.
WITH STRONG INDOMITABLE TEETH
ONE HALF THICK AND ROUNDED,
THE REMAINING HALF THIN and FINE FOR THE HAIR OF ANGELS

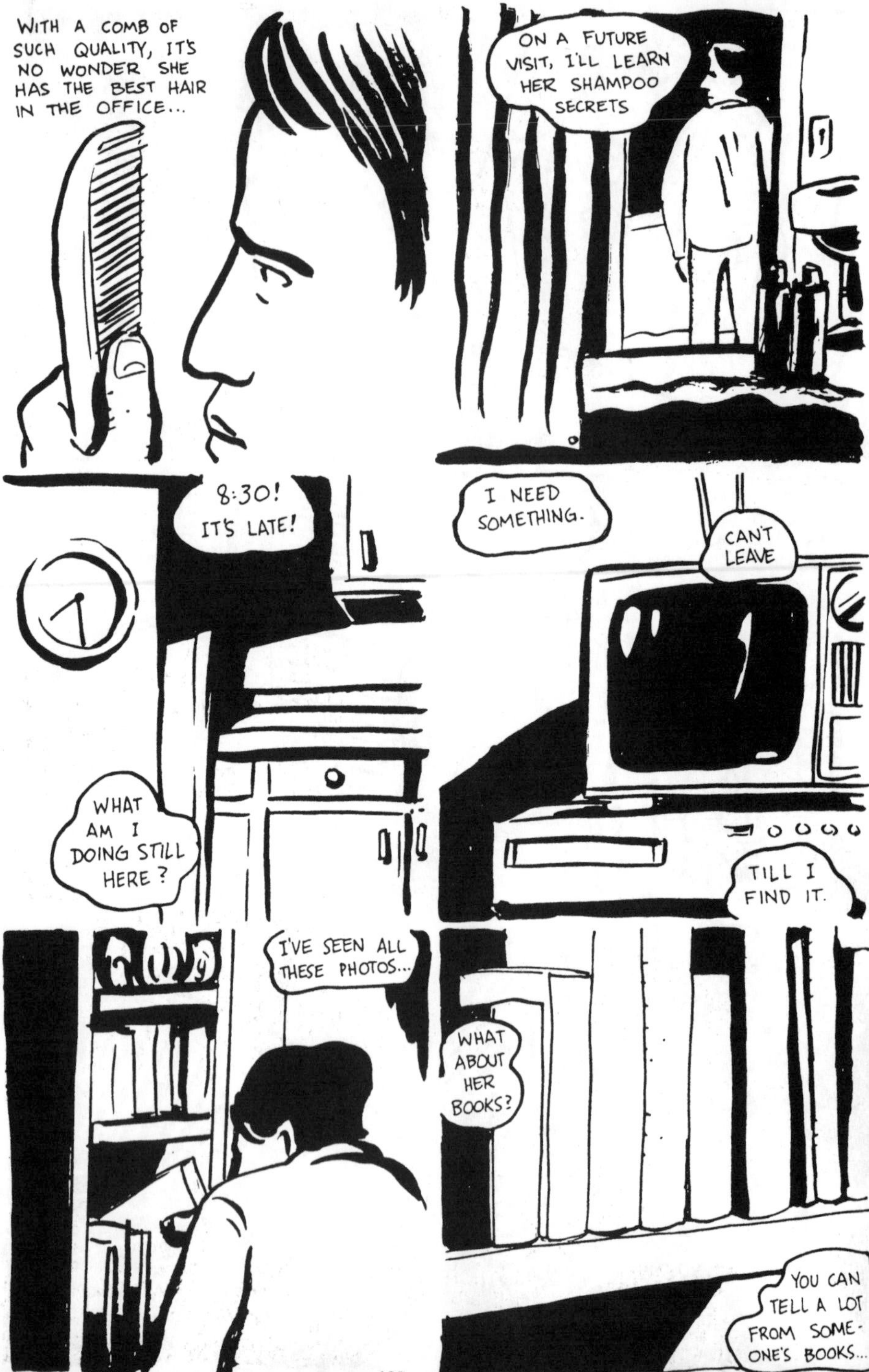

WITH A COMB OF SUCH QUALITY, IT'S NO WONDER SHE HAS THE BEST HAIR IN THE OFFICE...
ON A FUTURE VISIT, I'LL LEARN HER SHAMPOO SECRETS
8:30! IT'S LATE!
WHAT AM I DOING STILL HERE?
I NEED SOMETHING.
CAN'T LEAVE
TILL I FIND IT.
I'VE SEEN ALL THESE PHOTOS...
WHAT ABOUT HER BOOKS?
YOU CAN TELL A LOT FROM SOME-ONE'S BOOKS...

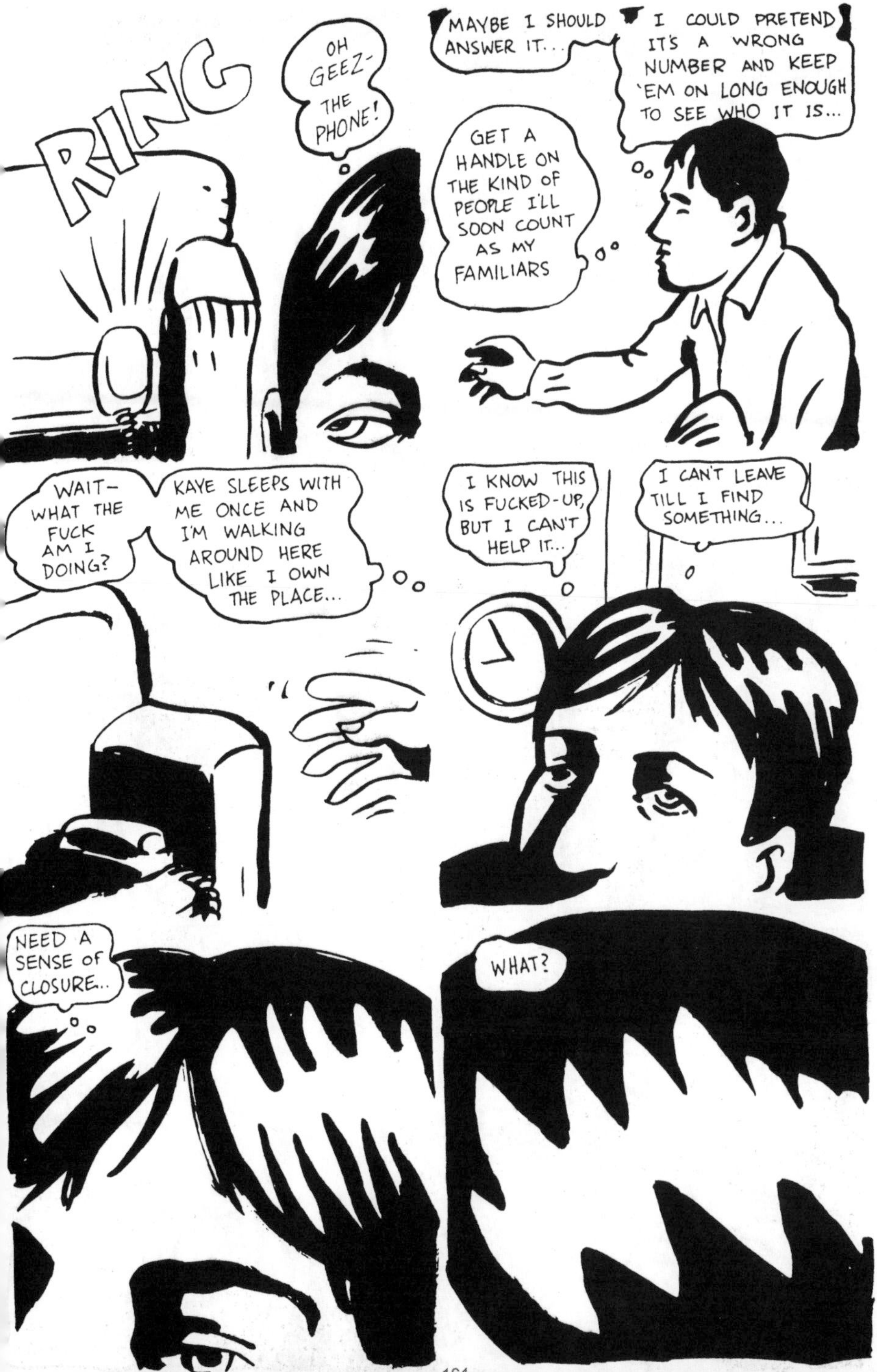
RING
OH GEEZ- THE PHONE!
MAYBE I SHOULD ANSWER IT...
I COULD PRETEND IT'S A WRONG NUMBER AND KEEP 'EM ON LONG ENOUGH TO SEE WHO IT IS...
GET A HANDLE ON THE KIND OF PEOPLE I'LL SOON COUNT AS MY FAMILIARS
WAIT- WHAT THE FUCK AM I DOING?
KAYE SLEEPS WITH ME ONCE AND I'M WALKING AROUND HERE LIKE I OWN THE PLACE...
I KNOW THIS IS FUCKED-UP, BUT I CAN'T HELP IT...
I CAN'T LEAVE TILL I FIND SOMETHING...
NEED A SENSE OF CLOSURE...
WHAT?

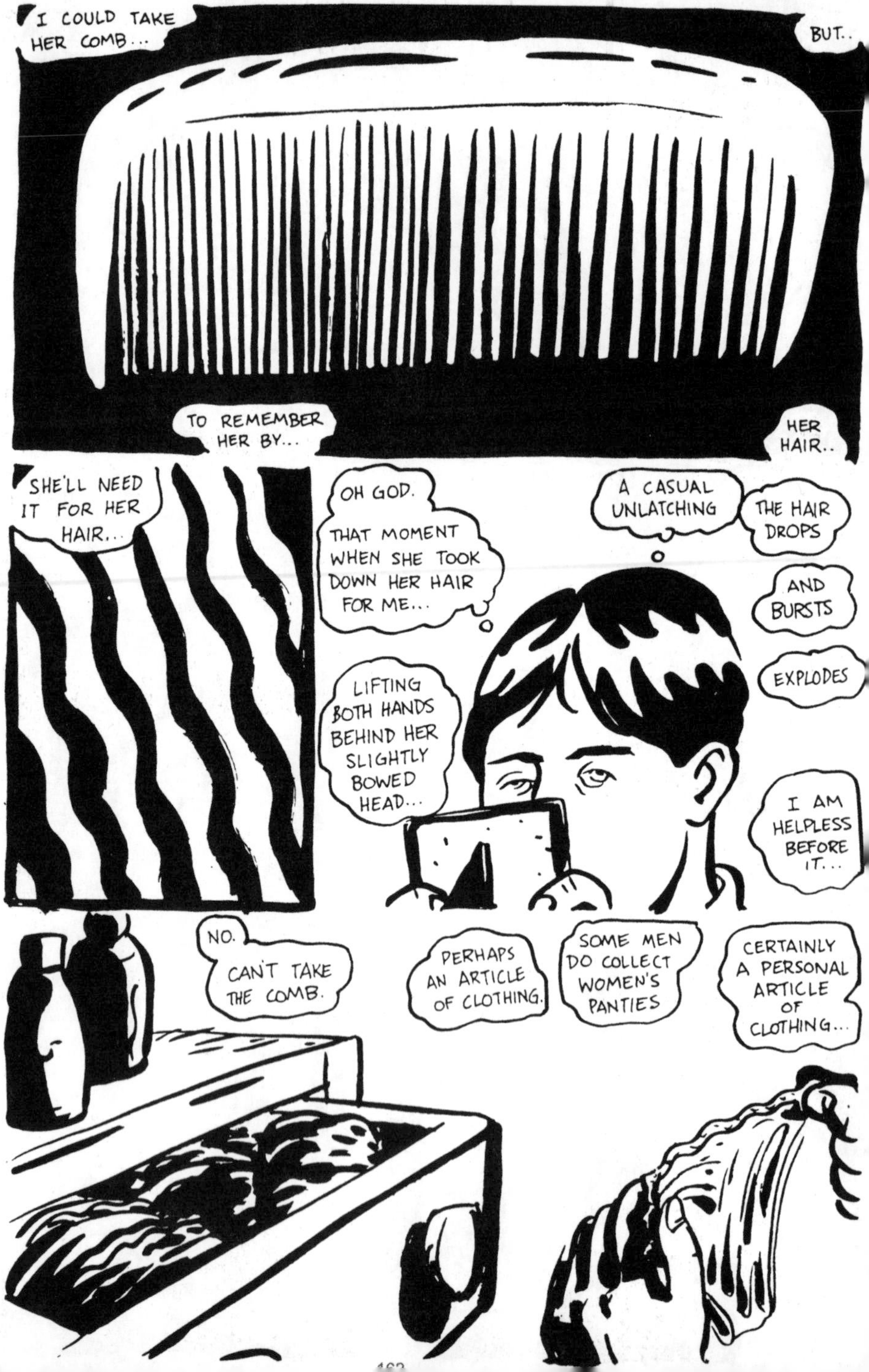
I COULD TAKE HER COMB...
BUT..
TO REMEMBER HER BY...
HER HAIR..
SHE'LL NEED IT FOR HER HAIR...
OH GOD.
THAT MOMENT WHEN SHE TOOK DOWN HER HAIR FOR ME...
LIFTING BOTH HANDS BEHIND HER SLIGHTLY BOWED HEAD...
A CASUAL UNLATCHING
THE HAIR DROPS
AND BURSTS
EXPLODES
I AM HELPLESS BEFORE IT...
NO.
CAN'T TAKE THE COMB.
PERHAPS AN ARTICLE OF CLOTHING.
SOME MEN DO COLLECT WOMEN'S PANTIES
CERTAINLY A PERSONAL ARTICLE OF CLOTHING...

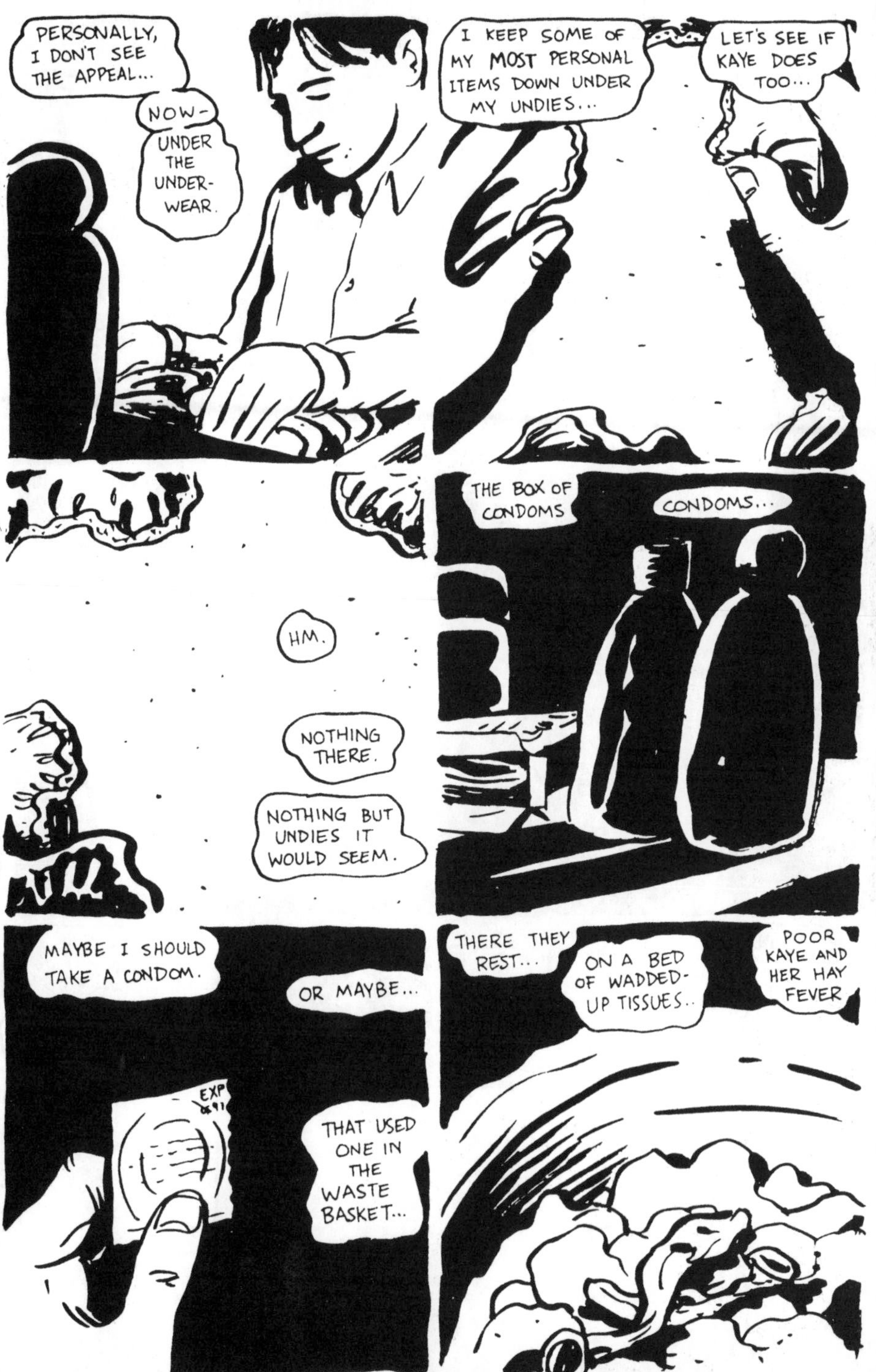
PERSONALLY, I DON'T SEE THE APPEAL...
NOW-
UNDER THE UNDER-WEAR.
I KEEP SOME OF MY MOST PERSONAL ITEMS DOWN UNDER MY UNDIES...
LET'S SEE IF KAYE DOES TOO...
HM.
NOTHING THERE.
NOTHING BUT UNDIES IT WOULD SEEM.
THE BOX OF CONDOMS
CONDOMS...
MAYBE I SHOULD TAKE A CONDOM.
OR MAYBE...
EXP
THAT USED ONE IN THE WASTE BASKET...
THERE THEY REST...
ON A BED OF WADDED-UP TISSUES..
POOR KAYE AND HER HAY FEVER

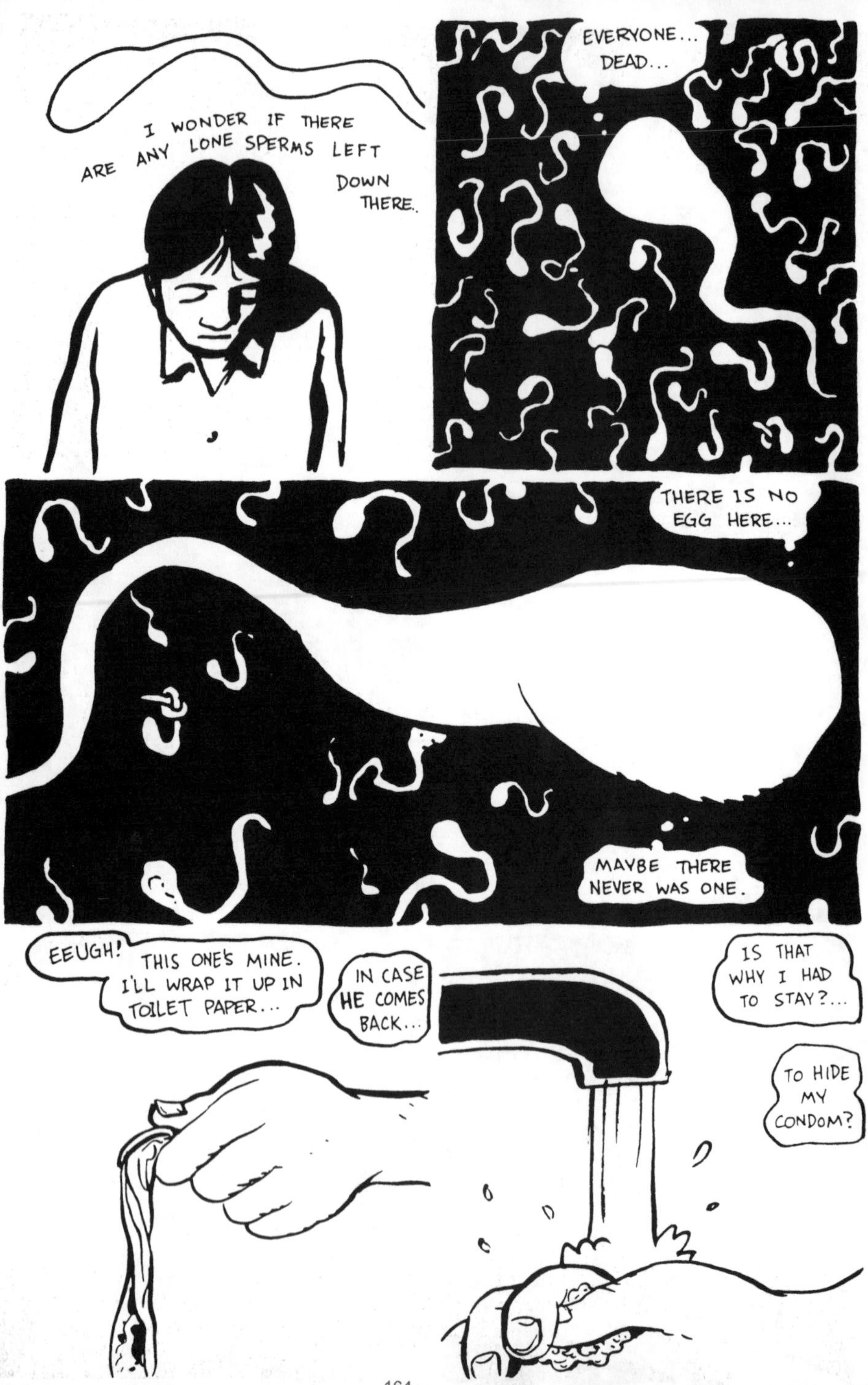
I WONDER IF THERE ARE ANY LONE SPERMS LEFT DOWN THERE.
EVERYONE... DEAD...
THERE IS NO EGG HERE...
MAYBE THERE NEVER WAS ONE.
EEUGH!
THIS ONE'S MINE. I'LL WRAP IT UP IN TOILET PAPER...
IN CASE HE COMES BACK...
IS THAT WHY I HAD TO STAY?...
TO HIDE MY CONDOM?

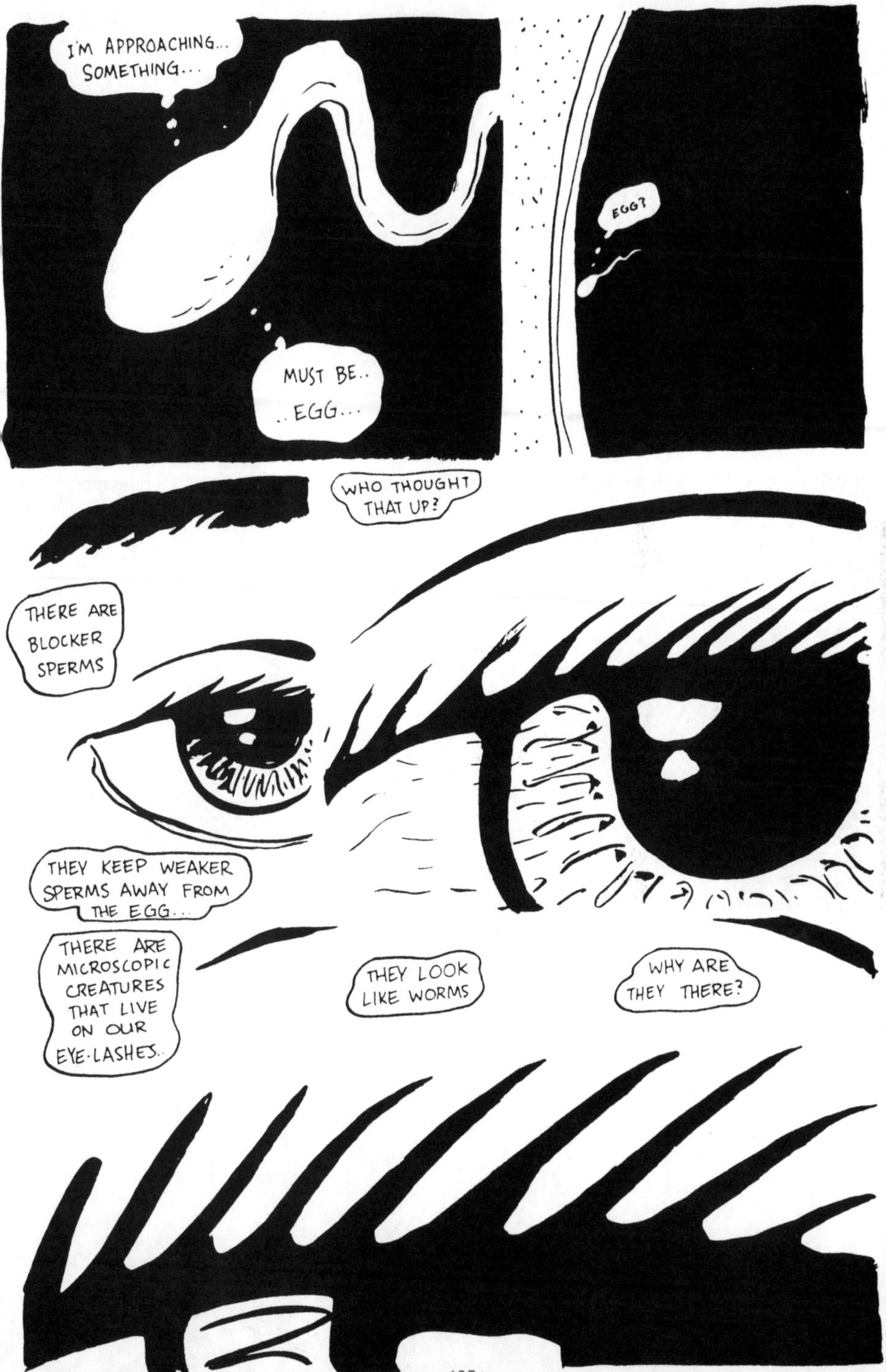
I'M APPROACHING... SOMETHING...
MUST BE.. ..EGG...
EGG?
WHO THOUGHT THAT UP?
THERE ARE BLOCKER SPERMS
THEY KEEP WEAKER SPERMS AWAY FROM THE EGG...
THERE ARE MICROSCOPIC CREATURES THAT LIVE ON OUR EYE-LASHES..
THEY LOOK LIKE WORMS
WHY ARE THEY THERE?

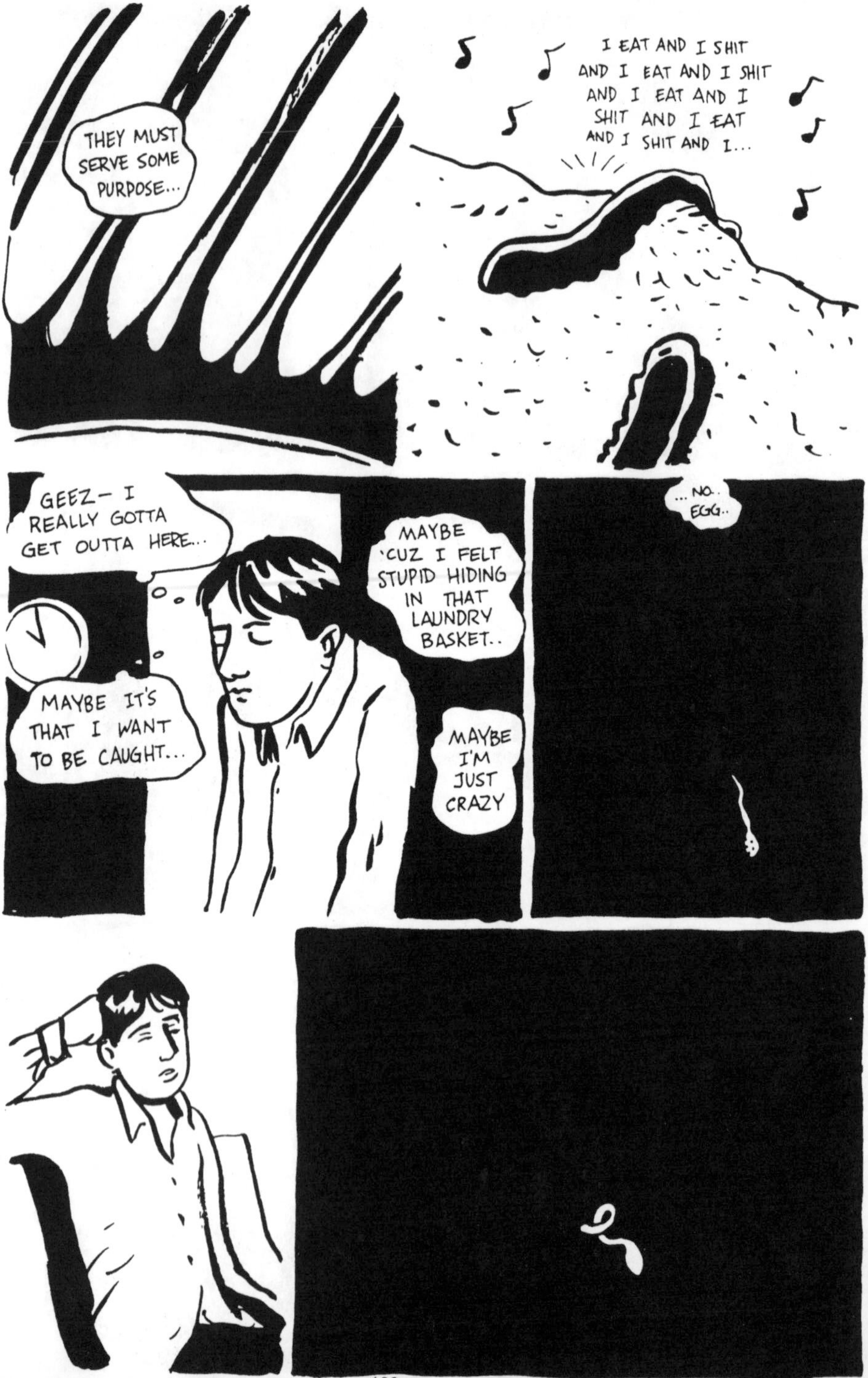
THEY MUST SERVE SOME PURPOSE...
I EAT AND I SHIT AND I EAT AND I SHIT AND I EAT AND I SHIT AND I EAT AND I SHIT AND I...
GEEZ— I REALLY GOTTA GET OUTTA HERE...
MAYBE IT'S THAT I WANT TO BE CAUGHT...
MAYBE 'CUZ I FELT STUPID HIDING IN THAT LAUNDRY BASKET..
MAYBE I'M JUST CRAZY
... NO.. EGG..

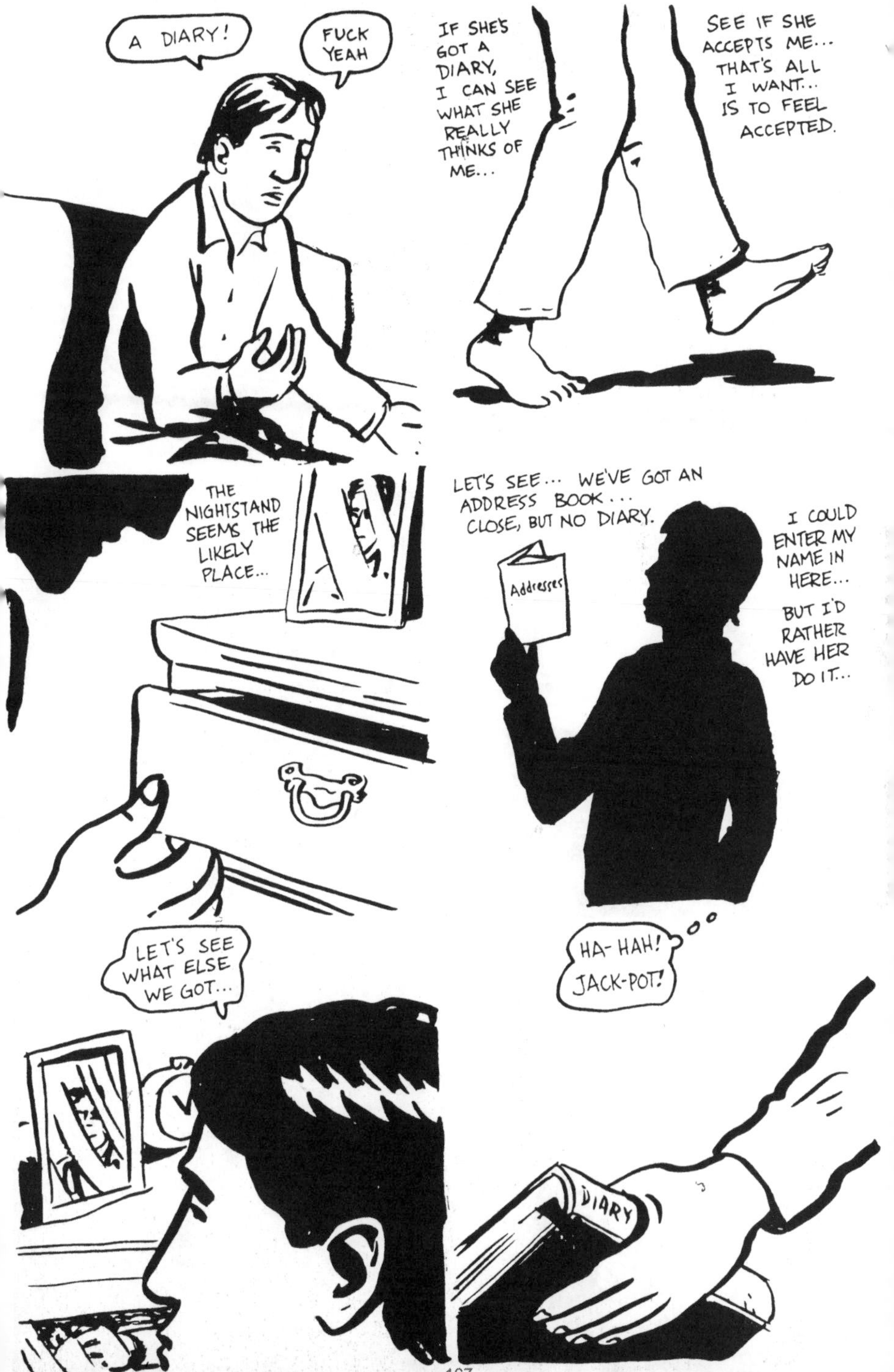
A DIARY!
FUCK YEAH
IF SHE'S GOT A DIARY, I CAN SEE WHAT SHE REALLY THINKS OF ME...
SEE IF SHE ACCEPTS ME... THAT'S ALL I WANT... IS TO FEEL ACCEPTED.
THE NIGHTSTAND SEEMS THE LIKELY PLACE...
LET'S SEE... WE'VE GOT AN ADDRESS BOOK... CLOSE, BUT NO DIARY.
Addresses
I COULD ENTER MY NAME IN HERE...
BUT I'D RATHER HAVE HER DO IT...
LET'S SEE WHAT ELSE WE GOT...
HA-HAH! JACK-POT!
DIARY

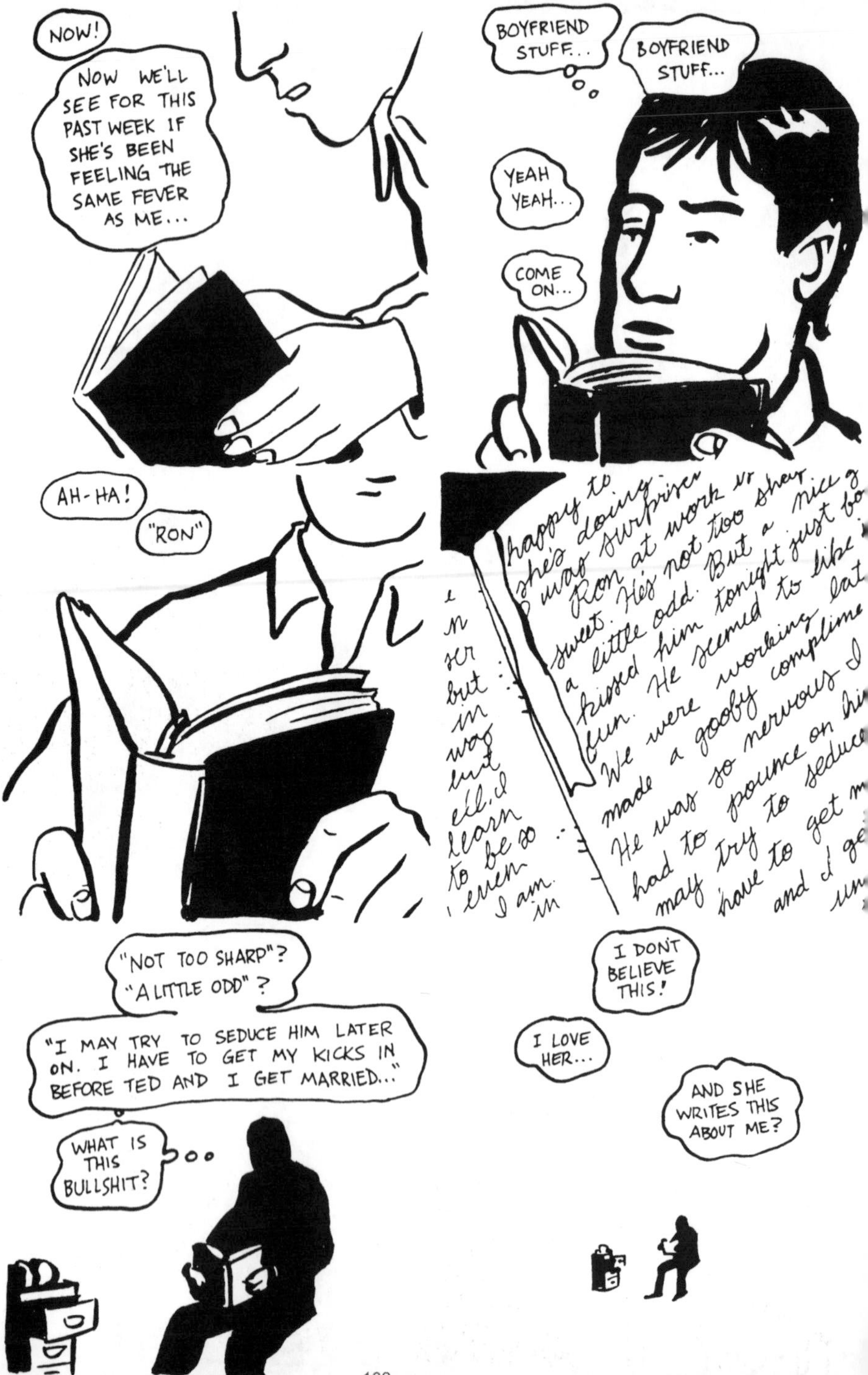

NOW!
NOW WE'LL SEE FOR THIS PAST WEEK IF SHE'S BEEN FEELING THE SAME FEVER AS ME...
BOYFRIEND STUFF...
BOYFRIEND STUFF...
YEAH YEAH...
COME ON...
AH-HA!
"RON"
"NOT TOO SHARP"? "A LITTLE ODD"?
"I MAY TRY TO SEDUCE HIM LATER ON. I HAVE TO GET MY KICKS IN BEFORE TED AND I GET MARRIED..."
WHAT IS THIS BULLSHIT?
I DON'T BELIEVE THIS!
I LOVE HER...
AND SHE WRITES THIS ABOUT ME?

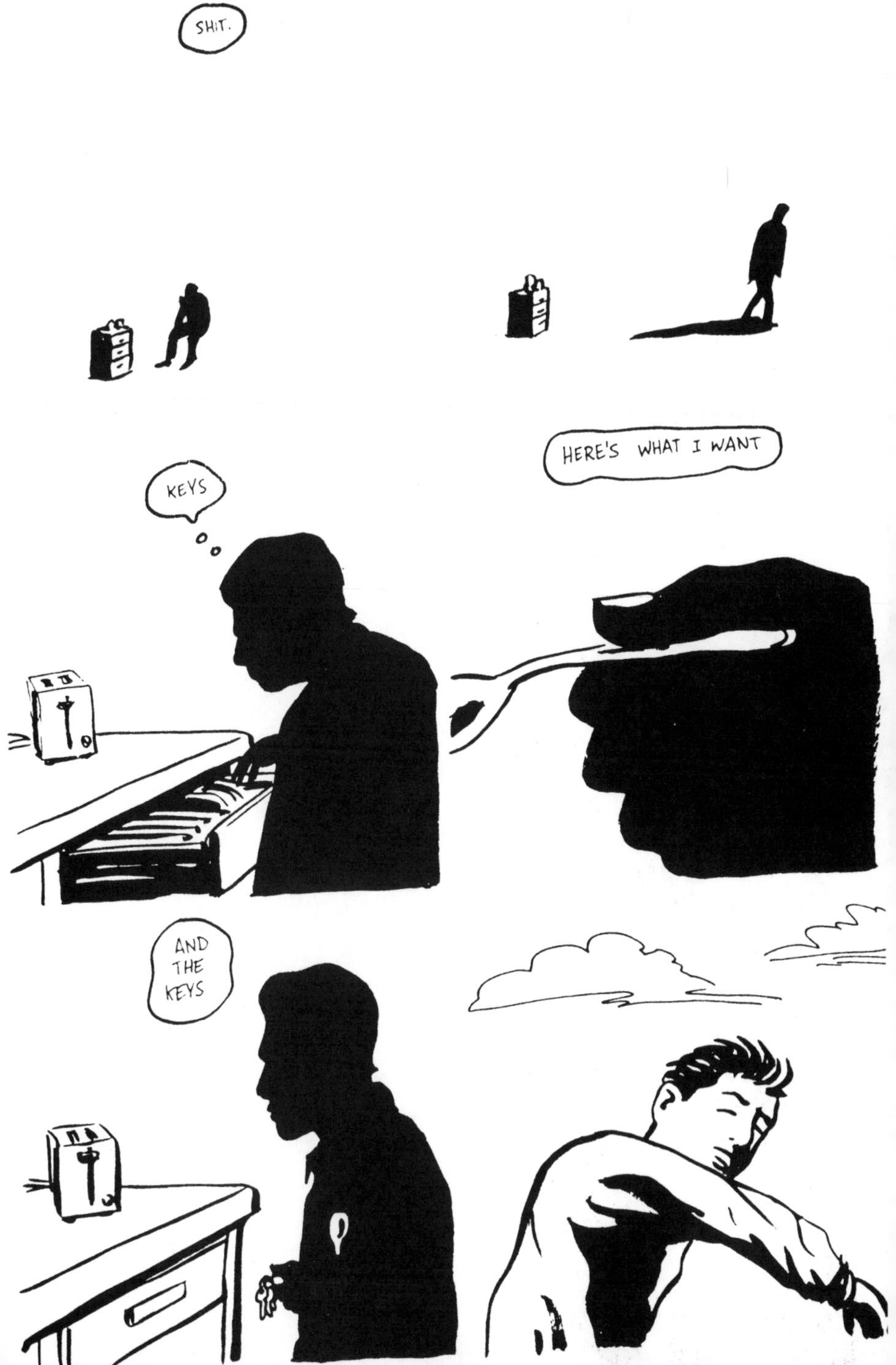
SHIT.
KEYS
HERE'S WHAT I WANT
AND THE KEYS

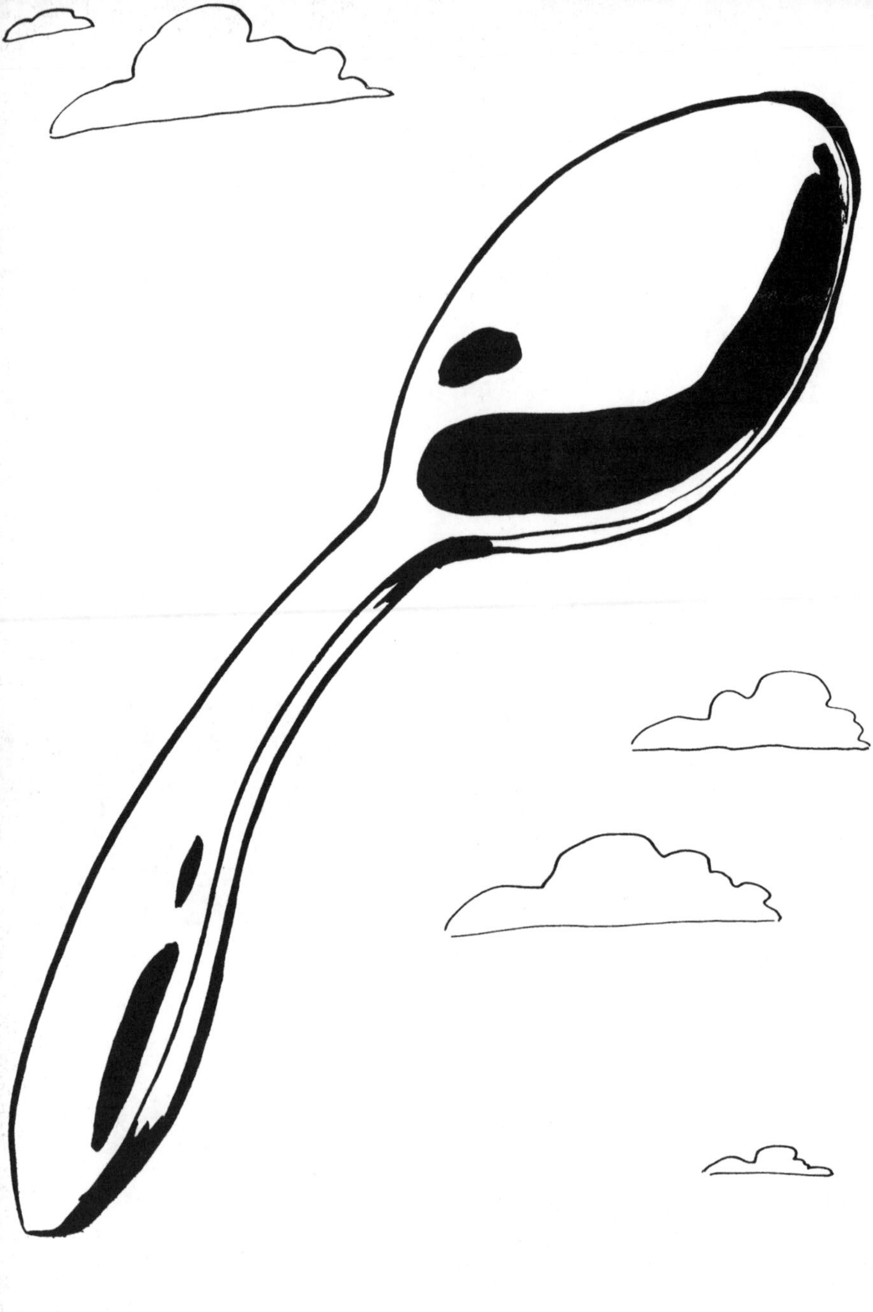

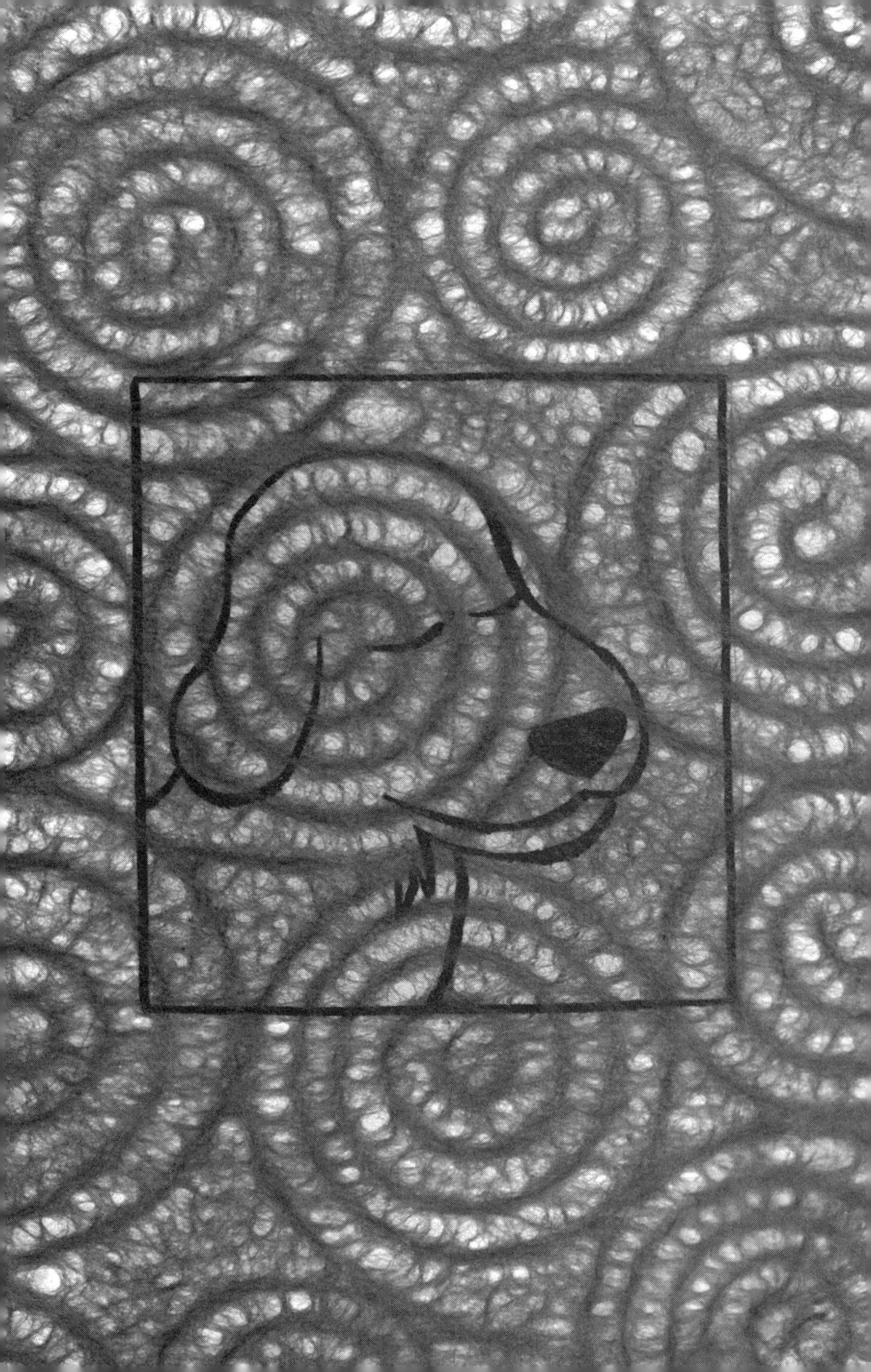

K. Thor Jensen

K. Thor Jensen is the Camper Van Beethoven of comics.

Okay, maybe not. I don't even know why I wrote that. I just always wanted to say it, so there you go.

[Restarting...]

K. Thor's Untitled 24-hour comic is a contemplative and beautiful story. Done entirely in a 24 hour period from March 10-11, 2002, the young artist's tale of Zen and personal discovery never feels rushed or strained. The style is simple, but full. The compositions are thoughtful and even challenging at times. Looking at such a gem, one can't help wondering if Thor might have it in him to set aside *100 days* at some point in the future and just keep going—without rest, without food even—and produce a 2,400 page graphic novel of equal consistency and beauty before lying down on a park bench and quietly expiring with the day.

My one regret in publishing this great little comic is that we can't possibly do justice to the cover of the original, hand-assembled mini, which was overlaid with a delicate, textured material that immeasurably adds to effect of the cover image. Ah well. I've got mine.

This comic was one of many 24-hour comics produced at a group event dubbed "Comics Lockdown", a gathering of 15 cartoonists over a long weekend in an apartment in Queens, New York. I knew a lot of the participants and they're a warm and supportive bunch. Yet somehow, it always felt to me like Thor created his 24-hour comic by himself. Perhaps the note that accompanied the copy he sent helped give me the impression.

> *Scott -*
>
> *One 24-hour comic. It is raining outside, I'm homeless and my heart hurts. Fuck this Zen shit, I need a beer.*
> *- KTJ*

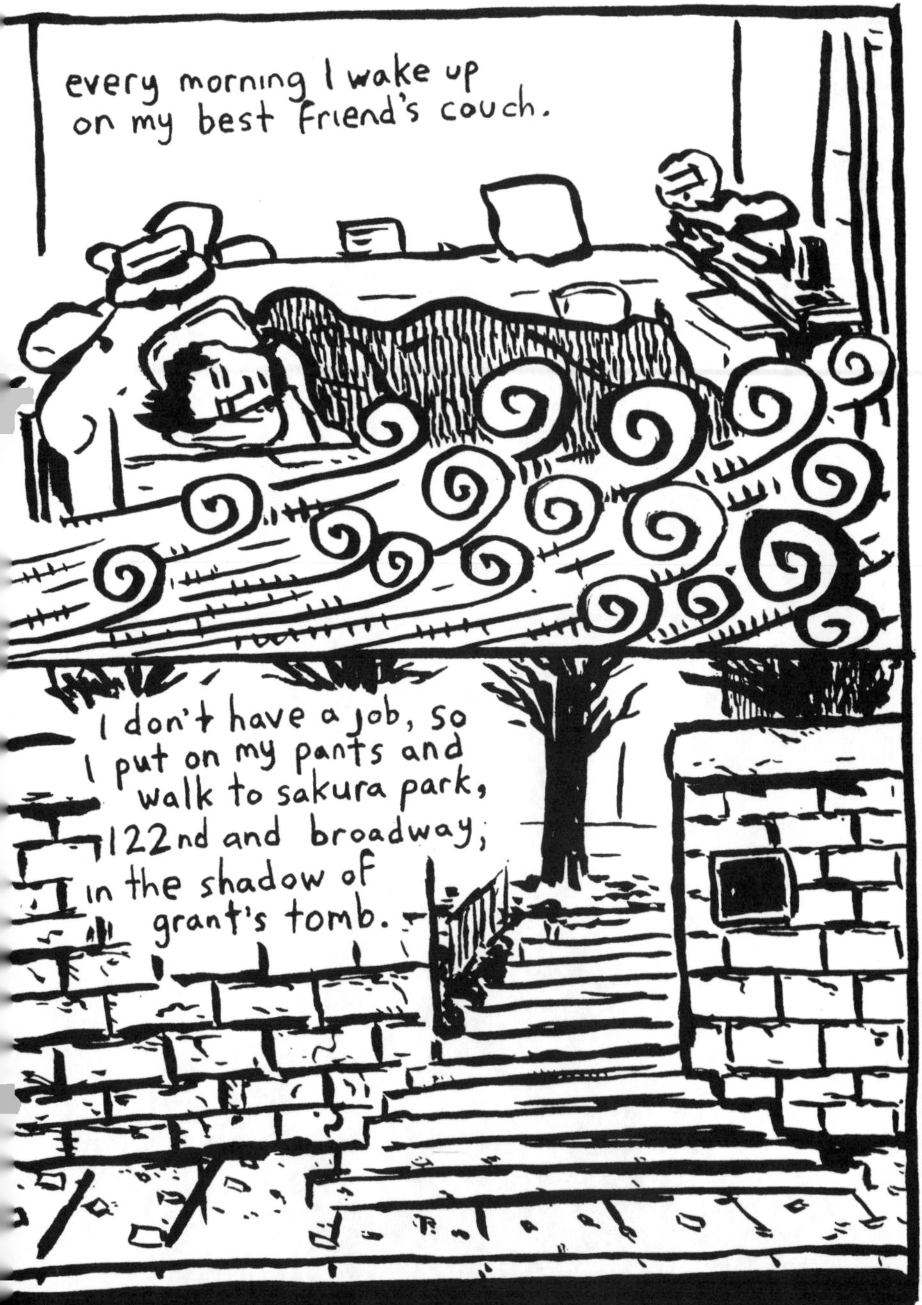
every morning I wake up on my best friend's couch.
I don't have a job, so I put on my pants and walk to sakura park, 122nd and broadway, in the shadow of grant's tomb.

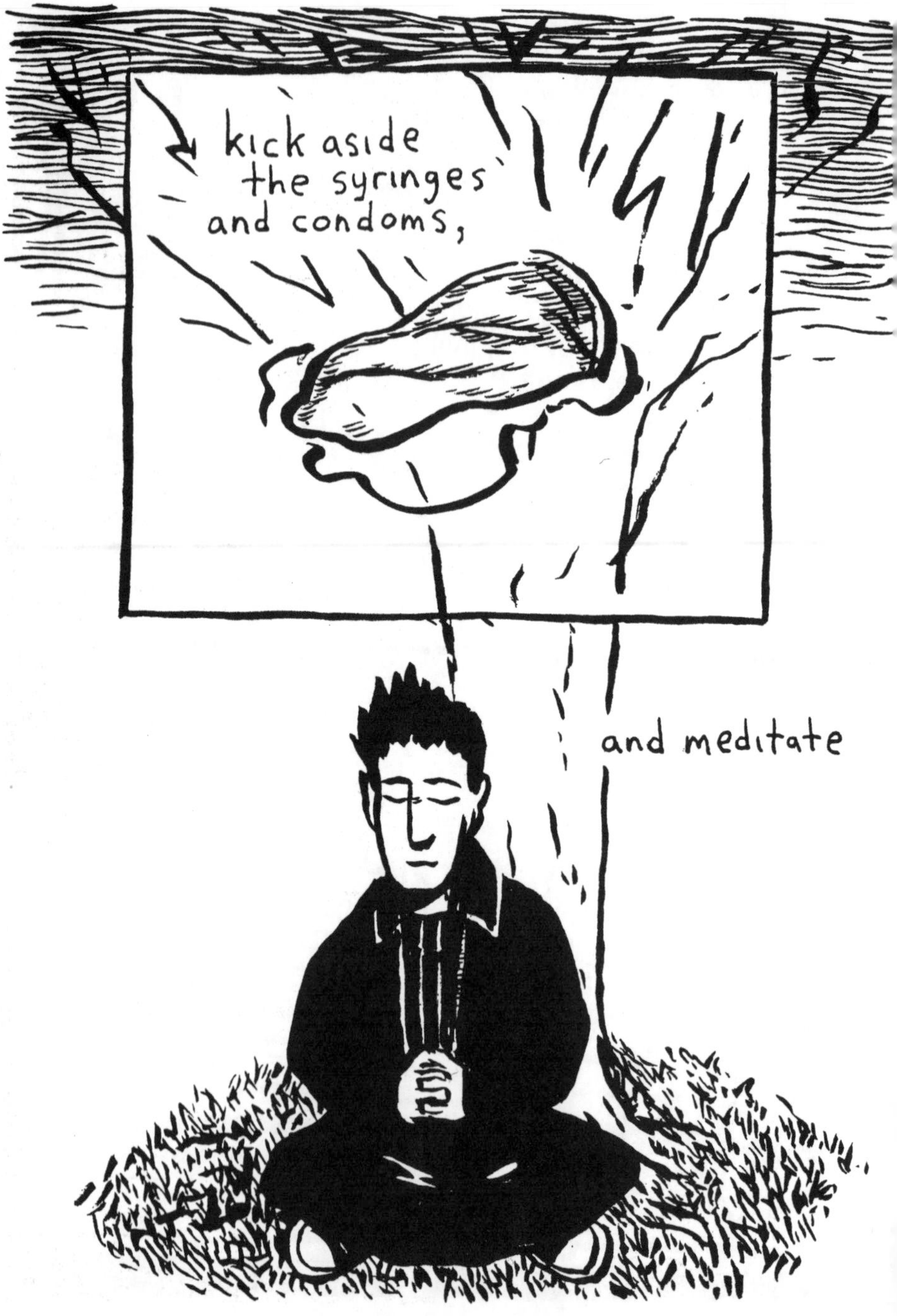
kick aside the syringes and condoms,
and meditate

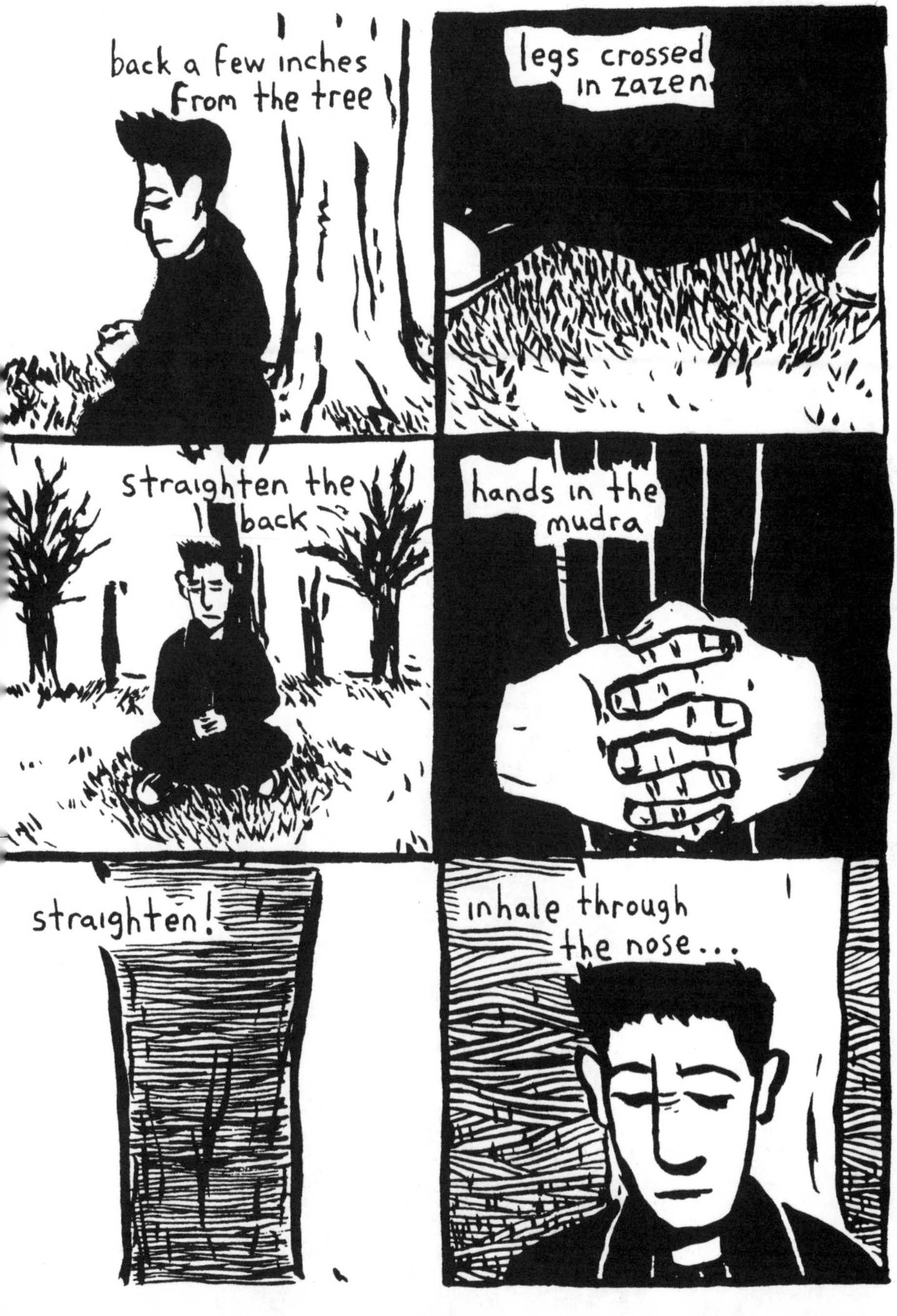
back a few inches from the tree
legs crossed in zazen
straighten the back
hands in the mudra
straighten!
inhale through the nose...

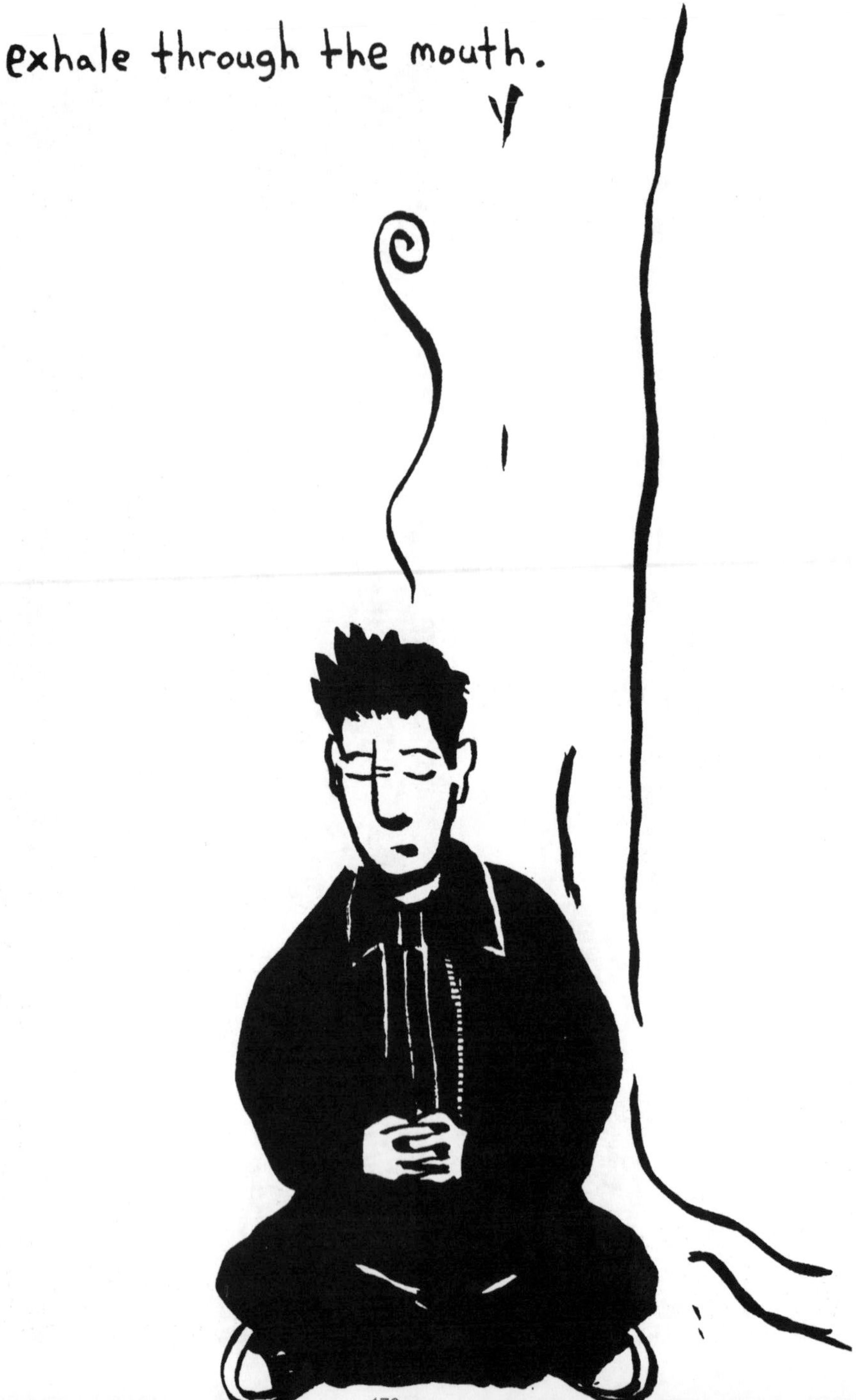
exhale through the mouth.

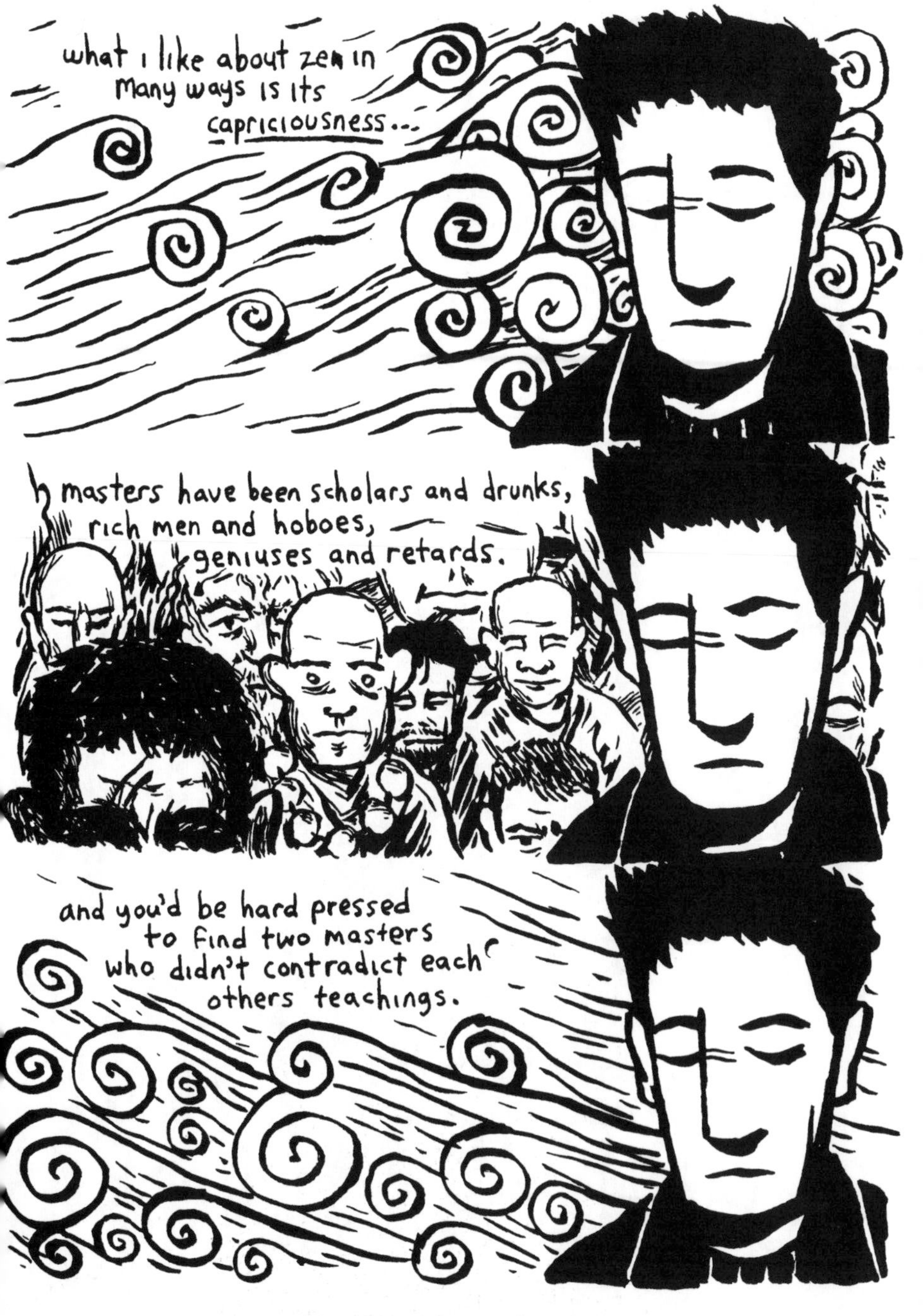
what i like about zen in many ways is its capriciousness...
masters have been scholars and drunks, rich men and hoboes, geniuses and retards.
and you'd be hard pressed to find two masters who didn't contradict each others teachings.

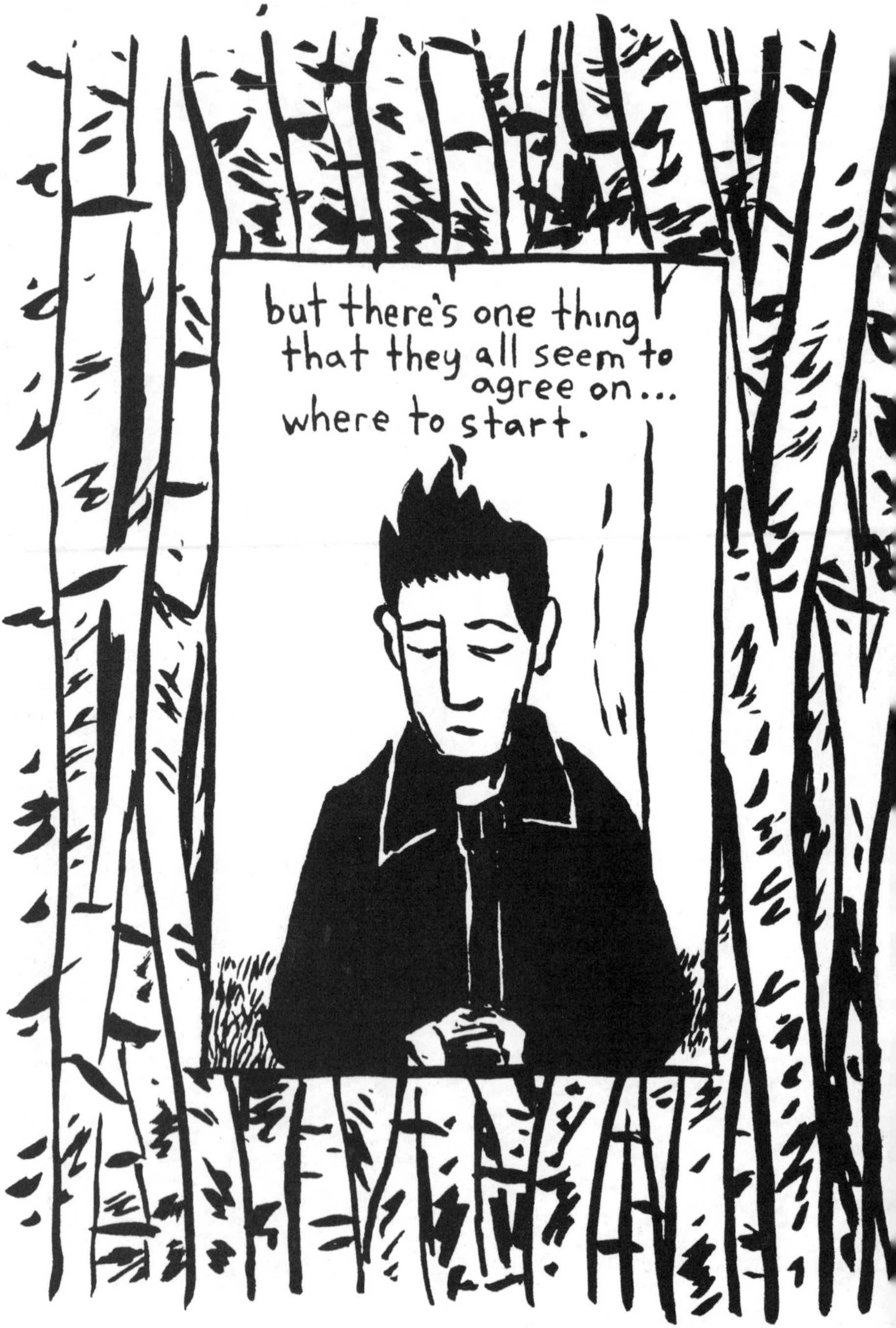
but there's one thing that they all seem to agree on...
where to start.

the first koan

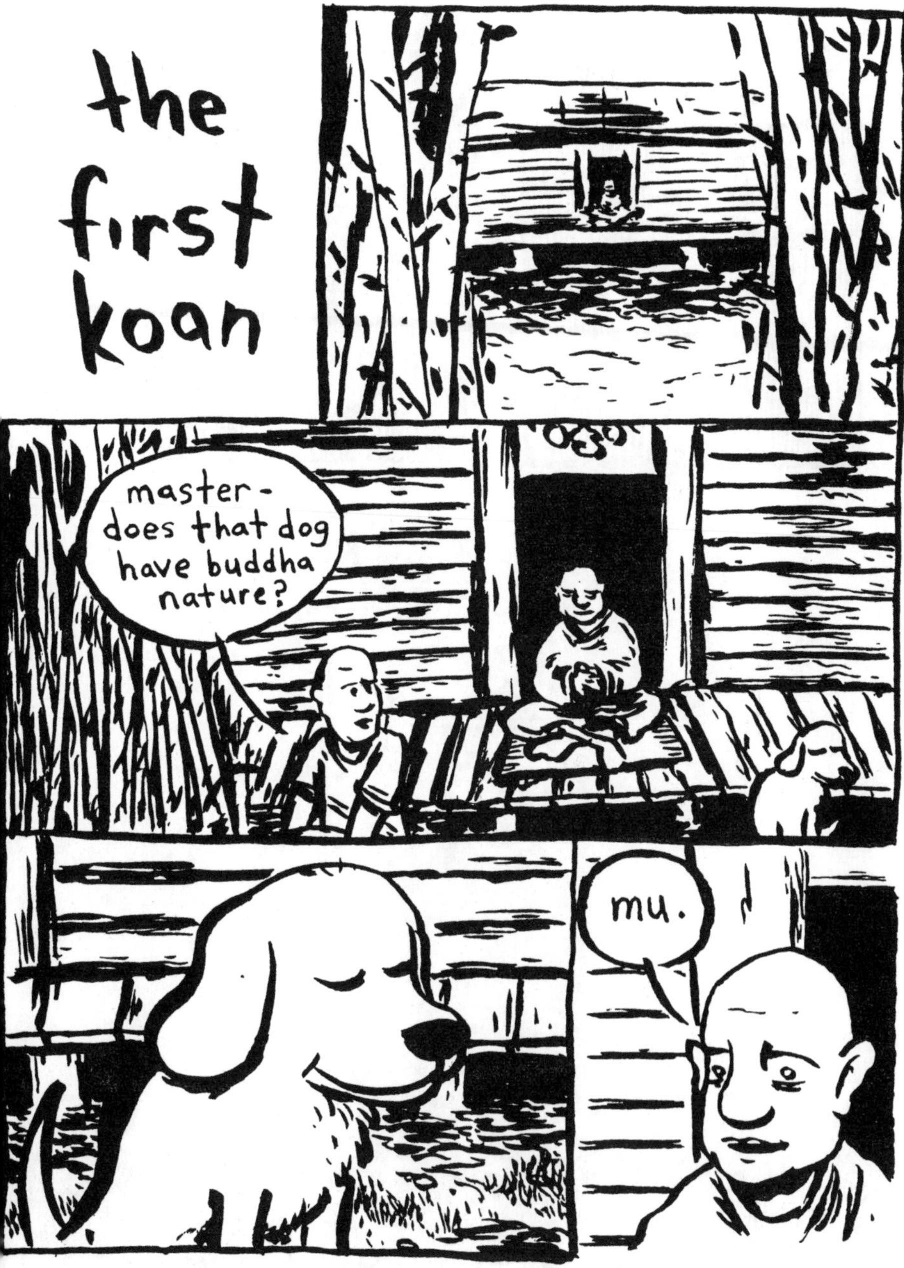
master - does that dog have buddha nature?
mu.

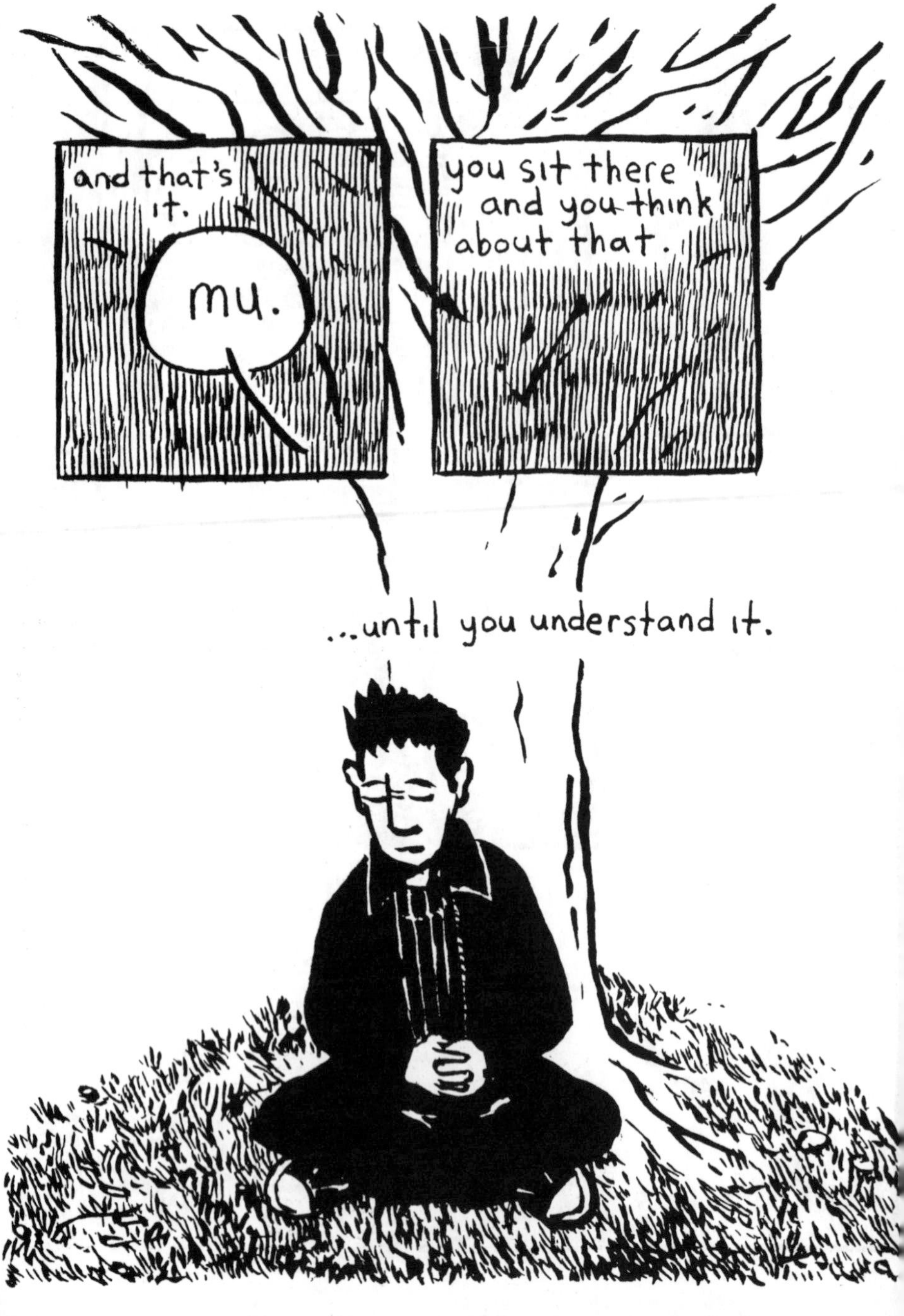
and that's it.
mu.
you sit there and you think about that.
...until you understand it.

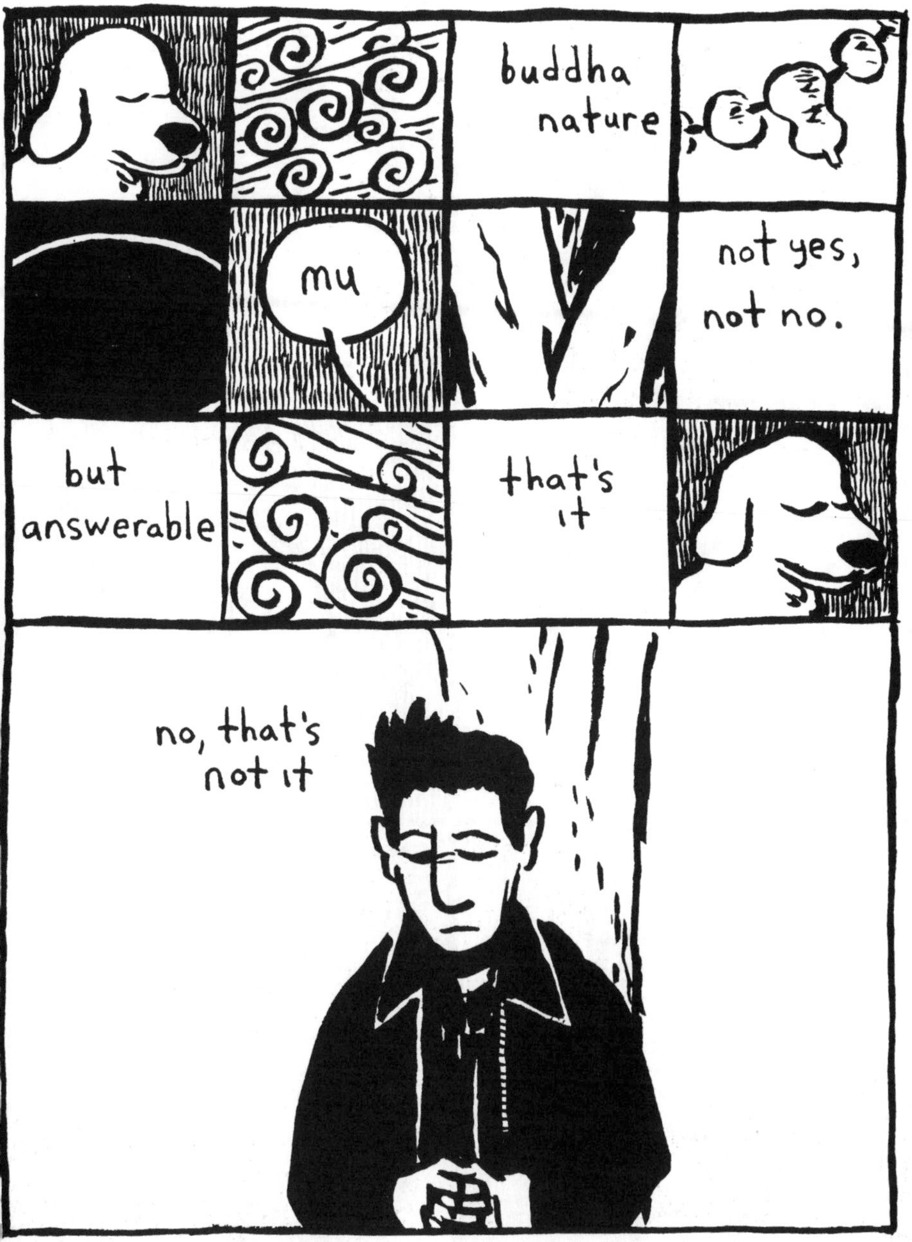
buddha nature
mu
not yes, not no.
but answerable
that's it
no, that's not it

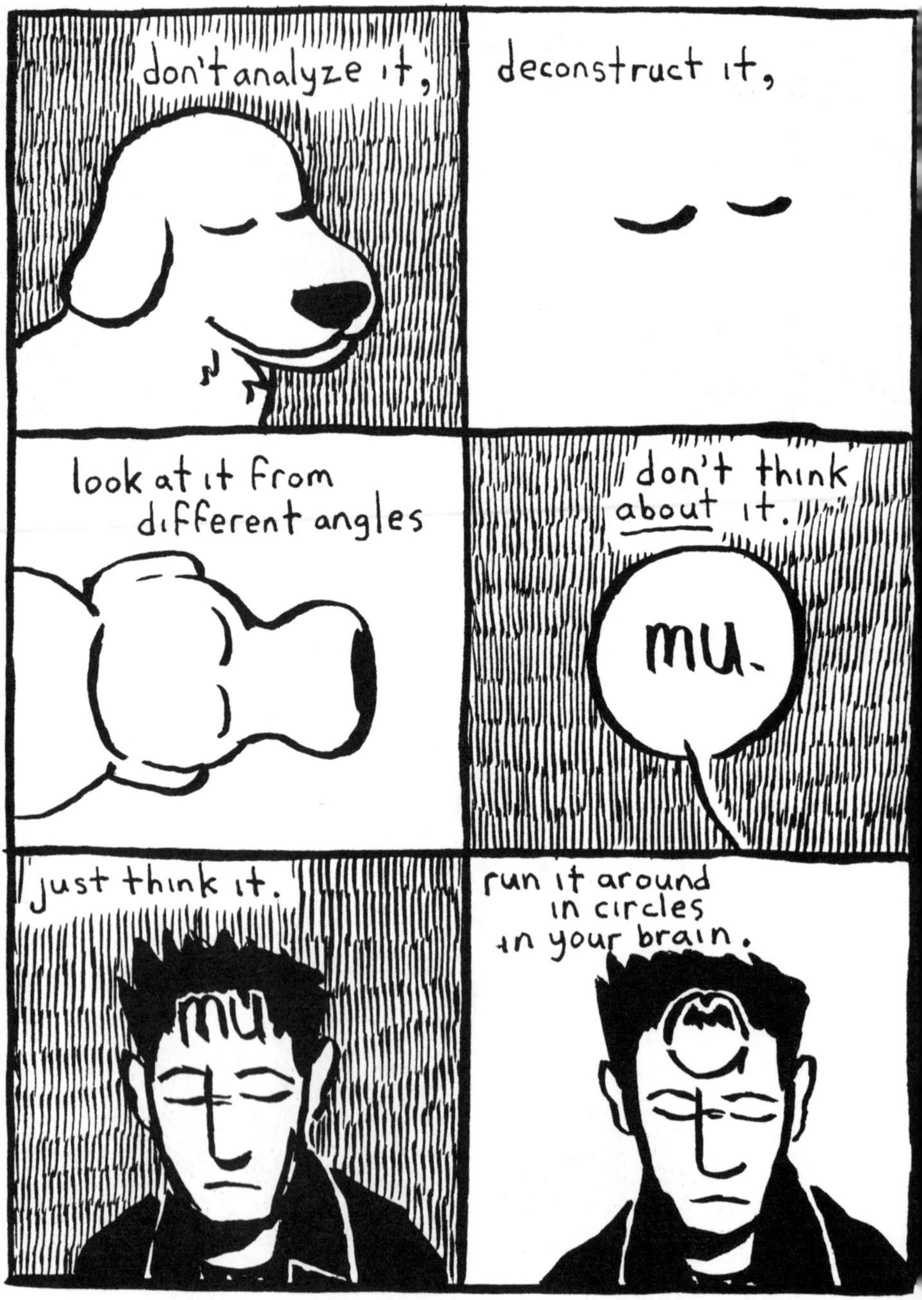
don't analyze it,
deconstruct it,
look at it from different angles
don't think about it.
mu.
just think it.
mu
run it around in circles in your brain.

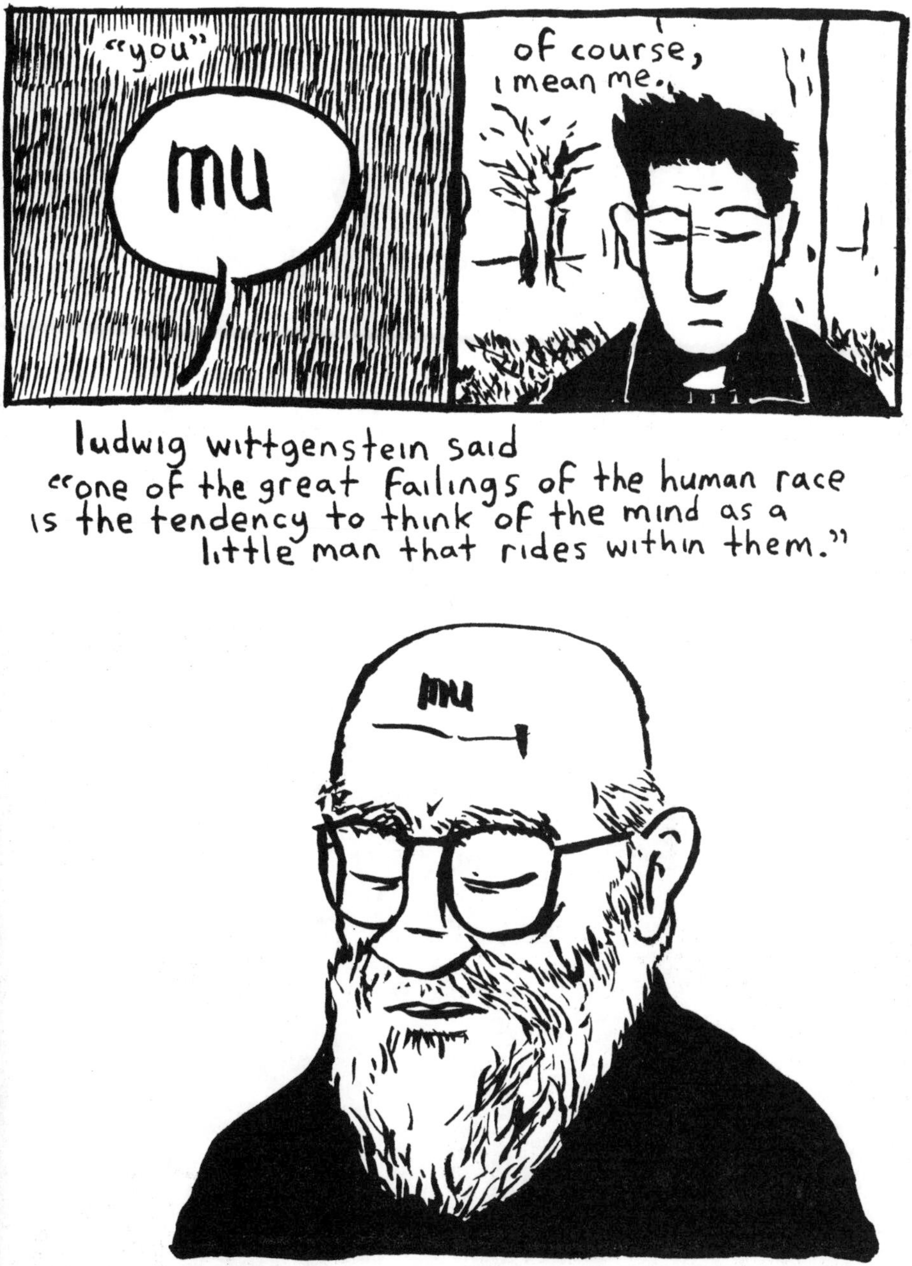
"you"
mu
of course, i mean me..
ludwig wittgenstein said
"one of the great failings of the human race is the tendency to think of the mind as a little man that rides within them."
mu

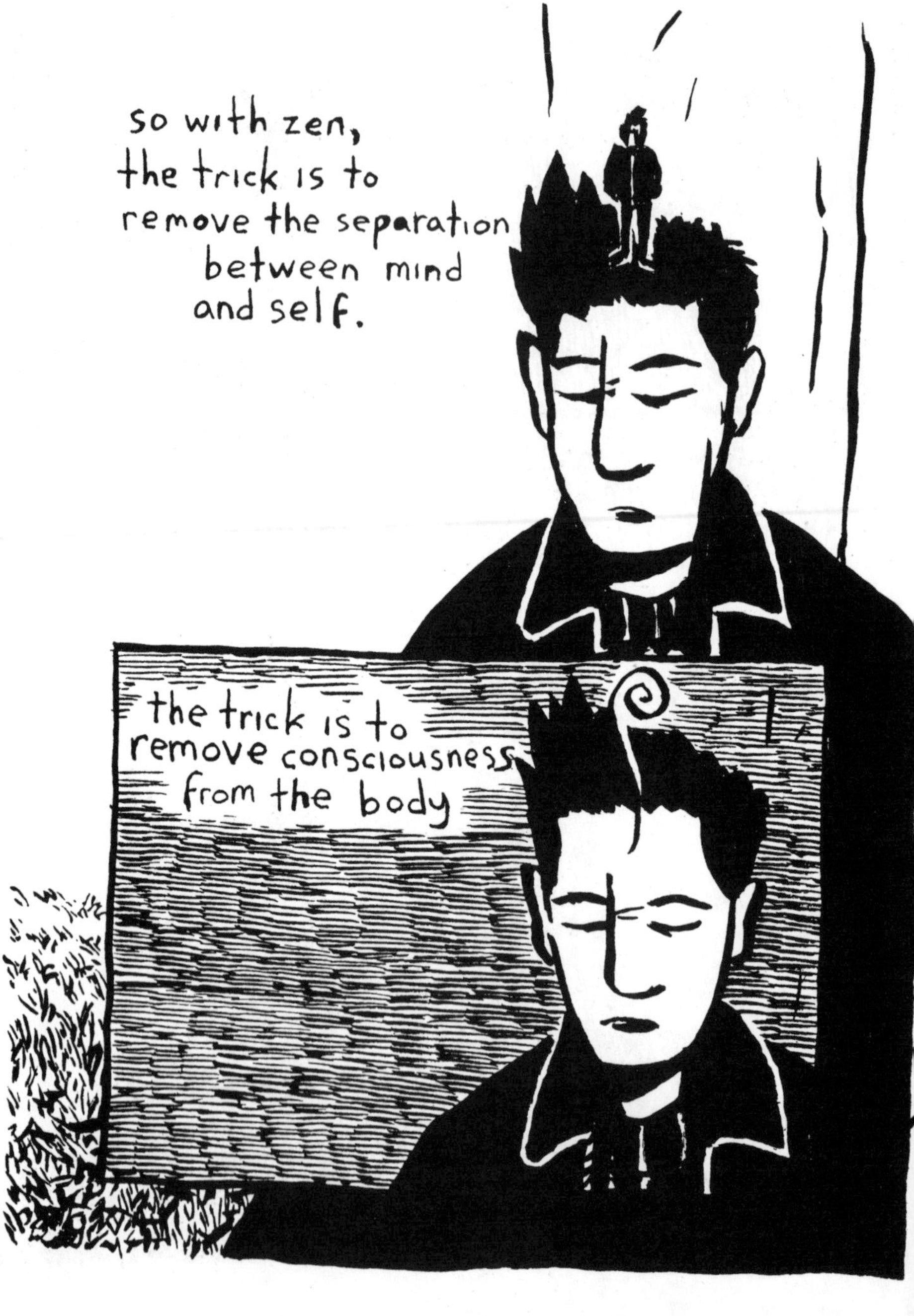
so with zen,
the trick is to
remove the separation
between mind
and self.
the trick is to
remove consciousness
from the body

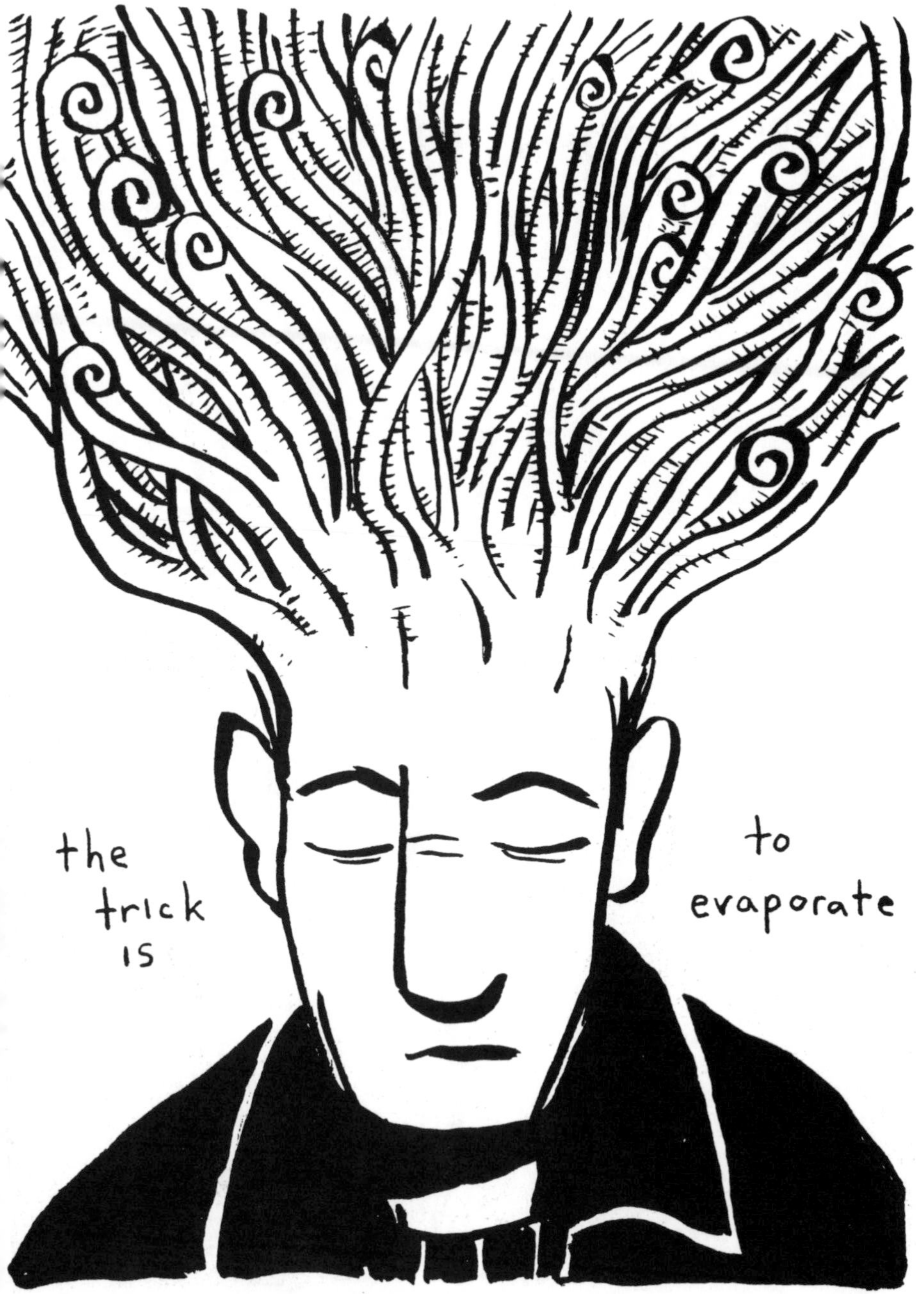
the trick is
to evaporate

and the trick,
of course

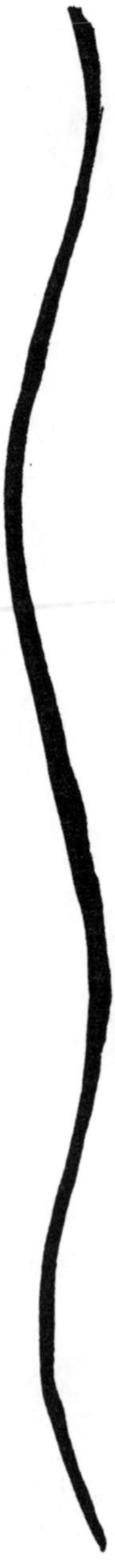

is that
there is
no trick.

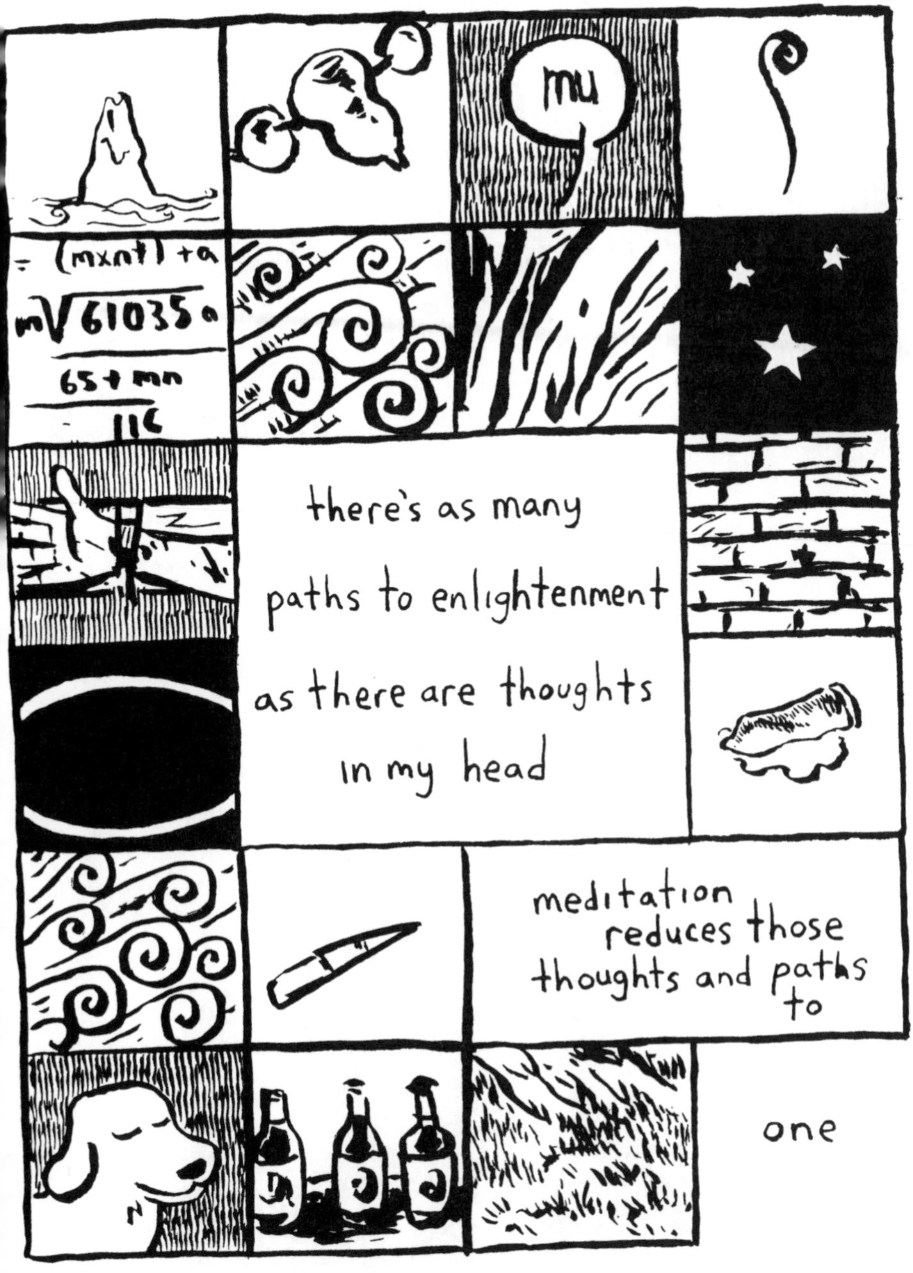
mu
(mxnt) +a
m√61035a
65+mn
11C
there's as many paths to enlightenment as there are thoughts in my head
meditation reduces those thoughts and paths to
one

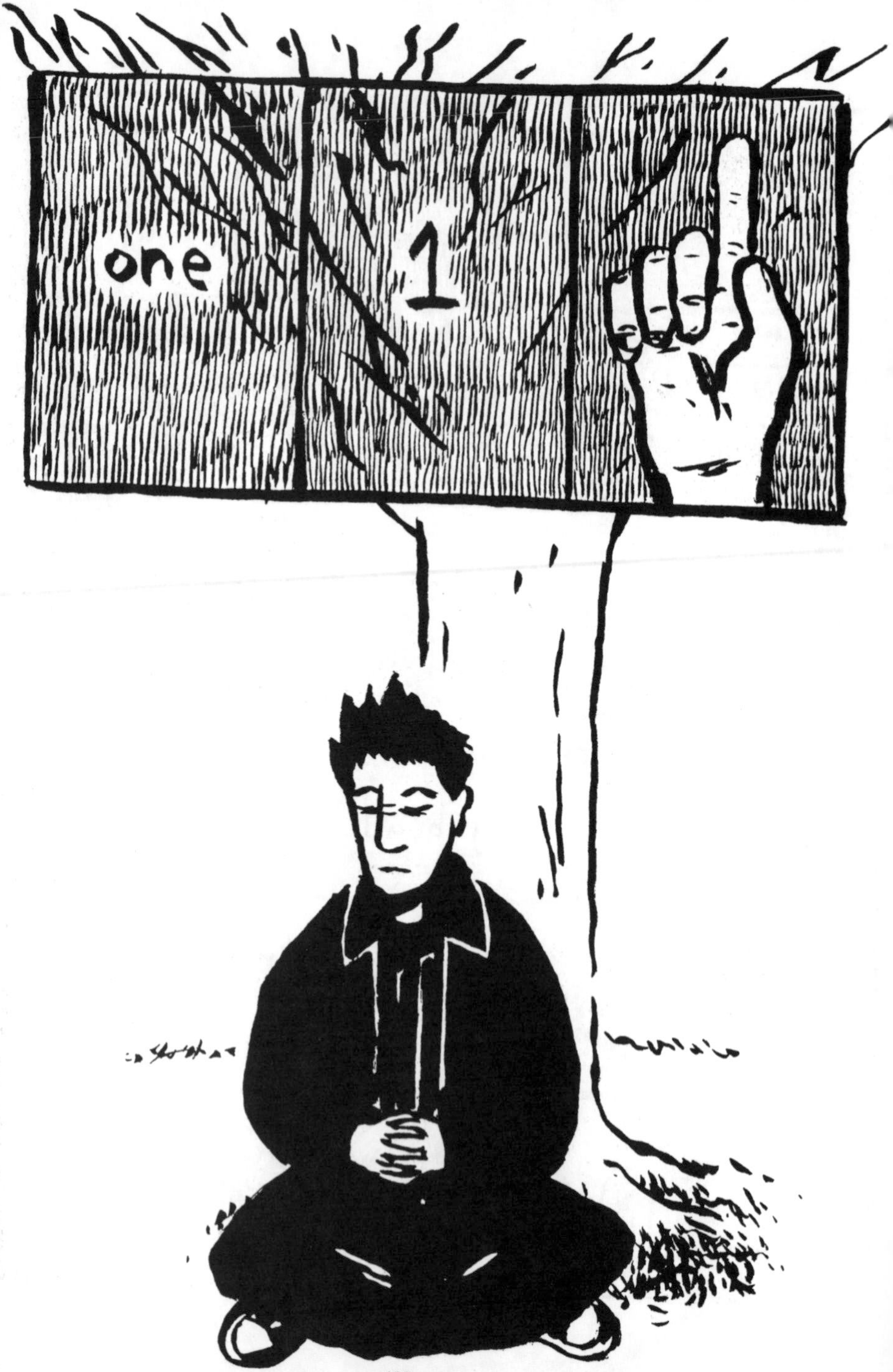
one
1

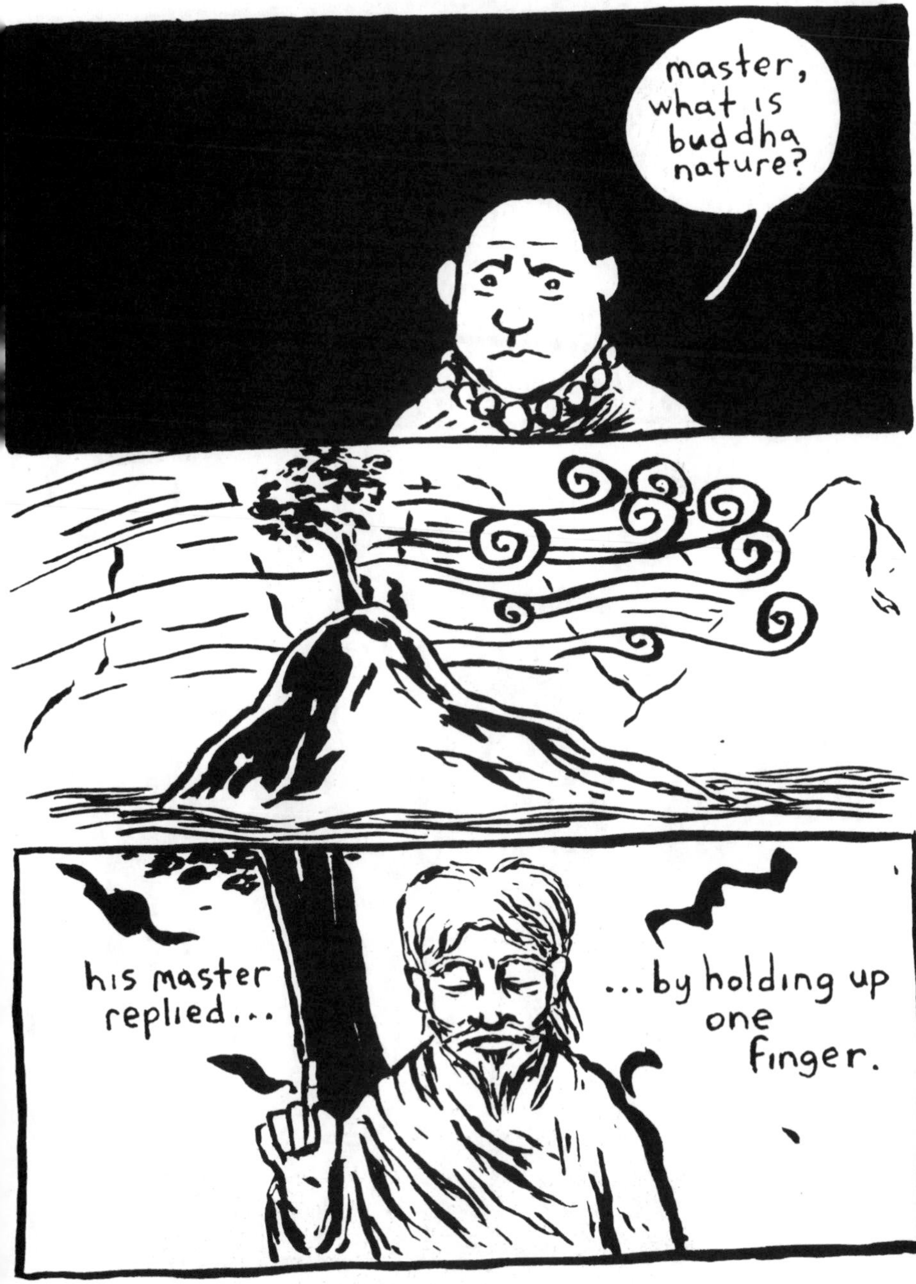
master, what is buddha nature?
his master replied...
...by holding up one finger.

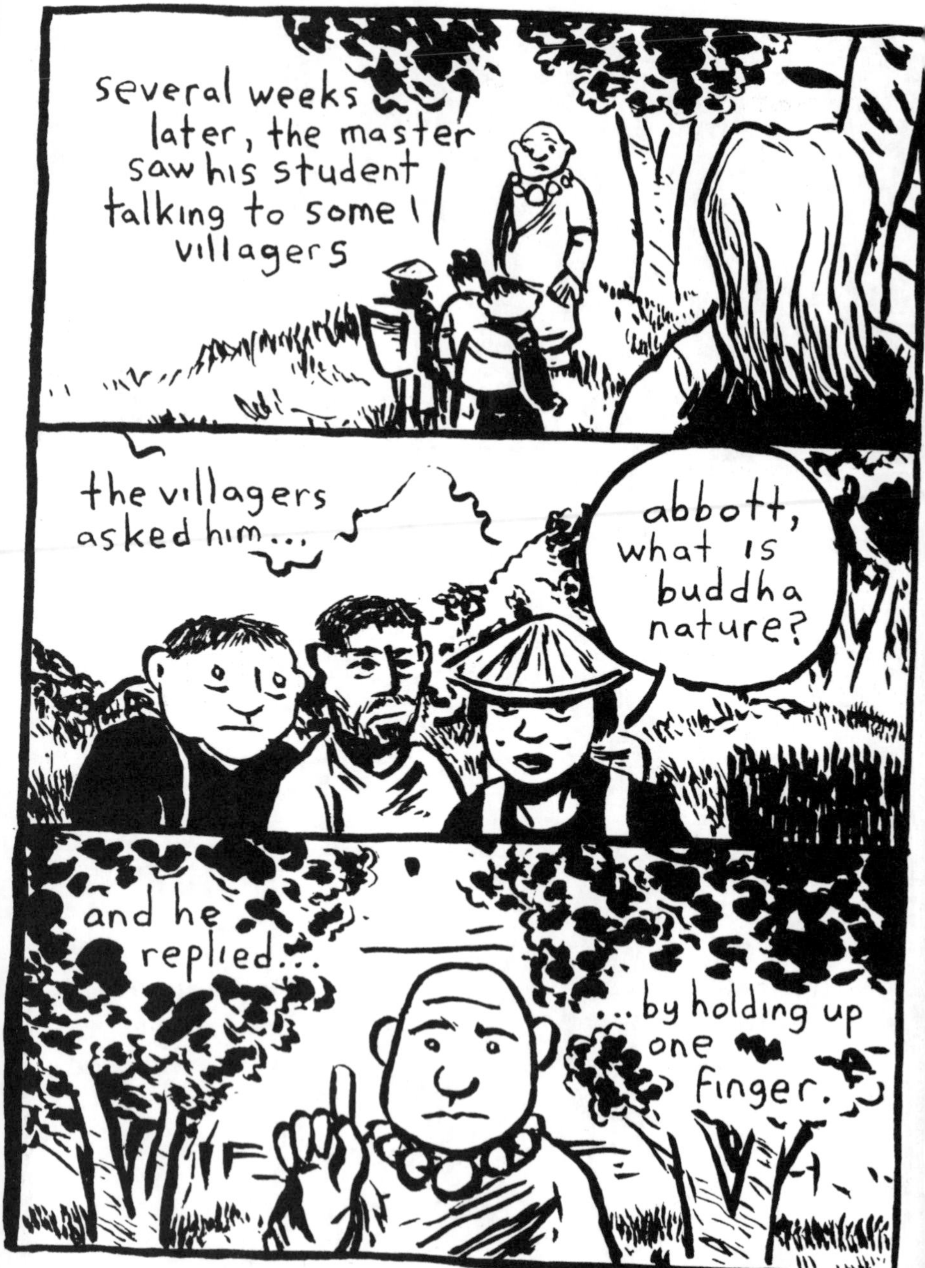
several weeks later, the master saw his student talking to some villagers
the villagers asked him...
abbott, what is buddha nature?
and he replied...
...by holding up one finger.

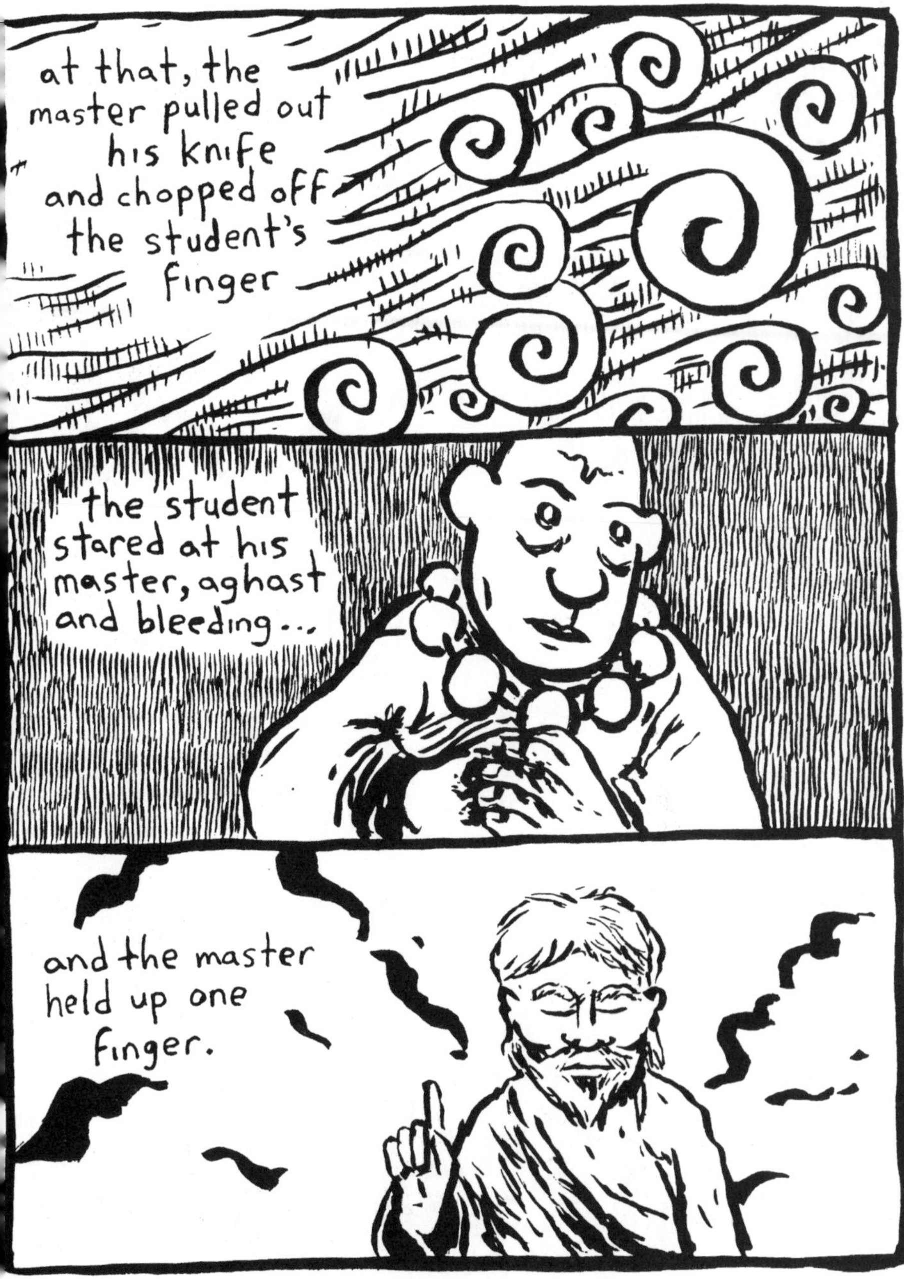
at that, the master pulled out his knife and chopped off the student's finger
the student stared at his master, aghast and bleeding...
and the master held up one finger.

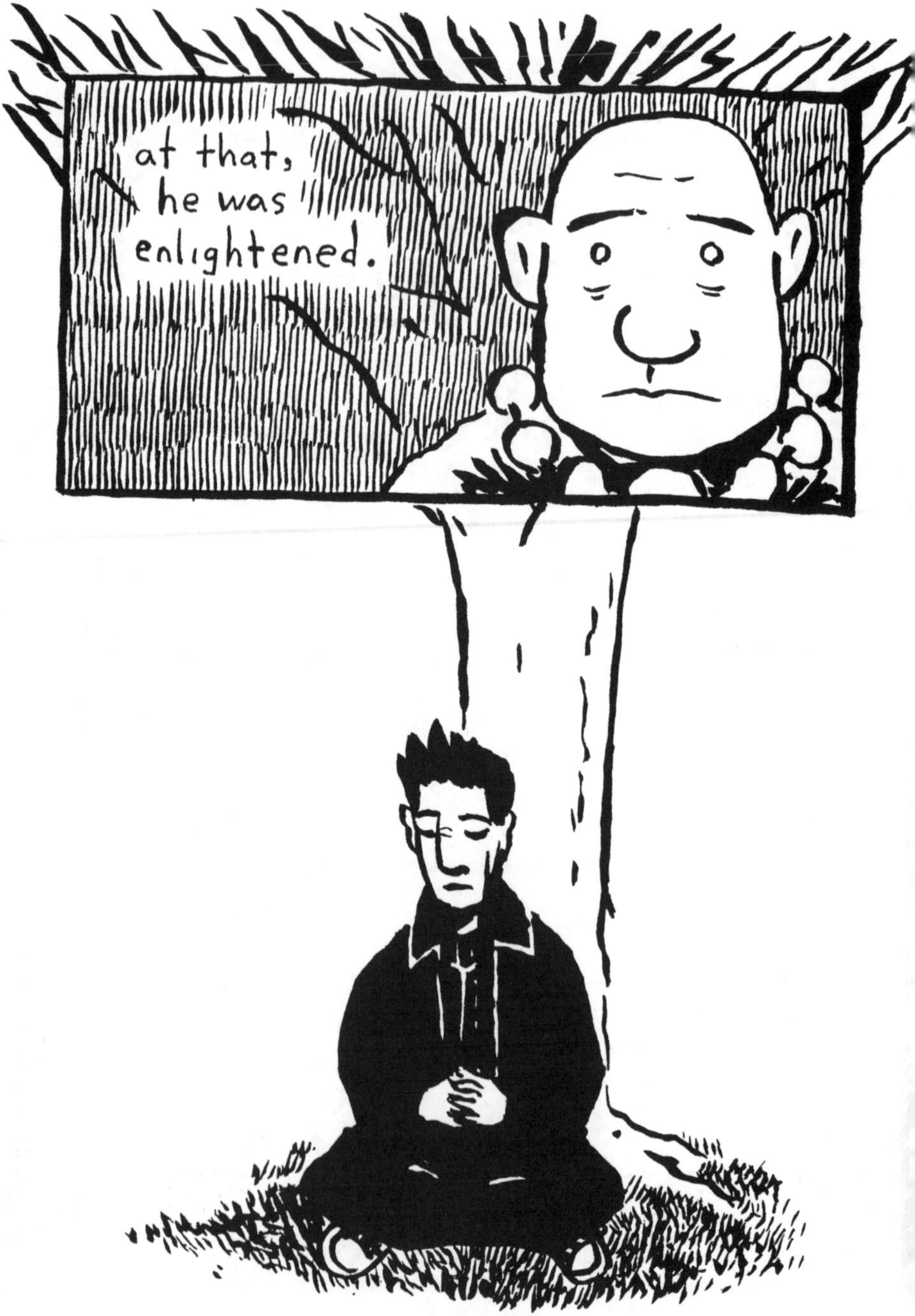
at that, he was enlightened.

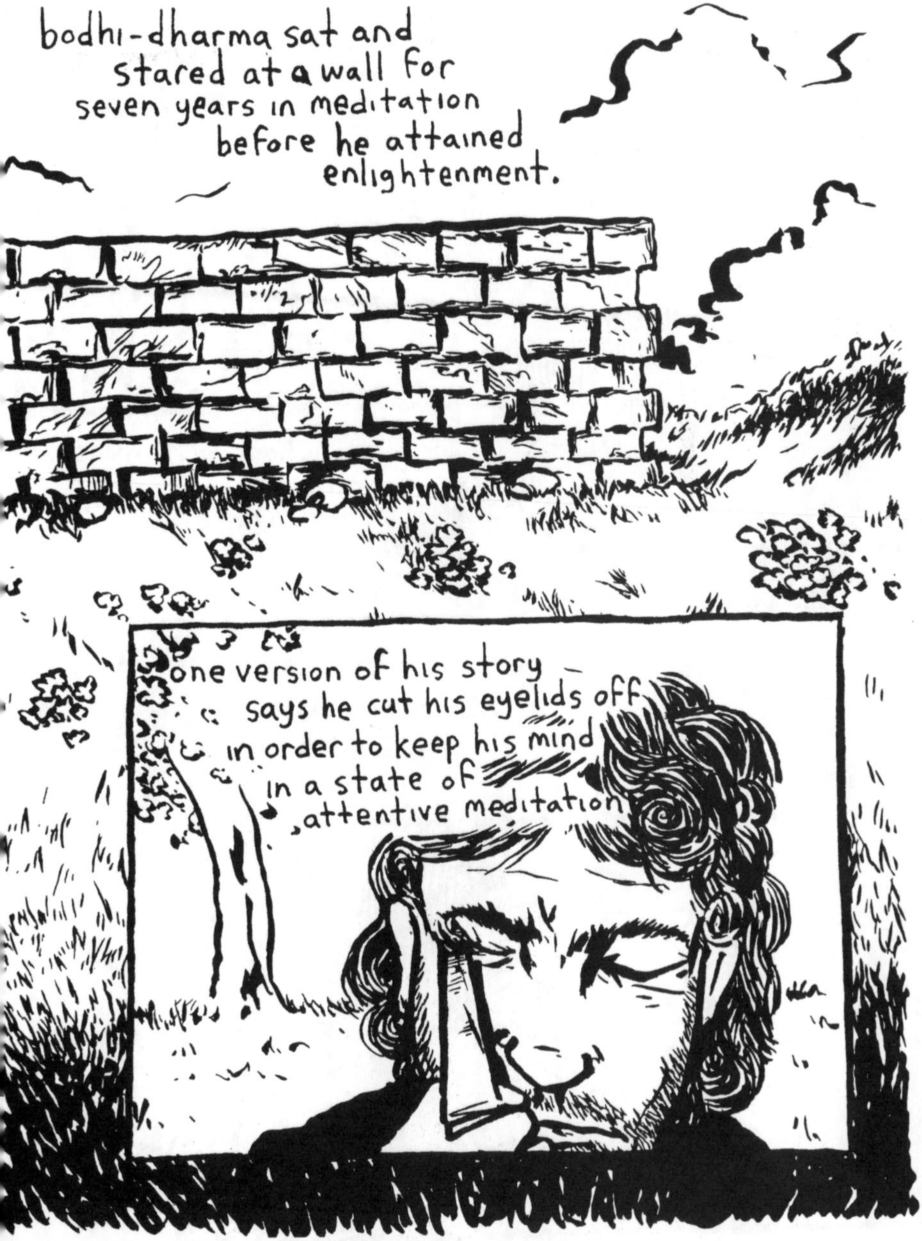
bodhi-dharma sat and stared at a wall for seven years in meditation before he attained enlightenment.
one version of his story says he cut his eyelids off in order to keep his mind in a state of attentive meditation

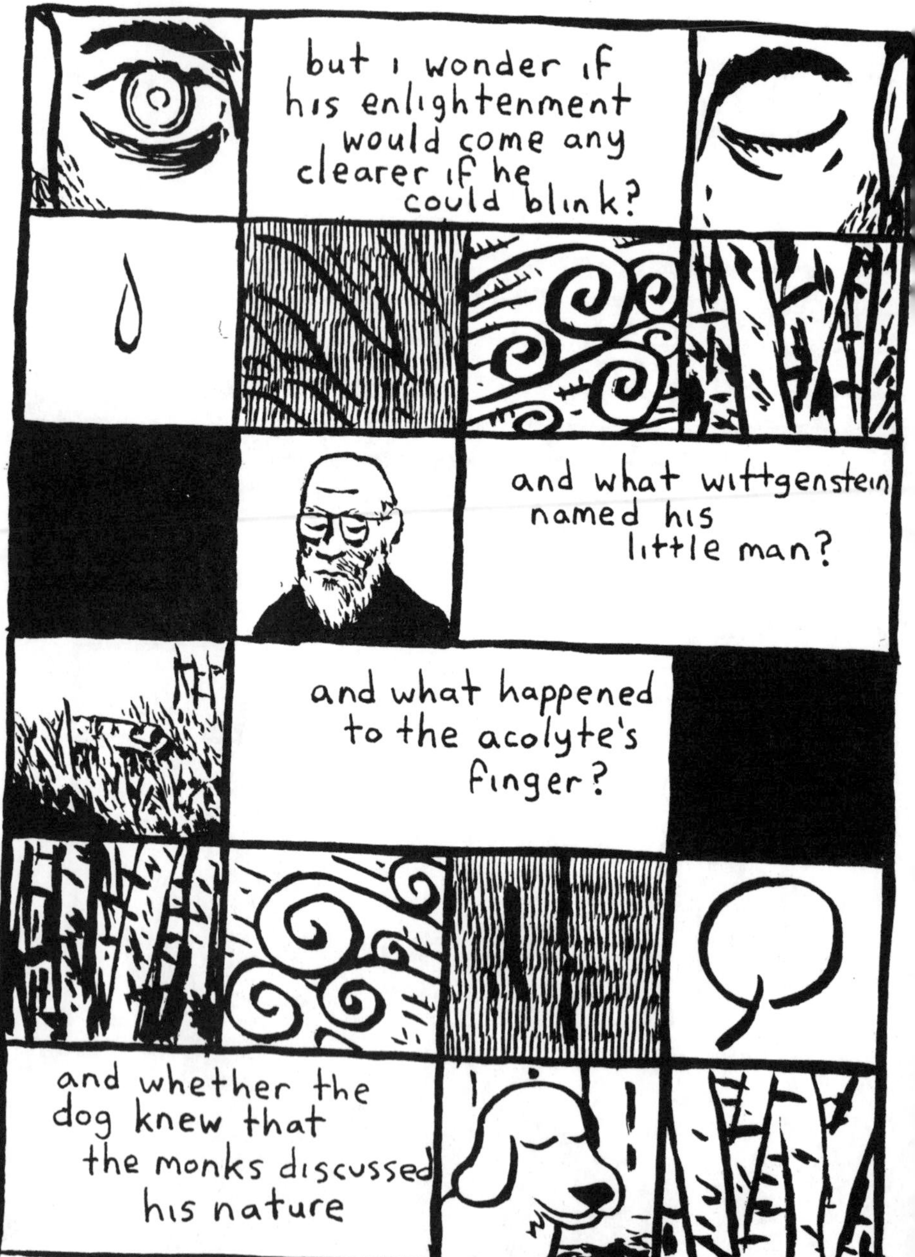
but i wonder if his enlightenment would come any clearer if he could blink?
and what wittgenstein named his little man?
and what happened to the acolyte's finger?
and whether the dog knew that the monks discussed his nature

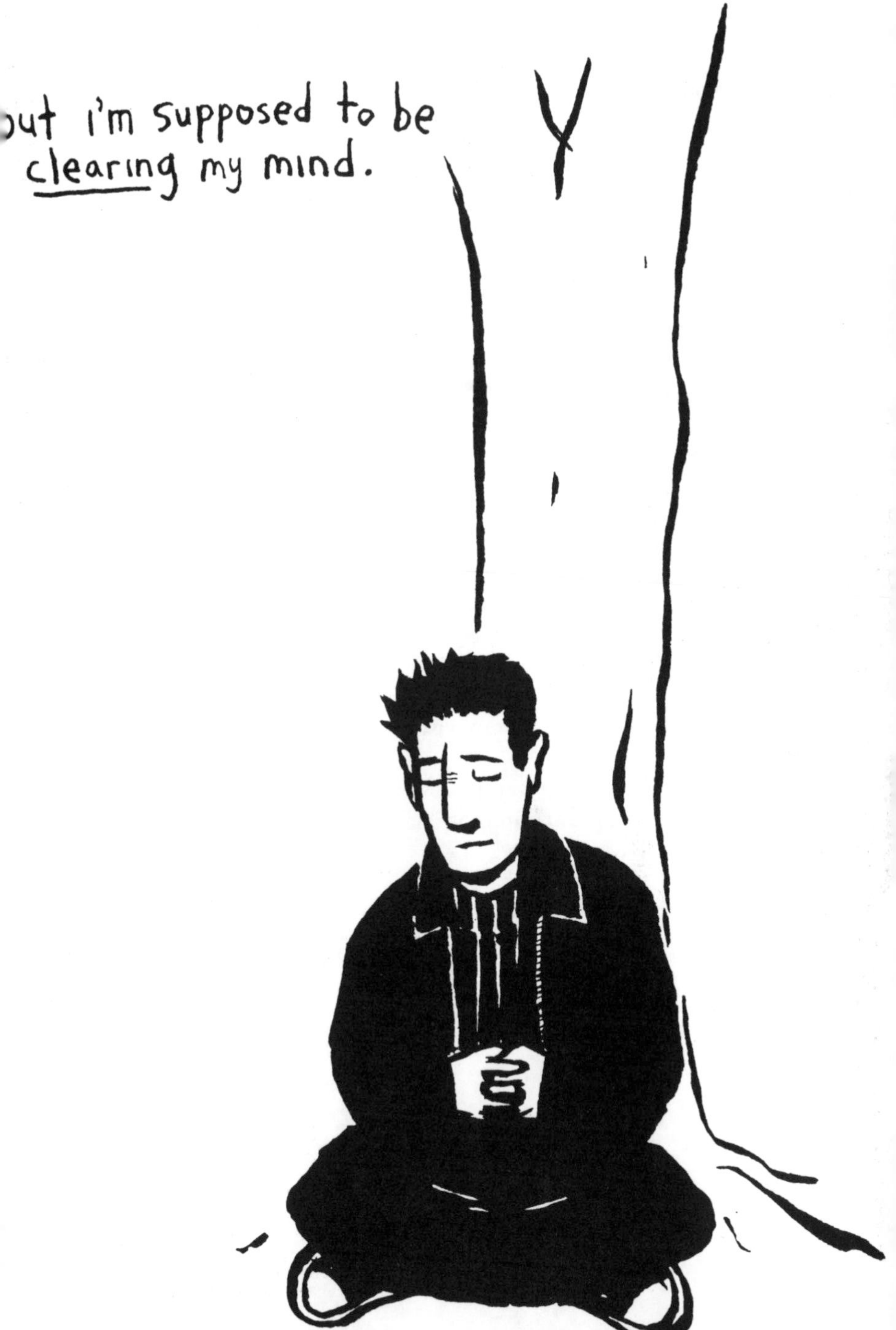

but i'm supposed to be clearing my mind.

AL DAVISON

It was at Comicon International 2002 in San Diego (a massive summer gathering of fans and pros which annually draws in about 50,000 attendees) when Al Davison handed me his gorgeous 24-hour comic "The Invisible Library". It felt so finished and perfect, I was amazed that anyone could produce such a work in a mere 24 hours. "This really took only a day?!" I asked. Al assured me that yes, it had.

I must have asked him at least three times.

U.K.-based Al Davison first came to prominence for many readers in the US through his 1990 autobiographical graphic novel The Spiral Cage in which he explored his life-long experience with Spina Bifida. Having overcome medical predictions at infancy that he would never walk to become an accomplished artist and teacher as well as a Black Belt in Karate, I suppose that the challenge to stay up drinking coffee and draw for 24-hours must have seemed laughably easy by comparison.

The Invisible Library is graphically powerful and inventive. Its imagery is haunting and memorable. Its linework is confident, smooth and lyrical.

It is, in my opinion, the best 24-hour comic to date.

So...

Think you can do better?

I'd like to see you try.

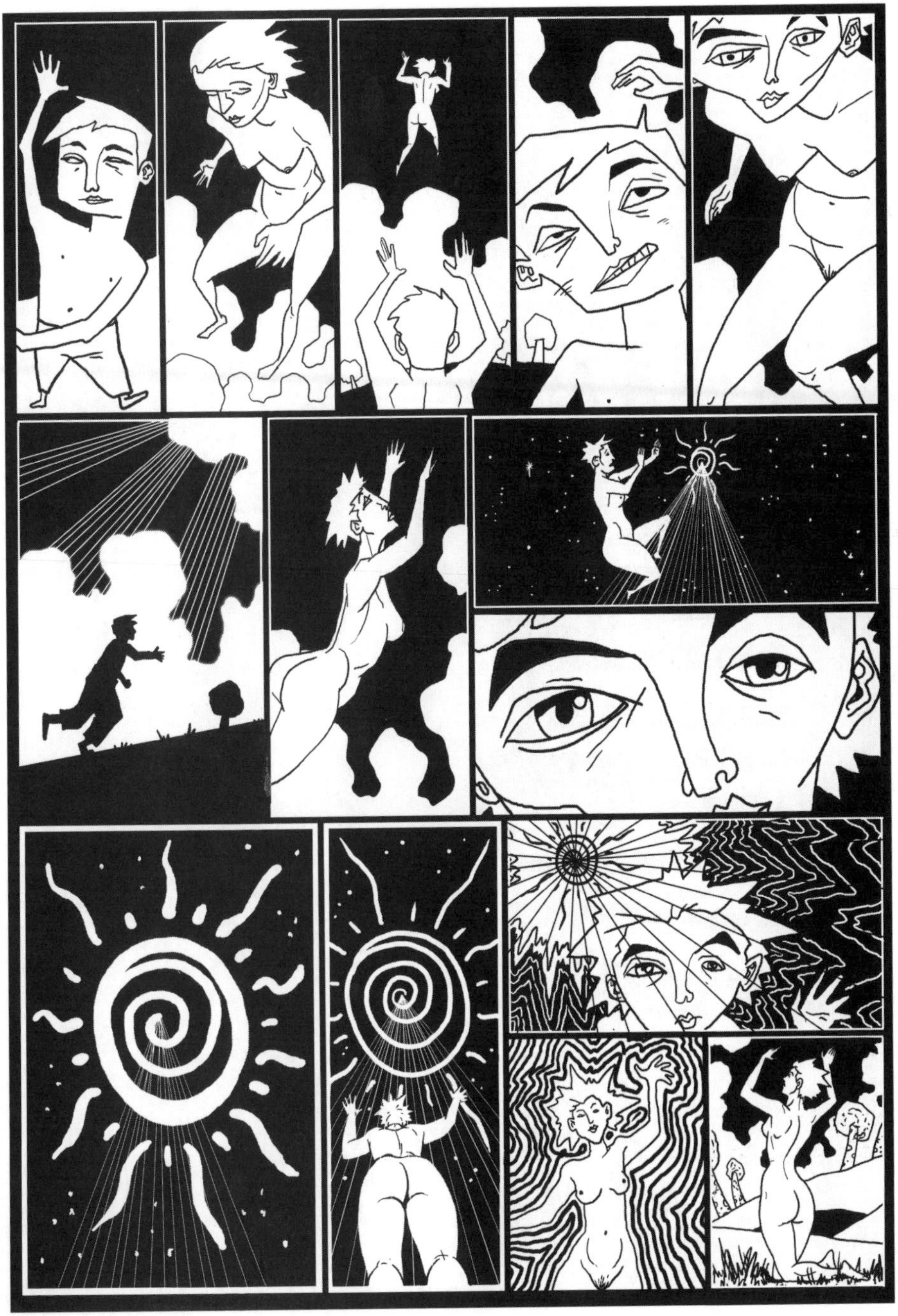

1

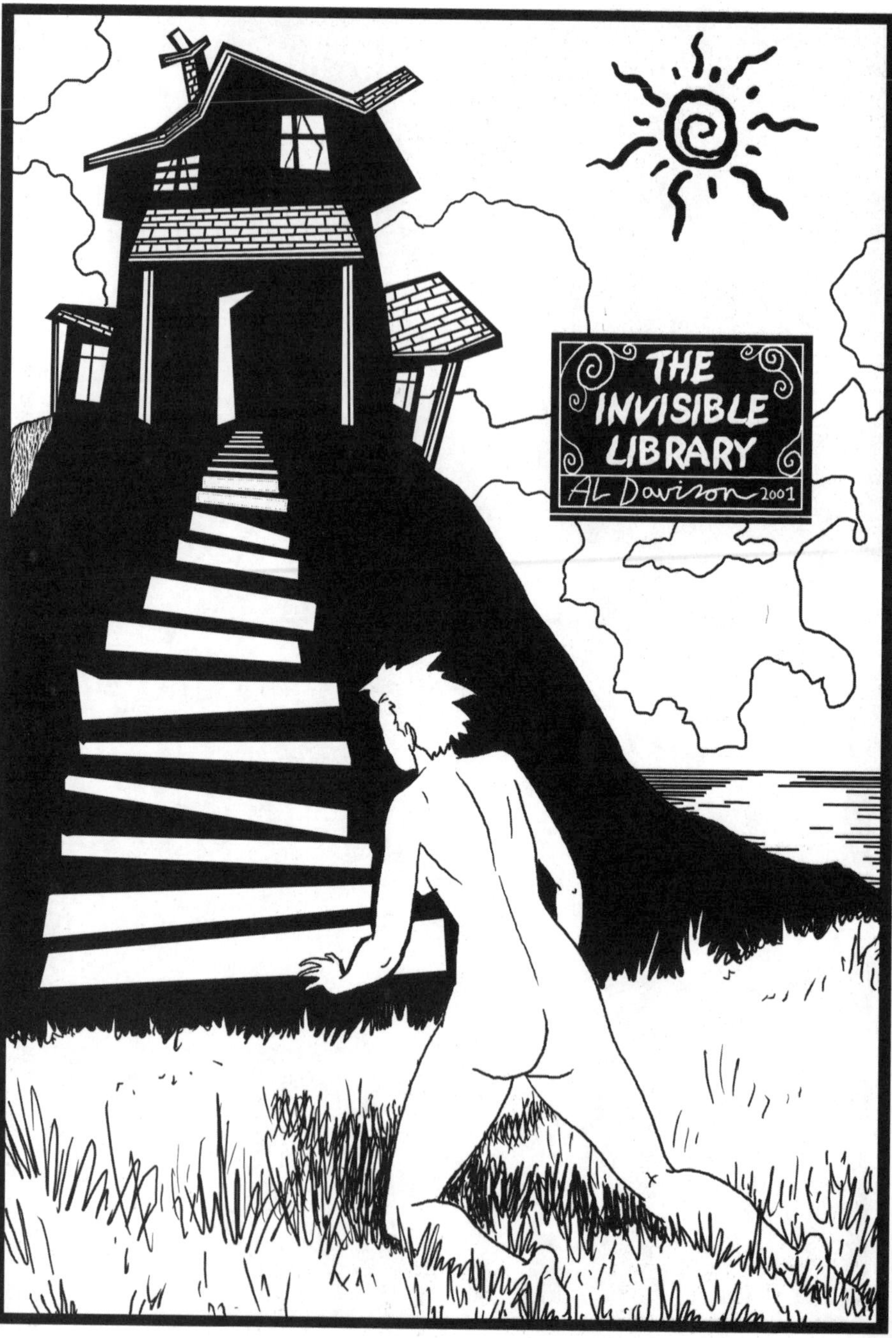
THE INVISIBLE LIBRARY
AL Davison 2001

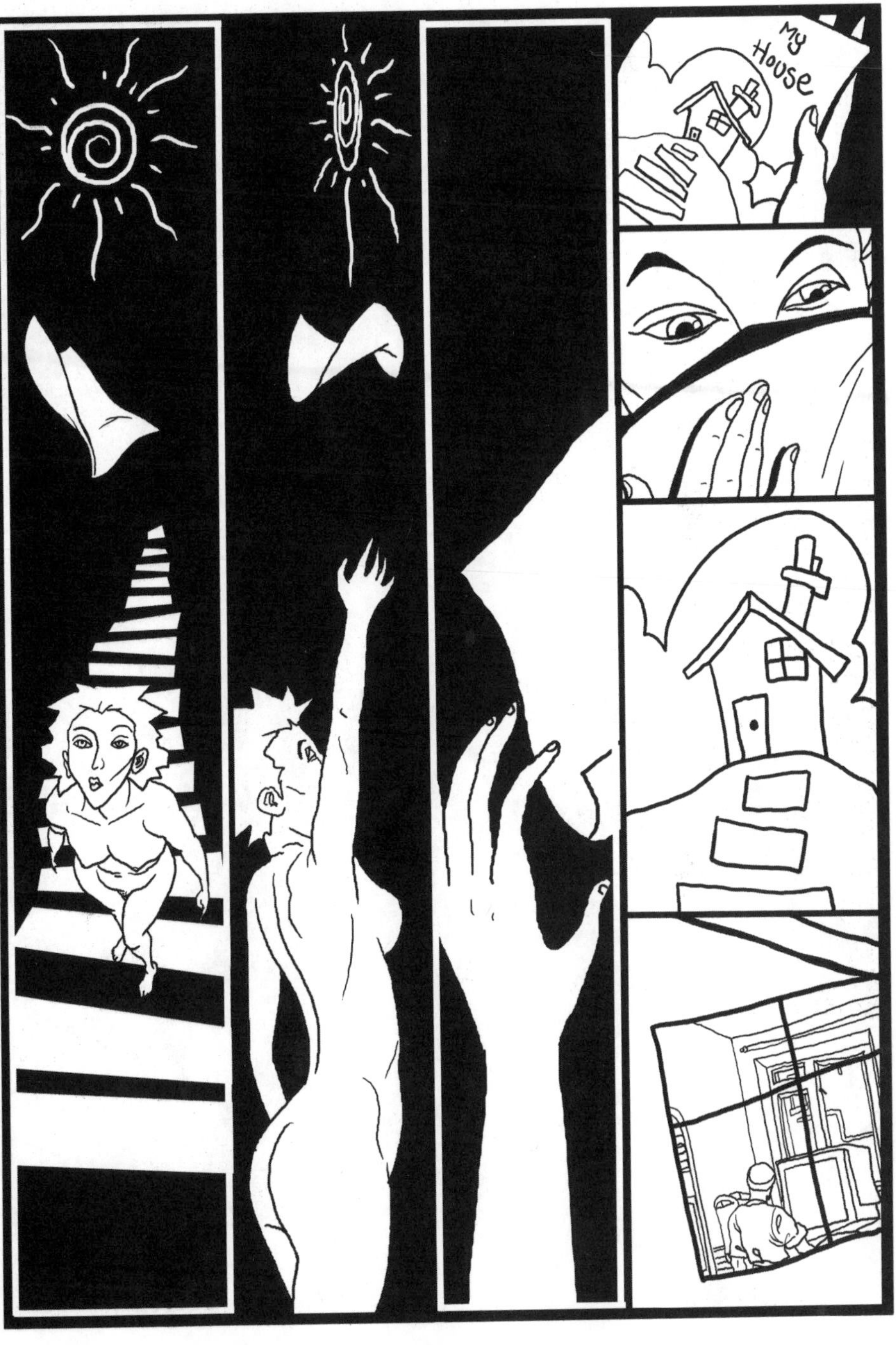
My House

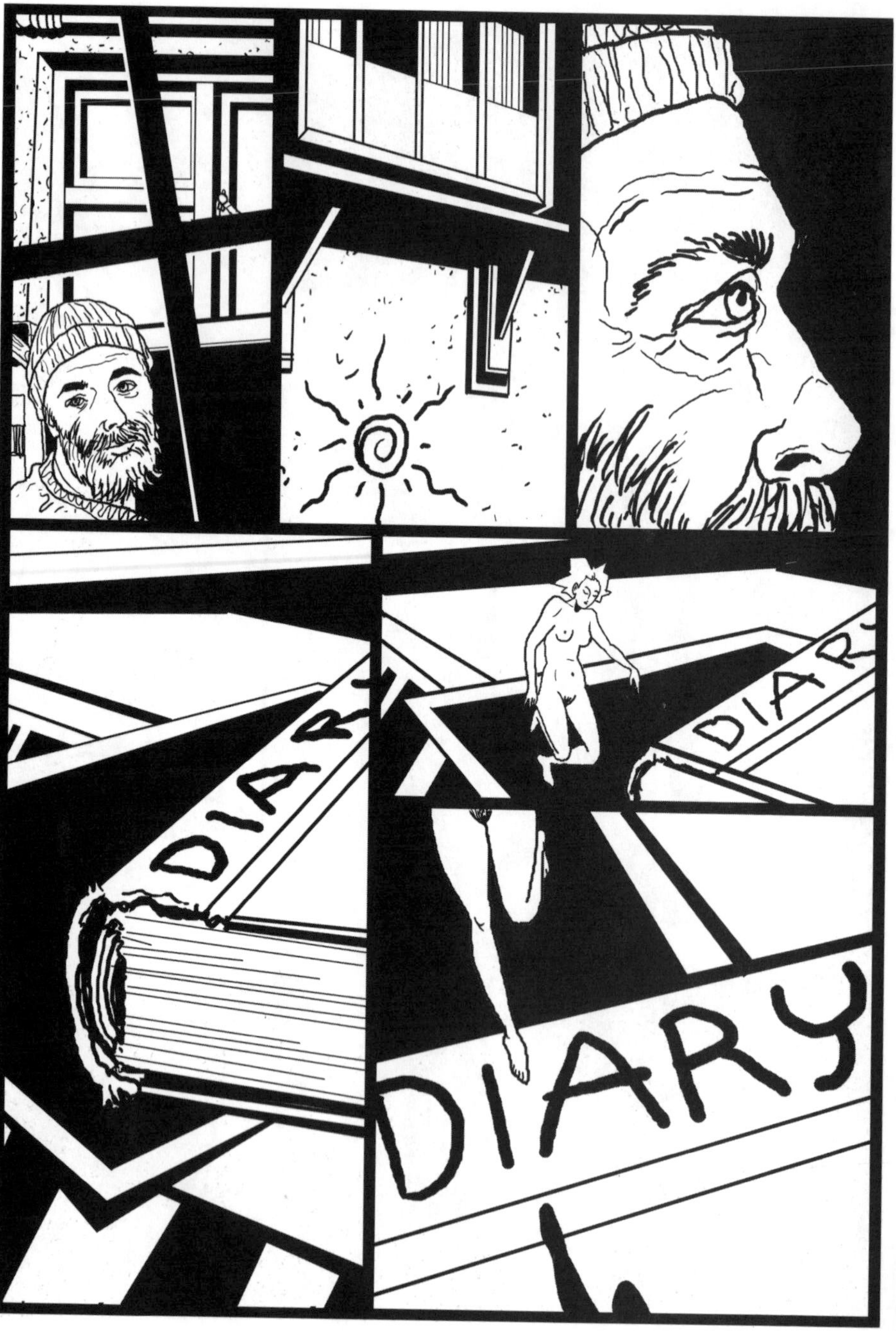
DIARY
DIARY
DIARY

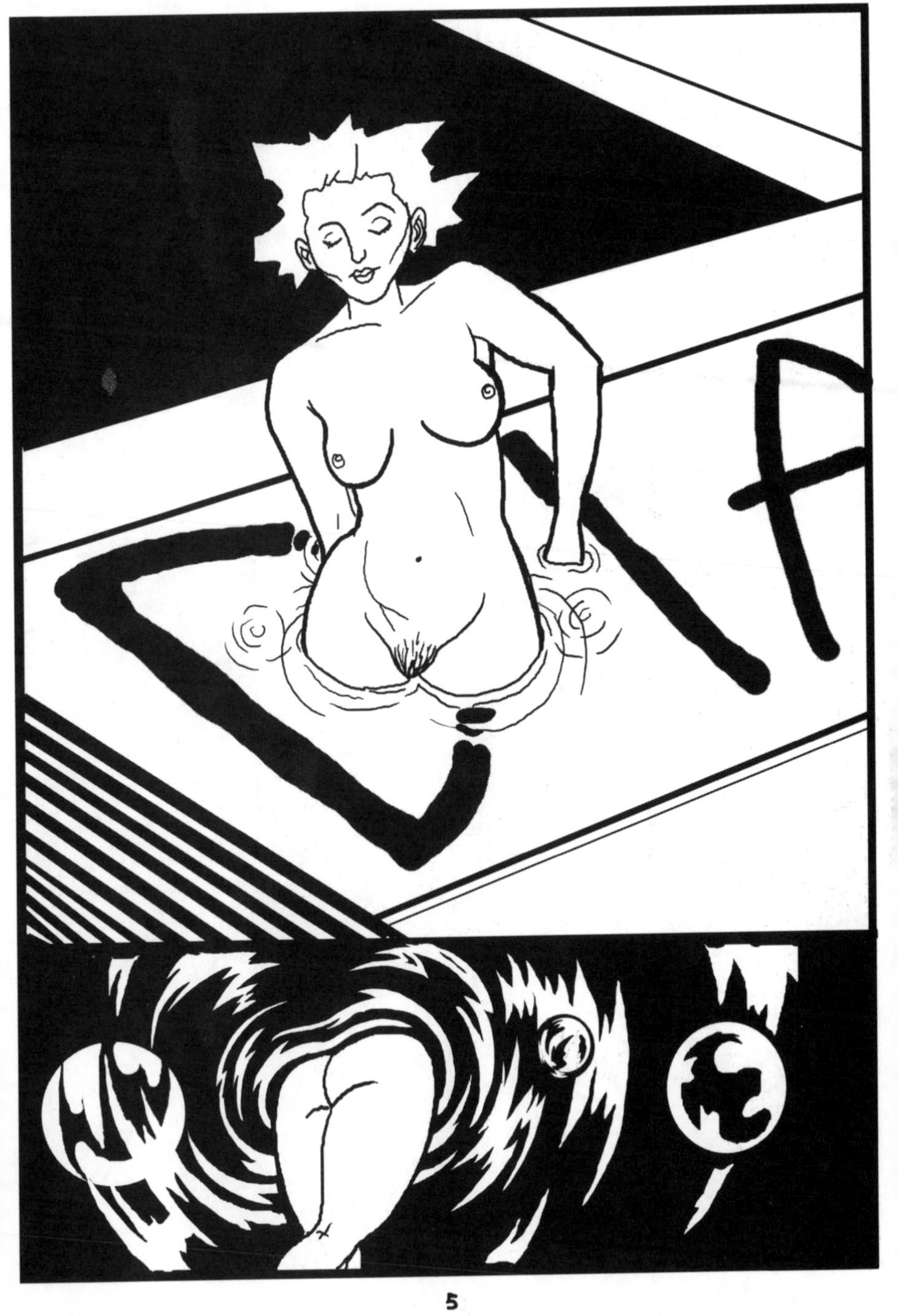

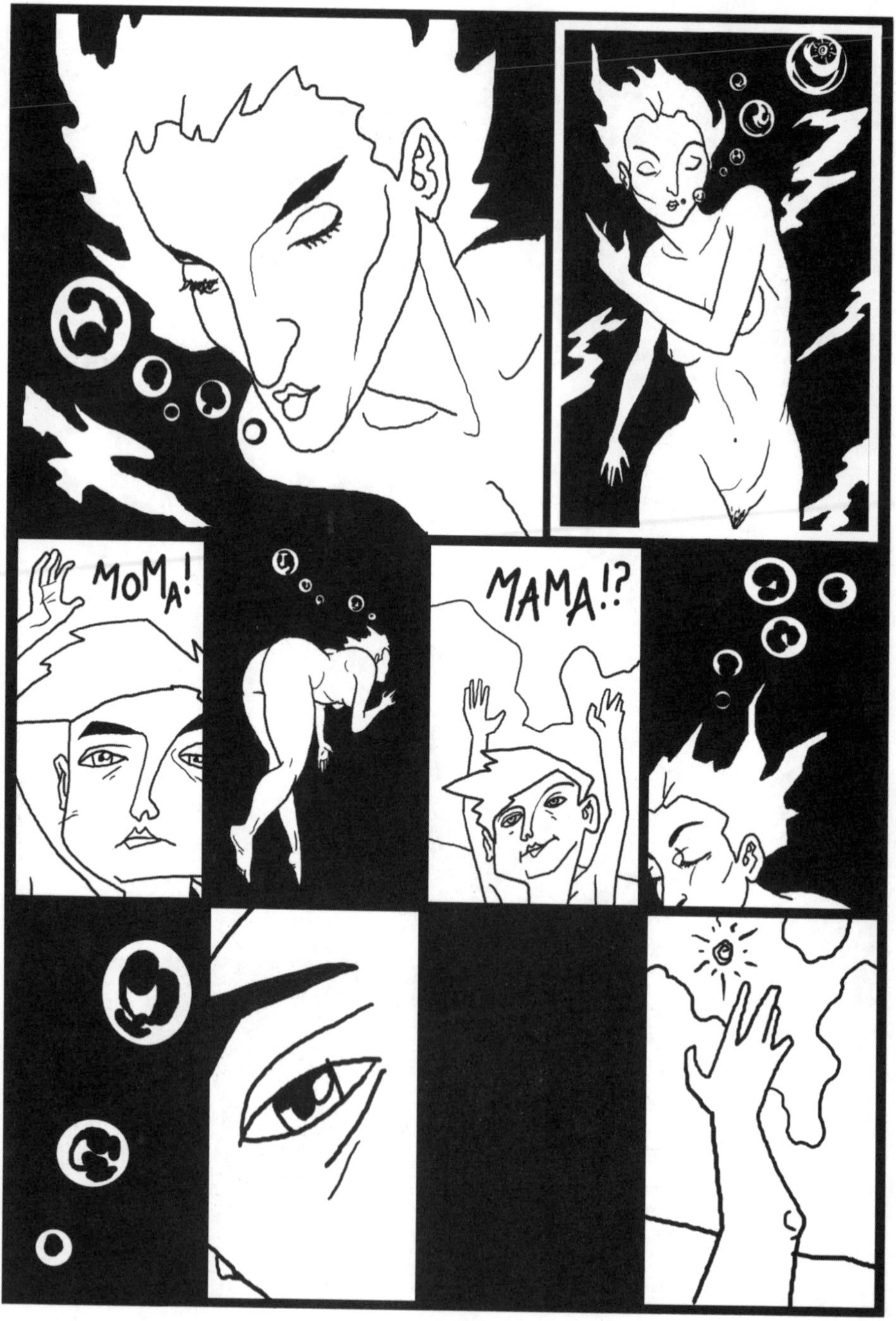
MOMA!
MAMA!?

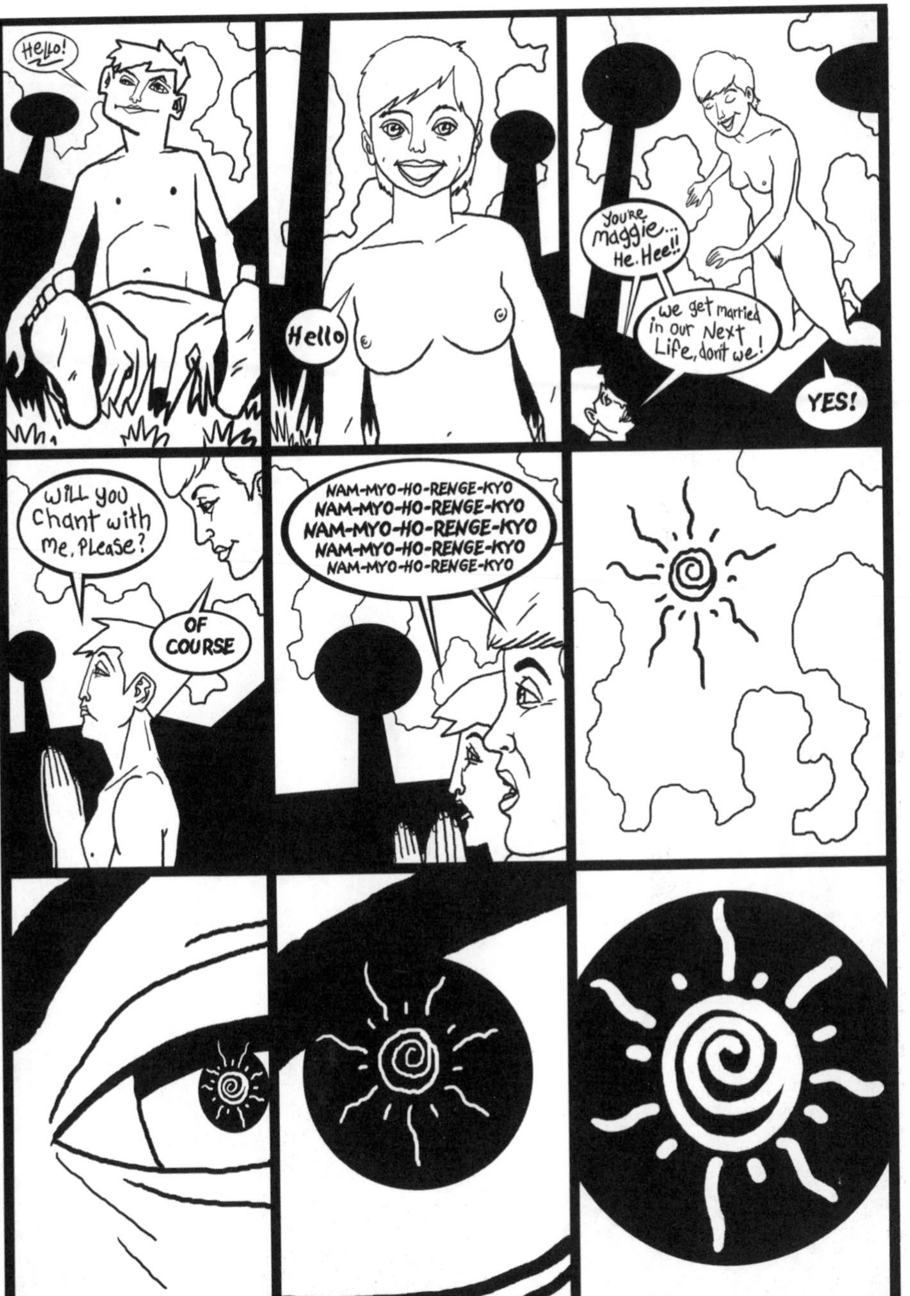
Hello!
Hello
You're maggie... He. Hee!!
we get married in our Next Life, don't we!
YES!
will you chant with me, please?
OF COURSE
NAM-MYO-HO-RENGE-KYO
NAM-MYO-HO-RENGE-KYO
NAM-MYO-HO-RENGE-KYO
NAM-MYO-HO-RENGE-KYO
NAM-MYO-HO-RENGE-KYO

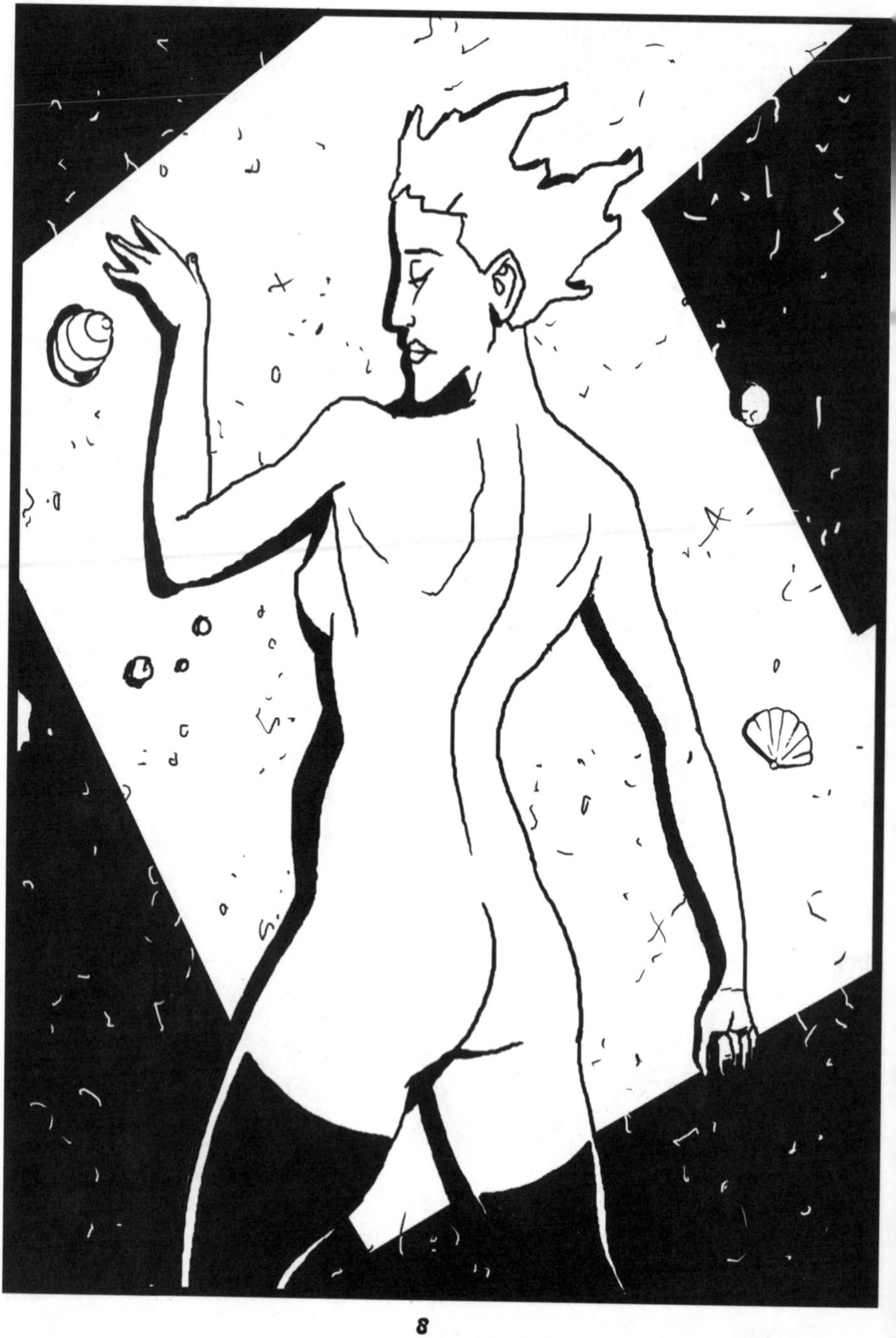

8

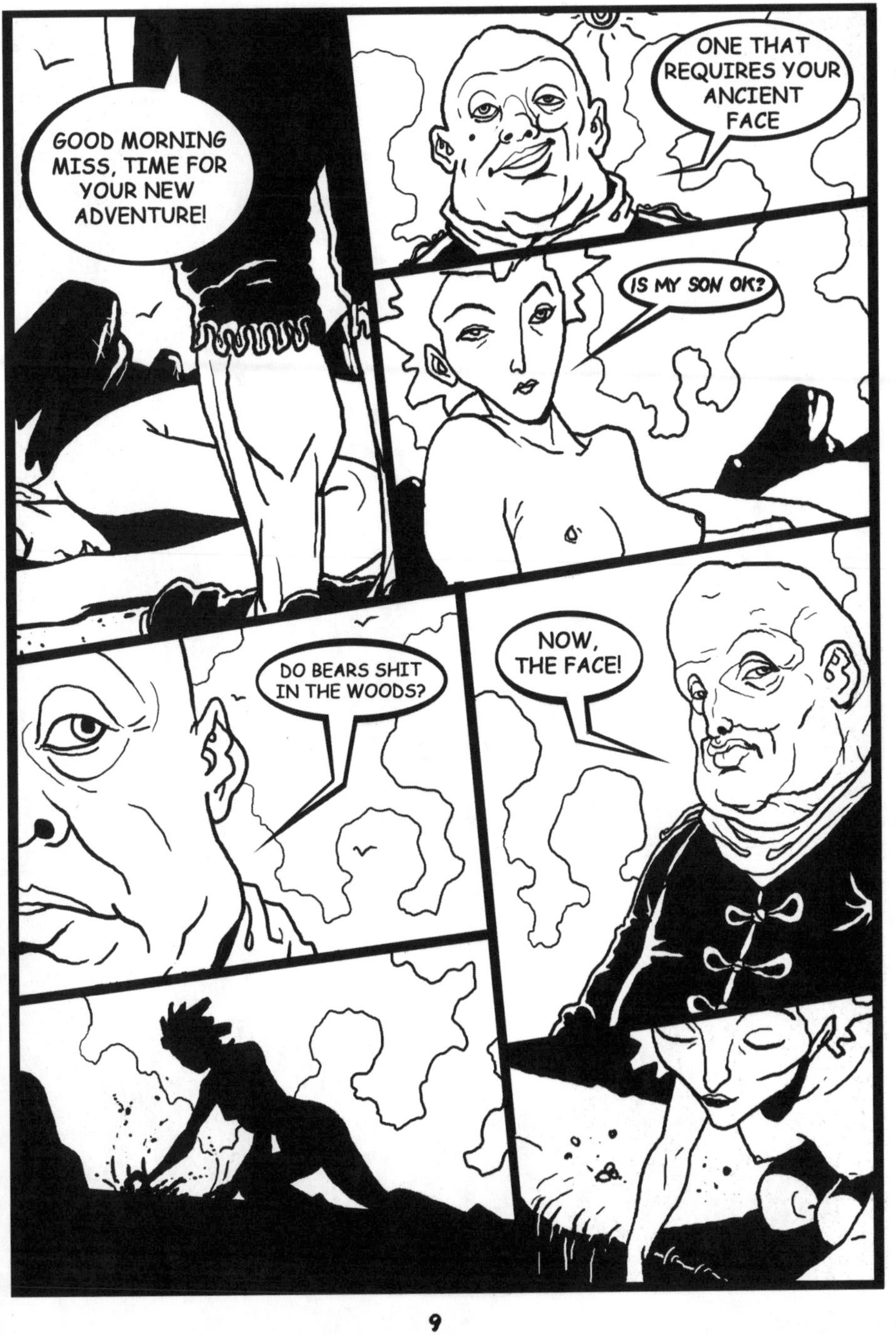
GOOD MORNING MISS, TIME FOR YOUR NEW ADVENTURE!
ONE THAT REQUIRES YOUR ANCIENT FACE
IS MY SON OK?
DO BEARS SHIT IN THE WOODS?
NOW, THE FACE!

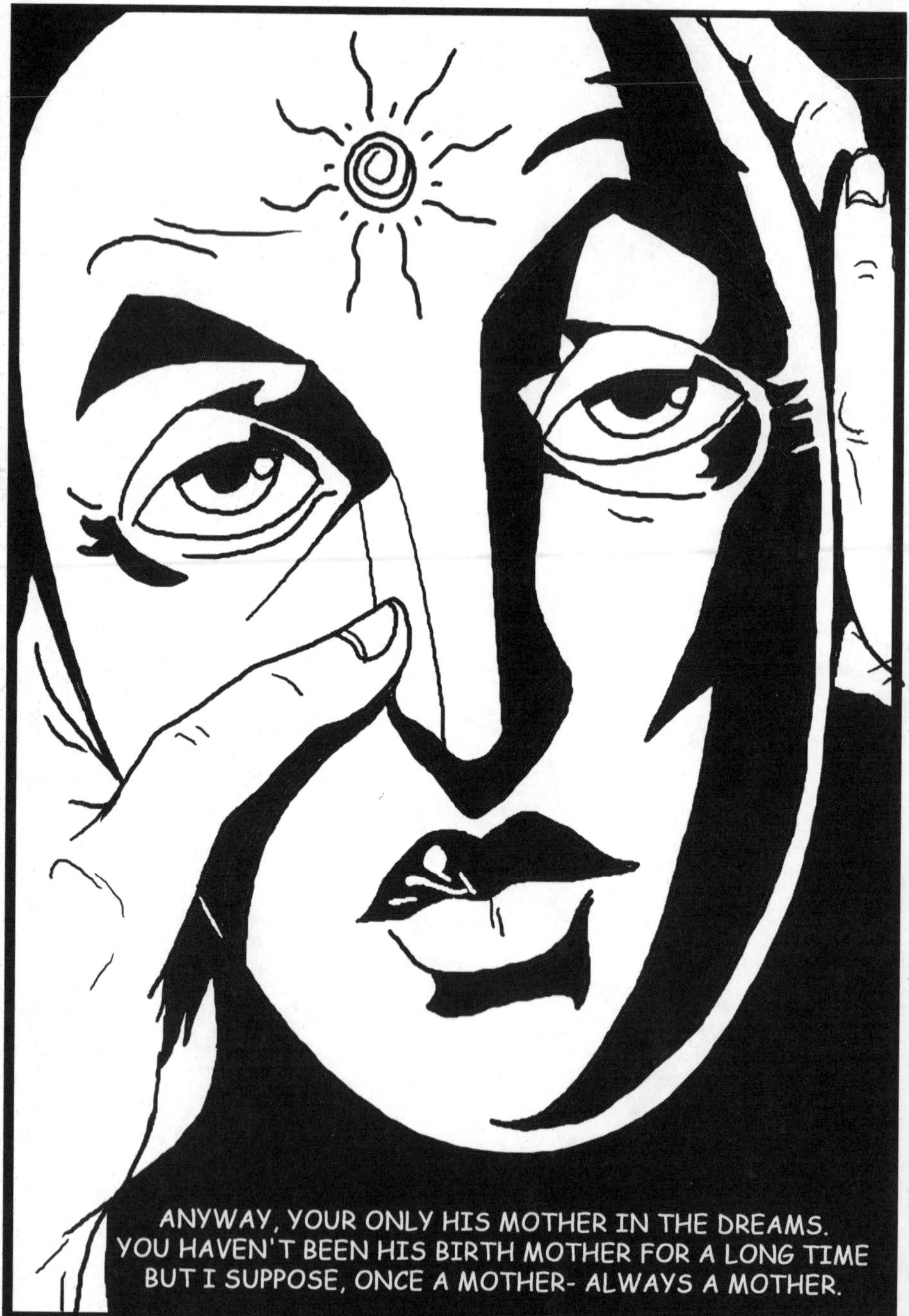
ANYWAY, YOUR ONLY HIS MOTHER IN THE DREAMS.
YOU HAVEN'T BEEN HIS BIRTH MOTHER FOR A LONG TIME
BUT I SUPPOSE, ONCE A MOTHER- ALWAYS A MOTHER.

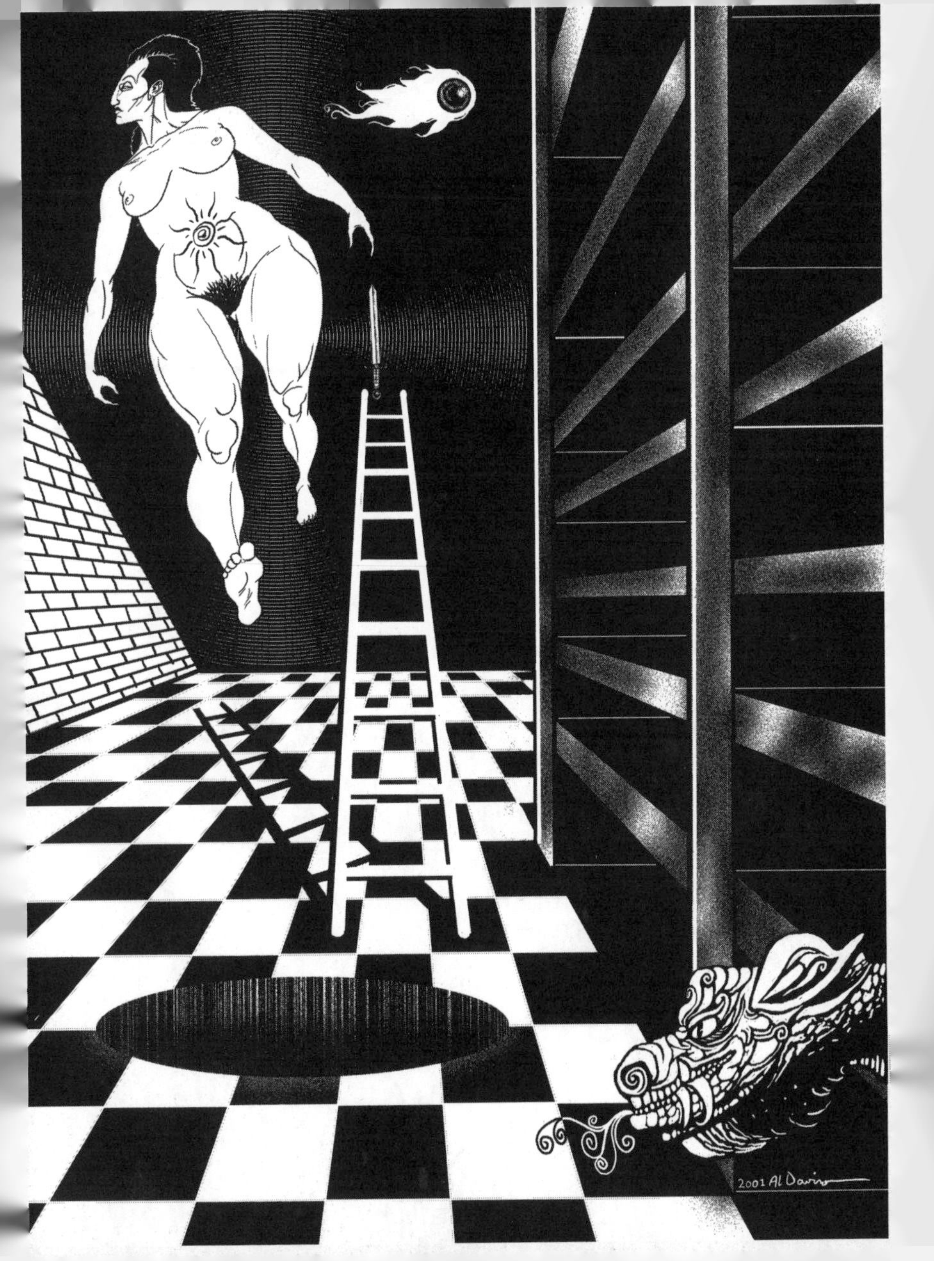
2001 Al Davison

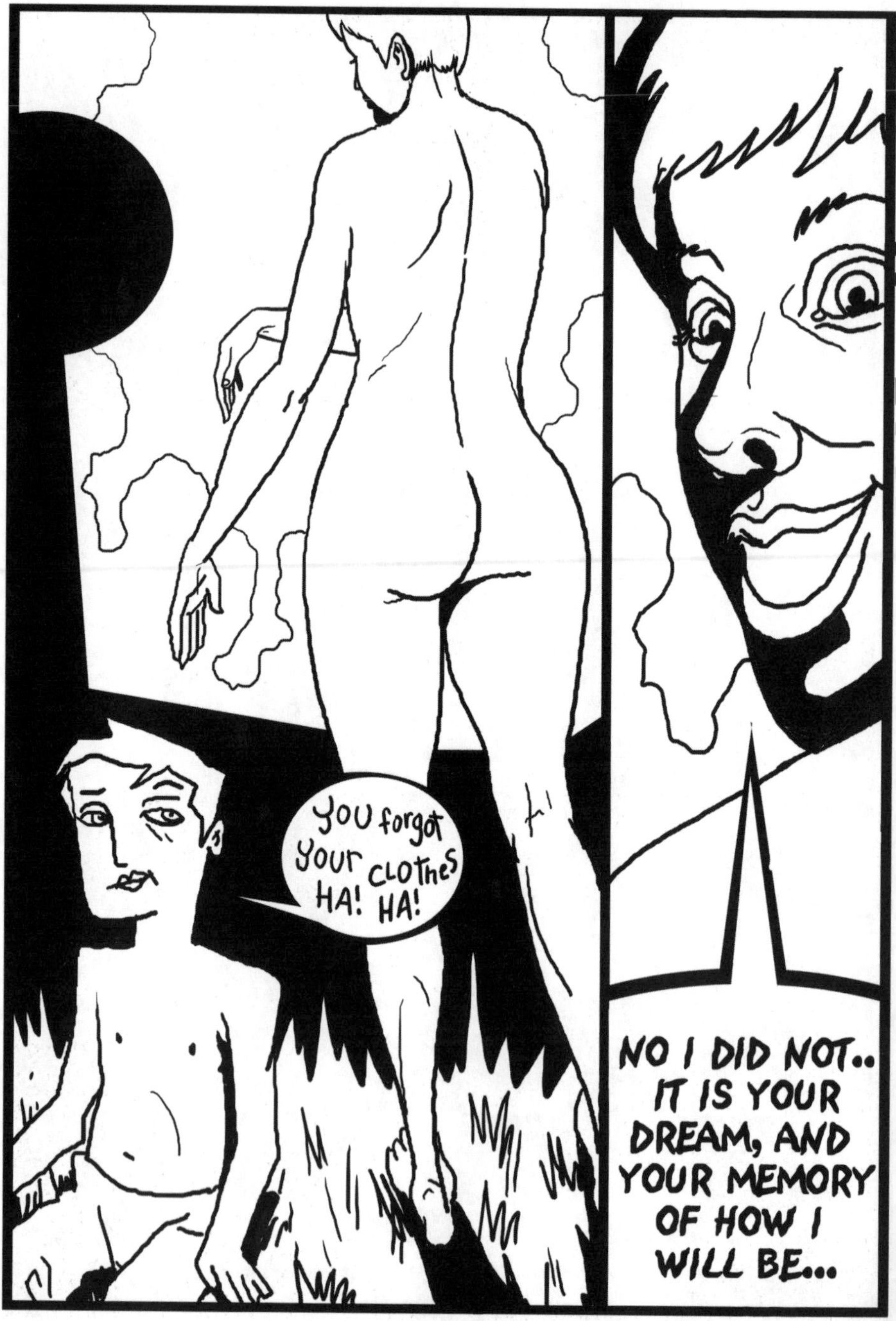
YOU forgot your clothes HA! HA!
NO I DID NOT.. IT IS YOUR DREAM, AND YOUR MEMORY OF HOW I WILL BE...

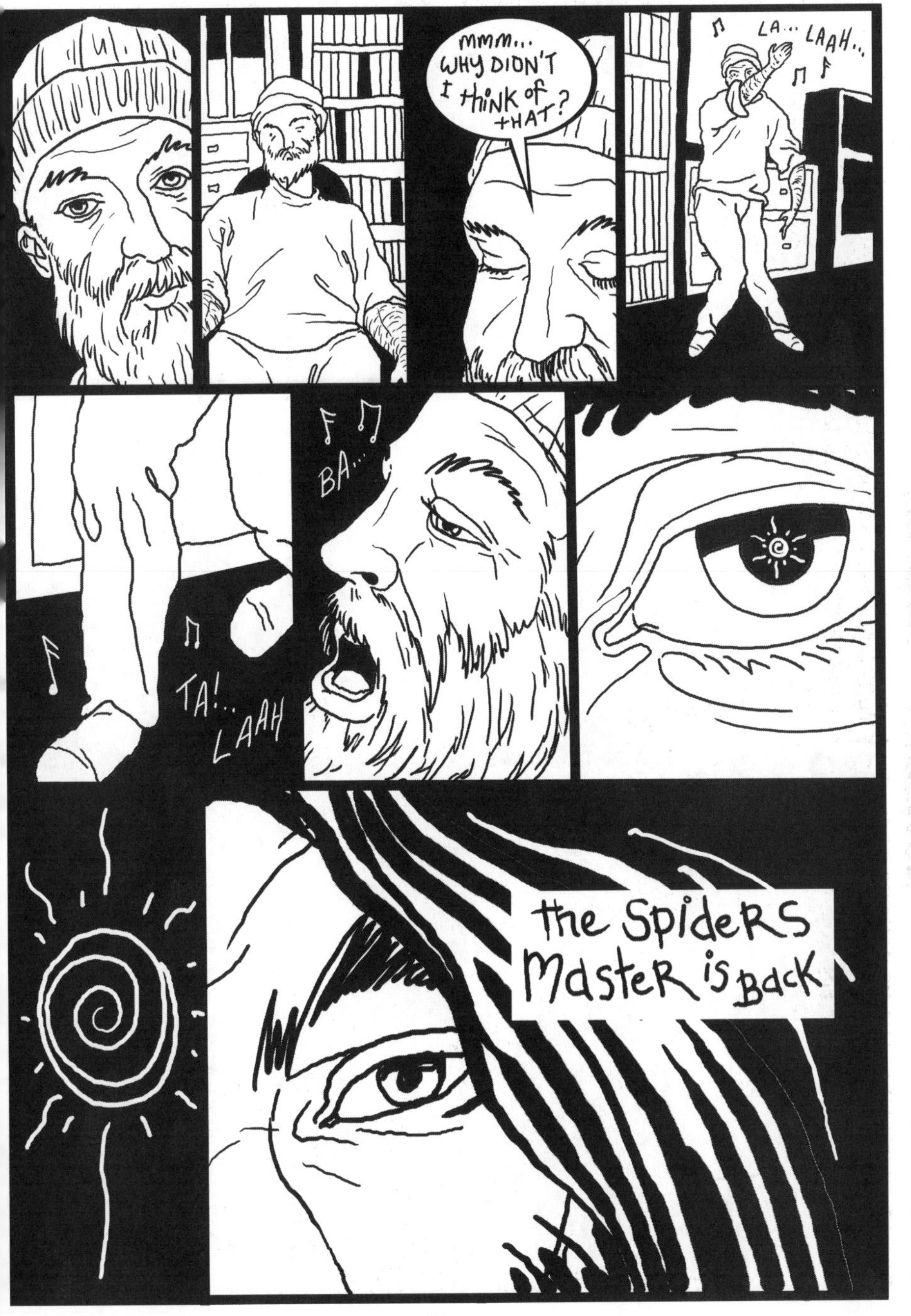
MMM... WHY DIDN'T I think of THAT?
LA... LAAH...
BA...
TA!... LAAH
the Spiders Master is Back

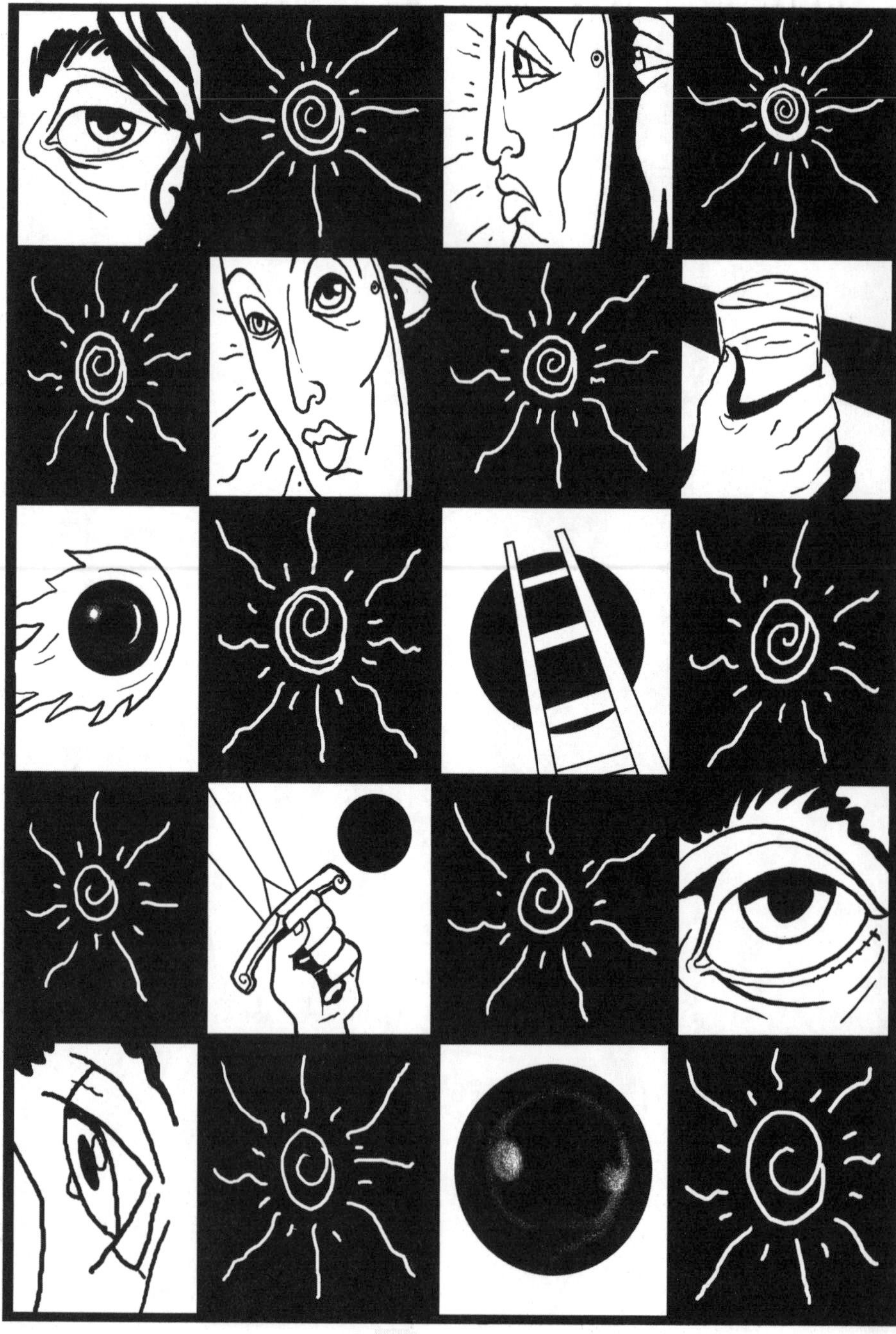

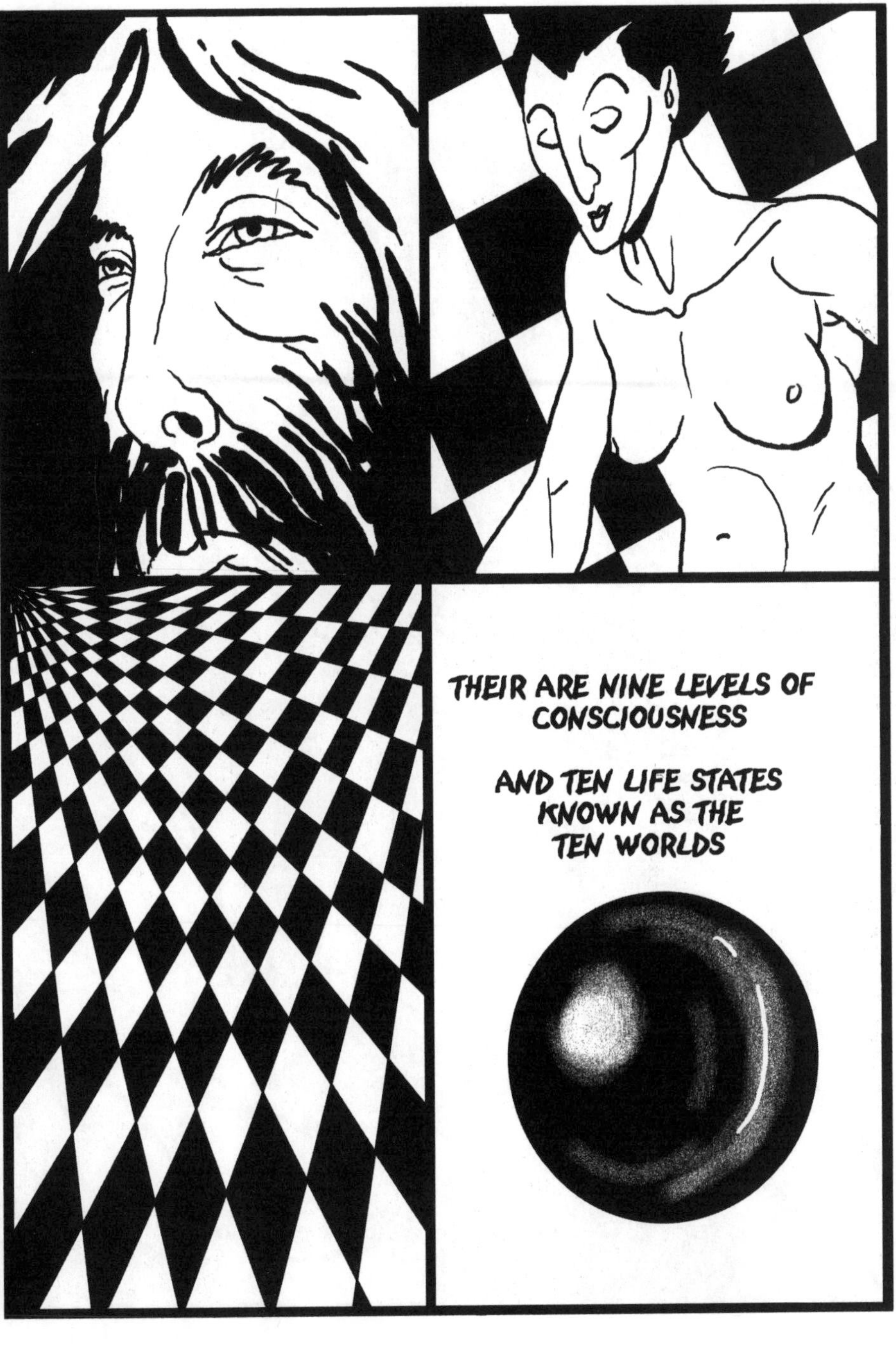
THEIR ARE NINE LEVELS OF CONSCIOUSNESS
AND TEN LIFE STATES KNOWN AS THE TEN WORLDS

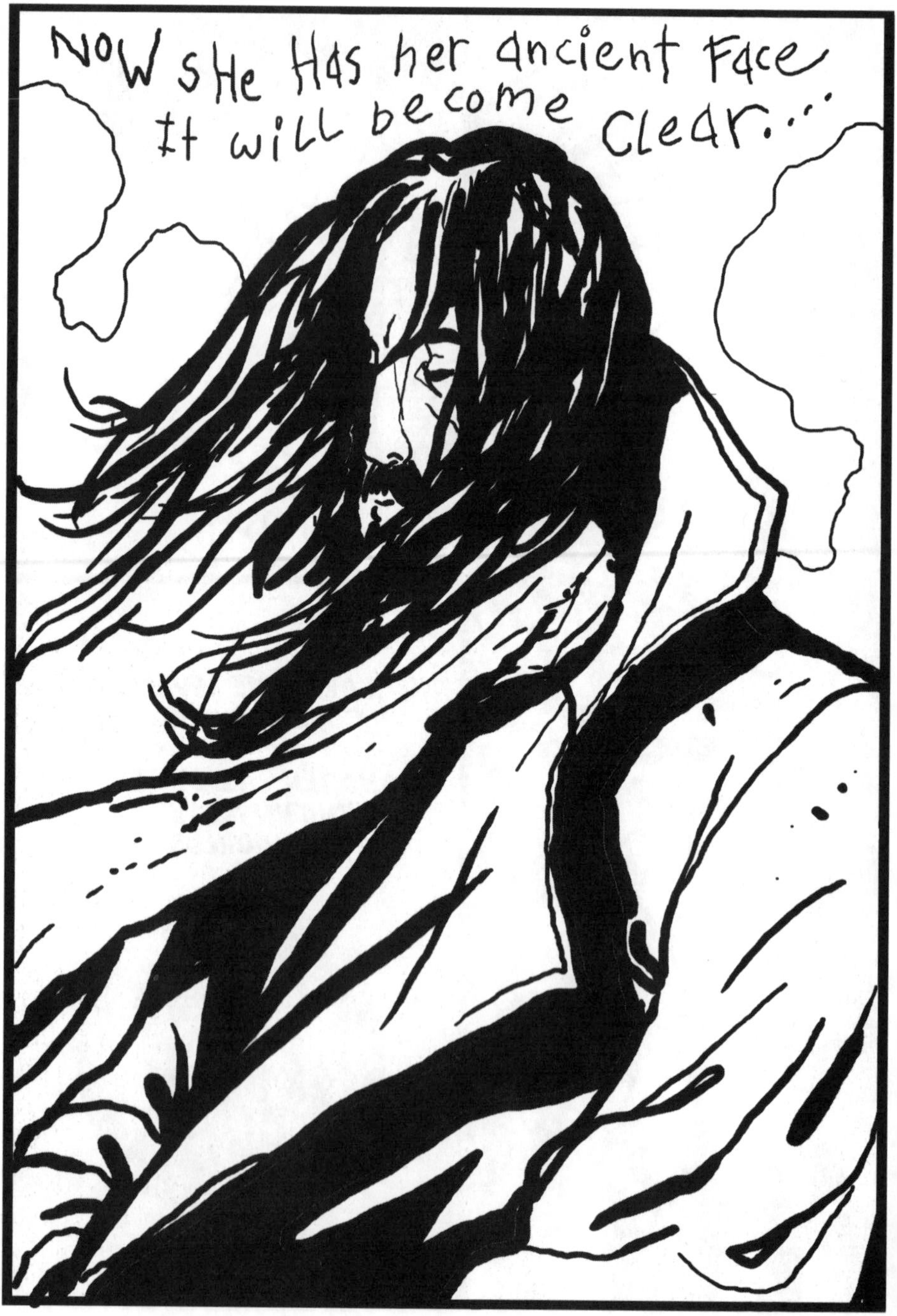
Now she has her ancient face
It will become clear...

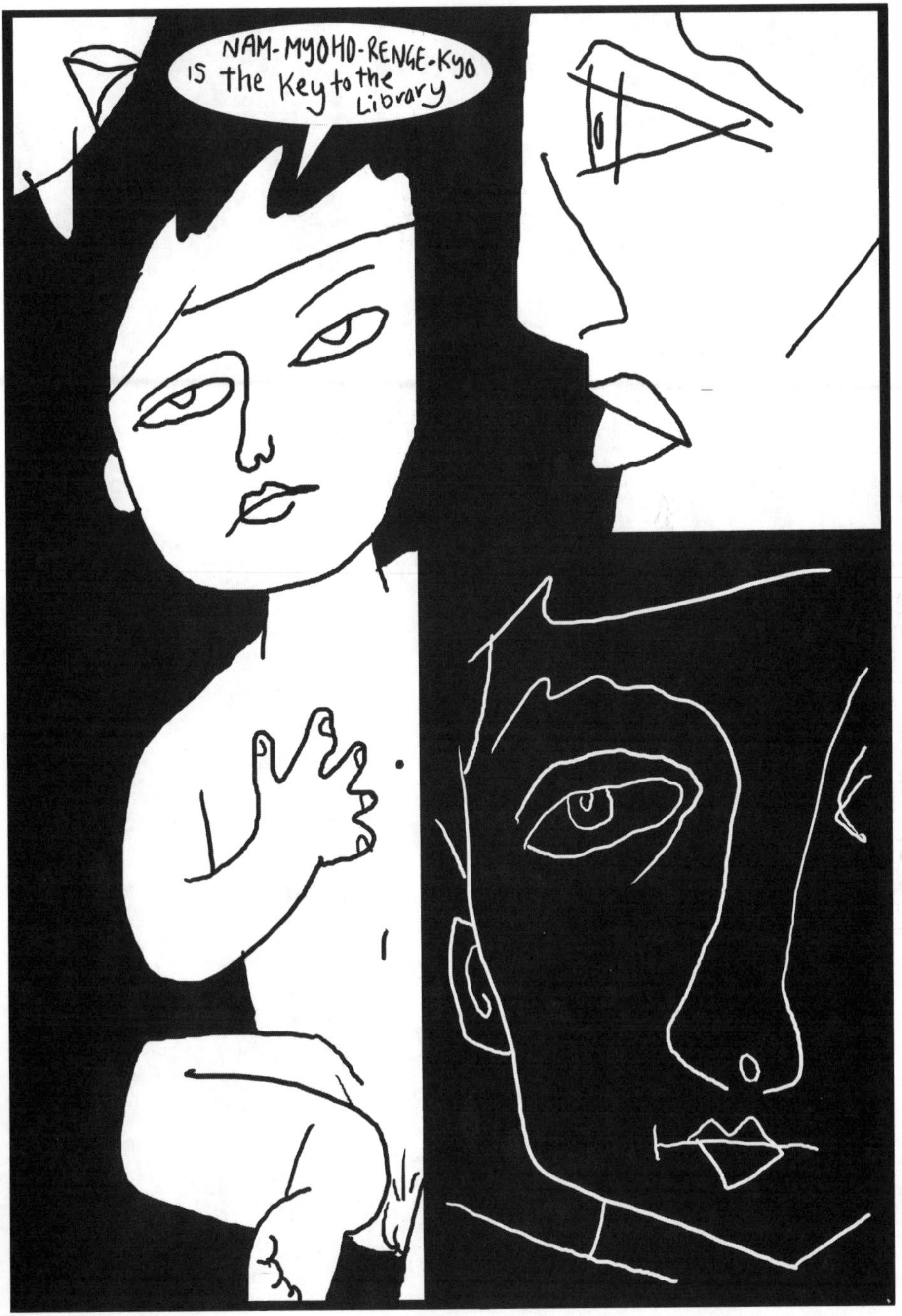
NAM-MYOHO-RENGE-KYO is the Key to the Library

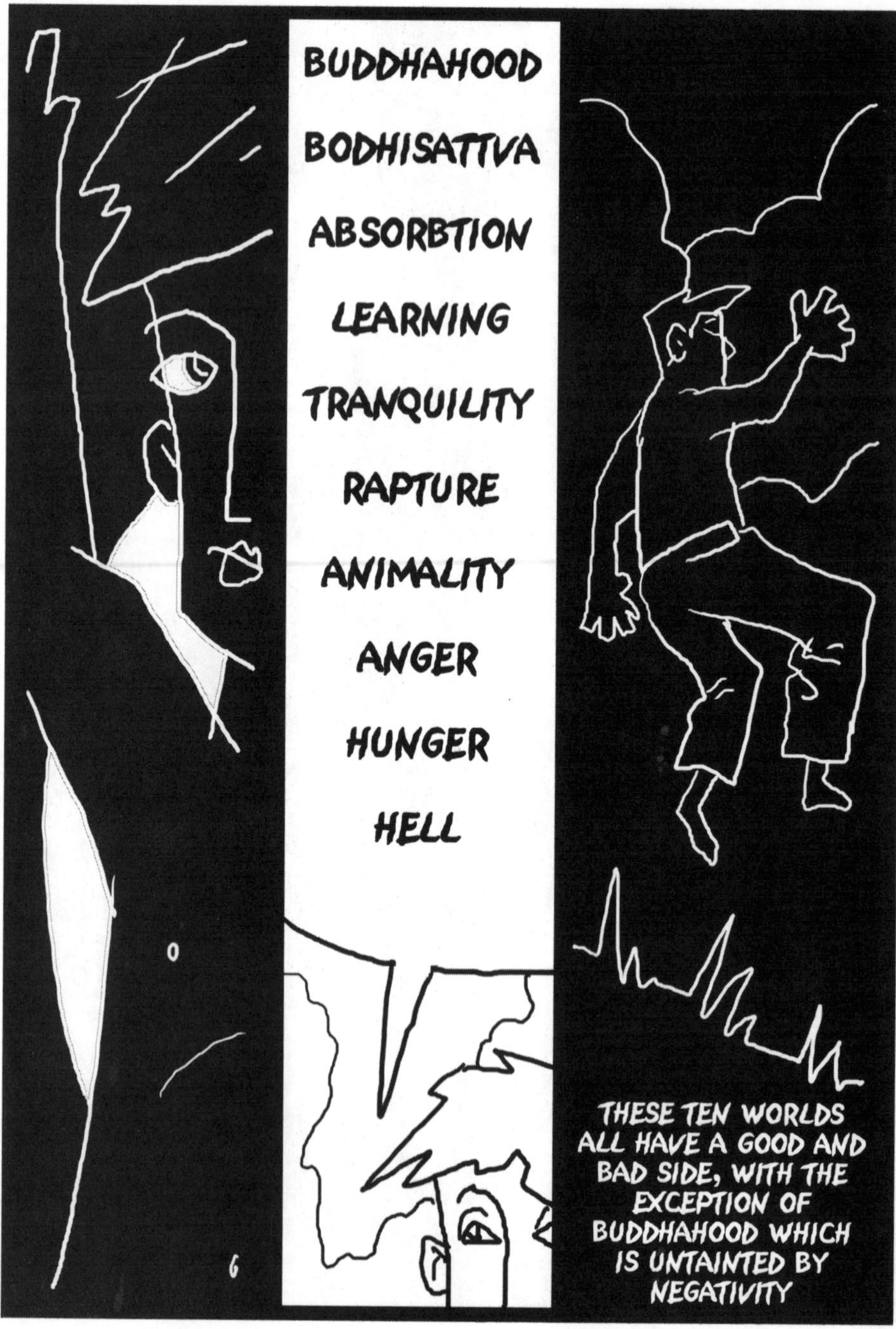
BUDDHAHOOD
BODHISATTVA
ABSORBTION
LEARNING
TRANQUILITY
RAPTURE
ANIMALITY
ANGER
HUNGER
HELL
THESE TEN WORLDS ALL HAVE A GOOD AND BAD SIDE, WITH THE EXCEPTION OF BUDDHAHOOD WHICH IS UNTAINTED BY NEGATIVITY

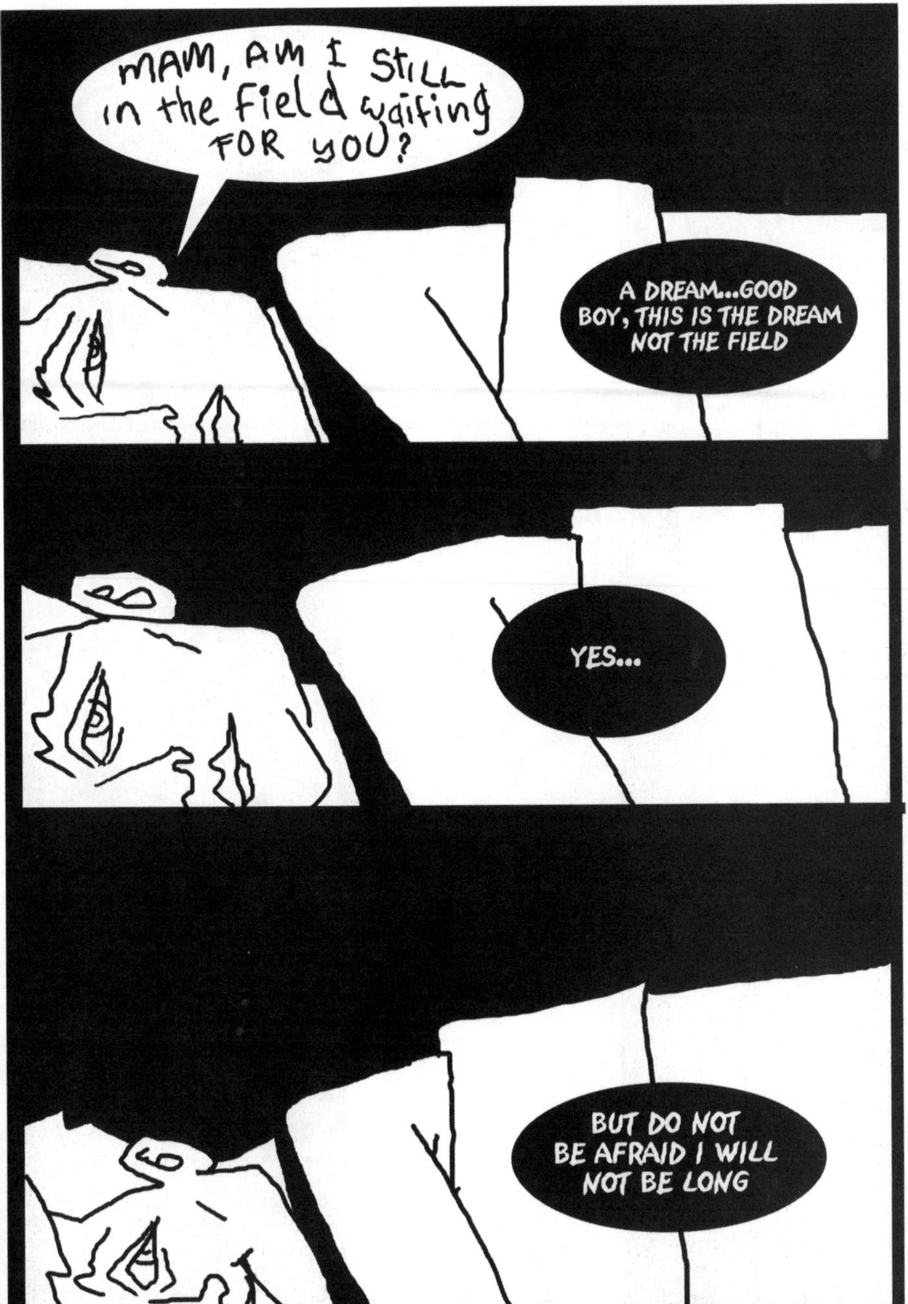
MAM, AM I STILL in the field waiting FOR YOU?
A DREAM...GOOD BOY, THIS IS THE DREAM NOT THE FIELD
YES...
BUT DO NOT BE AFRAID I WILL NOT BE LONG

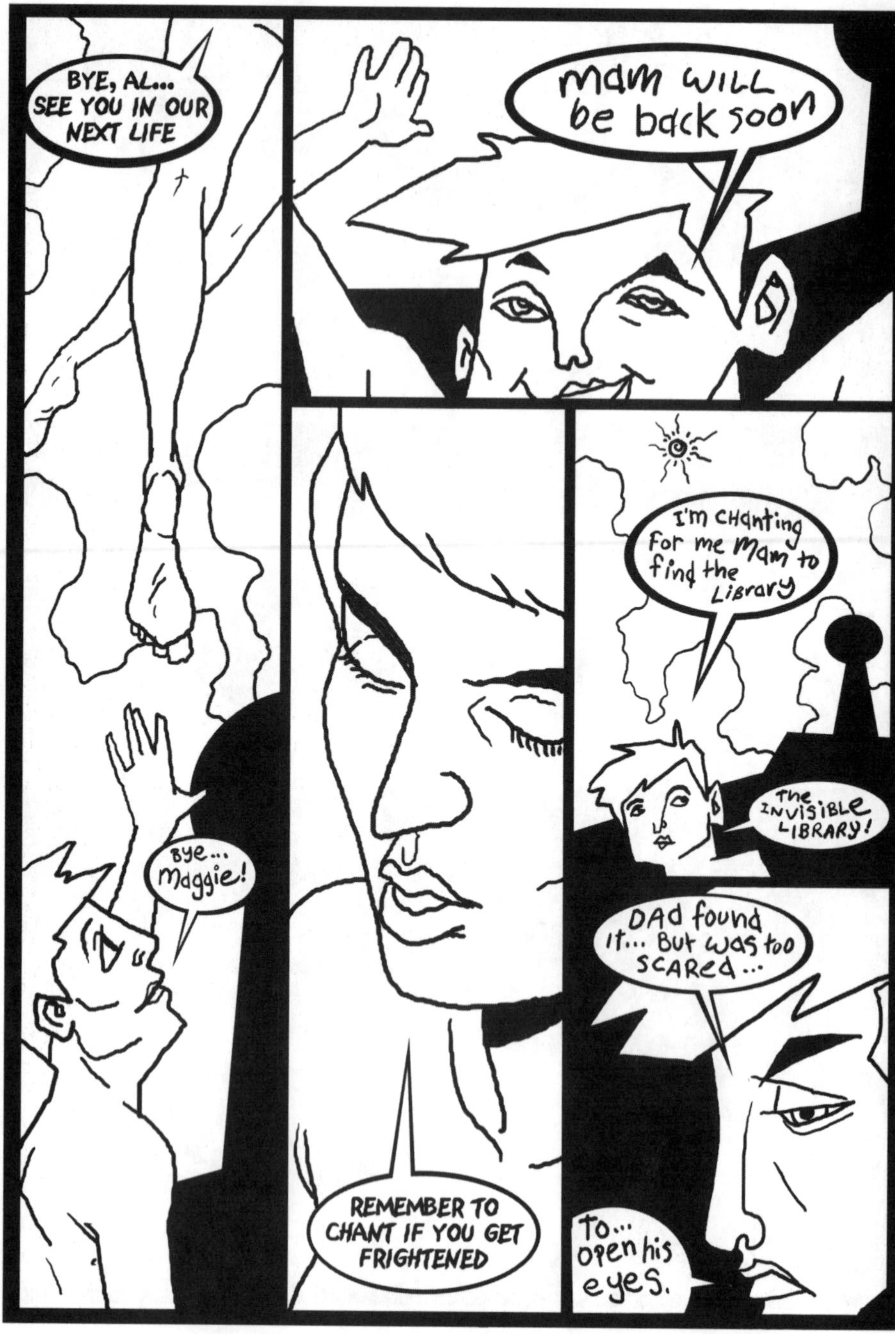
BYE, AL... SEE YOU IN OUR NEXT LIFE
Mam will be back soon
Bye... Maggie!
REMEMBER TO CHANT IF YOU GET FRIGHTENED
I'm chanting for me Mam to find the Library
The invisible library!
DAD found it... But was too scared...
To... open his eyes.

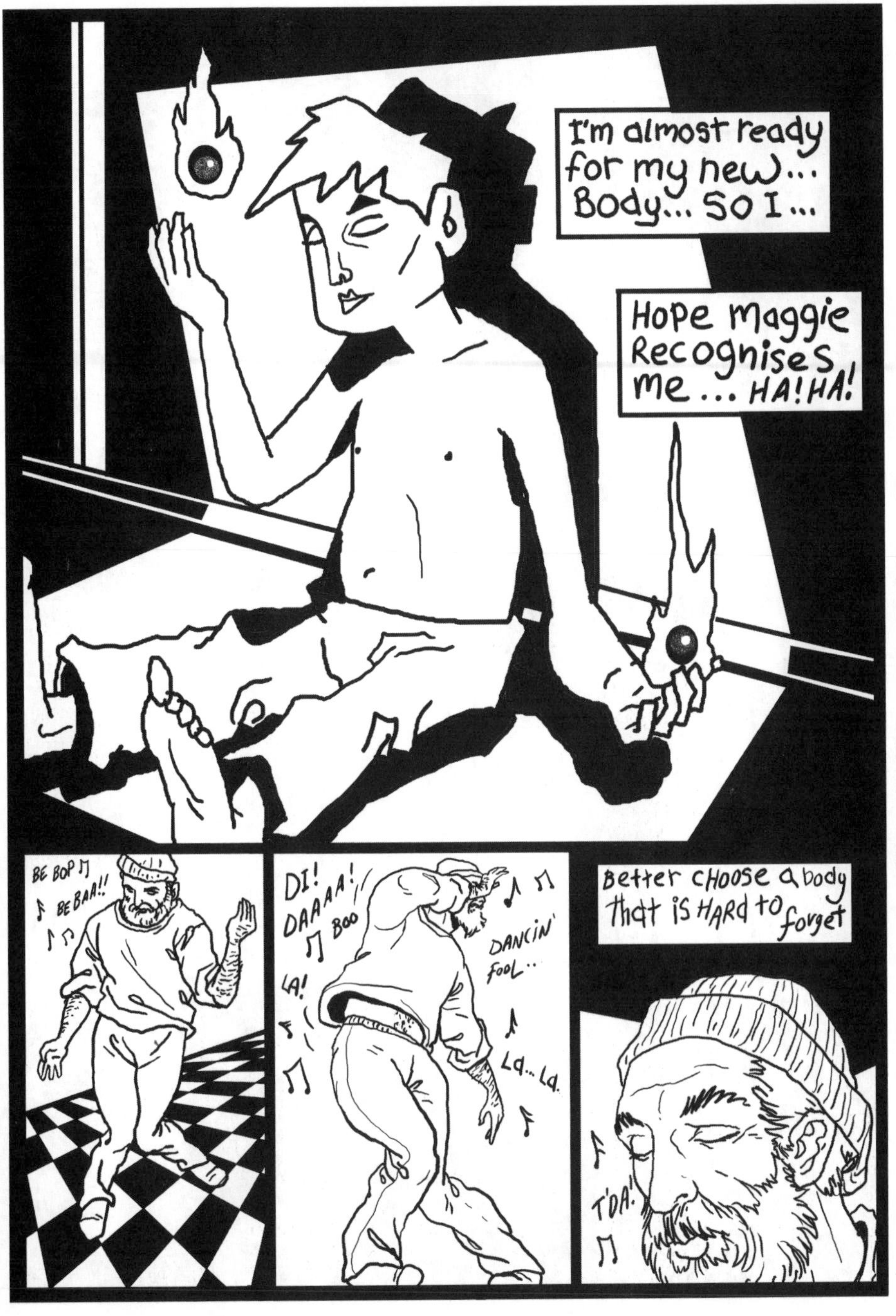
I'm almost ready for my new... Body... SO I...
Hope Maggie Recognises me... HA!HA!
BE BOP
BE BAA!!
DI! DAAAA! BOO
LA!
DANCIN' FOOL..
La... La.
Better choose a body that is HARD to forget
T'DA!

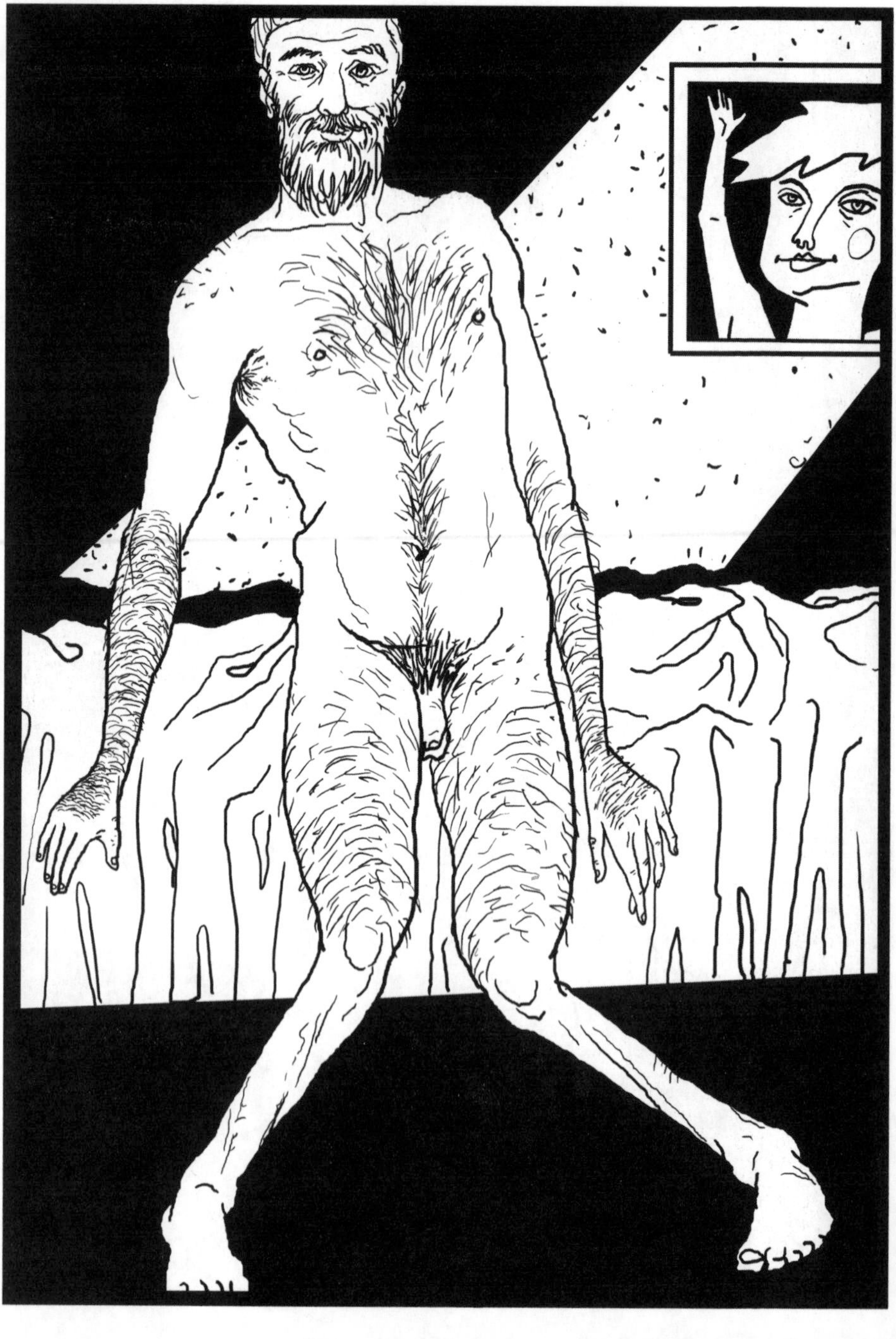

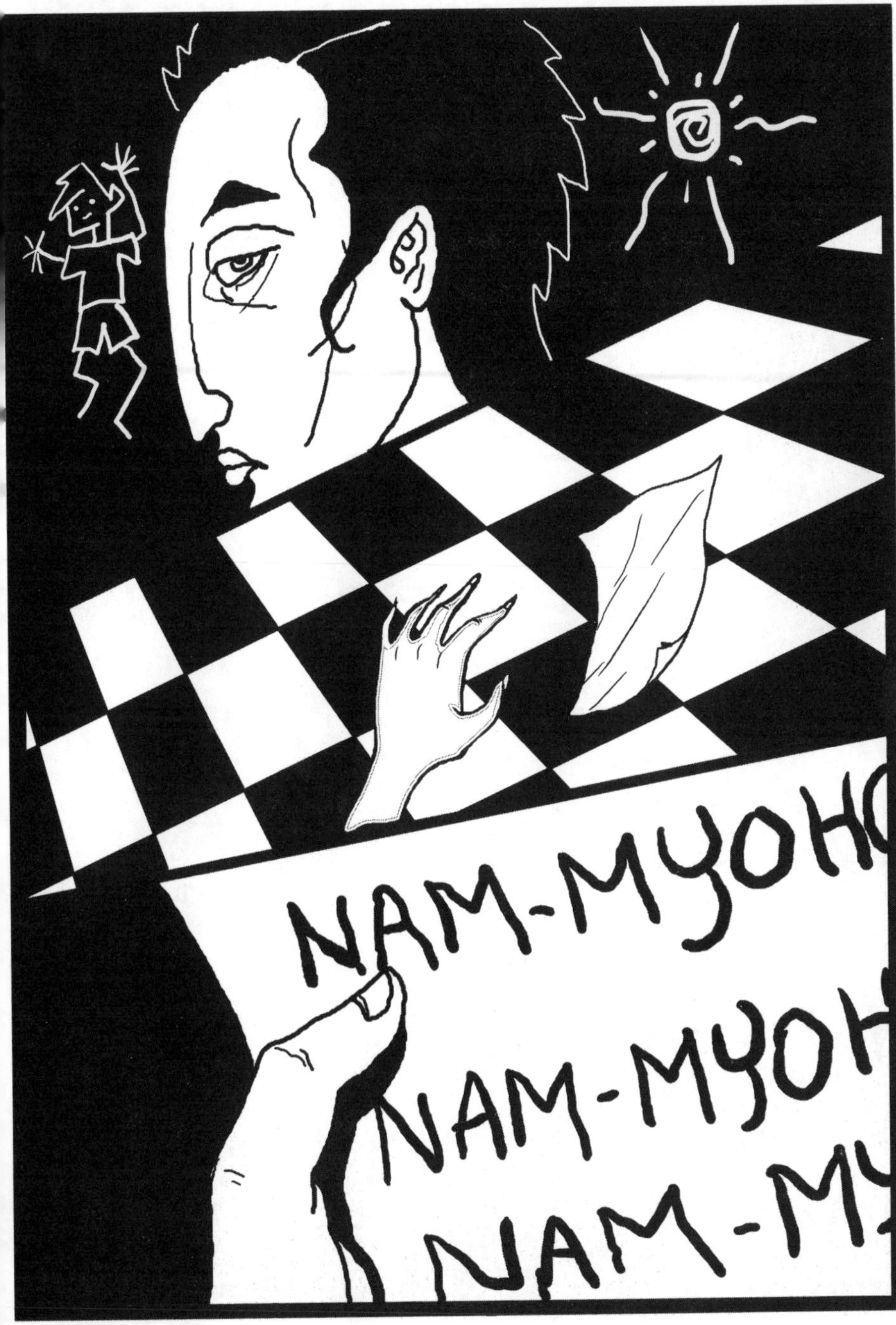
NAM-MYOHO
NAM-MYOH
NAM-MY

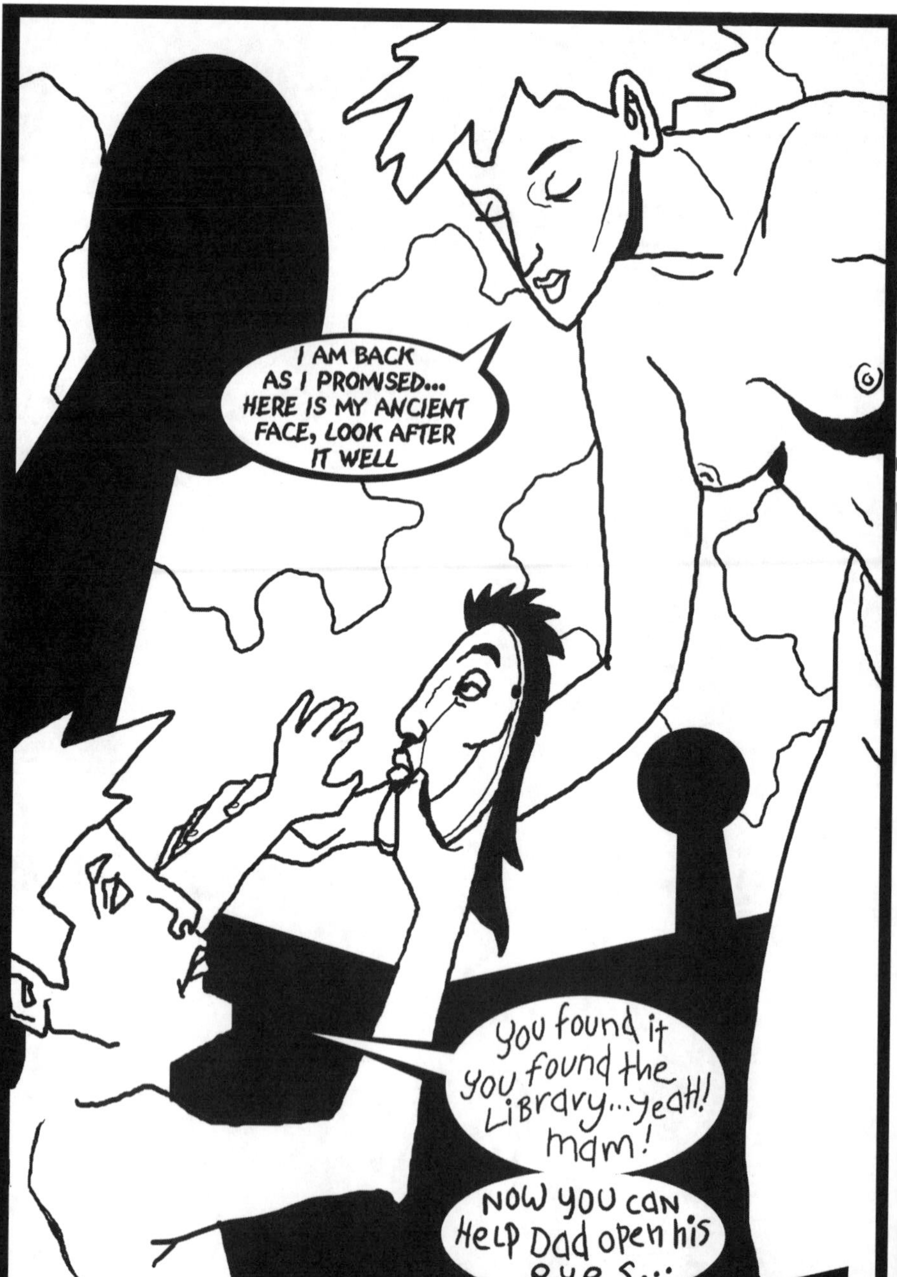
I AM BACK AS I PROMISED... HERE IS MY ANCIENT FACE, LOOK AFTER IT WELL
you found it you found the Library...yeah! mam!
NOW you can Help Dad open his eyes...
FIN.

ABOUT THE AUTHORS

SCOTT MCCLOUD has been writing and drawing comics since 1984. His book *Understanding Comics* is available in 15 languages (including English). His online comics can be found at scottmccloud.com.

With *Swamp Thing, Taboo, Tyrant*, his 24-hour comic, and 24+ years in comics under his belt, **STEVE BISSETTE** retired from comics in 1999. He writes, draws, works, lives in Vermont.

ALEXANDER GRECIAN is a multiple award-winning illustrator, copywriter and storyboard artist. Comic book credits include stories in *Negative Burn* and *The Factor*. He has also self-published two comics. Website: www.alexandergrecian.com

PAUL WINKLER, born 1970, is a musician, web developer, and occasional cartoonist. He hopes to participate in 24 Hour Comics Day 2004. He currently lives in Brooklyn, NY. Website: www.slinkp.com

JAKOB KLEMENČIČ lives in Ljubljana, Slovenia. He feels most at home on passenger trains (2nd class) between the Baltic and Black seas. E-mail: jakob.kemencic@ff.uni-lj.si

MATT MADDEN teaches comics and drawing at the School of Visual Arts. His most recent graphic novel is *Odds Off*, and his new work is the series *A Fine Mess*. Website: www.mattmadden.com.

NEIL GAIMAN is the writer of the popular Sandman comics and graphic novels, and the author of such best-selling and award-winning novels as *American Gods* and *Coraline*. Website: www.neilgaiman.com

Originally from the Northern Virginia suburbs, **DAVID LASKY** moved to Seattle in 1992, where he joined the ranks of a new wave of young "alternative cartoonists". He has since produced a number of experimental comic books, including a nine page adaptation of Joyce's *Ulysses*.

K. THOR JENSEN lives in New York City. His next book, *Red Eye, Black Eye*, will be released in late 2004. Website: www.shortandhappy.com

AL DAVISON is a vegetarian Buddhist black belt with Spina-Bifida. He is acclaimed for his autobiographical graphic novel *The Spiral Cage* and his illustrated dream diary *Spiral Dreams* among others. Website: www.astralgypsy.com

THERE ARE TWO GREAT HOLIDAYS ON THE COMICS CALENDAR

NOW THAT YOU'VE READ THE BOOK, YOU'RE PROBABLY THINKING THAT YOU'D LIKE TO DO A 24-HOUR COMIC *SOMEDAY.*

THIS IS THE DAY!

FOR MORE INFORMATION, SURF ON OVER TO:

WWW.24HOURCOMICS.COM

FREE COMIC BOOK DAY

PEOPLE WALK INTO COMIC BOOK STORES AND WALK OUT WITH SPECIAL EDITION COMIC BOOKS *WITHOUT PAYING A CENT.* IS THIS A DREAM? AN ILLUSION? A CRIME WAVE? NO, IT'S AN ALL-OUT ANNUAL EFFORT BY THE ENTIRE COMICS INDUSTRY TO GET COMICS INTO YOUR HAND.

www.FreeComicBookDay.com

Check out:

PANEL ONE:

COMIC BOOK SCRIPTS BY TOP WRITERS

Example scripts by some of comics top writers, including a script by **The Factor**'s Nat Gertler. Plus Neil Gaiman, Kurt Busiek, Dwayne McDuffie, Trina Robbins, Greg Rucka, Jeff Smith, Kevin Smith, and Marv Wolfman.

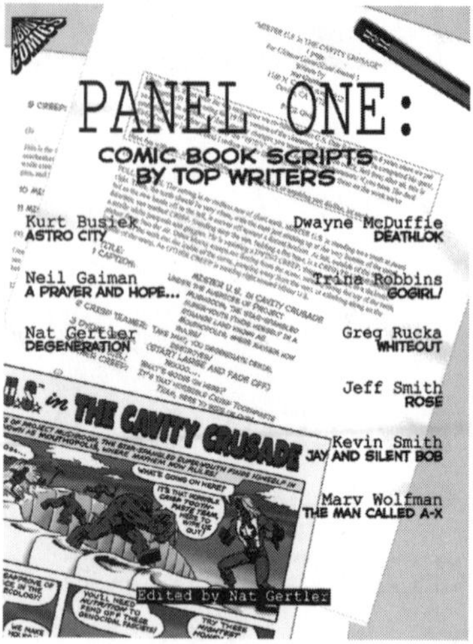

ABOUT COMICS
PANEL ONE:
COMIC BOOK SCRIPTS BY TOP WRITERS
Kurt Busiek
ASTRO CITY
Dwayne McDuffie
DEATHLOK
Neil Gaiman
A PRAYER AND HOPE...
Trina Robbins
GOGIRL!
Nat Gertler
DEGENERATION
Greg Rucka
WHITEOUT
Jeff Smith
ROSE
Kevin Smith
JAY AND SILENT BOB
Marv Wolfman
THE MAN CALLED A-X
THE CAVITY CRUSADE
Edited by Nat Gertler

ISBN: 0-9716338-0-0
Price: $19.95 US

Ask for it where you bought this book!

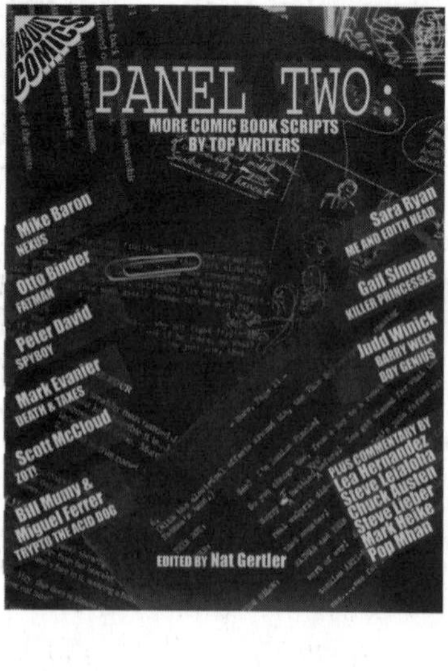

ABOUT COMICS
PANEL TWO:
MORE COMIC BOOK SCRIPTS BY TOP WRITERS
Mike Baron
NEXUS
Otto Binder
FATMAN
Peter David
SPYBOY
Mark Evanier
DEATH & TAXES
Scott McCloud
ZOT!
Bill Mumy & Miguel Ferrer
TRYPTO THE ACID DOG
Sara Ryan
ME AND EDITH HEAD
Gail Simone
KILLER PRINCESSES
Judd Winick
BARRY WEEN BOY GENIUS
PLUS COMMENTARY BY
Lea Hernandez
Steve Leialoha
Chuck Austen
Steve Lieber
Mark Heike
Pop Mhan
EDITED BY Nat Gertler

And while you're at it, check out the sequel. Scripts by Mike Baron, Otto Binder, Peter David, Mark Evanier, Scott McCloud, Bill Mumy & Miguel Ferrer, Sara Ryan, Gail Simone, and Judd Winick, plus commentary by a host of talented comics artists.

ISBN: 0-9716338-1-9
Price: $20.95 US

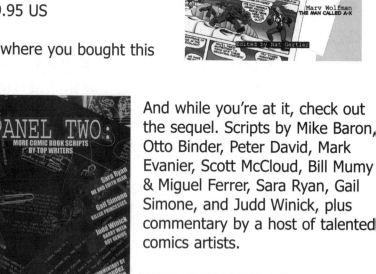

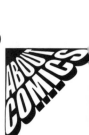

Other books in the ABOUT COMICS Reader Format:

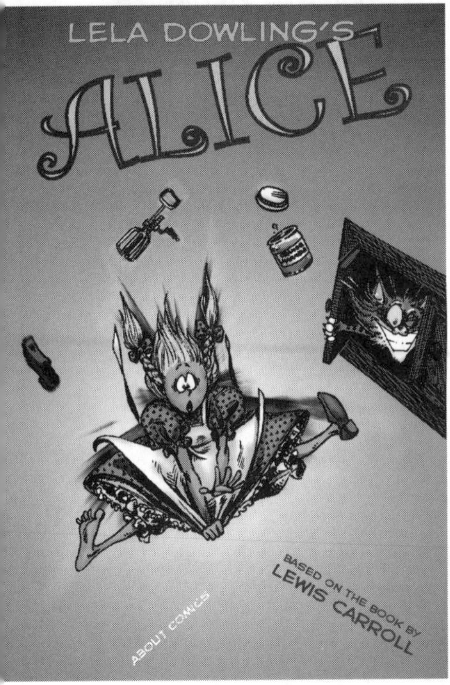

LELA DOWLING'S
ALICE
BASED ON THE BOOK BY
LEWIS CARROLL
ABOUT COMICS

Alice

A graphic novel adaptation of Alice In Wonderland, drawn in a delightful and attractive style by Lela Dowling. Over 100 pages long.

ISBN: 0-9716338-3-5
$8.95 US

The Liberty Project

Supervillains, captured by the government and given a chance to redeem themselves by working as heroes. Written by Kurt Busiek of *Astro City* and *Avengers/JLA*, drawn byJames W. Fry. 240 pages of super fun!

ISBN: 0-9716338-2-7
$11.95

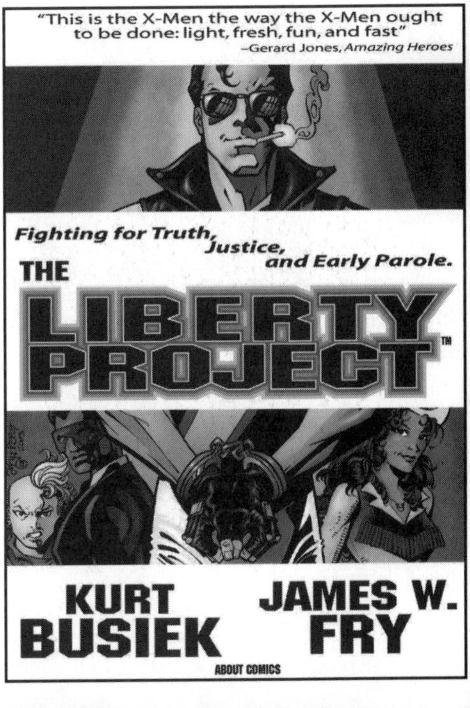

"This is the X-Men the way the X-Men ought to be done: light, fresh, fun, and fast"
–Gerard Jones, Amazing Heroes
Fighting for Truth, Justice, and Early Parole.
THE LIBERTY PROJECT™
KURT BUSIEK
JAMES W. FRY
ABOUT COMICS

Available July, 2004

Almost 500 pages of 24 Hour Comics goodness in one thick book.